The
Fisherman's
Bedside Book

Indeed my friend you will find Angling like the
virtue of humility, which has a calmness of
spirit and a world of other blessings
attendant on it.

Izaak Walton, *The Compleat Angler*

The Fisherman's Bedside Book

edited by
David and Gareth Pownall

Windward

Contents

First published in Great Britain 1980
by WHS Distributors (a division of
W. H. Smith & Son Ltd),
Burne House, 88/89 High Holborn,
London WC1V 6LS

ISBN 0 7112 0065 3

Devised, edited and designed by
Shuckburgh Reynolds Ltd
8 Northumberland Place,
London W2 5BS

This anthology
© Shuckburgh Reynolds Ltd 1980

Typesetting by SX Composing Ltd,
Rayleigh, Essex
Printed and bound by
Butler & Tanner Ltd,
Frome, Somerset

Designer: Roger Pring
Assistant designer: Mark Newcombe

Illustrations by: Rene Eyre,
Alan Folkard, Lucina Della Rocca Hay,
Carole Johnson, David Mallott,
Mark Newcombe, Sheilagh Noble,
Roger Pring

For Neil
who was caught by a pike
and a five pound note

Introduction

A sixteen-year old boy and a man in his early forties see most things differently, even their entertainments when shared. Fishing to my son is not what fishing is to me. He started it, having been lured by the sight of two lads catching an eel off the old quay at Lancaster; I followed, intrigued, amused but developing my interest through him. That was ten years ago. I suppose we have read as much as we have fished. It is the cheapest way to get onto most waters these days.

In all respects we learned what little we know together, the case being that he usually taught me after he had picked his technique up from friends or books. No better proof of Wordsworth's proposition that the Child is father to the Man has occurred within my experience. What we have gathered here is an amalgam of our tastes, a compromise between father and son; usually an interesting enough deal if family life is anything to go by.

Fishing is a simple business. The idea is straightforward: the catching of a fish by deceit is as ancient a mind-tingler as childhood itself. What has become complicated is technique, talk and tackle. In this anthology we have generally avoided pieces that blind with science and have concentrated on the pleasure and the idea, always trying to connect with the thing at the centre of angling – the fish itself. Many of the great names in fishing lore will not be found here, but they have plenty of exposure elsewhere. What we have looked for are illustrations of the way fishing moves the imagination and satisfies our lust for excitement.

We could easily fill these pages over again with the ones we decided to leave out, including the best fishing story of this century, Hemingway's *The Old Man and the Sea*, which won the Nobel Prize for Literature in 1954. That had to be rejected in favour of the excellent story, *Big Two-Hearted River*, an earlier work which we could publish in full. *The Old Man and the Sea* is a seamless book which should not be cut up. If you haven't read it, you should. Other stories of fine quality were put aside because they had been selected in previous anthologies and the devoted fishing-book collector will track them down in libraries and second-hand book shops.

Fishing and dreaming are not far apart. If the mind is employed on one it is receptive to the other. Although there is much strong, direct narrative in this selection and action between hunter and hunted is the most dominant theme, behind each tale there lies the enigmatic dream, the fish. It is always more than the sum of its physical self: target, trophy, totem, talisman, the fish has a multitude of identities in which it is cherished. Today we have added a further layer to the mysterious worship which the fish has always received from the men who set out to catch it. We are beginning to feel that this unteachable, inarticulate animal needs our protection. We must not destroy what fascinates us.

We have set out to provide an up-to-date, balanced selection of fishing tales, poems and extracts which will open up the themes of the sport—the stoical talent for disappointment, the heroic defeat of the great adversary, the obsessive tragedy, the romantic isolationist and his mourning-song, the antics of the benevolent eccentric, the tangles, tortures and triumphs of fishing adventure. We apologise for there being only three stories which feature a woman in action (find them yourself), and we think it a pity that something so dramatically satisfying as a woman, the Unknown, tussling with a fish, the Unseen, should not have been more fully explored in literature so far.

We have made the tales travel when we could find the quality to carry the reader to India, Russia, Chile, Alaska and other places. There is a paucity of translated fishing stories which is to be regretted. At the end of the business of putting the book together, one is left with images of peoples who live on the edge of nowhere angling for their existences who might have literatures of devotion to the fish that we will never read. But even from our ignorance we can guess with some accuracy that they will enshrine that supercharged moment when fish hits hook. We hope this anthology does the same.

David Pownall

Seven Marlin Swordfish in One Day

Zane Grey

San Clemente lies forty miles south of Santa Catalina, out in the Pacific, open to wind and fog, scorched by sun, and beaten on every shore by contending tides. Seen from afar, the island seems a bleak, long, narrow strip of drab rock rising from a low west end to the dignity of a mountain near the east end. Seen close at hand, it is still barren, bleak, and drab; but it shows long golden slopes of wild oats; looming, grey, lichen-coloured crags, where the eagles perch; and rugged deep cañons, cactus-covered on the south side and on the other indented by caves and caverns, and green with clumps of wild-lilac and wild-cherry and arbor vitae; and bare round domes where the wild goats stand silhouetted against the blue sky.

This island is volcanic in origin and structure, and its great caves have been made by blow-holes in hot lava. Erosion has weathered slope and wall and crag. For the most part these slopes and walls are exceedingly hard to climb. The goat trails are narrow and steep, the rocks sharp and ragged, the cactus thick and treacherous. Many years ago Mexicans placed goats on the island for the need of shipwrecked sailors, and these goats have traversed the wild-oat slopes until they are like a net-work of trails. Every little space of grass has its criss-cross of goat trails.

I rested high up on a slope, in the lee of a rugged rock, all rust-stained and grey-lichened, with a deep cactus-covered cañon to my left, the long, yellow, windy slope of wild oats to my right, and beneath me the Pacific, majestic and grand, where the great white rollers moved in graceful heaves along the blue. The shore-line, curved by rounded gravelly beach and jutted by rocky point, showed creeping white lines of foam, and then green water spotted by beds of golden kelp, reaching out into the deeps. Far across the lonely space rose creamy clouds, thunderheads looming over the desert on the mainland.

A big black raven soared by with dismal croak. The wind rustled the oats. There was no other sound but the sound of the sea—deep, low-toned, booming like thunder, long crash and continuous roar.

How wonderful to watch eagles in their native haunts! I saw a bald eagle sail by, and then two golden eagles winging heavy flight after him. There seemed to be contention or rivalry, for when the white-headed bird alighted the others swooped down upon him. They circled and flew in and out of the cañon, and one let out a shrill, piercing scream. They disappeared and I watched a lonely gull riding the swells. He at least was at home on the restless waters. Life is beautiful, particularly elemental life. Then far above I saw the white-tipped eagle and I thrilled to see the difference now in his flight. He was monarch of the air, king of the wind, lonely and grand in the blue. He soared, he floated, he sailed, and then, away across the skies he flew, swift as an arrow, to slow and circle again, and swoop up high and higher, wide-winged and free, ringed in the azure blue, and then like a thunderbolt he fell, to vanish beyond the crags.

Again I saw right before me a small brown hawk, poised motion-less, resting on the wind, with quivering wings, and he hung there, looking down for his prey—some luckless lizard or rat. He seemed suspended on wires. There, down like a brown flash he was gone, and surely that swoop meant a desert tragedy.

I heard the bleat of a lamb or kid, and it pierced the melancholy roar of the sea.

If there is a rapture on the lonely shore, there was indeed rapture here high above it, blown upon by the sweet, soft winds. I heard the bleat close at hand. Turning, I saw a she-goat with little kid scarce a foot high. She crossed a patch of cactus. The kid essayed to follow here, but found the way too thorny. He bleated—a tiny, pin-pointed bleat—and his mother turned to answer encouragingly. He leaped over a cactus, attempted another, and, failing, fell on the sharp prickers. He bleated in distress and scrambled out of that hard and painful place. The mother came around, and presently, reunited, they went on, to disappear.

The island seemed consecrated to sun and sea. It lay out of the latitude of ships. Only a few Mexican sheep-herders lived there, up at the east end where less-rugged land allowed pasture for their flocks. A little rain falls during the winter months, and soon dis-appears from the porous cañon-beds. Water-holes were rare and springs rarer. The summit was flat, except for some rounded domes of mountains, and there the deadly cholla cactus grew—not in profusion, but enough to prove the dread of the Mexicans for this species of desert plant. It was a small bush, with cones like a pine cone in shape, growing in clusters, and over stems and cones were fine steel-pointed needles with invisible hooks at the ends.

A barren, lonely prospect, that flat plateau above, an empire of the sun, where heat veils rose and mirages haunted the eye. But at sunset fog rolled up from the outer channel, and if the sun blasted the life on the island, the fog saved it. So there was war between sun and fog, the one that was the lord of day, and the other the dew-laden saviour of night.

South, on the windward side, opened a wide bay, Smugglers' Cove by name, and it was infinitely more beautiful than its name. A great curve indented the league-long slope of island, at each end of which low, ragged lines of black rock jutted out into the sea. Around this immense bare amphitheatre, which had no growth save scant cactus and patches of grass, could be seen long lines of shelves where the sea-levels had been in successive ages of the past.

Near the middle of the curve, on a bleached bank, stood a lonely little hut, facing the sea. Old and weather-beaten, out of place there, it held and fascinated the gaze. Below it a white shore-line curved away where the waves rolled in, sadly grand, to break and spread on the beach.

At the east end, where the jagged black rocks met the sea, I loved to watch a great swell rise out of the level blue, heave and come, slow-lifting as if from some infinite power, to grow and climb aloft till the blue turned green and sunlight showed through, and the long, smooth crest, where the seals rode, took on a sharp edge to send wisps of spray in the wind, and, rising sheer, the whole swell, solemn and ponderous and majestic, lifted its volume one beautiful instant, then curled its shining crest and rolled in and down with a thundering, booming roar, all the curves and contours gone in a green-white seething mass that climbed the reefs and dashed itself to ruin.

An extraordinary achievement and record fell to my brother R. C. It was too much good luck ever to come my way. Fame is a fickle goddess. R. C. had no ambition to make a great catch of swordfish. He angles for these big game of the sea more to furnish company for me than for any other reason. He likes best the golden, rocky streams where the bronze-back black-bass hide, or the swift, amber-coloured brooks full of rainbow trout.

I must add that in my opinion, and Captain Danielson's also, R. C. is a superior angler, and all unconscious of it. He has not my intimate knowledge of big fish, but he did not seem to need that. He is powerful in the shoulders and arms, his hands are strong and hard from baseball and rowing, and he is practically tireless. He never rested while fighting a fish. We never saw him lean the rod on the gunwale. All of which accounts for his quick conquering of a Marlin swordfish. We have yet to see him work upon a broadbill or a big tuna; and that is something Captain Dan and I are anticipating with much pleasure and considerable doubt.

August 31st dawned fine and cool and pleasant, rather hazy, with warm sun and smooth sea.

The night before we had sat in front of our tents above the beach and watched the flying-fish come out in twos and threes and schools, all the way down the rugged coast. I told the captain then that swordfish were chasing them. But he was sceptical.

This morning I remembered, and I was watching. Just at the

Glory Hole my brother yelled, "Strike!" I did not see the fish before he hit the bait. It is really remarkable how these swordfish can get to a bait on the surface without being seen. R. C. hooked the Marlin.

The first leap showed the fish to be small. He did not appear to be much of a jumper or fighter. He leaped six times, and then tried to swim out to sea. Slow, steady work of R. C.'s brought him up to the boat in fifteen minutes. But we did not gaff him. We estimated his weight at one hundred and thirty pounds. Captain Dan cut the leader close to the hook. I watched the fish swim lazily away, apparently unhurt, and sure to recover.

We got going again, and had scarce trolled a hundred yards when I saw something my companions missed. I stood up.

"Well, this starts out like your day," I remarked to my brother.

Then he saw a purple shape weaving back of his bait and that galvanized him into attention. It always thrilled me to see a swordfish back of the bait. This one took hold and ran off to the right. When hooked it took line with a rush, began to thresh half out, and presently sounded. We lost the direction. It came up far ahead of the boat and began to leap and run on the surface.

We followed while R. C. recovered the line. Then he held the fish well in hand; and in the short time of twelve minutes brought the leader to Dan's hand. The Marlin made a great splash as he was cut loose.

"Say, two swordfish in less than half an hour!" I expostulated. "Dan, this might be *the* day."

Captain Dan looked hopeful. We were always looking for that day which came once or twice each season.

"I'm tired," said my brother. "Now you catch a couple."

He talked about swordfish as carelessly as he used to talk about sunfish. But he was not in the least tired. I made him take up the rod again. I sensed events. The sea looked darkly rippling, inviting, as if to lure us on.

We had worked and drifted a little offshore. But that did not appear to put us out of the latitude of swordfish. Suddenly Captain Dan yelled, "Look out!" Then we all saw a blaze of purple back of R. C.'s bait. Dan threw out the clutch. But this Marlin was shy. He flashed back and forth. How swift! His motion was only a purple flash. He loomed up after the teasers. We had three of these flying-fish out as teasers, all close to the boat. I always wondered why the swordfish appear more attracted to the teasers than to our hooked baits only a few yards back. I made the mistake to pull the teasers away from this swordfish. Then he left us.

I was convinced, however, that this was to be R. C.'s day, and so, much to his amaze and annoyance, I put away my rod. No sooner had I quit fishing than a big black tail showed a few yards out from R. C.'s bait. Then a shining streak shot across under the water, went behind R. C.'s bait, passed it, came again. This time I saw him plainly. He was big and hungry, but shy. He rushed the bait. I saw him take it in his pointed jaws and swerve out of sight, leaving a boil on the surface. R. C. did not give him time to swallow the hook, but struck immediately. The fish ran off two hundred yards and then burst up on the surface. He was a jumper, and as he stayed in sight we all began to yell our admiration. He cleared the water forty-two times, all in a very few minutes. At the end of twenty-eight minutes R. C., with a red face and a bulging jaw, had the swordfish beaten and within reach of Captain Dan.

"He's a big one—over two hundred and fifty," asserted that worthy. "Mebbe you won't strike a bigger one."

"Cut him loose," I said, and my brother echoed my wish.

It was a great sight to see that splendid swordfish drift away from the boat—to watch him slowly discover that he was free.

"Ten o'clock! We'll hang up two records to-day!" boomed Captain Dan, as with big, swift hands he put on another bait for R. C.

"Do you fellows take me for a drag-horse?" inquired R. C. mildly. "I've caught enough swordfish for this year."

"Why, man, it's the day!" exlaimed Captain Dan, in amaze and fear.

"Humph!" replied my brother.

"But the chance of a record!" I added weakly. "Only ten o'clock. ... Three swordfish already. ... Great chance for Dan, you know. ... Beat the dickens out of these other fishermen."

"Aw, that's a lot of 'con'!" replied my brother.

Very eloquently then I elaborated on the fact that we were releasing the fish, inaugurating a sportsman-like example never before done there; that it really bid fair to be a wonderful day; that I was having a great chance to snap pictures of leaping fish; that it would be a favour to me for him to go the limit on this one occasion.

But R. C. shows no sign of wavering. He was right, of course, and I acknowledged that afterward to myself. On the instant, however, I racked my brain for some persuasive argument. Suddenly I had an inspiration.

"They think you're a dub fisherman," I declared forcefully.

"*They?*" My brother glared darkly at me.

"Sure," I replied hurriedly, with no intention of explaining that dubious *they*. "Now's your chance to fool them."

"Ahuh! All right, fetch on a flock of swordfish, and then some broadbills," remarked R. C. blandly. "Hurry, Dan! There's a fin right over there. Lead me to him! See."

Sure enough, R. C. pointed out a dark sickle fin on the surface.
I marvelled at the sight. It certainly is funny the luck some fishermen have! Captain Dan, beaming like a sunrise, swung the boat
around toward the swordfish.

That Marlin rushed the teasers. I pulled all three away from him,
while R. C. was reeling in his bait to get it close. Then the swordfish
fell all over himself after it. He got it. He would have climbed aboard
after it. The way R. C. hooked this swordfish showed that somebody
had got his dander up and was out to do things. This pleased me
immensely. It scared me a little, too, for R. C. showed no disposition
to give line or be gentle to the swordfish. In fact, it was real fight
now. And this particular fish appeared to have no show on earth—
or rather in the water—and after fourteen leaps he was hauled up
to the boat in such short order that if we had gaffed him, as we used
to gaff Marlin, we would have had a desperate fight to hold him.
But how easy to cut him free! He darted down like a blue streak.
I had no fair sight of him to judge weight, but Captain Dan said he
was good and heavy.

"Come on! Don't be so slow!" yelled R. C., with a roving eye
over the deep.

Captain Dan was in his element. He saw victory perched upon
the mast of the *Leta D.* He moved with a celerity that amazed me,
when I remembered how exasperatingly slow he could be, fooling
with kites. This was Captain Dan's game.

"The ocean's alive with swordfish!" he boomed. Only twice
before had I heard him say that, and he was right each time. I gazed
abroad over the beautiful sea, and, though I could not see any
swordfish, somehow I believed him. It was difficult now, in this
exciting zest of a record feat, to think of the nobler attributes of
fishing. Strong, earnest, thrilling business it was indeed for Captain
Dan.

We all expected to see a swordfish again. That was exactly what
happened. We had not gone a dozen boat-lengths when up out of
the blue depths lunged a lazy swordfish and attached himself to
R. C.'s hook. He sort of half lolled out in lazy splashes four or
five times. He looked huge. All of a sudden he started off, making
the reel hum. That run developed swiftly. Dan backed the boat
full speed. In vain! It was too late to turn. That swordfish run became
the swiftest and hardest I ever saw. A four-hundred-yard run, all
at once, was something new even for me. I yelled for R. C. to throw
off the drag. He tried, but failed. I doubted afterward if that would
have done any good. That swordfish was going away from there.
He broke the line.

"Gee! What a run!" I burst out. "I'm sorry. I hate to break off
hooks in fish."

"Put your hand on my reel," said R. C.

It was almost too hot to bear touching. R. C. began winding in the long slack line.

"Did you see that one?" he asked grimly.

"Not plain. But what I did see looked big."

"Say, he was a whale!" R. C.'s flashing eyes showed he had warmed to the battle.

In just ten minutes another swordfish was chasing the teasers. It was my thrilling task to keep them away from him. Hard as I pulled, I failed to keep at least one of them from him. He took it with a "wop," his bill half out of the water, and as he turned with a splash R. C. had his bait right there. Smash! The swordfish sheered off, with the bait shining white in his bill. When hooked he broke water about fifty yards out and then gave an exhibition of high and lofty tumbling, water-smashing, and spray-flinging that delighted us. Then he took to long, greyhound leaps and we had to chase him. But he did not last long, with the inexorable R. C. bending back on that Murphy rod. After being cut free, this swordfish lay on the surface a few moments, acting as if he was out of breath. He weighed about one hundred and fifty, and was a particularly beautiful specimen. The hook showed in the corner of his mouth. He did not have a scratch on his graceful bronze and purple and silver body. I waved my hat at him and then he slowly sank.

"What next?" I demanded. "This can't keep up. Something is going to happen."

But my apprehension in no wise disturbed R. C. or Captain Dan.

They proceeded to bait up again, to put out the teasers, to begin to troll; and then almost at once a greedy swordfish appeared, absolutely fearless and determined. R. C. hooked him. The first leap showed the Marlin to be the smallest of the day so far. But what he lacked in weight he made up in activity. He was a great performer, and his forte appeared to be turning upside down in the air. He leaped clear twenty-two times. Then he settled down and tried to plug out to sea. Alas! that human steam-winch at the rod drew him right up to the boat, where he looked to weigh about one hundred and twenty-five pounds.

"Six!" I exclaimed, as we watched the freed fish swim away. "That's the record. . . . And all let go alive—unhurt. . . . Do you suppose anyone will believe us?"

"It doesn't make any difference," remarked my brother. "We know. That's the best of the game—letting the fish go alive."

"Come on!" boomed Dan, with a big flying-fish in his hands. "You're not tired."

"Yes, I am tired," replied R. C.

"It's early yet," I put in, "We'll clinch the record for good. Grab the rod. I'll enjoy the work for you."

R. C. resigned himself, not without some remarks anent the insatiable nature of his host and boatman.

We were now off the east end of Clemente Island, that bleak and ragged corner where the sea, whether calm or stormy, contended eternally with the black rocks, and where the green and white movement of waves was never still. When almost two hundred yards off the yellow kelp-beds I saw a shadow darker than the blue water. It seemed to follow the boat, rather deep down and far back. But it moved. I was on my feet, thrilling.

"That's a swordfish!" I called.

"No," replied R. C.

"Some wavin' kelp, mebbe," added Dan doubtfully.

"Slow up a little," I returned. "I see purple."

Captain Dan complied and we all watched. We all saw an enormous colourful body loom up, take the shape of a fish, come back of R. C.'s bait, hit it and take it.

"By George!" breathed R. C. tensely. His line slowly slipped out a little, then stopped.

"He's let go," said my brother.

"There's another one," cried Dan.

With that I saw what appeared to be another swordfish, deeper down, moving slowly. This one also looked huge to me. He was right under the teasers. It dawned upon me that he must have an eye on them, so I began to pull them in.

As they came in the purple shadow seemed to rise. It was a swordfish and he resembled a gunboat with purple outriggers. Slowly he came onward and upward, a wonderful sight.

"Wind your bait in!" I yelled to R. C.

Suddenly Dan became like a jumping-jack. "He's got your hook," he shouted to my brother. "He's had it all the time."

The swordfish swam now right under the stern of the boat so that I could look down upon him. He was deep down, but not too deep to look huge. Then I saw R. C.'s leader in his mouth. He had swallowed the flying-fish bait and had followed us for the teasers. The fact was stunning. R. C., who had been winding in, soon found out that his line went straight down. He felt the fish. Then with all his might he jerked to hook that swordfish.

Just then, for an instant my mind refused to work swiftly. It was locked round some sense of awful expectancy. I remembered my camera in my hands and pointed it where I expected something wonderful about to happen.

The water on the right, close to the stern, bulged and burst with a roar. Upward even with us, above us, shot a tremendously large, shiny fish, shaking and wagging, with heavy slap of gills.

Water deluged the boat, but missed me. I actually smelled that fish, he was so close. What must surely have been terror for me, had I actually seen and realized the peril, gave place to flashing thought of the one and great chance for a wonderful picture of a swordfish close to the boat. That gripped me. While I changed the focus on my camera I missed seeing the next two jumps. But I heard the heavy sousing splashes and the yells of Dan and R. C., with the shrill screams of the ladies.

When I did look up to try to photograph the next leap of the swordfish I saw him, close at hand, monstrous and animated, in a surging, up-sweeping splash. I heard the hiss of the boiling foam. He lunged away, churning the water like a sudden whirl of a ferry-boat wheel, and then he turned squarely at us. Even then Captain Dan's yell did not warn us. I felt rather than saw that he had put on full speed ahead. The swordfish dived towards us, went under, came up in a two-sheeted white splash, and rose high and higher, to fall with a cracking sound. Like a flash of light he shot up again, and began wagging his huge purple-barred body, lifting himself still higher, until all but his tail stood ponderously above the surface; and then, incredibly powerful, he wagged and lashed upright in a sea of hissing foam, mouth open wide, blood streaming down his wet sides and flying in red spray from his slapping gills—a wonderful and hair-raising spectacle. He stayed up only what seemed a moment. During this action and when he began again to leap and smash towards us, I snapped my camera three times upon him. But I missed seeing some of his greatest leaps because I had to look at the camera while operating it.

"Get back!" yelled Dan hoarsely.

I was so excited I did not see the danger of the swordfish coming aboard. But Captain Dan did. He swept the girls back into the cabin doorway, and pushed Mrs R. C. into a back corner of the cockpit. Strange it seemed to me how pale Dan was!

The swordfish made long, swift leaps right at the boat. On the last he hit us on the stern, but too low to come aboard. Six feet closer to us would have landed that huge, maddened swordfish right in the cockpit! But he thumped back, and the roar of his mighty tail on the water so close suddenly appalled me. I seemed to grasp how near he had come aboard at the same instant that I associated the power in his tail with a havoc he would have executed in the boat. It flashed over me that he would weigh far over three hundred.

When he thumped back the water rose in a sounding splash, deluging us and leaving six inches in the cockpit. He sheered off astern, sliding over the water in two streaks of white running spray, and then up he rose again in a magnificent wild leap. He appeared maddened with pain and fright and instinct to preserve his life.

Again the fish turned right at us. This instant was the most terrifying. Not a word from R. C.! But out of the tail of my eye I saw him crouch, ready to leap. He grimly held on to his rod, but there had not been a tight line on it since he struck the fish.

Yelling warningly, Captain Dan threw the wheel hard over. But that seemed of no use. We could not lose the swordfish.

He made two dives into the air, and the next one missed us by a yard, and showed his great, glistening, striped body, thick as a barrel, and curved with terrible speed and power, right alongside the cockpit. He passed us, and as the boat answered to the wheel and turned, almost at right angles, the swordfish sheered too, and he hit us a sounding thud somewhere forward. Then he went under or around the bow and began to take line off the reel for the first time. I gave him up. The line caught all along the side of the boat. But it did not break, and kept whizzing off the reel. I heard the heavy splash of another jump. When we had turned clear round, what was our amaze and terror to see the swordfish, seemingly more tigerish than ever, thresh and tear and leap at us again. He was flinging bloody spray and wigwagging his huge body, so that there was a deep, rough splashing furrow in the sea behind him. I had never known any other fish so fast, so powerful, so wild with fury, so instinct with tremendous energy and life. Dan again threw all his weight on the wheel. The helm answered, the boat swung, and the swordfish missed hitting us square. But he glanced along the port side, like a toboggan down-hill, and he seemed to ricochet over the water. His tail made deep, solid thumps. Then about a hundred feet astern he turned in his own length, making a maelstrom of green splash and white spray, out of which he rose three-quarters of his huge body, purple-blazed, tiger-striped, spear-pointed, and, with the sea boiling white around him, he spun around, creating an indescribable picture of untamed ferocity and wild life and incomparable beauty. Then down he splashed with a sullen roar, leaving a red foam on the white.

That appeared the end of his pyrotechnics. It had been only a few moments. He began to swim off slowly and heavily. We followed. After a few tense moments it became evident that his terrible surface work had weakened him, probably bursting his gills, from which his life-blood escaped.

We all breathed freer then. Captain Dan left the wheel, mopping his pale, wet face. He gazed at me to see if I had realized our peril. With the excitement over, I began to realize. I felt a little shaky then. The ladies were all talking at once, still glowing with excitement. Easy to see they had not appreciated the danger! But Captain Dan and I knew that if the swordfish had come aboard—which he certainly would have done had he ever slipped his head over the gunwale—there would have been a tragedy on the *Leta D.*

"I never knew just how easy it could happen," said Dan. "No one ever before hooked a big fish right under the boat."

"With that weight, that tail, right after being hooked, he would have killed some of us and wrecked the boat!" I exclaimed, aghast.

"Well, I had him figured to come into the boat and I was ready to jump overboard," added my brother.

"We won't cut him loose," said Dan. "That's some fish. But he acts like he isn't goin' to last long."

Still, it took two hours longer of persistent, final effort on the part of R. C. to bring this swordfish to gaff. We could not lift the fish up on the stern and we had to tow him over to Mr. Jump's boat and there haul him aboard by block and tackle. At Avalon he weighed three hundred and twenty-eight pounds.

R. C. had caught the biggest Marlin in 1916—three hundred and four pounds, and this three-hundred-and-twenty-eight-pound fish was the largest for 1918. Besides, there was the remarkable achievement and record of seven swordfish in one day, with six of them freed to live and roam the sea again. But R. C. was not impressed. He looked at his hands and said:

"You and Dan put a job up on me. . . . Never again!"

From *Tales of Fishes*

Pike

Ted Hughes

Pike, three inches long, perfect
Pike in all parts, green tigering the gold.
Killers from the egg: the malevolent aged grin.
They dance on the surface among the flies.

Or move, stunned by their own grandeur
Over a bed of emerald, silhouette
Of submarine delicacy and horror.
A hundred feet long in their world.

In ponds, under the heat-struck lily pads—
Gloom of their stillness:
Logged on last year's black leaves, watching upwards.
Or hung in an amber cavern of weeds.

The jaws' hooked clamp and fangs
Not to be changed at this date;
A life subdued to its instrument;
The gills kneading quietly, and the pectorals.

Three we kept behind glass,
Jungled in weed: three inches, four,
And four and a half: fed fry to them—
Suddenly there were two. Finally one.

With a sag belly and the grin it was born with.
And indeed they spare nobody.
Two, six pounds each, over two feet long,
High and dry and dead in the willow-herb—

One jammed past its gills down the other's gullet:
The outside eye stared: as a vice locks—
The same iron in this eye
Though its film shrank in death.

A pond I fished, fifty yards across,
Whose lilies and muscular tench
Had outlasted every visible stone
Of the monastery that planted them—

Stilled legendary depth:
It was as deep as England. It held
Pike too immense to stir, so immense and old
That past nightfall I dared not cast

But silently cast and fished
With the hair frozen on my head
For what might move, for what eye might move.
The still splashes of the dark pond,

Owls hushing the floating woods
Frail on my ear against the dream
Darkness beneath night's darkness had freed,
That rose slowly towards me, watching.

It Came as a Big Surprise

Byron Rogers

There is an Angler's Prayer you still come across occasionally, painted on old mugs in fishing inns. It is a bit like a river itself, the couplet meandering towards a tired rhyme.

> *Lord, grant that I may catch a fish so big that even I,*
> *When speaking of it afterwards, may have no need to lie.*

This is an account of a man, "an excellent angler, and now with God", as Walton put it, who did just that. He caught a fish so big it would have needed two large men, their arms fully outstretched, to give cynics in saloon bars even a hint of its dimensions.

But he did more than that. He went fishing for salmon one day and caught something so peculiar, so far removed from even the footnotes of angling in Britain, that a grown man who was present ran off across the fields. Nobody would have thought it at all odd that day if the fisherman had been found trying to look up his catch in the Book of Revelations.

It needs a photograph. The fisherman is dead. His friends are beginning to die. If a photograph had not been taken few people would now believe what happened. A hundred years ago, ballads and hearsay would have wrecked it on the wilder shores of myth. As it is yellowing cuttings from the local paper, almost crumbling into carbon, are slowly unfolded from wallets. A print is unearthed reverently from under a pile of household receipts. It was on July 28, 1933, that Alec Allen caught his fish, but even that has been elbowed into myth. His obituary (far from the national press) says that it was on July 9. The *Guinness Book of Records* says that it was July 25. But the one contemporary cutting had no doubts. It was July 28. Appropriately it was a Friday.

The photograph is extraordinary. Allen, a short man in a Fairisle pullover and baggy trousers, leans against a wall beside a trestle. It is a typical Thirties snapshot slouch. His hands are in his pockets. There is a cigarette in his mouth. But of course you notice all this a long time afterwards, because of the thing dangling from the trestle.

At first it looks like the biggest herring in the history of the sea. It towers over the man by a good four feet. It is a fish certainly, but the head ends in a dark snout. The body appears to be armoured. The surroundings, a farm gate, the field beyond, underline the oddness. In a farmyard a man is posing beside a thing the size of a basking shark. Alec Allen had caught himself a Royal Sturgeon in the River Towy, at Nantgaredig, near Carmarthen. It was nine feet two inches long, had a girth of 59 inches, and weighed 388 pounds.

Allen was a commercial traveller from Penarth in Glamorganshire. He was a well known sportsman and hockey referee. In later life he was to referee Olympic matches. But he was then in his

22

early forties, one of that oddly innocent breed who figure in Saki and Wodehouse, but who latterly seem to have become as extinct as the Great Auk, the sporting bachelor. His great delight was fishing, but in him it was more than a delight.

His great friend was Alderman David Price of Nantgaredig, who died last year aged 74. He had known Allen all his life. All they had ever talked about, he recalled with wonder, was fishing.

In 1933 Allen was traveller for a firm of fishing tackle manufacturers. His father, also a great fisherman, was a traveller for a wallpaper firm. Father and son somehow contrived it that they could travel together in the same car. Both their commercial beats were West Wales, but a West Wales wonderfully concentrated between the rivers Wye, Teify and Towy. When their friends talk about the Allens it is with amusement. It was notorious that their business rounds were engineered for fishing.

Off-stage Hitler was ranting, Stalin drawing up lists of victims, Ramsay MacDonald droned his platitudes, and the dole queues lengthened. But in West Wales the Allens went their way, in a car full of tackle and wallpaper, their itineraries perfectly arranged to end in fishing inns beside rivers. The thing has an idyllic quality. It may have been a bit tough on you if your wallpaper shop was nowhere near a river, but nobody seems to have complained. In time the son succeeded the father as wallpaper salesman, but the itineraries did not change.

The two had rented a stretch of the Towy since 1928. This included some of the deepest pools in the river. But the summer of 1933 had been dry, and the water level was low. Walking by one of the pools that July Alec Allen noted enormous waves suddenly cross it. It puzzled him but at the time he would have discounted any suspicion that they had been made by a living thing. After all it was 15 miles to the sea, and tidal water ended two miles lower down.

A few days later Allen returned to the pool. It was evening and he had a friend with him, Edwin Lewis of Crosshands. There was a third man, his name lost to history, watching on the bank. Allen began fishing. It was a quiet evening. But then he felt a slight tug on his line. He pulled on it but to no effect.

Alderman Price was fond of telling what happened next, "Alec used to tell me that he thought he'd hooked a log. He couldn't see what it was, except that it was something huge in the shadows. Then the log began to move upstream." A faint smile would come over Price's face.

"Now Alec knew that logs don't move upstream."

Allen had still no idea of what was in the river. A more imaginative man might have become frightened at that stage. His line was jerking out under a momentum he had never experienced. In the darkness of the pool he had hooked something which moved with the force of a shark.

He played it for 20 minutes, letting the line move out when it went away. When it came back he retreated up the bank. But there was no channel of deep water leading away from the pool. If there had been, no salmon line made would have held his catch. Then he saw it.

Suddenly the creature leapt out of the water. Maddened, it crashed into a shallow run. It was there under them, threshing in the low water. Allen was confronted by a bulk that was just not possible. The sightseer ran shouting for his life.

But Lewis ran forward with the gaff. He stuck it into the fish, but the fish moved. It straightened the steel gaff. Then the great tail flicked up and caught Lewis, and threw him into the air on to the bank. Just one flick, but it nearly broke the man's leg.

There was a large rock on the bank. Allen dropped the rod (it had been a freak catch, the hook snagging in the fish's head, a sturgeon having no mouth) and tugged at the rock. With it in his hands he waded out, and dropped it on the head, lifting it again and pounding at it. The creature began to die. The two men looked down at it. Neither had any idea what it was.

But in death it provided them with an even greater problem: how were they to get it out of the river? Allen ran to a nearby farm. There then occurred one of those rare moments which cannot help but be pure comedy. Allen asked could he borrow a horse and cart. The farmer, naturally, asked why. Allen said he had caught a fish.

It ended with farmer, farmer's friends, dogs, horse, cart and all going back to the bank.

"I can remember it now," said Alderman Price. "Alec came running to my house. I had never seen him so excited. All he would say was, 'Well, I've caught something this time that you'll never beat.' I went back with him. They'd pulled it up on to the trestle you see in the photographs, and the news had got round. People were coming in cars and in carts. They were ferrying children across the river.

"It had these big scales, I remember. Very slimy. It was a sort of black and white in colour. No, I wasn't frightened." He was in the habit of pausing at that point. "It was dead."

As the anglers gathered it was determined that the thing out of the river was a sturgeon. Vague memories stirred. Was it not the law that a sturgeon was the King's prerogative?

A telegram was sent to Buckingham Palace inquiring after the King the next day. A stiff little reply came the same day, that the King was not in residence. Such trivia did not deter a man who had hooked the biggest fish in recorded angling history. Allen sold the sturgeon to a fishmonger from Swansea for two pounds ten shillings.

That worked out at something like a penny ha'penny a pound, and this at a time when Scotch salmon at Billingsgate was fetching two and six a pound. More than 40 years later Allen's friends, who had helped him load the thing on to the train, were still bitter about the deal.

There had been so much caviar in the sturgeon that some of it had fallen on to the farm yard where it was eaten by those of the farmer's pigs with a taste for the good life. History does not relate what happened to the pigs subsequently. But selling the fish did get rid of one problem. There were no refrigerators in the Valley, and 388 pounds of sturgeon was a lot of fish.

Allen fished on until his death in 1972 at the age of 77. In photographs the lean figure became stocky. Spectacles were added. Catches got held up regularly to the camera, something he could never have done that wild July night when he was content just to pose beside his fish. So did he consider the rest of his fishing life to be a sort of epilogue?

Brian Rudge, who now runs the fishing tackle firm on whose

behalf Allen meandered through West Wales, knew him well. "I think he saw the incident as more of a joke than anything. He wasn't a man who was easily impressed. I think, you know, that as far as he was concerned it was a bit of a nuisance. He was out salmon fishing. The sturgeon had got in his way."

Alderman Price heard Allen talk about it a few times. "It was usually when he heard anglers going on about their catches. He wasn't a boasting man but sometimes he couldn't resist saying, 'Well, I suppose this would be the biggest fish I ever caught.' And then of course they'd say, 'Good God.'"

Yet outside the valley and angling circles it was a small fame. There was no mention of it in the national press that July.

It was a small item even in the *Carmarthen Journal.* The august organ rose to its greatest heights of sensationalism. "Two anglers had an exciting time while fishing in the River Towy," the report began.

In March, 1972, Allen died suddenly at the home in Penarth he had shared with a spinster sister. But there was a passage in his will which surprised his friends almost as much as the catching of the sturgeon. Though he had talked little about the incident, he left instructions that his body be cremated and the ashes put into the river at the spot out of which he had pulled Leviathan.

"I called on David Price one day," said Ronald Jones, the former Chief Constable of Dyfed, and another of Allen's friends, "and said what a pity it was about Alec. 'Aye,' said Dai, 'I've got him there on the mantlepiece.' It was the casket, you see. We were all surprised. Nobody's ever heard of anyone wanting that done before."

"I suppose it was a romantic touch," said Brian Rudge, "but he wasn't the sort of man who'd like people to gather round a grave."

It was a grey wet day when they put the ashes into the water. A dozen of his old friends, contacted by phone or letter, gathered on the bank. No clergyman or minister had agreed to take part, their religion not recognising a river as consecrated ground.

Despite the hymns in the rain, it would seem to have had pagan overtones. Among the first things a people names are rivers. River gods are the oldest. A man who had pulled out of a river its largest living thing would seem to be assuaging something very old in having himself put back in its place.

"We said the Lord's Prayer," said the Chief Constable, "as we committed the ashes to the waters he'd fished for 50 years. But then as the wind carried them I saw a trout leap into the air just where they were drifting.

"And I said to Dai: 'Look, Alec's there.'"

From *The Sunday Telegraph*

Caviare

H. and G. Papashvily

From the early nineteenth century upper class society, particularly in St Petersburg, affected foreign manners and clothes, spoke French almost exclusively and Russian, if at all, with an artificial accent, engaged German tutors, Parisian governesses and English nurses, and sent the family washing to Western Europe to be laundered. But this all-pervasive snobbery changed the basic cuisine very little. Russian foodstuffs, climate and customs did not adapt to continental standards. Chefs came and went, a few new dishes were introduced, a few old ones improved, but generally the traditional fare seemed to suit the Russians best. By the middle of the century this traditional fare had been stabilized into what is often considered the finest cuisine in Russian history. From that time until the outbreak of World War I, Russians of nobility and wealth passed their day in an elaborate ritual of four separate meals, reaching a climax in a feast of small dishes—the famous *zakuska*—and a splendid dinner. Let us follow such a day from meal to meal.

The day began with tea, a strong essence made in a china pot and diluted in the cup to the desired strength with briskly boiling water from the samovar, an ornate brass urn heated by a charcoal fire in a vertical tube at the centre. Milk was sometimes added, and a piece of sugar broken from the loaf with small silver pincers. Women drank their tea from a cup, men from a glass set in an engraved or filigreed metal holder with a handle. With the tea went sweet buns, plain rolls, or bread with butter and perhaps a slice of cheese.

About noon a simple lunch was prepared, usually fish or meat and a vegetable with, perhaps, a plain pudding for a sweet. Often only the women and children of the family appeared at the table. The men would be lunching at some male stronghold—at the club, at the officers' mess, or at a restaurant. In Moscow, the restaurant might be Testov's, for oblong pies stuffed with gelatinous sturgeon spine, eggs and mushrooms; or the Slaviansky Bazaar, for clear, rich, deep orange sterlet soup; or the Moscovi Traktir, for *kotlety pozharskie* of minced chicken.

Dinner, the main meal of the day, could be eaten at any time from late afternoon to mid-evening. It began with *zakuska*, an array of "small bites" accompanied by vodka, set out in advance on a table in the hall, the parlour or an alcove in the reception room. In some households, particularly in Moscow which was considered more Russian than St Petersburg, the *zakuska* table was a permanent fixture, constantly replenished, always available.

Because *zakuska* is so typically Russian an institution, it is worth special attention. The custom probably originated in country houses on vast estates, to which guests came over long distances on bad roads, often in below-zero weather. People might arrive at any hour, frequently unexpected, usually hungry. *Zakuska* offered a practical way to give them sustenance and keep them in good spirits until dinner could be prepared.

As time passed, the *zakuska* grew increasingly lavish, with more and varied dishes. It became commonplace for visitors from abroad to mistake it for the full dinner and partake so heartily that they could not eat the meal that followed. By the last decades of the nineteenth century the composition and content of the *zakuska* table had evolved from a culinary exercise into an esoteric art form that embraced the techniques of mosaic, collage, sculpture, easel painting and taxidermy. Each dish was lavishly decorated— a wreath of turnip rosebuds for the pâté, carrot daisies blooming in the aspic, unsalted butter lilies for the bread, a silver chain of onion rings encircling a herring, spring onions transmuted into white peacocks spreading green fan-tails.

An over-all plan combining both functional and aesthetic principles was worked out for the table, which was usually oval and placed so that guests might surround it comfortably while sampling the scores of dishes. Some foods, such as the fish, cheeses and meats, were more or less grouped together; others, such as pickles and breads, were set at several convenient points. To keep within this framework and yet achieve a balance of taste, texture and colour—so that the dark smoked eel was close to the pink salmon, the hard, thin sausage beside a creamy ivory cheese, a bowl of crisp green pickles near the golden sprats—called for a discerning eye and a skilled hand.

The most important item on the table was caviar, offered in a variety and an amount that was an indication of both the host's solvency and the guests' consequence. One noble family had a cut-glass barrel that held 20 kilograms—about 45 pounds—and was refilled daily. It was served from a crystal dish with a silver spoon, since base metals impaired the flavour.

In earlier times the roes of many kinds of fish—shad, mullet, whiting, codfish, catfish—had been considered delicacies. By the nineteenth century, however, fashions in food had changed and the most popular were the roe of four species of sturgeon, called caviar from the Turkish word for roe, *khavyah*.

From the Volga sterlet came the rarest of all caviars—a golden roe that was traditionally reserved for the imperial table. Of the three other sturgeons from which roe is taken, the *Beluga*, largest in size, produces the largest eggs, which may vary after processing from almost black to grey, touched by a pearly lustre. *Sevruga* and *Osetrova* sturgeon, smaller both in body and in the size of their eggs, sometimes yield a darker roe. While the large grey Beluga egg was, and is, generally considered the choicest caviar available, the quality of caviar depends not only on the variety of sturgeon, but also on the individual fish—its age, genetic composition, food supply, environment—and on the treatment of the roe.

For the finest caviar, the roe is sieved by hand to remove membranes and is lightly salted; the Russian word for the best grade, *malossol*, means just that—lightly salted. Less choice roes are more heavily salted and pressed into bricks called *Pausnaia*. Freezing permanently destroys the cellular composition of the roe used in producing caviar, and at temperatures above 45°F (7°C) caviar soon spoils. Today, caviar is generally pasteurized and vacuum-packed in glass and tin, but in earlier times its transport to Moscow and St Petersburg required containers that had to be carefully warmed in winter and chilled in summer.

From *The Cooking of Russia*

The Escape of Ika

H. E. Towner Coston

Towner Coston's book The Swift Trout *tells the parallel life-stories of two fish which were bred on the same trout-farm. One grows up in an English river; the other, Ika, is shipped to New Zealand.*

The pohutokawas, the Maori Christmas trees, were in full bloom, their scarlet blossoms making a blaze of colour amongst the dull tones of green and brown. Ra, in happy mood, sparkled ceaselessly on the turquoise of the lake and everywhere roused a ready response.

In the pahs, the Maori wahines were busy about their preparations for the haka. There would be many guests; and a guest in a Maori household must always be made welcome. Even if the hosts themselves have to go short, a guest must always be fed, no matter how unwanted.

Now it was a time of plenty. The maize was not yet ripe, but the kumaras could be dug, and many tuna hung drying in the sun.

Trout brought in by the successful Maori fishermen must be cured. These were split open, soaked in strong brine for twenty-four hours, then hung in the sun until tacky. Then in a lean-to affair, made of the boughs of green manuka, a fire was kindled and green wood and sawdust heaped on until the place filled with acrid smoke. Now the split fish were hung inside on improvised rafters until they should be sufficiently smoked to keep until the haka.

As if by magic, the blowflies appeared. The mere killing of a fish sufficed to conjure them up, and now, with all this food in preparation, they hovered about the pahs in swarms. But every one was happy. There would be plenty kai, plenty haka, and much korero (talk). Treasured kiwi feather mats were produced and shaken out, and the more elaborately woven ones, their herbal dyes still unfaded, showed something of the glory that had departed. In place of the slightly dark-skinned European in rather nondescript clothes, there would stand vital figures, their fine bodies exposed, and once again the real Maori would live.

Rewi and Tiki were kept busy. Both were noted fishermen and to them had been delegated much of the responsibility for supplying the pah with trout.

Rewi was glad of the feathers of Matuku. Between them they caught many fine fish, and he was more than glad to think that he could use legitimate methods in their capture. His favourite fishing spot in the evening was just where the Golden River flowed out of the lake. Overlooking this spot was the Ranger's office. It was no place for the practice of underhand methods.

It was late in the evening when Rewi and Tiki came down the slope to where their dinghy was drawn up on the sand. The shadows were lengthening fast as they loaded their rods and tackle on board and shoved off.

Owing to the number of fishermen standing waist deep in the waters which covered the spit, they had to make a detour, and tiny wavelets slapped against the hull as the oars bent to the pull of the brawny-armed Tiki.

There was another boat already anchored in the stream when they arrived, but still plenty of room, so it mattered little.

A heavy chunk of iron was dropped over the bows, the oars were shipped and the boat swung round, fretting at the rope which held it. Then Rewi and Tiki went leisurely about their business of the evening.

Sitting side by side on the middle thwart, facing the stern, they tied on their strong lake casts and Rewi produced the flies. Carefully they fingered them over and each selected one, mounting it carefully on the cast. Then, each putting his rod out on the opposite side, they began to harl.

The four-inch wood reels had their ratchets set at "off" and the fly was allowed to drift back very slowly on the current. Skilled hands weaved the rods so that the fly was moving at a rate somewhat less than that of the current, and the vibrations of the tip kept it swimming in a lifelike manner.

Sometimes they caught fish while letting out their lines, but usually the strike came when they had worked them part of the distance back again. It was not fishing of the most ethical kind and called for no fine skill in casting. It was quite legitimate, and they were not seeking exercise, but food and a bit of sport during which they could sit and smoke and talk, and enjoy the pleasant evening.

A hundred yards of line were slipped off the reels and checked. Slowly, in little jerks, like the erratic darting of the kokopu, the flies were reeled in again.

Many times they repeated the performance. Then Tiki had a strike. A silver streak leaped out of the water as the hook was driven home, and Rewi reeled in frantically to avoid a tangle.

The fight was sparkling but shortlived, and the rainbow was quickly lifted into the boat. It was not a large fish, but a plump one of about three and a half pounds.

Again the lines reached slowly out. By now the sun was gone and dusk was rapidly spreading over the land. Along the shore line, an occasional light would flare up as some fisherman lit his pipe. Now and then came a darting flash over the surface as a lucky one engaged in a fight or extracted the hook from a captive.

Ika's restlessness had brought him once more into the lake, but after the quiet of his pool in the river he found it unattractive. Certainly the water was calm and food was plentiful. But the constant disturbance caused by chugging launches and spluttering outboard motors, and the omnipresent danger from the flashing spoons which were dragged in their wake, turned his thoughts back to the river again. He was now feeling the pull of the current once more and keeping to the deeper water beyond the spit.

Ika was in no hurry. Now that his longings were definitely stilled he dawdled along, at peace with the world, except for these distractions.

In this pleasant state he came to where the main flow of the river swept through the narrows, and was intrigued by the food he found there. Presently he became aware of numbers of odd kokopus working one after another up and down the current. In the half-light they looked very lifelike.

Ika was a big fish and liked substantial foods.

One flashed past him, but it was going too fast for him to bother with it. Then another came flickering along, its progress slow and hesitant as if at any second it would change its mind and make for the nearest boulder or swim off downstream. Ika struck.

Bang! He came up with a jerk. The sharp point of the hook went home in his jaw. He became possessed of a terrible fear.

Another kokopu flashed swiftly by, but it was unseen. Making the most of the current, Ika turned his powerful body and made off downstream. Breathing would become difficult if he kept it up too long, but for the moment he was only concerned to get away from the pressure which was holding him.

Rewi yelled. He knew he had hooked into no small fish.

"Kapai! Te ika nui—the big fish," he cried excitedly as he felt the weight of Ika.

Although Ika rushed to the surface several times and made long runs for the waving fronds of weed, he could not shake out the hook. His head wagged savagely, but he was powerless.

The fight was long and arduous. Rewi and Tiki, wise in the ways of these waters, knew they had no rainbow on and were rather surprised. The capture of a brown trout here in these days was something of an event. Tiki yelled the news to a boat which hovered near by, watching the fight.

At last, Ika, the strength gone from his fine body, turned belly up and was led up to the boat.

Tiki leaned down and lifted him out of the water just as the other boat came alongside, its occupants eagerly curious to see the big brown trout. They knew that when a brown trout was captured here it was usually a big one.

"What's he weigh, Tiki?" asked one.

"Blowed if I know," was the rejoinder. "You got any scales?"

The occupant of the other boat signified that he had, and Tiki, having extracted the hook, reached over to hand the ika to him to be weighed. In the light of the torch, Ika looked a beautiful sight, one to make the pulse of the most stolid quicken.

The boats had drifted slightly apart as soon as the pull of the oars in the second boat ceased. The stretch was a long one and Ika was heavy on an outstretched arm. Ika was exhausted but not dead.

Suddenly the nearness of the water brought a flash of hope back into his heart. With one convulsive kick he came to life in the out-stretched hand and felt himself slipping.

"Look out!" yelled Riwi. But it was too late. At the mere sensation of slipping Ika found enough strength to give one more flip of his tail. There was a dull splash and he disappeared from view, leaving three amazed and concerned faces peering down as if to catch a last glimpse of him.

Rewi's grin faded and Tiki started shamefacedly to explain how it all happened. For a while Rewi was inconsolable. However, they continued fishing and a fine rainbow of five pounds made him smile again, though he still shook his head regretfully over the lost fish, which grew larger the more he thought about it.

Ika must have been twice blest by Tangaroa, the god of the seas and the fishes. Twice when death seemed inevitable he had escaped, nay, if his escape whilst still unborn in the spawning beds be taken into consideration, he was thrice blest.

Ika was not aware of his good fortune. All he knew was a deathly sickness, a tiredness which made every fin movement a conscious effort, and the exertion of his gills as they laboured to restore the oxygen balance in his blood. As he lay on the bottom he rolled in his weakness, and had not the strength to travel farther.

This feeling soon passed, however, though he remained weak and tired for some days. A few hours later, his respiration and strength restored, he suddenly came to life, and swam off to seek a place far removed from these seductive dangers.

From *The Swift Trout*

The Mahseer

Jocelyn Lane

*The British Raj is the social and political setting for
Jocelyn Lane's account of big mahseer fishing in India.
The mahseer is a giant minnow classified in the Order
Cypriniformes. The book was published in 1954.*

Though many anglers would probably endorse the opinion expressed by Francis Francis that "the wild rush of a twenty-pound salmon thrills through the frame as nothing else in the nature of sport does," not a few of those who have fished for both would hand the palm to a mahseer of comparable weight. However this may be, the mahseer is entitled to his special niche among sporting freshwater fish that take the fly.

I feel, myself, that there is little cause to take sides regarding the relative sporting merits of these two rivals, since in my view both stand supreme in their different ways. We can however hold the scales between them and see how their merits pan out, weight for weight.

The most impressive characteristic of a hooked mahseer is the startling tug he gives on seizing the fly or bait and the sustained headlong rush that follows it without a pause. In this he puts all he has got, and when and if he is brought to close quarters again, rush follows rush, each only slightly less furious and protracted than the last. In this way his strength, great though it is, is relatively soon exhausted. He then takes to boring deep in the water, near at hand. The first rush of a mahseer is a fair criterion of his weight, whereas it may only be possible to estimate the weight of a salmon as the fight progresses. And herein lies the superiority of the salmon's tactics—his grand leaps, his never-say-die determination and staying powers; and finally when he does come to gaff what fish can vie with the stream-lined beauty of a big fresh-run salmon, or sea trout?

I would say then, that the initial phases of the battle with a big mahseer are unsurpassed for their thrills and that the later phases of the struggle with a salmon of the same size are equally so.

The "mighty mahseer", though a somewhat grandiloquent title, is not without its aptness. The name has been interpreted as Great Mouth, *maha* meaning great—hence Maharajah. A mahseer of 119 lbs. was caught by Col. Rivett-Carnac in the Cauvery river in 1919, and I have a photo of a so-called Tigris salmon—(*Barbus seich*) a near relative of the mahseer—weighing 140 lbs., caught on a 2 in. spoon by Major F. B. Lane in Iraq, also in 1919. Larger ones have been taken with paste or meat baits. The record mahseer proper was caught by J. de Wet van Ingen of Mysore in 1946 on the upper reaches of the Cubbany river; and weighed 120 lbs.

Many wildly improbable stories are told of these wild fish, and so often repeated that one comes almost to believe in them. There is for instance the hardy perennial about the fisherman whose fly was taken by a swallow and the swallow by a mahseer. What happened after that varies with the version. Possibly the mahseer took the fisherman. In any case there is no need to exaggerate the feats of these fish, which are quite astonishing enough in reality.

As an example, I may quote the following experience of an old friend of mine, "T." He was fishing from one of the bridges on a well known irrigation canal in Northern India, which at that point was about fifty yards wide and ran straight as could be between high banks to the next bridge, just visible in the distance. He was using a salmon rod, with 200 yards of backing on the reel. The fish took in midstream and went off at full speed, taking half the backing with him in no time. "T." put extra pressure on the drum with his fingers till they were blistered. He then tried pressing his sleeve against the line—with no better effect. The line cut into the cloth, and the fish still raced on. A moment or two later the last of the two hundred yards of backing ran off, and with a sharp snap broke from the reel. All this happened without a pause, in a matter of seconds. How big that fish was and how far it travelled it would be interesting to know.

The mahseer, though a carp, is very different in appearance, dash and vigour from its British namesakes. Being a carp it grows its teeth not in the mouth but in its throat. Embedded in the muscles of the gullet are two semi-circular bones hinged together to form a ring and on each of the bones are grouped clusters of strong, closely-packed teeth coated with a highly polished enamel. I have in my possession a set of them removed from a mahseer of about 14 lbs. The ring of bone is nearly $3\frac{1}{2}$ inches in diameter, and some of the teeth are three-quarters of an inch long and correspondingly thick. In this vice the fish is not only able to crush up large water-snails, crabs and shells but the heaviest spoon-bait, as if it were made of cardboard. In comparison with this ominous outfit, the salmon's dentition shrinks into insignificance. The mahseer's lips are leathery and actuated by powerful muscles, so that it is capable of seizing and killing a small fish by sheer compression. A curious feature of the mouth is that the upper lip can be protruded, owing to the presence of an extending membrane, as may be seen, and can then be turned downwards to form a sort of inverted cup. This contrivance, acting after the manner of a vacuum-cleaner, enables the fish to suck up even minute objects, such as grains of rice, one by one, with extraordinary rapidity.

The scales of the mahseer are extremely large and thick, and the fins too a good deal bigger in proportion to the body than those of the salmon family. Immediately above the anal fin the girth of the body is considerably greater than round the tail end. This abrupt drop, so to speak, detracts from the streamlining of the fish as seen in profile. H. S. Thomas attributed the powerful rush of the mahseer to the comparatively large superficial area covered by its fins. Judging however by what is now known of the function of the fins, one may safely say that the momentum displayed by this fish is due rather to the abnormal strength of its supple frame, as a whole. As regards the fins the more likely explanation is that their large size enables the fish to maintain its balance and position in the heavy streams it frequents. I have watched mahseer, of sixty pounds and over, lying poised almost motionless in terrific currents where no ordinary fish would linger purposely.

Notwithstanding the leathery nature of their lips mahseer are quite sensitive in the matter of taste. One day while out fishing with a friend I decided to put this to the test for my own satisfaction. We were sitting on a high rock overlooking a pool which we knew contained a number of mahseer, including some big ones, and had just finished our lunch, consisting mainly of sardine sandwiches. Leaving my friend to watch, I went to the rapids near the head of the pool and emptied the dregs of a sardine tin into the water. Before long a number of mahseer had collected and my friend could see others ranging from one to two pounds working their way up stream towards me. None of the big ones, however, put in an appearance, probably because they were lying in the depths well out of the way of temptation. Undoubtedly the fish had been attracted from some distance by the taste of the sardine oil carried well down into the pool by the rapid water above—and a fly soon caused some of them to regret it. I need hardly add that never before or since have I resorted to such depths of delinquency.

Though usually shy of any unnatural movements within their ken, mahseer grow accustomed to them more readily than trout, where they are of frequent occurrence. At least, that has been my impression.

A striking example of this adaptability is their behaviour in what is known to Hindus as the Sacred Pool—an artificial basin about twenty yards wide, adjoining a well-known Hindu temple on the Ganges. This temple stands in grand surroundings at the mouth of a gorge, where the river breaks through the Himalayan foothills into the plains. The pool is connected with the river by a channel through which the fish have free passage in and out, and is spanned by a low bridge reminiscent of the Chinese Willow Pattern. From the bridge these fish, varying in weight from five to fifty pounds, and packed almost as thickly as sardines, are hand-fed by the pilgrims. When a fistful of grain is thrown in, the mass surges and huge fish rise above the surface of the water, gliding over the backs of the smaller ones to secure their share of the grain. The strange thing is that the fish do not remain permanently in the pool but are constantly changing places with wild ones from the river; and yet, without any restraint or compulsion, they quickly adopt habits directly contrary to instinct.

My first visit to the pool was quite an incidental one, preparatory to fishing in the neighbourhood. Anyone with a rod in the vicinity of the temple was naturally regarded with disfavour by the priests and pilgrims, so I made my way upstream to a promising pool; and almost immediately got into a fish. The hooking of a big mahseer under normal conditions may be likened to the hooking of an express train, but this fish merely sank to the bottom of the pool and stood on its head, lazily waving its tail end. I might have been fast in Asia for all the effect my salmon rod had on it at first, and it took a prolonged tug-of-war to bring it eventually up to the surface. I towed its twelve pounds of inertia shorewards, embraced it with a thumb under each gill cover, and managed to strand it safely. Sad to say, I had killed a sacred fish that had wandered from its sanctuary, and, according to the Hindu belief in transmigration, had violated the soul of its saintly inmate. Not wishing to incur the odium of the gods, or of the local priesthood, I slipped it back carefully and walked on several hundred yards further upstream, consoling myself with the thought that, according to Plato, only the souls of the stupidest entered into fish.

Having wandered thus far from the sacred pool I may as well carry this narrative to its sequel. Just as I was preparing to make my first cast I heard some monkeys chattering excitedly at the top of a bluff behind me. Out of curiosity I climbed up to investigate, and came upon a strange scene. In a small glade stood an Indian, clad, or almost unclad, in the garb of an ascetic. His back was towards me and near him was an artificial cave of rocks, evidently his temporary abode—while at a safe distance crouched a troop of monkeys. In one hand he held some nuts, and in the other a stone. He threw a few nuts to the monkeys and while they were squabbling over them followed these up with the stone, chuckling in a most unholy way as the monkeys scrambled up the nearest trees. I caught his attention and enquired in my best vernacular if there was any objection to my fishing in the pool below.

To my amazement he answered in perfect English, with only a slight accent, "No, sir. Not a bit, as long as I don't see you doing it."

On questioning him I found that he had been educated at a public school and at Cambridge. "Whatever brought you here?" I asked.

He waved his arm towards the towering mountains across the river. "Where else would I find anything like this? Here I am free. My board and lodging are free. I am free from the tyranny of money and free from care."

"But what do you do with yourself all day?" I enquired.

"When I am not amusing myself with the monkeys I sit and contemplate the infinity of Nature and lose myself in it all. Contemplation deadens the sense of time, you know."

"Don't you feel very lonely?" I asked.

"One of your poets has answered that question. I can't remember the whole verse but one line sticks in my memory. 'There is society where none intrudes.' Perhaps you know who wrote it?"

"Byron," I said, "*Childe Harold*. You mean the verse that goes on:

'To mingle with the Universe, and feel
What I can ne'er express, yet cannot all conceal.' "

"Yes, that's the one," he said, with a charming smile. "It answers all your questions in a nutshell."

Here I left this strange embodiment of Eastern philosophy and returned to the pool. What happened there has something to do with a spoon—and so nothing to do with this book.

A small tributary, the River Song, which flows through the dense forests of the Doon Valley, joins the Ganges close to the Sacred Pool. It is an Elysian stream for the fly fisherman—brisk, boulder-strewn and wadeable almost throughout its length—and it holds plenty of small mahseer up to five pounds in weight, which readily take the fly. A 'basket,' of which I have a snapshot, of five fish weighing $12\frac{1}{2}$ lbs. was no more than an average one, but on the day I made this catch I was to learn that there were bigger fish in the Song than ever came out of it.

Near its mouth there was a nice pool spanned by a wooden footbridge. With an angler's curiosity, I made for the bridge to see what was to be seen in the pool, and, shading my eyes from the glare, peered down into the depths. At first the pool seemed to be empty. Then my attention was arrested by a dark object near the bottom that seemed to be moving slightly, and I discovered to my astonishment that I was looking at a huge mahseer of about seventy pounds. It was an exciting moment. I shouted to my orderly to bring my spinning rod, but to my surprise the answer came from the opposite side of the river.

"Ho-oo. Don't kill the fish. Don't kill the fish."

The next moment a frantic Forest Guard, fully turbaned and badged, appeared running through the bushes. He arrived, panting, on the bridge and began to gabble excitedly. The pith of his complaint was this.

The Viceroy was expected to arrive in the neighbourhood, shortly, on a fishing trip, and sport must be good. It was only with infinite pains, and by dint of much ground-baiting with grain, that the 'big fish' had been enticed from the main river into this secluded pool, where it was being fed daily to keep it *cooshy* till the great day came. And now a total stranger had suddenly appeared from nowhere and was about to kill His Excellency's fish. No wonder the 'poor' man was dithering with panic at this unexpected threat to all his dreams of untold *buksheesh*. Reluctantly I left him with his charge and wandered off ruminating.

Those in high places are naturally in a position to get their pick of sport, but it might surprise them if they knew how much of it is made to order.

To return to the habits of the mahseer. Like many other river and lake fish they are addicted to moving more or less in shoals. So much so that when a fish is hooked several more are likely to put in an appearance and follow it almost right up to the net. As the spawning season approaches mahseer travel long distances and sometimes ascend several thousand feet to find suitable water. Dropping back as the water falls, they are then cut off completely from the fry which they otherwise would make short work of. They do not spawn once and for all during the season, like the salmon, but lay their eggs in batches, repeating this procedure two or three times at intervals.

A curious belief persists among Indian fishermen—and by this I mean the Indians themselves—that mahseer have a taste for a dish of hailstones, and occasionally even die from a surfeit of them.

At any rate there can be no doubt that hail often brings them on the rise without any other apparent cause. Of this I have had plenty of ocular proof, and in one instance while unhooking my fly from a small mahseer, caught in a hailstorm, I actually found a hailstone still in its mouth; though whether it had been accepted as a separate tit-bit, or sucked in with the fly, it was impossible to know.

And now as to fishing and fly-fishing tactics.

The fishing season ranges roughly from autumn to spring; that is to say, throughout the colder months. Even so, sport is not at its best during the warmest hours of the day. One may knock off from nine in the morning to about four in the afternoon, and again at sunset, without missing much. To my mind, the cream of mahseer fishing, from the sporting point of view, is to be had in the turbulent rivers that flow through the lower gorges and valleys of the Himalaya, but very large fish are also to be caught much further south in some of the big rivers, such as the Cauvery.

A good gillie is a great asset. I have in mind the Gurkha and the Garhwali, both jolly companions with a keen sense of humour. Their methods may be primitive but the spirit of sport is there. Most of their villages are sited near mountain rivers and they are adepts at partially damming backwaters, forming a line and driving the fish into the shallows. Here the fun begins, as is evident from their shouts of excitement when the fish escape between their legs while they are scooping them out—call it poaching if you like. In some parts of the higher ranges their methods have much in common with those of dry-fly fishing. More than once I have come across villagers fishing with a bamboo and using some succulent flower of the forest as bait. This they cast across stream and work as a floating fly, with evident success. Without hesitation, provided that they can swim, they will take to the water, even in rapids, to rescue a fly or spoon from a snag.

Then there is the Arab fisherman of the Tigris and Euphrates. He will take you out in his coracle and provide you with sport of a novel and somewhat alarming type. My first attempt at coracle

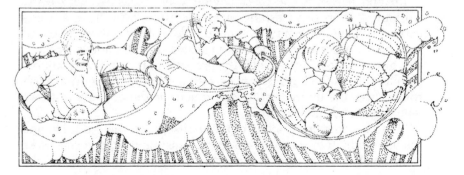

management in those wide, swirling waters was a nightmare. I have recollections of revolving like a top, clockwise and anti-clockwise, in the eddies, where all sense of the points of the compass was lost. Give me a craft with a well-defined starboard and larboard for choice. Even when out with an expert navigator there was always the possibility, or so I felt, of being yanked overboard, rod and all, by a 'Tigris salmon' of perhaps 130 lbs. or so in weight. Nor was it much consolation to know that one might eventually land up on the shores of the alleged Garden of Eden itself, at the head of the Persian Gulf.

Those who fish for mahseer with the fly, only have to deal mainly with mahseer minor; that is to say, with fish of not more than 5 lbs. in weight—the larger ones having at this stage taken permanently to predacious habits, cannibalism or bottom feeding. Popular flies vary in their colour schemes as much as Paris fashions, or as the tackle shops can make them. Black flies, and those incorporating jungle cock's feathers, are much in vogue. None the less, home-tied imitations of the natural flies will, in my experience, hold their own and more with the innumerable fancy favourites, and mahseer minor will suck them in as readily and daintily as any trout. For the bigger fish, up to ten pounds, any silvery fly is acceptable, especially if it be a near imitation of a miniature fish, though a spoon or live bait is preferable.

The most suitable tackle for the fly takers is much the same as that used for lake trout. It is just as well to remember that you may hook a big 'un unexpectedly at any time, and in this connection anything up to 150 yards of backing is a wise insurance against risks. At the same time it is most important that the reel should not be overloaded, or recovery may be difficult and result in a regrettable dilemma. Personal experience is a potent teacher and I have never forgotten my dismay on one occasion at finding myself with a reel crammed to the brim and ten yards of unrecovered line still attached to a tired mahseer of bulky proportions.

Up and across is the most paying way of casting with a fly, working it as in trout fishing at home. Those who have any experience of salmon fishing will have little difficulty about so-called striking. In other words the fish, provided that the line is straight, sees to the matter himself, and the pressure of the hook, if you hold on hard, drives the barb home. As with a salmon, the sight of a fish rolling over the fly may prove too much for the angler's restraint —and the result a clean miss.

The two enemies-in-chief of the mahseer are the crocodile and the otter, which in some Indian rivers runs the crocodile very close as a spoil-sport of the worst type. Once while fishing in the

Himalayan foothills I happened on a big dog otter who gave me an object lesson in the destructive methods of his kind. I had hardly started to fish when a small, dark object caught my eye, appearing and disappearing in the water about 200 yards downstream, and my field glasses showed that it was an otter. He was working his way towards me so I took cover behind a big boulder and kept the glasses on him. Presently he caught a fish and brought it to the bank. I could see him lying on a flat rock with one foot holding down the fish, which he chewed a little, and then left. A minute or so later he surfaced again with another fish in his mouth. This time he took it into the shallows, where he sat up and, after taking a good look round to see that the coast was clear, grasped it between his paws, gave it a crunch and dropped it. He then dived and continued to swim towards me. Within every twenty yards or so he had a fish, which he treated in the same way, systematically hunting the water that I had hoped to fish later. When he arrived opposite to me I rose and waved my arms at him, whereupon he dived in a flash and came up in mid-stream. After pausing a moment to have a look at me he gave a loud whistle and disappeared, eventually emerging on the opposite bank a hundred yards away. There he sat up at full stretch, like a pet dog, to make sure what I was up to, and feeling rather dubious about it whistled loudly again and ran along the bank for about thirty yards, where, to my disgust, he took to the river and calmly went on fishing upstream.

I was not the only witness of this scene. Already a fishhawk had carried off one of the dead fish, and another was patrolling overhead, keeping an eye on me as I made my way down the bank to take stock of the damage. I counted ten mutilated fish and probably there were more, all of about one pound in weight and all chewed in the head or shoulder. The total number of fish this single otter must have destroyed did not bear thinking about.

The otter is an attractive creature in many ways, but to describe him as the fisherman's friend, as some have, is hardly fair to the trout.

Big mahseer, as I have said, rarely take a fly. The following account therefore of a tussle with one that did do so may be worth relating, if only for this reason.

The setting was a gorge in the Himalaya a few miles above the Sacred Pool already mentioned. Here the mahseer fishing is at its best and the river, which in places is a hundred yards wide and strewn with huge boulders, has all the features of an Alpine torrent on a gigantic scale. I was fishing a long pool with a heavy fall at its head, which churned up the water on the far side for a distance of some fifty yards. It was a wild scene and the roar of the fall echoing and re-echoing from the cliffs of the narrow gorge was awe-inspiring. On the near side the current eddied in a deep, glassy backwater at the edge of which stood a rock about the size of a big haystack. From the top of this I could cover the smoother water with my 16 ft. salmon rod.

As an experiment I was trying a very big salmon fly, a Wilkinson. I had made two or three casts and the fly was swinging round into the middle of the eddy when three great grey shapes rose almost imperceptibly from the depths, gliding slowly upwards side by side towards the fly. I judged the smallest to be a fish of 35 to 40 lbs., and the largest from 50 to 60. What happened next was too quick for me to follow. In my excitement I gave the fly a jerk that nearly brought it out of the water, and whether it was jealousy, or the sudden dart of the fly, that roused them it is impossible to say, but all three made a rush for it. There was a prodigious swirl and one of them took it, almost wrenching the rod, not to mention myself, into the water. The reel did not screech, it shrieked, and fifty yards of line ripped through the eddy in a few seconds and were gone downstream before I could bring the butt to bear. Directly the fish stopped, somehow or other I slid and bumped down the side of the rock and, reeling up as I went, scrambled along the stony beach to a point where the line entered the water about thirty feet from the bank. I could make no impression on the fish or feel anything but the throbbing of the current on the line. Obviously I was fast in a snag. Had I been alone that would have been the end of it, but now my orderly who was with me came to the rescue. Without a word he stripped and very pluckily swam out from one rock to another to try and clear the line. The current proved too strong, and after a dive or two he came back to tell me that the fish had taken the line under a submerged tree trunk which he could not move. Not to be defeated, he went off with his kukri and cut down a forked pole from a tree near by, with which he managed eventually to work the line free.

There was no mistake about the fish being still there. No sooner had the line straightened than he started off on another mad rush downstream, stripping off all the backing I had recovered and much more, while I followed as best I could, trying to keep in touch with him. It was no cross-country canter; it was a breath-taking obstacle race. Boulders, breast high, blocked the way and had to be surmounted before I got abreast of the fish some hundred yards further downstream. Directly I brought side strain to bear on him he changed his tactics and cut straight across the river, making the longest non-stop run of all. Anxiously I watched the lengthening line threading its way between the rocks, till the main current caught and drowned it, sweeping it downstream in a deep curve.

The fish ran on irresistibly, only stopping more than a hundred yards away near the opposite bank. I could do nothing but raise the rod as high as possible and hang on. A little further down, steep bluffs barred the way, and from below them came the roar of another pool. What was to happen next? The answer was not long in coming. The rod began to bob in little jerks and an ominous grating sensation passed down it. Suddenly the tension ceased. I reeled in frantically, and then more and more slowly as the loose backing floated down the current; and I knew that all was over. The best man had won.

Is it better to have hooked and lost? Painful though it may be, I think it is. I still have the remnant of the backing, and I still have that reel. It is a reel with a famous name, and to me a perpetual memento of fights such as that described; for one of the cross-bars is scored by the line throughout its length, each score telling of the rush of a big mahseer.

From *Fly Fisherman's Pie*

The Mighty Mahseer

The legends which the British spread about the big mahseer were sufficient to attract the Transworld Fishing Expedition which, in 1977, went to India from America to see whether the larger specimens were still around.

The term "Mighty Mahseer" first appeared in 1903, incorporated into the title of a book on angling in India, written by an Englishman who used the nom de plume Skene Dhu. But long before this book was published, the mahseer, that most magnificent of India's many freshwater game fish, had already captured the hearts and imaginations of generations of British sportsmen.

Having learned their fishing in the trout and salmon waters of England and Scotland, these anglers learned to prize and covet the noble mahseer, not only for the large size it attained but also for its indomitable fighting spirit.

In fact, as early as 1873, H. S. Thomas, the Izaac Walton of Indian angling literature, had stated his belief that, pound for pound, the mahseer was a fish superior in sporting qualities even to the "lordly salmon", and coming from an Englishman that was indeed high praise.

Subsequently, many books were written by Englishmen on angling in India. But reports of the capture of monster fish—mahseer over 75 lbs.—are rarely recorded. Major A. St. J. Macdonald, the doyen of Himalayan and Burmese mahseer angling, published photographs of "a brace of grandmothers" of 75 and 55 lbs. But he then went on to say ". . . indeed there must be few anglers in India who would need more than five fingers to count the fish they have caught over 50 lbs."

The record mahseer taken by Mr. J. deWet van Ingen in 1946 weighed 120 lbs and was significantly the last large mahseer recorded. Decline of the mahseer started when the British left India in 1947. Due to massive hydro-electric power schemes and intensive fish-farming, not to mention illegal netting, poisoning and dynamiting, the larger mahseer found itself on the verge of extinction. Whilst searching the shelves of an antiquarian bookshop in Salisbury, three fishing companions of long standing came across several of the books mentioned earlier and were astonished to find such a fish had been virtually forgotten for 30 years. The Transworld Fishing Expedition was born. But it took four years of planning by Bob Hewitt and brothers Martin and Andrew Clarke before the team's Land Rover began its trans-Asian journey to India. The trials and tribulations of obtaining sponsorship for such a venture were long and wearisome, and it was not until the team approached ABU in Britain that what had once been a dream became reality. Once the tackle sponsorship had been secured, other sponsors came forward. The team left London on September 1st, 1977, for a gruelling 7,000 mile drive through ten countries, across the blazing heat of the Middle Eastern plateau, to India.

January 1978 found the team in Bangalore, the beautiful Garden City capital of the state of Karnataka. It was here that the team was introduced to a Mr. P. L. N. Shetty, a keen angler and Honorary Secretary of the Wildlife Association of Southern India. Concerned over the drastic decline of large mahseer, W.A.S.I. had leased a 14-mile stretch of the river Cauvery. It was from this river that the van Ingen family had taken many large fish, though they themselves had long given up the pursuit of large mahseer due to irreparable damage done to this river by damming and dynamiting. Reports suggested, however, that local fishermen had recently taken large mahseer and indeed Mr. Shetty himself had taken a 50-pounder from the protected waters surrounding the old British power station at Bluff.

As it was too early in the season to venture into the W.A.S.I.-owned stretch of the river, it was suggested that we try Bluff. It was here that the team met its guide, Sundar Raj, an extremely accomplished local fisherman who explained that the fishing had been protected for 70 years, and that it was not uncommon to see large mahseer turning on the surface of the lake that fed the anicut leading to the power station.

After twelve long, biteless days, the season started with a bang when Sundar, fishing from a boat with Robert, hooked into what could only have been a monster. Unfortunately, his unfamiliarity with ABU sophistication had caused him to screw up the drag on his hand-held reel so tight that it could not yield line. Still clutching the top joint of an Atlantic 484 beachcaster that he had borrowed from the team in preference to his short bamboo stick, he was pulled out of the boat, over Robert's head, and disappeared down-stream in a bow-wave for about 20 yards before the hook straightened. Minutes later he struggled safely ashore, soaking wet and breathless.

Fishing continued a little apprehensively. On the next day the team caught its first mahseer. The 28 lb. fish put up an unbe-lievable fight on Andrew's Atlantic 443S and Ambassadeur 6500C, stripping off well over 100 yards of 0.40 mm line on its initial headlong rush into the lake. 25 minutes later, after five sizzling runs, the magnificent golden fish was deftly landed. Jubilation was mixed with relief as, after five long months, the team had at last found a place where big mahseer still lived.

The fish came in steadily over the next three weeks. Robert took a 34-pounder the next day. A few days later, it was Martin's turn, taking a long male fish of 42 lbs. in the middle of the night. The team's stay at Bluff was culminated by two marvellous fish: one of 55 lbs. falling to Andrew and then, the "pièce de résistance," an incredible 77 lbs. fish which fell to Sundar's own bait of spun fig! All the other fish were taken on a paste made from ground millet known locally as Ragi. The 77-pounder was rushed to Mysore to be skinned by a firm of renowned taxidermists, none other than the famous van Ingen brothers. They were extremely surprised to discover that the big fish were still at large.

And so to Sangam, site of the W.A.S.I. reserve stretch of the Cauvery river, set deep in the jungles of Southern Karnataka. The journey alone convinced the team that if monsters were to be had, surely this remote river valley was where they were to be found. At first glance the team realised that this would not be an easy task. The river ran through impenetrable jungle, though the rock-strewn rapids and slow, deep pools were ideal territory for mahseer. No facilities were available and all supplies had to be brought in in advance. The first camp was made at a place known as Moshelli Halla. Roughly translated this means "Crocodile Deep".

We had been advised that live-baiting with "chilwa", a term used to describe an infinite variety of small fish, and spinning, were the appropriate tactics. For two long and very hot weeks, the team fished on the baking rocks with very little success, taking ten fish in the 10–20 lbs. range. After the first week, the team instructed the W.A.S.I. guards to ground-bait two pools down-stream with ragi, in the belief that other baits might meet with more success.

This was the first time that ragi had been tried on this part of the river and it was with little confidence that we broke camp and moved down-stream to Ounti Gundu, Canarese for "The Single Stone". A camp was made under the shade of two huge mutthi trees directly opposite the swims that had been fed. It was here that the Code 3 Atlantics and Ambassadeurs were really tested to their limits. After taking many fish between 20 and 30 lbs. Ounti Gundu was climaxed by a magnificent brace of 51 and 56 lbs. caught by Martin and Robert respectively. But just how big did they grow? The season was drawing to a close and the final programme was decided on. The team would return to the original camp, feed two more likely pools and, with considerable optimism, fish the more powerful Atlantic 463S and Ambassadeur 7000 outfits.

The first of these pools was the site of the unsuccessful fortnight's livebaiting, Moshelli Halla, and the second was a massive, mile-long pool at the end of a long series of rapids known as Galliborrai. And so it was on April 3rd 1978, four long years of planning, 12,000 miles of driving and eight weary months under the Indian sun paid off with a bonus that was beyond our wildest dreams.

The team split into two. Robert and Sundar went upstream to Moshelli Halla, while Martin and Andrew took up their positions at Galliborrai. At 09.00 a call came over the walkie-talkie. Robert had landed a huge bronze mahseer of 80 lbs. No sooner had the call been received when Martin struck into what would prove to be the largest mahseer caught for 32 years. From a rock in the middle of the pool, after an hour-long struggle, Martin succeeded in playing out and landing a golden mahseer which later tipped the scales at an unbelievable 92 lbs.

This proved that the W.A.S.I. sanctuary had established the fact that the "Mighty Mahseer", if protected, can once again assume its status as the premier sporting fish of Asia.

From *The Abu Catalogue, 1979*

Boiled Trout

Izaak Walton

*Izaak Walton's rugged recipe for boiled trout is a
trencherman's challenge. Note his instruction that the
fish should not be washed after gutting, presumably to
keep the flavour of blood.*

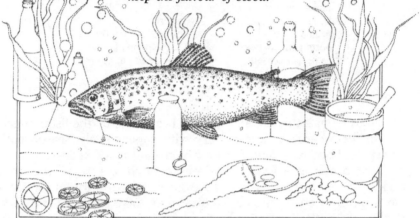

T ake your trout, wash, and dry him with a clean napkin; then
open him, and having taken out his guts, and all the blood,
wipe him very clean within, but wash him not, and give him three
scotches with a knife to the bone, on one side only. After which
take a clean kettle, and put in as much hard stale beer (but it must
not be dead), vinegar, and a little white wine and water as will
cover the fish you intend to boil; then throw into the liquor a good
quantity of salt, the rind of a lemon, a handful of sliced horseradish root, with a handsome light faggot of rosemary, thyme, and
winter savory. Then set your kettle upon a quick fire of wood: and
let your liquor boil up to the height before you put in your fish: and
then, if there be many, put them in one by one, that they may not
so cool the liquor as to make it fall. And whilst your fish is boiling,
beat up the butter for your sauce with a ladle full or two of the
liquor it is boiling in. And being boiled enough, immediately pour
the liquor from the fish: and being laid in a dish, pour your butter
upon it; and strewing it plentifully over with shaved horseradish,
and a little pounded ginger, garnish the sides of your dish, and the
fish itself, with a sliced lemon or two, and serve it up.

A grayling is also to be dressed exactly after the same manner,
saving that he is to be scaled, which a trout never is: and that must
be done either with one's nails, or very lightly and carefully with a
knife, for fear of bruising the fish. And note, that these kinds of
fish, a trout especially, if he is not eaten within four or five hours
after he be taken, is worth nothing.

From *The Complete Angler*

Trout with Shrimp

Robert Carrier

4 large fresh trout	4 oz. *100 g.* shelled shrimps
salt and freshly ground	4–6 tablespoons double cream
black pepper	
2 oz. *50 g.* butter	*Garnish:*
8 oz *225 g.* small	4 thin slices lemon
button mushrooms	2 tablespoons finely
juice of ½–1 lemon	chopped parsley

1. Clean trout if this has not already been done by the fishmonger. Wash them carefully and pat dry with paper towels. Season both inside and out with salt and freshly ground black pepper.

2. Melt butter in a frying pan large enough to take all the trout side by side. When it is hot, lay trout in pan and fry gently for 4 to 5 minutes on each side, or until they flake easily with a fork. Take care not to let butter burn.

3. Meanwhile, trim mushrooms; wipe them clean and slice them thinly. Sprinkle with lemon juice.

4. When trout are cooked, transfer them to a large, heated, serving dish and keep hot in a slow oven.

5. Add sliced mushrooms to butter remaining in frying pan and sauté gently for 3 minutes.

6. Add shrimps to pan and continue to sauté until heated through, about 3 minutes longer.

7. Stir in cream; bring almost to the boil and simmer until slightly thickened. Taste for seasoning, adding more salt, freshly ground black pepper or lemon juice if necessary.

8. Spoon sauce over trout. Garnish each fish with a slice of lemon and sprinkle with finely chopped parsley.

Serves 4.

From *Cooking for You*

The Inmates' Fishing Trip

Ken Kesey

*A group of voluntary patients in an American mental
hospital arrange a boat-fishing trip for sea-running salmon.
The narrator is a very tall Red Indian who thinks a lot
but doesn't say much. He is under treatment as well.*

We crossed a bridge over the Siuslaw. There was just enough
mist in the air that I could lick out my tongue to the wind
and taste the ocean before we could see it. Everyone knew we were
getting close and didn't speak all the way to the docks.

The captain who was supposed to take us out had a bald grey
metal head set in a black turtleneck like a gun turret on a U-boat;
the cold cigar sticking from his mouth swept over us. He stood
beside McMurphy on the wooden pier and looked out to sea as he
talked. Behind him and up a bunch of steps, six or eight men in
windbreakers were sitting on a bench along the front of the bait
shop. The captain talked loudly, half to the loafers on his one side
and half to McMurphy on the other side, firing his copper-jacket
voice someplace in between.

"Don't care. Told you specifically in the letter. You don't have a
signed waiver clearing me with proper authorities, I don't go out."
The round head swivelled in the turret of his sweater, beading
down that cigar at the lot of us. "Look there. Bunch like that at sea,
could go to diving overboard like rats. Relatives could sue me for
everything I own. I can't risk it."

McMurphy explained how the other girl was supposed to get all
those papers up in Portland. One of the guys leaning against the
bait shop called, "What other girl? Couldn't Blondie there handle
the lot of you?" McMurphy didn't pay the guy any mind and went
on arguing with the captain, but you could see how it bothered the
girl. Those men against the shop kept leering at her and leaning
close together to whisper things. All our crew, even the doctor,
saw this and got to feeling ashamed that we didn't do something.
We weren't the cocky bunch that was back at the service station.

McMurphy stopped arguing when he saw he wasn't getting any
place with the captain, and turned around a couple of times,
running his hand through his hair.

"Which boat have we got rented?"

"That's it there. The *Lark*. Not a man sets foot on her till I have
a signed waiver clearing me. Not a man."

"I don't intend to rent a boat so we can sit all day and watch it
bob up and down at the dock," McMurphy said. "Don't you have a
phone up there in your bait shack? Let's go get this cleared up."

They thumped up the steps onto the level with the bait shop and
went inside, leaving us clustered up by ourselves, with that bunch

of loafers up there watching us and making comments and sniggering and goosing one another in the ribs. The wind was blowing the boats at their moorings, nuzzling them up against the wet rubber tyres along the dock so they made a sound like they were laughing at us. The water was giggling under the boards, and the sign hanging over the door to the bait shack that read "SEAMAN'S SERVICE—CAPT BLOCK, PROP" was squeaking and scratching as the wind rocked it on rusty hooks. The mussels that clung to the pilings, four feet out of water marking the tide line, whistled and clicked in the sun.

The wind had turned cold and mean, and Billy Bibbit took off his green coat and gave it to the girl, and she put it on over her thin little T-shirt. One of the loafers kept calling down, "Hey you, Blondie, you like fruitcake lids like that?" The man's lips were kidney-coloured and he was purple under his eyes where the wind'd mashed the veins to the surface. "Hey you, Blondie," he called over and over in a high, tired voice, "hey you, Blondie . . . hey you, Blondie . . . hey you, Blondie . . ."

We bunched up closer together against the wind.

"Tell me, Blondie, what've they got *you* committed for?"

"Ahr, she ain't committed, Perce, she's part of the *cure*!"

"Is that right, Blondie? You hired as part of the *cure*? Hey you, Blondie."

She lifted her head and gave us a look that asked where was that hard-boiled bunch she'd seen and why weren't they saying something to defend her? Nobody would answer the look. All our hard-boiled strength had just walked up those steps with his arm around the shoulders of that bald-headed captain.

She pulled the collar of the jacket high around her neck and hugged her elbows and strolled as far away from us down the dock as she could go. Nobody went after her. Bill Bibbit shivered in the cold and bit his lip. The guys at the bait shack whispered something else and whooped out laughing again.

"Ask 'er. Perce—go on."

"Hey, Blondie, did you get 'em to sign a waiver clearing you with proper authorities? Relatives could sue, they tell me, if one of the boys fell in and drown while he was on board. Did you ever think of that? Maybe you'd better stay here with us, Blondie."

"Yeah, Blondie; my relatives wouldn't sue. I promise. Stay here with us fellows, Blondie."

I imagined I could feel my feet getting wet as the dock sank with shame into the bay. We weren't fit to be out here with people. I wished McMurphy would come back out and cuss these guys good and then drive us back where we belonged.

The man with the kidney lips folded his knife and stood up and brushed the whittle shavings out of his lap. He started walking towards the steps. "C'mon now, Blondie, what you want to mess with these bozos for?"

She turned and looked at him from the end of the dock, then back at us, and you could tell she was thinking his proposition over when the door of the bait shop opened and McMurphy came shoving past the bunch of them, down the steps.

"Pile in, crew, it's all set! Gassed and ready and there's bait and beer on board."

He slapped Billy on the rear and did a little hornpipe and commenced slinging ropes from their snubs.

"Ol' Cap'n Block's still on the phone, but we'll be pulling off as quick as he comes out. George, let's see if you can get that motor warmed up. Scanlon, you and Harding untie that rope there. Candy! What you doing off down there? Let's get with it, honey, we're shoving off."

We swarmed into the boat, glad for anything that would take us away from those guys standing in a row at the bait shop. Billy took the girl by the hand and helped her on board. George hummed over the dashboard up on the bridge, pointing out buttons for McMurphy to twist or push.

"Yeah, these pukers, puke boats, we call them," he said to McMurphy, "they joost as easy like driving the ottomobile."

The doctor hesitated before climbing aboard and looked towards the shop where all the loafers stood milling towards the steps.

"Don't you think, Randle, we'd better wait . . . until the captain—"

McMurphy caught him by the lapels and lifted him clear of the dock into the boat like he was a small boy. "Yeah, Doc," he said, "wait till the captain *what?*" He commenced to laugh like he was drunk, talking in an excited, nervous way. "Wait till the captain comes out and tells us that the phone number I gave him is a flophouse up in Portland? You bet. Here, George, damn your eyes; take hold of this thing and get us out of here! Sefelt! Get that rope loose and get on. George, come *on.*"

The motor chugged and died, chugged again like it was clearing its throat, then roared full on.

"*Hoowee!* There she goes. Pour the coal to 'er, George, and all hands stand by to repel boarders!"

A white gorge of smoke and water roared from the back of the boat, and the door of the bait shop crashed open and the captain's head came booming out and down the steps like it was not only dragging his body behind it but the bodies of the eight other guys as well. They came thundering down the dock and stopped right at the boil of foam washing over their feet as George swung the big boat out and away from the docks and we had the sea to ourselves.

A sudden turn of the boat had thrown Candy to her knees, and Billy was helping her up and trying to apologize for the way he'd acted on the dock at the same time. McMurphy came down from the bridge and asked if the two of them would like to be alone so they could talk over old times, and Candy looked at Billy and all he could do was shake his head and stutter. McMurphy said in that case that he and Candy'd better go below and check for leaks and the rest of us could make do for a while. He stood at the door down to the cabin and saluted and winked and appointed George captain and Harding second in command and said, "Carry on, mates," and followed the girl out of sight into the cabin.

The wind lay down and the sun got higher, chrome-plating the east side of the deep green swells. George aimed the boat straight out to sea, full throttle, putting the docks and that bait shop farther and farther behind us. When we passed the last point of the jetty and the last black rock, I could feel a great calmness creep over me, a calmness that increased the farther we left land behind us.

The guys had talked excitedly for a few minutes about our piracy of the boat, but now they were quiet. The cabin door opened once long enough for a hand to shove out a case of beer, and Billy opened us each one with an opener he found in the tackle box, and passed them around. We drank and watched the land sinking in our wake.

A mile or so out George cut the speed to what he called a trolling idle, put four guys to the four poles in the back of the boat, and the rest of us sprawled in the sun on top of the cabin or up on the bow and took off our shirts and watched the guys trying to rig their poles. Harding said the rule was a guy got to hold a pole till he got one strike, then he had to change off with a man who hadn't had a chance. George stood at the wheel, squinting out through the salt-caked windshield, and hollered instructions back how to fix up the reels and lines and how to tie a herring into the herring harness and how far back to fish and how deep:

"And take that number *four* pole and you put twelve ounces on him on a rope with a breakaway rig—I show you how in joost a minute—and we go after that *big* fella down on the bottom with that pole, by golly!"

Martini ran to the edge and leaned over the side and stared down into the water in the direction of his line. "Oh. Oh, my God," he said, but whatever he saw was too deep down for the rest of us.

There were other sports boats trolling up and down the coast, but George didn't make any attempt to join them; he kept pushing steadily straight on out past them, towards the open sea. "You bet," he said. "We go out with the commercial boats, where the real *fish* is."

The swells slid by, deep emerald on one side, chrome on the other. The only noise was the engine sputtering and humming, off and on, as the swells dipped the exhaust in and out of the water, and the funny, lost cry of the raggedy little black birds swimming around asking one another directions. Everything else was quiet. Some of the guys slept, and the others watched the water. We'd been trolling close to an hour when the tip of Sefelt's pole arched and dived into the water.

"George! Jesus, George, give us a hand!"

George wouldn't have a thing to do with the pole; he grinned and told Sefelt to ease up on the star drag, keep the tip pointed up, *up*, and work hell outa that fella!

"But what if I have a seizure?" Sefelt hollered.

"Why, we'll simply put hook and line on you and use you for a lure," Harding said. "Now work that fella, as the captain ordered, and quit worrying about a seizure."

Thirty yards back of the boat the fish broke into the sun in a shower of silver scales, and Sefelt's eyes popped and he got so excited watching the fish he let the end of his pole go down, and the line snapped into the boat like a rubber band.

"*Up*, I told you! You let him get a straight pull, don't you see? Keep that tip *up* . . .*up*! You had you one big silver there, by golly."

Sefelt's jaw was white and shaking when he finally gave up the pole to Fredrickson. "Okay—but if you get a fish with a hook in his mouth, that's my godblessed fish!"

I was as excited as the rest. I hadn't planned on fishing, but after seeing that steel power a salmon has at the end of a line I got off the cabin top and put on my shirt to wait my turn at a pole.

Scanlon got up a pool for the biggest fish and another for the first fish landed, four bits from everybody that wanted in it, and he'd no more'n got his money in his pocket than Billy drug in some awful thing that looked like a ten-pound toad with spines on it like a porcupine.

"That's no fish," Scanlon said. "You can't win on that."

"It isn't a b-b-bird."

"That there, he's a *ling* cod," George told us. "He's one good eating fish you get all his warts off."

"See there. He is too a fish. P-p-pay up."

Billy gave me his pole and took his money and went to sit up close to the cabin where McMurphy and the girl were, looking at the closed door forlornly. "I wu-wu-wu-wish we had enough poles to go around," he said, leaning back against the side of the cabin.

I sat down and held the pole and watched the line swoop out into the wake. I smelt the air and felt the four cans of beer I'd drunk shorting out dozens of control leads down inside me: all around, the chrome sides of the swells flickered and flashed in the sun.

George sang out for us to look up ahead, that here come just what we been looking for. I leaned around to look, but all I saw was a big drifting log and those black seagulls circling and diving around the log, like black leaves caught up in a dust devil. George speeded up some, heading into the place where the birds circled, and the speed of the boat dragged my line until I couldn't see how you'd be able to tell if you did get a bite.

"Those fellas, those cormorants, they go after a school of *candle* fishes," George told us as he drove. "Little white fishes the size of your finger. You dry them and they burn joost like a candle. They are *food* fish, chum fish. And you bet where there's a big school of them candle fish you find the silver salmon feeding."

He drove into the birds, missing the floating log, and suddenly all around me the smooth slopes of chrome were shattered by diving birds and churning minnows, and the sleek silver-blue torpedo backs of the salmon slicing through it all. I saw one of the backs check its direction and turn and set course for a spot thirty yards behind the end of my pole, where my herring would be. I braced, my heart ringing, and then felt a jolt up both arms as if somebody'd hit the pole with a ball bat, and my line went burning off the reel from under my thumb, red as blood. "Use the star drag!" George yelled at me, but what I knew about star drags you could put in your eye so I just mashed harder with my thumb until the line turned back to yellow, then slowed and stopped. I looked around, and there were all three of the other poles whipping around just like mine, and the rest of the guys scrambling down off the cabin at the excitement and doing everything in their power to get underfoot.

"Up! Up! Keep the tip up!" George was yelling.

"McMurphy! Get out here and look at this."

"Godbless you, Fred, you got my blessed fish!"

"McMurphy, we need some help!"

I heard McMurphy laughing and saw him out of the corner of my eye, just standing at the cabin door, not even making a move to do anything, and I was too busy cranking at my fish to ask him for help. Everyone was shouting at him to do something, but he wasn't moving. Even the doctor, who had the deep pole, was asking McMurphy for assistance. And McMurphy was just laughing. Harding finally saw McMurphy wasn't going to do anything, so he got the gaff and jerked my fish into the boat with a clean, graceful motion like he's been boating fish all his life. He's big as my leg, I thought, big as a fence post! I thought. He's bigger'n any fish we ever got at the falls. He's springing all over the bottom of the boat like a rainbow gone wild! Smearing blood and scattering scales like little silver dimes, and I'm scared he's gonna flop overboard. McMurphy won't make a move to help, Scanlon grabs the fish and wrestles it down to keep it from flopping over the side. The girl comes running up from below, yelling it's her turn, dang it, grabs my pole, and jerks the hook into me three times while I'm trying to tie on a herring for her.

"Chief. I'll be damned if I ever saw anything so *slow*! Ugh, your thumb's bleeding. Did that monster bite you? Somebody fix the Chief's thumb—hurry!"

"Here we go into them again." George yells, and I drop the line off the back of the boat and see the flash of the herring vanish in the dark blue-grey charge of a salmon and the line go sizzling down into the water. The girl wraps both arms around the pole and grits her teeth. "*Oh* no you don't, dang you! *Oh* no . . . !"

She's on her feet, got the butt of the pole scissored in her crotch and both arms wrapped below the reel and the reel crank knocking against her as the line spins out: "*Oh* no you don't!" She's still got on Billy's green jacket, but that reel's whipped it open and everybody on board sees the T-shirt she had on is gone—everybody gawking, trying to play his own fish, dodge mine slamming around the boat bottom, with the crank of that reel fluttering her breast at such a speed the nipple's just a red blur!

Billy jumps to help. All he can think to do is reach around from behind and help her squeeze the pole tighter in between her breasts until the reel's finally stopped by nothing more than the pressure of her flesh. By this time she's flexed so taut and her breasts look so firm I think she and Billy could both turn loose with their hands and arms and she'd *still* keep hold of that pole.

This scramble of action holds for a space, a second there on the sea—the men yammering and struggling and cussing and trying to tend their poles while watching the girl; the bleeding, crashing battle between Scanlon and my fish at everybody's feet; the lines all tangled and shooting every which way with the doctor's glasses-on-a-string tangled and dangling from one line ten feet off the back of the boat, fish striking at the flash of the lens, and the girl cussing for all she's worth and looking now at her bare breasts, one white and one smarting red—and George takes his eyes off where he's going and runs the boat into that log and kills the engine.

While McMurphy laughs. Rocking farther and farther backward against the cabin top, spreading his laugh out across the water— laughing at the girl, at the guys, at George, at me sucking my bleeding thumb, at the captain back at the pier and the bicycle

rider and the service-station guys and the five thousand houses
and the Big Nurse and all of it. Because he knows you have to
laugh at the things that hurt you just to keep yourself in balance,
just to keep the world from running you plumb crazy. He knows
there's a painful side; he knows my thumb smarts and his girl
friend has a bruised breast and the doctor is losing his glasses, but
he won't let the pain blot out the humour no more'n he'll let the
humour blot out the pain.

I notice Harding is collapsed beside McMurphy and is laughing
too. And Scanlon from the bottom of the boat. At their own selves
as well as at the rest of us. And the girl, with her eyes still smarting
as she looks from her white breast to her red one, she starts
laughing. And Sefelt and the doctor, and all.

It started slow and pumped itself full, swelling the men bigger
and bigger. I watched, part of them, laughing with them—and
somehow not with them. I was off the boat, blown up off the water
and skating the wind with those black birds, high above myself,
and I could look down and see myself and the rest of the guys, see
the boat rocking there in the middle of those diving birds, see
McMurphy surrounded by his dozen people, and watch them, us,
swinging a laughter that rang out on the water in ever-widening
circles, farther and farther, until it crashed up on beaches all over
the coast, on beaches all over all coasts, in wave after wave after
wave.

The doctor had hooked something off the bottom on the deep pole,
and everybody else on board except George had caught and landed
a fish by the time he lifted it up to where we could even see it—just
a whitish shape appearing, then diving for the bottom in spite of
everything the doctor tried to do to hold it. As soon as he'd get it
up near the top again, lifting and reeling at it with tight, stubborn
little grunts and refusing any help the guys might offer, it would
see the light and down it would go.

George didn't bother starting the boat again, but came down to
show us how to clean the fish over the side and rip the gills out so
the meat would stay sweeter. McMurphy tied a chunk of meat to
each end of a four-foot string, tossed it in the air, and sent two
squawking birds wheeling off. "Till death do them part."

The whole back of the boat and most of the people in it were
dappled with red and silver. Some of us took our shirts off and
dipped them over the side and tried to clean them. We fiddled
around this way, fishing a little, drinking the other case of beer,
and feeding the birds till afternoon, while the boat rolled lazily
around the swells and the doctor worked with his monster from
the deep. A wind came up and broke the sea into green and silver

chunks, like a field of glass and chrome, and the boat began to rock and pitch about more. George told the doctor he'd have to land his fish or cut it loose because there was a bad sky coming down on us. The doctor didn't answer. He just heaved harder on the pole, bent forward and reeled the slack, and heaved again.

Billy and the girl had climbed around to the bow and were talking and looking down in the water. Billy hollered that he saw something, and we all rushed to that side, and a shape broad and white was becoming solid some ten or fifteen feet down. It was strange watching it rise, first just a light colouring, then a white form like fog under water, becoming solid, alive . . .

"Jesus God," Scanlon cried, "that's the doc's fish!"

It was on the side opposite the doctor, but we could see by the direction of his line that it led to the shape under the water.

"We'll never get it in the boat," Sefelt said. "And the wind's getting stronger."

"He's a big flounder," George said. "Sometimes they weigh two, three hundred. You got to lift them in with the winch."

"We'll have to cut him loose, Doc," Sefelt said and put his arm across the doctor's shoulders. The doctor didn't say anything; he had sweated clear through his suit between his shoulders, and his eyes were bright red from going so long without glasses. He kept heaving until the fish appeared on his side of the boat. We watched it near the surface for a few minutes longer, then started getting the rope and gaff ready.

Even with the gaff in it, it took another hour to drag the fish into the back of the boat. We had to hook him with all three other poles, and McMurphy leaned down and got a hand in his gills, and with a heave he slid in, transparent white and flat, and flopped down to the bottom of the boat with the doctor.

"That was something." The doctor panted from the floor, not enough strength left to push the huge fish off him. "That was . . . certainly something."

The boat pitched and cracked all the way back to shore, with McMurphy telling grim tales about shipwrecks and sharks. The waves got bigger as we got closer to shore, and from the crests clots of white foam blew swirling up in the wind to join the gulls. The swells at the mouth of the jetty were combing higher than the boat, and George had us all put on life jackets. I noticed all the other sports boats were in.

We were three jackets short, and there was a fuss as to who'd be the three that braved that bar without jackets. It finally turned out to be Billy Bibbit and Harding and George, who wouldn't wear one anyway on account of the dirt. Everybody was kind of surprised that Billy had volunteered, took his life jacket off right away when we found we were short, and helped the girl into it, but everybody was even more surprised that McMurphy hadn't insisted that he be one of the heroes; all during the fuss he'd stood with his back against the cabin, bracing against the pitch of the boat, and watched the guys without saying a word. Just grinning and watching.

We hit the bar and dropped into a canyon of water, the bow of the boat pointing up the hissing crest of the wave going before us, and the rear down in the trough in the shadow of the wave looming behind us, and everybody in the back hanging on the rail and looking from the mountain that chased behind to the streaming black rocks of the jetty forty feet to the left, to George at the wheel. He stood there like a mast. He kept turning his head from the front to the back, gunning the throttle, easing off, gunning again, holding us steady riding the uphill slant of that wave in front. He'd told us before we started the run that if we went over that crest in *front*, we'd surfboard out of control as soon as the prop and rudder broke water, and if we slowed down to where that wave *behind* caught up it would break over the stern and dump ten tons of water into the boat. Nobody joked or said anything funny about the way he kept turning his head back and forth like it was mounted up there on a swivel.

Inside the mooring the water calmed to a choppy surface again, and at our dock, by the bait shop, we could see the captain waiting with two cops at the water's edge. All the loafers were gathered behind them. George headed at them full throttle, booming down on them till the captain went to waving and yelling and the cops headed up the steps with the loafers. Just before the prow of the boat tore out the whole dock, George swung the wheel, threw the prop into reverse, and with a powerful roar snuggled the boat in against the rubber tyres like he was easing it into bed. We were already out tying up by the time our wake caught up; it pitched all the boats around and slopped over the dock and whitecapped around the docks like we'd brought the sea home with us.

The captain and the cops and the loafers came tromping back down the steps to us. The doctor carried the fight to them by first off telling the cops they didn't have any jurisdiction over us, as we were a legal, government-sponsored expedition, and if there was anyone to take the matter up with it would have to be a federal agency. Also, there might be some investigation into the number of life jackets that the boat held if the captain really planned to make trouble. Wasn't there supposed to be a life jacket for every man on board, according to the law? When the captain didn't say anything the cops took some names and left, mumbling and confused, and as soon as they were off the pier McMurphy and the

captain went to arguing and shoving each other around. Mc-
Murphy was drunk enough he was still trying to rock with the roll
of the boat and he slipped on the wet wood and fell in the ocean
twice before he got his footing sufficient to hit the captain one up
alongside of his bald head and settle the fuss. Everybody felt better
that that was out of the way, and the captain and McMurphy both
went to the bait shop to get more beer while the rest of us worked
at hauling our fish out of the hold. The loafers stood on that upper
dock, watching and smoking pipes they'd carved themselves. We
were waiting for them to say something about the girl again,
hoping for it, to tell the truth, but when one of them finally did
say something it wasn't about the girl but about our fish being
the biggest halibut he'd ever seen brought in on the Oregon coast.
All the rest nodded that that was sure the truth. They came
edging down to look it over. They asked George where he learned
to dock a boat that way, and we found out George'd not just run
fishing boats but he'd also been captain of a PT boat in the Pacific
and got the Navy Cross. "Shoulda gone into public office," one of
the loafers said. "Too dirty," George told him.

They could sense the change that most of us were only suspect-
ing; these weren't the same bunch of weak-knees from a nuthouse
that they'd watched take their insults on the dock this morning.
They didn't exactly apologize to the girl for the things they'd said,
but when they ask to see the fish she'd caught they were just as
polite as pie. And when McMurphy and the captain came back
out of the bait shop we all shared a beer together before we drove
away.

From *One Flew Over the Cuckoo's Nest*

Piping in the Salmon

J. F. Todhunter

The small kirk of St Fergus, at Dalarossie in Inverness-shire, stands miles from the main road, on a promontory overlooking the Findhorn. There could hardly be a more beautiful site: it stands in isolation, its granite walls and slated roof flanked on two sides by farmland and on the other two by the river. Its well-kept churchyard is surrounded by a sturdy stone dyke, over which the tall tombstones gaze sternly, like chessmen, into the river ten yards below.

Under their gaze is a salmon pool, named, I need hardly add, Church Pool, in which salmon rest before tackling the tumbling, fast-running water, which turns through a right-angle round the point on which the church stands. The church is little used these days. The ruins of crofts and school bear witness to the size of the former population of the glen, now alas, long gone.

But last September, there was a rare event at the church—a wedding. No ordinary wedding, either, but that of a local laird, which had brought guests from all over the county. The church holds a mere seventy-two people, and there was an overflow of guests waiting outside. My wife and I were fishing the opposite bank of the Findhorn and for once the water was almost perfect after a spate and there was a tremendous run of autumn salmon. During the morning we had had four fish, and just before lunch I had beaten our previous family record with a fish of 17½ lb. Considering my advancing years, I was convinced that my fish would retain the record for the remainder of our fishing lives!

We went up to the Church Pool just after two o'clock in the afternoon. I went to the head of the pool and started fishing where the white water broke round the bend and my wife went further down to fish the tail. For a short while we fished, listening to the rush of the water and the dimly-heard murmur of the marriage service only 25 yards away on the other bank, when suddenly there was a screech from my wife, which might well have startled the minister, and she was into a big fish that had taken with enthusiasm her size 6 double-hooked Garry Dog.

The screech was loud enough to be heard by the waiting wedding guests on the opposite bank, and in no time at all there was an interested audience, with buttonholes and wedding hats, leaning on the churchyard wall and watching the battle below!

My wife succeeded in stopping the fish from going out of the tail of the pool, into a rushing torrent full of boulders, where she would surely have lost him and kept him trying to fight his way upstream, against the strong current. Twice, by sheer brute force, he pulled his way to the head of the pool and got his nose into the white water foaming over the rocks, and twice, with her heart in her mouth, she forced him to turn his head and back away before he could cut the cast on a sharp rock face.

The banks of the pool are steep and the water deep, and a fish is difficult to gaff or net unless one can get out to a sandy spit near the tail, to which a tired fish can be led. I just managed to reach this spit without getting wet, when, after twenty minutes of unrelenting struggle, my wife relaxed the pressure and let the tiring fish drop downstream. I was ready with the net in the water, and as he drifted slowly back, I had him in it. The subdued and decorous cheers from the spectators opposite were much appreciated.

I waded gingerly back, carrying in the net what I could feel at once was the heaviest fish either of us had ever caught, a great cock fish with a kype like a rhinocerous horn! I staggered up the bank and, having despatched him, hung him on my spring balance. He weighed just 18½ lb. My unbeatable family record had lasted just two hours!

"Well done," said I to my wife, as I held the fish up in the air, "I wish we had some way to celebrate this."

As I spoke, as if waiting for the cue, the doors of the church opposite were thrown open, and the bride and bridegroom emerged preceded by a piper, whose joyful music came singing across the water to us. His music was for the happiness of the new husband and wife, but it could not have been more appropriate for us at that moment. It was a wonderful moment, and the nicest wish my wife and I could think to send to the bride and bridegroom was that in their married life they may often experience such moments of happiness, excitement and success, all combined. Certainly, we are grateful to them for, fortuitously, providing the pipe music at exactly the right moment. It crowned the occasion for us, and made it one we shall certainly never forget.

from *Trout and Salmon*

Fish and the Shadow

Ezra Pound

The salmon-trout drifts in the stream,
The soul of the salmon-trout floats over the stream
Like a little wafer of light.

The salmon moves in the sun-shot, bright shallow sea. . . .
As light as the shadow of the fish
       that falls through the water,
She came into the large room by the stair,
Yawning a little she came with the sleep still upon her.
"I am just from bed. The sleep is still in my eyes.
Come. I have had a long dream."
And I: "That wood?
And two springs have passed us."
"Not so far, no, not so far now,
There is a place—but no one else knows it—
A field in a valley . . .
                          Qu'ieu sui avinen,
Ieu lo sai."

She must speak of the time
Of Arnaut de Mareuil, I thought, *"qu'ieu sui avinen"*.

Light as the shadow of the fish
That falls through the pale green water.

Big Two-Hearted River

Ernest Hemingway

The train went on up the track out of sight, around one of the hills of burnt timber. Nick sat down on the bundle of canvas and bedding the baggage man had pitched out of the door of the baggage car. There was no town, nothing but the rails and the burned-over country. The thirteen saloons that had lined the one street of Seney had not left a trace. The foundations of the Mansion House hotel stuck up above the ground. The stone was chipped and split by the fire. It was all that was left of the town of Seney. Even the surface had been burned off the ground.

Nick looked at the burned-over stretch of hillside, where he had expected to find the scattered houses of the town and then walked down the railroad track to the bridge over the river. The river was there. It swirled against the log piles of the bridge. Nick looked down into the clear, brown water, coloured from the pebbly bottom, and watched the trout keeping themselves steady in the current with wavering fins. As he watched them they changed their positions by quick angles, only to hold steady in the fast water again. Nick watched them a long time.

He watched them holding themselves with their noses into the current, many trout in deep, fast moving water, slightly distorted as he watched far down through the glassy convex surface of the pool, its surface pushing and swelling smooth against the re-sistance of the log-driven piles of the bridge. At the bottom of the pool were the big trout. Nick did not see them at first. Then he saw them at the bottom of the pool, big trout looking to hold themselves on the gravel bottom in a varying mist of gravel and sand, raised in spurts by the current.

Nick looked down into the pool from the bridge. It was a hot day. A kingfisher flew up the stream. It was a long time since Nick had looked into a stream and seen trout. They were very satisfactory. As the shadow of the kingfisher moved up the stream, a big trout shot upstream in a long angle, only his shadow marking the angle, then lost his shadow as he came through the surface of the water, caught the sun, and then, as he went back into the stream under the surface, his shadow seemed to float down the stream with the current, unresisting, to his post under the bridge where he tightened facing up into the current.

Nick's heart tightened as the trout moved. He felt all the old feeling.

He turned and looked down the stream. It stretched away, pebbly-bottomed with shallows and big boulders and a deep pool as it curved away around the foot of a bluff.

Nick walked back up the ties to where his pack lay in the cinders beside the railway track. He was happy. He adjusted the pack harness around the bundle, pulling straps tight, slung the pack on his

back, got his arms through the shoulder straps and took some of the pull off his shoulders by leaning his forehead against the wide band of the tump-line. Still, it was too heavy. It was much too heavy. He had his leather rod-case in his hand and leaning forward to keep the weight of the pack high on his shoulders he walked along the road that paralleled the railway track, leaving the burned town behind in the heat, and then turned off around a hill with a high, fire-scarred hill on either side on to a road that went back into the country. He walked along the road feeling the ache from the pull of the heavy pack. The road climbed steadily. It was hard work walking up-hill. His muscles ached and the day was hot, but Nick felt happy. He felt he had left everything behind, the need for thinking, the need to write, other needs. It was all back of him.

From the time he had gotten down off the train and the baggage man had thrown his pack out of the open car door things had been different. Seney was burned, the country was burned over and changed, but it did not matter. It could not all be burned. He knew that. He hiked along the road, sweating in the sun, climbing to cross the range of hills that separated the railway from the pine plains.

The road ran on, dipping occasionally, but always climbing. Nick went on up. Finally the road after going parallel to the burnt hillside reached the top. Nick leaned back against a stump and slipped out of the pack harness. Ahead of him, as far as he could see, was the pine plain. The burned country stopped off at the left with the range of hills. On ahead islands of dark pine trees rose out of the plain. Far off to the left was the line of the river. Nick followed it with his eye and caught glints of the water in the sun.

There was nothing but the pine plain ahead of him, until the far blue hills that marked the Lake Superior height of land. He could hardly see them, faint and far away in the heat-light over the plain. If he looked too steadily they were gone. But if he only half-looked they were there, the far-off hills of the height of land.

Nick sat down against the charred stump and smoked a cigarette. His pack balanced on top of the stump, harness holding ready, a hollow moulded in it from his back. Nick sat smoking, looking out over the country. He did not need to get his map out. He knew where he was from the position of the river.

As he smoked, his legs stretched out in front of him, he noticed a grasshopper walk along the ground and up on to his woollen sock. The grasshopper was black. As he had walked along the road, climbing, he had started many grasshoppers from the dust. They were all black. They were not the big grasshoppers with yellow and black or red and black wings whirring out from their black wing sheathing as they fly up. These were just ordinary hoppers, but all a sooty black in colour. Nick had wondered about them as he walked, without really thinking about them. Now, as he watched the black hopper that was nibbling at the wool of his sock with its fourway lip, he realized that they had all turned black from living in the burned-over land. He realized that the fire must have come the year before, but the grasshoppers were all black now. He wondered how long they would stay that way.

Carefully he reached his hand down and took hold of the hopper by the wings. He turned him up, all his legs walking in the air, and looked at his jointed belly. Yes, it was black too, iridescent where the back and head were dusty.

"Go on, hopper," Nick said, speaking out loud for the first time. "Fly away somewhere."

He tossed the grasshopper into the air and watched him sail away to a charcoal stump across the road.

Nick stood up. He leaned his back against the weight of his pack where it rested upright on the stump and got his arms through the shoulder straps. He stood with the pack on his back on the brow of the hill looking out across the country toward the distant river and then struck down the hillside away from the road. Underfoot the ground was good walking. Two hundred yards down the hillside the fire line stopped. Then it was sweet fern, growing ankle high, to walk through, and clumps of jack pines; a long undulating country with frequent rises and descents, sandy underfoot and the country alive again.

Nick kept his direction by the sun. He knew where he wanted to strike the river and he kept on through the pine plain, mounting small rises to see other rises ahead of him and sometimes from the top of a rise a great solid island of pines off to his right or his left. He broke off some sprigs of the heathery sweet fern, and put them under his pack straps. The chafing crushed it and he smelled it as he walked.

He was tired and very hot, walking across the uneven, shadeless pine plain. At any time he knew he would strike the river by turning off to his left. It could not be more than a mile away. But he kept on toward the north to hit the river as far upstream as he could go in one day's walking.

For some time as he walked Nick had been in sight of one of the big islands of pine standing out above the rolling high ground he was crossing. He dipped down and then as he came slowly up to the crest of the ridge he turned and made toward the pine trees.

There was no underbrush in the island pine trees. The trunks of the trees went straight up or slanted toward each other. The trunks were straight and brown without branches. The branches were high above. Some interlocked to make a solid shadow on the brown forest floor. Around the grove of trees was a bare space. It was brown and soft underfoot as Nick walked on it. This was the over-lapping of the pine needle floor, extending out beyond the width of the high branches. The trees had grown tall and the branches moved high, leaving in the sun this bare space they had once covered with shadow. Sharp at the edge of this extension of the forest floor commenced the sweet fern.

Nick slipped off his pack and lay down in the shade. He lay on his back and looked up into the pine trees. His neck and back and the small of his back rested as he stretched. The earth felt good against his back. He looked up at the sky, through the branches, and then shut his eyes. He opened them and looked up again. There was a wind high up in the branches. He shut his eyes again and went to sleep.

Nick woke stiff and cramped. The sun was nearly down. His pack was heavy and the straps painful as he lifted it on. He leaned over with the pack on and picked up the leather rod-case and started out from the pine trees across the sweet fern swale, toward the river. He knew it could not be more than a mile.

He came down a hillside covered with stumps into a meadow. At the edge of the meadow flowed the river. Nick was glad to get to the river. He walked upstream through the meadow. His trousers were soaked with the dew as he walked. After the hot day, the dew had come quickly and heavily. The river made no sound. It was too fast and smooth. At the edge of the meadow, before he mounted to a piece of high ground to make camp, Nick looked down the river at the trout rising. They were rising to insects come from the swamp on the other side of the stream when the sun went down. The trout jumped out of water to take them. While Nick walked through the little stretch of meadow alongside the stream, trout had jumped high out of water. Now as he looked down the river, the insects must be settling on the surface, for the trout were feeding steadily all down the stream. As far down the long stretch as he could see, the trout were rising, making circles all down the surface of the water, as though it were starting to rain.

The ground rose, wooded and sandy, to overlook the meadow, the stretch of river and the swamp. Nick dropped his pack and rod-case and looked for a level piece of ground. He was very hungry and he wanted to make his camp before he cooked. Between two jack-pines, the ground was quite level. He took the axe out of the pack and chopped out two projecting roots. That levelled a piece of ground large enough to sleep on. He smoothed out the sandy soil with his hand and pulled all the sweet fern bushes by their roots. His hands smelled good from the sweet fern. He smoothed the up-rooted earth. He did not want anything making lumps under the blankets. When he had the ground smooth, he spread his three blankets. One he folded double, next to the ground. The other two he spread on top.

With the axe he slit off a bright slab of pine from one of the stumps and split it into pegs for the tent. He wanted them long and solid to hold in the ground. With the tent unpacked and spread on the ground, the pack, leaning against a jack-pine, looked much smaller. Nick tied the rope that served the tent for a ridge-pole to the trunk of one of the pine-trees and pulled the tent up off the ground with the other end of the rope and tied it to the other pine. The tent hung on the rope like a canvas blanket on a clothes line. Nick poked a pole he had cut up under the back peak of the canvas and then made it a tent by pegging out the sides. He pegged the sides out taut and drove the pegs deep, hitting them down into the ground with the flat of the axe until the rope loops were buried and the canvas was drum tight.

Across the mouth of the tent Nick fixed cheesecloth to keep out mosquitoes. He crawled inside under the mosquito bar with various things from the pack to put at the head of the bed under the slant of the canvas. Inside the tent the light came through the brown canvas. It smelled pleasantly of canvas. Already there was something mysterious and home-like. Nick was happy as he crawled inside the tent. He had not been unhappy all day. This was different though. Now things were done. There had been this to do. Now it was done. It had been a hard trip. He was very tired. That was done. He had made his camp. He was settled. Nothing could touch him. It was a good place to camp. He was there, in the good place. He was in his home where he had made it. Now he was hungry.

He came out, crawling under the cheesecloth. It was quite dark outside. It was lighter in the tent.

Nick went over to the pack and found, with his fingers, a long nail in a paper sack of nails, in the bottom of the pack. He drove it into the pine tree, holding it close and hitting it gently with the flat of the axe. He hung the pack up on the nail. All his supplies were in the pack. They were off the ground and sheltered now.

Nick was hungry. He did not believe he had ever been hungrier. He opened and emptied a can of pork and beans and a can of spaghetti into the frying-pan.

"I've got a right to eat this kind of stuff, if I'm willing to carry it," Nick said. His voice sounded strange in the darkening woods. He did not speak again.

He started a fire with some chunks of pine he got with the axe from a stump. Over the fire he stuck a wire grill, pushing the four legs down into the ground with his boot. Nick put the frying-pan on the grill over the flames. He was hungrier. The beans and spaghetti warmed. Nick stirred them and mixed them together. They began to bubble, making little bubbles that rose with difficulty to the surface. There was a good smell. Nick got out a bottle of tomato catchup and cut four slices of bread. The little bubbles were coming faster now. Nick sat down beside the fire and lifted the frying-pan off. He poured about half the contents out into a tin plate. It spread slowly on the plate. Nick knew it was too hot. He poured on some tomato catchup. He knew the beans and spaghetti were still too hot. He looked at the fire, then at the tent, he was not going to spoil it all by burning his tongue. For years he had never enjoyed fried bananas because he had never been able to wait for them to cool. His tongue was very sensitive. He was very hungry. Across the river in the swamp, in the almost dark, he saw a mist rising. He looked at the tent once more. All right. He took a full spoonful from the plate.

"Chrise," Nick said. "Geezus Chrise," he said happily.

He ate the whole plateful before he remembered the bread. Nick finished the second plateful with the bread, mopping the plate shiny. He had not eaten since a cup of coffee and a ham sandwich in the station restaurant at St. Ignace. It had been a very fine experience. He had been that hungry before, but had not been able to satisfy it. He could have made camp hours before if he had wanted to. There were plenty of good places to camp on the river. But this was good.

Nick tucked two big chips of pine under the grill. The fire flared up. He had forgotten to get water for the coffee. Out of the pack he got a folding canvas bucket and walked down the hill, across the edge of the meadow, to the stream. The other bank was in the white mist. The grass was wet and cold as he knelt on the bank and dipped the canvas bucket into the stream. It bellied and pulled hard in the current. The water was ice cold. Nick rinsed the bucket and carried it full up to the camp. Up away from the stream it was not so cold.

Nick drove another big nail and hung up the bucket full of water. He dipped the coffee pot half full, put some more chips under the grill on to the fire and put the pot on. He could not remember which way he made coffee. He could remember an argument about it with Hopkins, but not which side he had taken. He decided to bring it to a boil. He remembered now that was Hopkins's way. He had once argued about everything with Hopkins. While he waited for the coffee to boil, he opened a small can of apricots. He liked to open cans. He emptied the can of apricots out into a tin cup. While he watched the coffee on the fire, he drank the juice syrup of the apricots, carefully at first to keep from spilling, then meditatively, sucking the apricots down. They were better than fresh apricots.

The coffee boiled as he watched. The lid came up and coffee and grounds ran down the side of the pot. Nick took it off the grill. It was a triumph for Hopkins. He put sugar in the empty apricot cup and poured some of the coffee out to cool. It was too hot to pour and he used his hat to hold the handle of the coffee pot. He would not let it steep in the pot at all. Not the first cup. It should be straight Hopkins all the way. Hop deserved that. He was a very serious coffee drinker. He was the most serious man Nick had ever known. Not heavy, serious. That was a long time ago. Hopkins spoke without moving his lips. He had played polo. He made millions of dollars in Texas. He had borrowed car fare to go to Chicago, when the wire came that his first big well had come in. He could have wired for money. That would have been too slow. They called Hop's girl the Blonde Venus. Hop did not mind because she was not his real girl. Hopkins said very confidently that none of them would make fun of his real girl. He was right. Hopkins went away when the telegram came. That was on the Black River. It took eight days for the telegram to reach him. Hopkins gave away his .22 calibre Colt automatic pistol to Nick. He gave his camera to Bill. It was to remember him always by. They were all going fishing again next summer. The Hop Head was rich. He would get a yacht and they would all cruise along the north shore of Lake Superior. He was excited but serious. They said good-bye and all felt bad. It broke up the trip. They never saw Hopkins again. That was a long time ago on the Black River.

Nick drank the coffee, the coffee according to Hopkins. The coffee was bitter. Nick laughed. It made a good ending to the story. His mind was starting to work. He knew he could choke it because he was tired enough. He spilled the coffee out of the pot and shook the grounds loose into the fire. He lit a cigarette and went inside the tent. He took off his shoes and trousers, sitting on the blankets, rolled the shoes up inside the trousers for a pillow and got in between the blankets.

Out through the front of the tent he watched the glow of the fire, when the night wind blew on it. It was a quiet night. The swamp was perfectly quiet. Nick stretched under the blanket comfortably. A mosquito hummed close to his ear. Nick sat up and lit a match. The mosquito was on the canvas, over his head. Nick moved the match quickly up to it. The mosquito made a satisfactory hiss in the flame. The match went out. Nick lay down again under the blanket. He turned on his side and shut his eyes. He was sleepy. He felt sleep coming. He curled up under the blanket and went to sleep.

PART TWO

In the morning the sun was up and the tent was starting to get hot. Nick crawled out under the mosquito netting stretched across the mouth of the tent, to look at the morning. The grass was wet on his hands as he came out. He held his trousers and his shoes in his hands. The sun was just up over the hill. There was the meadow, the river and the swamp. There were birch trees in the green of the swamp on the other side of the river.

The river was clear and smoothly fast in the early morning. Down about two hundred yards were three logs all the way across the stream. They made the water smooth and deep above them. As Nick watched, a mink crossed the river on the logs and went into the swamp. Nick was excited. He was excited by the early morning and the river. He was really too hurried to eat breakfast, but he knew he must. He built a little fire and put on the coffee pot.

While the water was heating in the pot he took an empty bottle and went down over the edge of the high ground to the meadow. The meadow was wet with dew and Nick wanted to catch grasshoppers for bait before the sun dried the grass. He found plenty of good grasshoppers. They were at the base of the grass stems. Sometimes they clung to a grass stem. They were cold and wet with the dew, and could not jump until the sun warmed them. Nick picked them up, taking only the medium-sized brown ones, and put them into the bottle. He turned over a log and just under the shelter of the edge were several hundred hoppers. It was a grasshopper lodging house. Nick put about fifty of the medium browns into the bottle. While he was picking up the hoppers the others warmed in the sun and commenced to hop away. They flew when they hopped. At first they made one flight and stayed stiff when they landed, as though they were dead.

Nick knew that by the time he was through with breakfast they would be as lively as ever. Without dew on the grass it would take him all day to catch a bottle full of good grasshoppers and he would have to crush many of them, slamming at them with his hat. He washed his hands at the stream. He was excited to be near it. Then he walked up to the tent. The hoppers were already jumping stiffly in the grass. In the bottle, warmed by the sun, they were jumping in a mass. Nick put in a pine stick as a cork. It plugged the mouth of the bottle enough, so the hoppers could not get out and left plenty of air passage.

He had rolled the log back and knew he could get grasshoppers there every morning.

Nick laid the bottle full of jumping grasshoppers against a pine trunk. Rapidly he mixed some buckwheat flour with water and stirred it smooth, one cup of flour, one cup of water. He put a handful of coffee in the pot and dipped a lump of grease out of a can and slid it sputtering across the hot skillet. On the smoking skillet he poured smoothly the buckwheat batter. It spread like lava, the grease spitting sharply. Around the edges the buckwheat cake began to firm, then brown, then crisp. The surface was bubbling slowly to porousness. Nick pushed under the browned under surface with a fresh pine chip. He shook the skillet sideways and the cake was loose on the surface. I won't try and flop it, he thought. He slid the chip of clean wood all the way under the cake, and flopped it over on to its face. It sputtered in the pan.

When it was cooked Nick regreased the skillet. He used all the batter. It made another big flapjack and one smaller one.

Nick ate a big flapjack and a smaller one, covered with apple butter. He put apple butter on the third cake, folded it over twice, wrapped it in oiled paper and put it in his shirt pocket. He put the apple butter jar back in the pack and cut bread for two sandwiches.

In the pack he found a big onion. He sliced it in two and peeled the silky outer skin. Then he cut one half into slices and made onion sandwiches. He wrapped them in oiled paper and buttoned them in the other pocket of his khaki shirt. He turned the skillet upside down on the grill, drank the coffee, sweetened and yellow brown with the condensed milk in it, and tidied up the camp. It was a good camp.

Nick took his fly rod out of the leather rod-case, jointed it, and shoved the rod-case back into the tent. He put on the reel and threaded the line through the guides. He had to hold it from hand to hand, as he threaded it, or it would slip back through its own weight. It was a heavy, double tapered fly line. Nick had paid eight dollars for it a long time ago. It was made heavy to lift back in the air and come forward flat and heavy and straight to make it possible to cast a fly which has no weight. Nick opened the aluminium leader box. The leaders were coiled between the damp flannel pads. Nick had wet the pads at the water cooler on the train up to St. Ignace. In the damp pads the gut leaders had softened and Nick unrolled one and tied it by a loop at the end of the heavy fly line. He fastened a hook on the end of the leader. It was a small hook; very thin and springy.

Nick took it from his hook book, sitting with the rod across his lap. He tested the knot and the spring of the rod by pulling the line taut. It was a good feeling. He was careful not to let the hook bite into his finger.

He started down to the stream, holding his rod, the bottle of grasshoppers hung from his neck by a thong tied in half hitches around the neck of the bottle. His landing net hung by a hook from his belt. Over his shoulder was a long flour sack tied at each corner into an ear. The cord went over his shoulder. The sack flapped against his legs.

Nick felt awkward and professionally happy with all his equipment hanging from him. The grasshopper bottle swung against his chest. In his shirt the breast pockets bulged against him with the lunch and his fly book.

He stepped into the stream. It was a shock. His trousers clung tight to his legs. His shoes felt the gravel. The water was a rising cold shock.

Rushing, the current sucked against his legs. Where he stepped in, the water was over his knees. He waded with the current. The gravel slid under his shoes. He looked down at the swirl of water below each leg and tipped up the bottle to get a grasshopper.

The first grasshopper gave a jump in the neck of the bottle and went out into the water. He was sucked under in the whirl by Nick's right leg and came to the surface a little way downstream. He floated rapidly, kicking. In a quick circle, breaking the smooth surface of the water, he disappeared. A trout had taken him.

Another hopper poked his face out of the bottle. His antennae wavered. He was getting his front legs out of the bottle to jump. Nick took him by the head and held him while he threaded the slim hook under his chin, down through his thorax and into the last segments of his abdomen. The grasshopper took hold of the hook with his front feet, spitting tobacco juice on it. Nick dropped him into the water.

Holding the rod in his right hand he let out line against the pull of the grasshopper in the current. He stripped off line from the reel with his left hand and let it run free. He could see the hopper in the little waves of the current. It went out of sight.

There was a tug on the line. Nick pulled against the taut line. It was his first strike. Holding the now living rod across the current, he brought in the line with his left hand. The rod bent in jerks, the trout pumping against the current. Nick knew it was a small one. He lifted the rod straight up in the air. It bowed with the pull.

He saw the trout in the water jerking with his head and body against the shifting tangent of the line in the stream.

Nick took the line in his left hand and pulled the trout, thumping tiredly against the current, to the surface. His back was mottled the clear, water-over-gravel colour, his side flashing in the sun. The rod under his right arm, Nick stooped, dipping his right hand into the current. He held the trout, never still, with his moist right hand, while he unhooked the barb from his mouth, then dropped him back into the stream.

He hung unsteadily in the current, then settled to the bottom beside a stone. Nick reached down his hand to touch him, his arm to the elbow under water. The trout was steady in the moving stream, resting on the gravel, beside a stone. As Nick's fingers touched him, touched his smooth, cool, underwater feeling he was gone, gone in a shadow across the bottom of the stream.

He's all right, Nick thought. He was only tired.

He had wet his hand before he touched the trout, so he would not disturb the delicate mucus that covered him. If a trout was touched with a dry hand, a white fungus attacked the unprotected spot. Years before when he had fished crowded streams, with fly fishermen ahead of him and behind him, Nick had again and again come on dead trout, furry with white fungus, drifted against a rock, or floating belly up in some pool. Nick did not like to fish with other men on the river. Unless they were of your party, they spoiled it.

He wallowed down the stream, above his knees in the current, through the fifty yards of shallow water above the pile of logs that crossed the stream. He did not rebait his hook and held it in his hand as he waded. He was certain he could catch small trout in the shallows, but he did not want them. There would be no big trout in the shallows this time of day.

Now the water deepened up his thighs sharply and coldly. Ahead was the smooth dammed-back flood of water above the logs. The water was smooth and dark; on the left, the lower edge of the meadow; on the right the swamp.

Nick leaned back against the current and took a hopper from the bottle. He threaded the hopper on the hook and spat on him for good luck. Then he pulled several yards of line from the reel and tossed the hopper out ahead on to the fast, dark water. It floated down toward the logs, then the weight of the line pulled the bait under the surface. Nick held the rod in his right hand, letting the line run out through his fingers.

There was a long tug. Nick struck and the rod came alive and dangerous, bent double, the line tightening, coming out of water, tightening, all in a heavy, dangerous, steady pull. Nick felt the moment when the leader would break if the strain increased and let the line go.

The reel racheted into a mechanical shriek as the line went out in a rush. Too fast. Nick could not check it, the line rushing out, the reel note rising as the line ran out.

With the core of the reel showing, his heart feeling stopped with the excitement, leaning back against the current that mounted icily his thighs. Nick thumbed the reel hard with his left hand. It was awkward getting his thumb inside the fly reel frame.

As he put on pressure the line tightened into sudden hardness and beyond the logs a huge trout went high out of water. As he jumped, Nick lowered the tip of the rod. But he felt, as he dropped the tip to ease the strain, the moment when the strain was too great; the hardness too tight. Of course, the leader had broken. There was no mistaking the feeling when all spring left the line and it became dry and hard. Then it went slack.

His mouth dry, his heart down, Nick reeled in. He had never seen so big a trout. There was a heaviness, a power not to be held, and then the bulk of him, as he jumped. He looked as broad as a salmon.

Nick's hand was shaky. He reeled in slowly. The thrill had been too much. He felt, vaguely, a little sick, as though it would be better to sit down.

The leader had broken where the hook was tied to it. Nick took it in his hand. He thought of the trout somewhere on the bottom, holding himself steady over the gravel, far down below the light, under the logs, with the hook in his jaw. Nick knew the trout's teeth would cut through the snell of the hook. The hook would imbed itself in his jaw. He'd bet the trout was angry. Anything that size would be angry. That was a trout. He had been solidly hooked. Solid as a rock. He felt like a rock, too, before he started off. By God, he was a big one. By God, he was the biggest one I ever heard of.

Nick climbed out on to the meadow and stood, water running down his trousers and out of his shoes, his shoes squelchy. He went over and sat on the logs. He did not want to rush his sensations any.

He wriggled his toes in the water, in his shoes, and got out a cigarette from his breast pocket. He lit it and tossed the match into the fast water below the logs. A tiny trout rose at the match, as it swung around in the fast current. Nick laughed. He would finish the cigarette.

He sat on the logs, smoking, drying in the sun, the sun warm on his back, the river shallow ahead entering the woods, curving into the woods, shallows, light glittering, big water-smooth rocks, cedars along the bank and white birches, the logs warm in the sun, smooth to sit on, without bark, grey to the touch; slowly the feeling of disappointment left him. It went away slowly, the feeling of disappointment that came sharply after the thrill that made his shoulders ache. It was all right now. His rod lying out on the logs, Nick tied a new hook on the leader, pulling the gut tight until it grimped into itself in a hard knot.

He baited it, then picked up the rod and walked to the far end of the logs to get into the water, where it was not too deep. Under and beyond the logs was a deep pool. Nick walked around the shallow shelf near the swamp shore until he came out on the shallow bed of the stream.

On the left, where the meadow ended and the woods began, a great elm tree was uprooted. Gone over in a storm, it lay back into the woods, its roots clotted with dirt, grass growing in them, rising

a solid bank beside the stream. The river cut to the edge of the up-
rooted tree. From where Nick stood he could see deep channels, like
ruts, cut in the shallow bed of the stream by the flow of the current.
Pebbly where he stood and pebbly and full of boulders beyond;
where it curved near the tree roots, the bed of the stream was marly
and between the ruts of deep water green weed fronds swung in the
current.

Nick swung the rod back over his shoulder and forward, and the
line, curving forward, laid the grasshopper down on one of the
deep channels in the weeds. A trout struck and Nick hooked him.

Holding the rod far out toward the uprooted tree and sloshing
backward in the current, Nick worked the trout, plunging, the rod
bending alive, out of the danger of the weeds into the open river.
Holding the rod, pumping alive against the current, Nick brought
the trout in. He rushed, but always came, the spring of the rod
yielding to the rushes, sometimes jerking under water, but always
bringing him in. Nick eased downstream with the rushes. The rod
above his head he led the trout over the net, then lifted.

The trout hung heavy in the net, mottled trout back and silver
sides in the meshes. Nick unhooked him; heavy sides, good to hold,
big undershot jaw, and slipped him, heaving and big sliding, into
the long sack that hung from his shoulders in the water.

Nick spread the mouth of the sack against the current and it
filled, heavy with water. He held it up, the bottom in the stream,
and the water poured out through the sides. Inside at the bottom
was the big trout, alive in the water.

Nick moved downstream. The sack out ahead of him sunk heavy
in the water, pulling from his shoulders.

It was getting hot, the sun hot on the back of his neck.

Nick had one good trout. He did not care about getting many
trout. Now the stream was shallow and wide. There were trees
along both banks. The trees of the left bank made short shadows on
the current in the forenoon sun. Nick knew there were trout in each
shadow. In the afternoon, after the sun had crossed toward the
hills, the trout would be in the cool shadows on the other side of the
stream.

The very biggest ones would lie up close to the bank. You could
always pick them up there on the Black. When the sun was down
they all moved out into the current. Just when the sun made the
water blinding in the glare before it went down, you were liable to
strike a big trout anywhere in the current. It was almost impossible
to fish then, the surface of the water was blinding as a mirror in the
sun. Of course, you could fish upstream, but in a stream like the
Black, or this, you had to wallow against the current and in a deep
place, the water piled up on you. It was no fun to fish upstream

with this much current.

Nick moved along through the shallow stretch watching the banks for deep holes. A beech tree grew close beside the river, so that the branches hung down into the water. The stream went back in under the leaves. There were always trout in a place like that.

Nick did not care about fishing that hole. He was sure he would get hooked in the branches.

It looked deep though. He dropped the grasshopper so the current took it under water, back in under the overhanging branch. The line pulled hard and Nick struck. The trout threshed heavily, half out of water in the leaves and branches. The line was caught. Nick pulled hard and the trout was off. He reeled in and holding the hook in his hand, walked down the stream.

Ahead, close to the left bank, was a big log. Nick saw it was hollow; pointing up river the current entered it smoothly, only a little ripple spread each side of the log. The water was deepening. The top of the hollow log was grey and dry. It was partly in the shadow.

Nick took the cork out of the grasshopper bottle and a hopper clung to it. He picked him off, hooked him and tossed him out. He held the rod far out so that the hopper on the water moved into the current flowing into the hollow log. Nick lowered the rod and the hopper floated in. There was a heavy strike. Nick swung the rod against the pull. It felt as though he were hooked into the log itself, except for the live feeling.

He tried to force the fish out into the current. It came, heavily.

The line went slack, and Nick thought the trout was gone. Then he saw him, very near, in the current, shaking his head, trying to get the hook out. His mouth was clamped shut. He was fighting the hook in the clear flowing current.

Looping the line with his left hand, Nick swung the rod to make the line taut and tried to lead the trout toward the net, but he was gone, out of sight, the line pumping. Nick fought him against the current, letting him thump in the water against the spring of the rod. He shifted the rod to his left hand, worked the trout upstream, holding his weight, fighting on the rod, and then let him down into the net. He lifted him clear of the water, a heavy half circle in the net, the net dripping, unhooked him and slid him into the sack.

He spread the mouth of the sack and looked down in at the two big trout alive in the water.

Through the deepening water, Nick waded over to the hollow log. He took the sack off, over his head, the trout flopping as it came out of water, and hung it so the trout were deep in the water. Then he pulled himself up on the log and sat, the water from his trousers and boots running down in the stream. He laid his rod

down, moved along to the shady end of the log and took the sandwiches out of his pocket. He dipped the sandwiches in the cold
water. The current carried away the crumbs. He ate the sandwiches and dipped his hat full of water to drink, the water running
out through his hat just ahead of his drinking.

It was cool in the shade, sitting on the log. He took a cigarette out
and struck a match to light it. The match sunk into the grey wood,
making a tiny furrow. Nick leaned over the side of the log, found
a hard place and lit the match. He sat smoking and watching the
river.

Ahead the river narrowed and went into a swamp. The river
became smooth and deep and the swamp looked solid with cedar
trees, their trunks close together, their branches solid. It would not
be possible to walk through a swamp like that. The branches grew
so low. You would have to keep almost level with the ground to
move at all. You could not crash through the branches. That must
be why the animals that lived in swamps were built the way they
were, Nick thought.

He wished he had brought something to read. He felt like reading. He did not feel like going on into the swamp. He looked down
the river. A big cedar slanted all the way across the stream. Beyond
that the river went into the swamp.

Nick did not want to go in there now. He felt a reaction against
deep wading with the water deepening up under his armpits, to
hook big trout in places impossible to land them. In the swamp the
banks were bare, the big cedars came together overhead, the sun
did not come through, except in patches; in the fast deep water, in
the half light, the fishing would be tragic. In the swamp fishing was
a tragic adventure. Nick did not want it. He did not want to go
down the stream any farther to-day.

He took out his knife, opened it and stuck it in the log. Then he
pulled up the sack, reached into it and brought out one of the trout.
Holding him near the tail, hard to hold, alive, in his hand, he
whacked him against the log. The trout quivered, rigid. Nick laid
him on the log in the shade and broke the neck of the other fish the
same way. He laid them side by side on the log. They were fine trout.

Nick cleaned them, slitting them from the vent to the tip of the
jaw. All the insides and the gills and tongue came out in one piece.
They were both males; long grey-white strips of milt, smooth and
clean. All the insides clean and compact, coming out all together.
Nick tossed the offal ashore for the minks to find.

He washed the trout in the stream. When he held them back up
in the water they looked like live fish. Their colour was not gone yet.
He washed his hands and dried them on the log. Then he laid the
trout on the sack spread out on the log, rolled them up in it, tied the

bundle and put it in the landing net. His knife was still standing, blade stuck in the log. He cleaned it on the wood and put it in his pocket.

Nick stood up on the log, holding his rod, the landing net hanging heavy, then stepped into the water and splashed ashore. He climbed the bank and cut up into the woods, toward the high ground. He was going back to camp. He looked back. The river just showed through the trees. There were plenty of days coming when he could fish the swamp.

From *First Forty-Nine Stories*

Ancient Anglers

Charles Chenevix Trench

The Turkana tribe of northern Kenya live in an incredibly harsh desert. They seldom have enough to eat, and when the rains fail, they die. Their country bounds on three sides Lake Rudolf, which teems with excellent edible fish; but until a benign government taught a few of the Turkana to fish, some forty years ago, it had never occurred to them to catch and eat those fish. Crocodiles, yes! Delicious! But fish! Whoever heard of people eating *fish*? Why, the idea was just laughable! And laugh they did, loud and long, when first it was put to them.

Fishing seems, indeed, to be a method of food procurement characteristic of fairly advanced cultures, invented long after hunting. The earliest Palaeolithic fishermen used spears and harpoons, at first perhaps to kill fish which had been stranded by a receding flood. Then, perhaps after many millennia, they learned that to spear a fish you must aim off for refraction. Nets must have been invented long after harpoons; and somewhere between the two primitive man thought of catching fish with a baited line. There are no hooks dating from Palaeolithic times, but there are horn, shell, flint, and bone gorges. A gorge resembles a thick nail, pointed at both ends. It is embedded in a bait so as to pass easily down the fish's throat, but when the line is jerked, the gorge is jammed across the fish's gullet. It was probably with such instruments that Palaeolithic men angled: we do not know if they used a rod, but from the use of a hand-line it is an easy and obvious development to tie one end of the line to a long stick in order to reach the deep water where the big fish lie.

The next step was to use a gorge shaped like a hooked arrow-head. Several of these, made of flint, are in museums. Hooks came much later. In the Berlin Museum there is the earliest known hook, made from the upper mandible of an eagle, notched down to its base. When once one had the idea it was not difficult to find natural objects which would serve the purpose. There are in museums Maori hooks made of human bone. There are Mohave hooks made from the thorn of the barrel-cactus. Natives of New Guinea used hooks made from the clawed hind legs of a fearsome-looking, but quite harmless, insect known to science as *Eurycantha latro*. In La Musée de la Pêche at La Bussière there are two objects described as flint hooks of the Middle Stone Age. There are bronze hooks, barbed and eyed, among Mycenean remains, and also depicted in tomb paintings from ancient Egypt.

Although it is sometimes blurred, there is a distinction between fishing for food and angling for sport. The sporting angler uses the method which gives him most pleasure, even though it may not be the best way of filling his basket. Thus the angler may not be a fool, but is unquestionably a sportsman. The most purely sporting anglers in the world today are those coarse-fishermen who return to the water every fish they catch.

Perhaps the first sporting angler found that rod and line was more fun than using a fish-spear or a net. The distinction is made perfectly clear by two Egyptian drawings: one, of about 2000 BC, shows a man fishing who is obviously poor—a slave, perhaps, or a professional fisherman. Another, dating from about 1400 BC, shows a gentleman of leisure angling. Clearly he is angling for pleasure, since his appearance, clothes, and demeanour makes it quite obvious that he could easily have afforded to buy fish or to pay men to catch them for him.

Angling was certainly practised in Homeric Greece. There is in Homer, who is believed to have lived between 1050 and 850 BC, one unquestionable reference to an angler "letting down with a long rod his baits to the little fishes below, casting into the deep the horn of an ox, and as he catches each flings it up writhing". What on earth was the ox-horn for?

It hardly seems suitable material for a gorge, and in any case hooks were then in use. It has been suggested that the hook was made from the ring which would be produced when a thin section of a hollow ox-horn is sawn off. But this, being cut across the grain, would have no strength whatever. There may have been an artificial bait made of horn, a sort of spinner. The most likely suggestion is that the end of the line, where it is joined to the hook, was protected against the fishes' teeth by a tube of the hollow horn, which may also have held the lead. In 1904 there was reported from Egypt a similar device, made from a hollow maize stalk, to protect the line against a large fish's teeth. (The bait, incidentally, was a live rat.) Being translucent and of a dark olive colour, the tube of ox-horn would not be very conspicuous. But it does seem strange that such a gadget should have been used in angling for *small* fish.

The respectability of angling in ancient Greece is attested by a vase-painting of Heracles angling—though, to be sure, the heroes not infrequently indulged in pastimes which were far from respectable. His very short rod is probably just artistic licence: there was no room on the vase for a long one.

The Greeks, not content with inventing democracy, also invented fly-fishing. Claudius Aelianus, the author of a book on natural history written in the fifth century AD, describes a practice which is obviously not new, but quite well established. Since "Aelian's" work is believed to have been cribbed from a writer of the first century AD, it may well be that fly-fishing for trout was practised by Greeks before the birth of Christ. Anyway, this is what Aelian has to say about it:

"I have heard of a Macedonian way of catching fish, and it is this: between Beroea and Thessalonica runs a river called the Astraeus, and in it there are fish with speckled skins. . . . These fish feed on a fly peculiar to the country, which hovers on the river.

"When the fish observes a fly on the surface, it swims quietly up, afraid to stir the water above, lest it should scare away its prey; then coming up by its shadow, it opens its mouth gently and gulps down the fly, like a wolf carrying off a sheep from the fold or an eagle a goose from the farmyard; having done this it goes below the rippling water.

"Now though the fishermen know of this, they do not use these flies at all for bait for fish; for if a man's hand touch them, they lose their natural colour, their wings wither, and they become unfit food for the fish. . . .

"They fasten red wool round a hook and fix on to the wool two feathers which grow under a cock's wattles, and which in colour are like wax. Their rod is six feet long, and their line is the same length. Then they throw their snare, and the fish, attracted and maddened by the colour, comes straight at it, thinking to get a dainty mouthful and enjoys a bitter repast, a captive."

There are, broadly speaking, two kinds of trout-flies: imitation flies, which purport to resemble the natural insect and are, presumably, taken by the trout as such; and fancy flies, which bear no resemblance to any living creature but appeal presumably to the trout's curiosity or aggressive instinct rather than to his hunger. In the latter category are all those flashy objects glittering with brightly dyed feathers, with gold and silver tinsel—Butchers, Zulus, Grouse-and-this, Mallard-and-that, Teal-and-the-other. When one considers the extraordinary difficulty of imitating with silk, fur, and feather, all attached to a steel hook, anything so light, delicate and ephemeral as a water-fly, it is very surprising that the earliest trout-flies of which we have any knowledge were imitation flies.

Elsewhere Aelian describes fishing with hook and line as being the most skilful and the most becoming for free men—surely a hint of angling for sport, rather than primarily for food. He recommended horsehair for lines, and for artificial flies "feathers, chiefly white, or black, or various. They use two wools, red and blue." Added to the list of angler's equipment are "corks . . . and a shaved wand, and a dog-wood rod". Also, mysteriously, the "horns and hide of a she-goat". Can this have been used for camouflaging the angler? Or as a raincoat?

For the thyme-scented grayling, which Balkan anglers rate higher than the trout, Aelian recommended dapping with a natural insect, indeed with a mosquito. But there must be some misunderstanding, for it is inconceivable that an insect as small as a mosquito could be impaled on the hooks of that day.

The Romans, on the whole, were not great sportsmen. They liked eating game and fish, but seldom exerted themselves to kill or catch it, and when they did, they all too frequently cheated. Mark Antony, for instance, wishing to make a good impression on Cleopatra who was, uncharacteristically, a keen and successful angler, hired a diver to attach fish to his hook. But the lady was not deceived: she hired a diver to attach a salted fish to Mark Antony's hook, which he duly struck and landed to general ridicule. Iniquitous! But hardly more lamentable than the Younger Pliny: fishing fascinated him: he could watch people doing it for hours. He fairly spread himself on the beauties of the countryside, the joys of the pastoral life, the delights of river and lake. But when it came to actually angling himself, it was really too much trouble; the best he could do was to drop a line into Lake Como from his bedroom window. Nor was Martial made of sterner stuff. He makes, however, a curious, isolated reference to fly-fishing or dapping, for a sea-fish known as 'scarus' which has not been identified.

Plutarch came nearer the root of the matter. When a friend was banished from Rome, Plutarch congratulated him on escaping the noise, dust, smells, vices, and intrigues of Rome and being able to settle down in a quiet Aegean island where there was plenty of unspoilt nature and good fishing. The friend's reaction is not recorded. Plutarch knew something about fishing, or at least about tackle. He recommended a whole cane rod, tough and pliable, strong enough to hold a powerful fish, but not so thick as to throw an alarming shadow over the water. The line should be of white horse-hair, with as few knots as possible, as these make it visible to the fish.

The passage in question is interesting in that it is the first which recommends a certain subtlety in angling and precautions lest the fish take fright. Plutarch, if not himself a practical angler, had certainly talked to some who were. The line was about as long as the rod, and fastened to its top: a running line was unknown to the ancients. The "hairs" of which the line was made were taken from a stallion's tail, which are supposed to be stronger than those of a mare or gelding. Plutarch had a theory, unsupported by modern science or indeed by observation of a mare's habits, that the hairs of a mare's tail were weakened by her urine. The hook was barbed, not eyed, of bronze, iron, or sometimes bone.

One of the best eating fishes in the Mediterranean is the grey mullet. Roman anglers fished for him with a paste made of flour and curds, flavoured with mint, the scent of which was supposed to attract the mullet. . . . "He nibbles and plucks at the bait with the tip of his mouth, and straightaway the fisher strikes."

Although many Italian lakes and rivers held trout, which are common also in the colder streams of the Balkans, no Greek or Latin author except Aelian mentions the fish which are now considered to be the most sporting and best eating of any which live in fresh water. Ausonius, the fourth-century poet, gives a vivid description of trout-fishing, with bait, on the Moselle.

A young angler, "leaning over the waters beneath the rock, lowers the arching top of his supple rod, as he casts the hooks sheathed in deadly baits". The trout seize the bait, "and the rod ducks to the jerky twitch of the quivering horse-hair. With one stroke the boy snatches his prey slant-wise from the waters."

Elsewhere he makes the first mention in classical literature of the pike, which he despises as the coarsest food of the meanest tavern.

When every scrap of angling lore of the ancient Greeks and Romans has been collected, one must admit that angling occupied a very small place in their world. The paucity of references in the literature of a thousand years indicates that it was not the sport of the masses but was, rather, the occasion for a few urban intellectuals to rhapsodize over country life, and even, occasionally, without unduly exerting themselves, to catch a few fish.

The pleasures of the table appealed to them more strongly: after all, there were plenty of slaves to do the drudgery of actually fishing. They paid more attention to the management of stew-ponds than to the technique of angling.

Tribute must, however, be paid to a sixth-century author, Cassianus Bassus, for developing a ground-baiting technique which in a more sceptical age has not, perhaps, been sufficiently exploited. "Get three limpets and, having taken out the fish, inscribe on the shells 'Jehovah, God of Armies'; you will immediately see the fish come to the place in surprising numbers." Try it.

The Chinese, during the same period, were far better anglers. The first reference in Chinese literature to the rod comes from the *Shih Ching*, or Book of Odes, written between the eleventh and the seventh centuries BC. A lovelorn maiden bewails her lover's absence: "With your long and tapering bamboo rods you angle in the Ch'i. How should I not think of you? But I am too far away to reach you." Lines, according to another ode, were made of twisted silk thread. "When he went a-fishing", mourns an angler's wife, "I arranged his line for him. What did he take in angling? Bream and tench, bream and tench, while the people looked on to see."

In the fifth century there is a mention of a float made of pith: the moment the angler saw it sink, he knew a fish was on. In the fourth century BC, "By making a line of cocoon silk, the hook of a sharp needle, the rod of a branch of bramble or dwarf bamboo, and using a grain of cooked rice as a bait, one can catch a whole cart-load of fish."

At about the time of Christ, the Emperor Wu, with deplorable and unsportsmanlike ostentation, angled with a golden hook, a white silk line, and a goldfish as bait. In the district of Lu angling was a popular sport. They used cinnamon bark for bait, forged [sic] golden and silver hooks and lines ornamented with kingfisher feathers. Could this have been a sort of artificial lure or fly, or were the citizens of Lu codding a stranger? The use of cinnamon bark and of aromatic cassia suggests a belief that fish were attracted by sense of smell.

Unquestionably China produced the first "fishing story". A grandson of Confucius actually witnessed, with his own eyes, the capture in the Yellow River of a fish the size of a cart. The fortunate angler had first baited his hook, unsuccessfully, with bream; then, by a happy inspiration, he baited it with half a sucking-pig, and was rewarded with instant success.

From *A History of Angling*

The "Bishop Browne" Story

Derek Barker

In that part of the Tay where the Earn flows in to join the larger stream and where the real estuary begins—three-quarters of a mile long at high tide, no salmon or sea trout had, until 1867, been taken by means of rod and line. After various experiments the late Bishop G. F. Browne, Bishop of Stepney, discovered that salmon could be taken with a blue or brown phantom minnow, and in the early morning of the last day but one of the rod season of 1868, a small expedition set forth from the mouth of the Earn, in a boat, with a personnel of three rods and a dour Scots boatman.

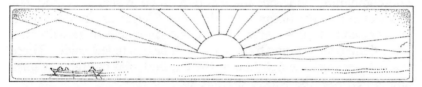

High tide that morning was at 10 a.m. and at 11.30 a.m. operations commenced. At 12.30 p.m. the middle rod was seen to drag and two seconds later the line went out at a speed that threatened to dispose of the rod and its owner. It is incidentally noted at the time that the middle rod was the weakest and that the line consisted of two trout lines spliced together to form a length of a hundred and twenty yards.

The fish decides to pull the boat all over the middle channel of the Tay before making at full speed for the mouth of the Earn, vigorously pursued by the boat. At the end of an hour and a half the fish decides to leave the Earn and makes for the north bank of the Tay, but on getting into the shallow water decides on a violent race to the southward, and at the first pause for breath the party finds itself among the shipping of Newburgh.

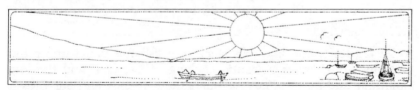

The fight goes on but at 3.30 p.m. there seems to be a definite weakening on the part of the fish. But alas for false hopes, the tide turns, a new surge of life begins and back we go to the westward with the tide, at a merry pace, and the party begins to think of food.

A cold rain begins to fall in the late afternoon and after four hours of gruelling fight all over the estuary the fish is seen. He leaps two feet out of the water, a monster, "as big as a well-grown boy." But the constant friction of the wet line on the rings has worn the threads and a strand breaks with a snap, leaving only twenty yards of whole line to defeat the biggest salmon ever seen.

Night falls and it is now 6.30. A strong salmon line has been spliced on to the trout line after frantic efforts and the party prepares for an all-night sitting. Various attempts are made to land "a non-combatant" who has had enough, to go in search of food, but it is not until two hours later that our friends are fortified with whisky and scones, after prodigious manoeuvring with the victualling boat. At nine o'clock the rain begins to feel colder. There is a wild feeling of temptation in the air, and wild thoughts of gaffs and lanterns on the water, are abroad.

However, by ten o'clock we still find them faithful, and we are now back in home waters, with still no sign of yielding on the part of either side. The fish still appears to have his strength and his opponents are now stoically committed to an indefinite life on the waters of the Tay.

At ten-thirty the line falls slack, the fish has come under the boat again. There is a frantic clicking of the reel, and the line comes in and in. . . . Alas for our gallant friends and our British Sporting Records, the tail-hook has broken.

A year later in 1869, near Newburgh where the Tay flows into the sea, a gigantic salmon of seventy-four pounds was taken in the nets, and in his mouth was the scar of a tail-hook.

Among the Sea Monsters

Hugh Copley

Lokoja,
West Africa
1914

Dear Charles,

You will see from my address that I am travelling again. As a matter of fact I am on my way back from Lagos where I have been for a couple of months on special work. I had quite a good time, plenty to do in the day-time and free week-ends to do what I liked in.

Lagos is the same as ever, hasn't changed one little bit from the first time I went there, four years ago. Naturally, I hadn't been there long before I began poking about to see if anybody had been sea fishing, but still found the same blissful ignorance as prevailed on my last visit. Harbour works certainly very much extended, but I hear they are getting trouble with silting and will have to build out an easterly arm—some job, looks for life.

I found the same old native fisherman who catered for me on my first visit, and my general purpose man got busy and found me a dug-out which would take me out fishing. This was an opportunity not to be despised, so I clinched the arrangements entered into by Hassan, my man. One trouble was that I know very little of their language, and they couldn't understand a word of Hausa, the language I know fairly well. However, Hassan seems to be able to make known my wants.

I used my heaviest greenheart spinning rod and largest spinning reel with heavy wire traces, and my home-made spinners, the gear I had been using for the big Giwan Rua, so felt really ready for the big stuff.

The first time we went out from the breakwater we began trolling, with the sea beautifully calm and as blue as a turquoise under the early morning sun. Both men paddled well with long easy strokes, quite different from our up-river boys, so that my bait did its work properly. I was so eager to begin that I hadn't really had time to get my few things put shipshape when I got such a wrench on the rod. I grabbed it of course and nearly turned the canoe over.

These canoes are very gimcrack affairs with only a foot freeboard, no keel, just hewn out of a tree with rough shapings for a bow and a stern. I sit flat in the bottom, facing astern, as I cannot kneel for long periods like my men do.

My fish went completely away, going so fast that my rod top was drawn down into the sea, and I could not for the life of me hold him, although I had the palm of my hand on the rim of the revolving drum of the reel until it nearly burnt into the flesh. I was only too glad when the fish stopped, and I could get my rod up to a safe angle. Almost before I could get my wits together the fish came towards me and passed right under the canoe. I seemed to reel for hours before the rod bent violently and away he went again.

This went on for ages, until I began to feel really annoyed that I couldn't subdue him. I put every bit of my strength into it until I thought the rod couldn't have stood the strain any longer, but would have gone at one of the joints. This, I think, really took all the strength out of him, and we got him so near that I could see his dim shape weaving about below us. He turned to and fro, but had to come up and was got on board by Hassan.

I was fully convinced that I had hooked the father of all whales, but the fish didn't weigh more than thirty-two pounds when we killed him. He was a deep fish, slate blue on top, with a blunt head and finlets like a mackerel, also the forked tail of that family. Here I had been nearly an hour over this small fish, and was thoroughly done, so what was I going to be like if I got into a real big one, which was my idea in life at that time?

However, this was much better than our previous experiences. When I was having a rest I saw a lot of silvery-looking fish jumping out of the water. They jumped out in a flock, so we went over to have a look. These fish, I should judge, were from six to twelve inches in length, swimming together in shoals. I was watching them with interest, really thinking what excellent bait they would be, when we saw a great rush into the middle of them, and out came the flock, wildly leaping from their pursuers. This meant business, so I rigged up another bait, and the two men took the dug-out round the outskirts of the shoal.

I could see down in the clear water dark blue shapes flashing underneath, so let the bait down astern. I distinctly saw three go for my bait; one got it, and away he went, but I only saw the belly flash of the other two out of the corner of my eye, as I had on my hands quite enough trouble for the immediate future. I never dreamt a fish had so much strength. When I tried to hold him he pulled yards off with savage primitive tugs. The upper three-quarters of my rod was horizontal to the water with the strain, and I held on, feeling quite a void round my heart region. When nearly two hundred yards had gone he stopped, but before I could congratulate myself he was away again, but this time my canoe boys had got the hang of things and gave me help by following the fish.

At the end of the second run my fish came clear out of the water and tugged until the line twanged and vibrated with the strain. I couldn't help letting out a yell. The fish never eased up, and I finally fought him back by instinct and not with a reasoning mind. I was really feeling physically distressed when I realised he was near the canoe and Hassan got him out.

This was a different fish from the other. He was long and slim like a torpedo, blue black on top with a silver belly flushed with yellow right down to the tail, which was forked like a mackerel, and I am sure this fish is the American Yellowtail. He was forty-five pounds when weighed, and I truly had had enough, especially as we were too far from land for my liking.

The men paddled for the shore whilst I got my strength back. With these two magnificent fish on board I really couldn't forbear to put a bait over and have another shot. I was sitting watching the water when, bang, I had another run, and the business began all over again, but this fish fought deep down nearly under the canoe. Things went on as I have described before, and I was fairly on top of my fish when he suddenly woke up and ran yards off. I gave him hell but could not make any impression, although he was coming up to the surface with a rush.

I was watching the rod tip when Hassan, with a chorus from the other men, yelled and pointed to a big fin sticking out of the water about one hundred yards away. I realised that the owner of that fin and myself were connected in some way and also that it was a shark. It took about three seconds for my mind to go over all the shark incidents I had ever read about, and I was not comforted. Still, something had to be done, as the shark wasn't doing anything much, and the only place my men wanted to go to was "Home, sweet Home" in the shortest time possible.

I therefore held hard, and nothing occurred. I might be holding hard until now for all the good I was doing. However, things did move; the line went slack, and the fin moved out seawards. I reeled in with a huge sigh and soon saw I was reeling in the head and shoulders only of my fish; the other part was also going seawards.

However, our troubles were only beginning, as when the fish's head got near a great shape came from under the canoe. My fish's head and shoulders disappeared into the shape, and my reel began to spin round faster than anybody could have thought possible. I had really and truly hooked a shark, but what the devil to do with him I hadn't the foggiest notion. There may be a book written on shark fishing to help soft-headed amateurs like myself when in such trouble, but if there is I have never read it. I simply clung on for all my life. Then the brute began to run. I felt a tremendous jar on my left arm and shoulders, the dug-out gave a lurch, and my rod came back straight. I never said "Thank God" with such thankfulness before, and believed every letter of those two small words.

I was feeling pretty frightened myself, but on turning round with a sickly grin I found three absolutely green niggers; so I took courage as I realised there were three more frightened men in my

little world than I myself. There was no more fishing, and no
urging was wanted on my part until we arrived at the shore.

My legs felt quite shaky on landing, so we found a shady spot
and had lunch. Through Hassan I had a long talk with the men
and finally, after treating them well in the matter of a monetary
present, got them to promise they would be there the next Sunday.
They took the yellowtail, whilst I took the other fish, which was
quite good eating. I felt the effects next day on my shoulders, and
also in my groin, where the butt of the rod rested during my
fishing. I therefore tied a piece of stuffed leather as big as a tennis
ball on to the butt end of the rod to act as a cushion, and it was a
great success, but even then there is a danger that one might
hurt one's inside.

When out the next Sunday morning we didn't get any luck
until we saw a school of small fish being crashed, and, as soon as
we could troll a bait round the school, I got a run, which resulted
in a twenty-five pound yellowtail. By the time the fight was over
the school had either gone a long distance out to sea or gone down
for good. Owing to my crazy craft I was frightened to go out far to
sea in case of accidents, as if we got upset there are too many
sharks, so we kept as near to the bar as possible. This day I saw
some fish leaping clear out of the water in magnificent jumps, so
we trolled round the neighbourhood and got into one without
much difficulty. There was a terrific long run, and then out of the
water and up into the air came five feet of silver. The fish seemed
to my astonished eyes to go up and up, but when he came down
again the line was slack.

On examining the bait, I found the hook of the tail triangle,
although it was of large dimension, pulled out straight. I then
removed all three triangles and used one large hook, a number ten
nought, and again tried my luck. I got another strike, so gave it
back to him; another long run, then out of the water again came
the fish with his mouth wide open, rattling his gills.

At the top of the jump I saw my hook flung quite another
twenty feet into the air. I yelled like an Indian, when the beggar
jumped, quite involuntarily.

As there seemed quite a number of these fish about working on
the bar, I baited up again and got another strike, with a repetition
of the jumping performance, but this time the line whistled when
he entered the water again. By encouraging my men we settled
down to the fight. Seven times the fish came out of the water,
sideways, all ways; but I felt he was weakening himself by these
acrobatics and felt confident he was ours.

The fish went finally deep and was really coming in when I felt
an irresistible force take and shake it like a terrier does a rat. The

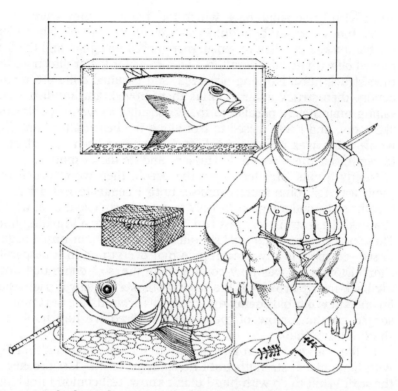

line went slack, and we got in a bleeding head and a small part of the shoulders only. I could have wept with annoyance, but could only swear hard to relieve my feelings. It seems as if every fish as soon as it is weak or fights down will be taken by those accursed brutes. We never got another run. I am convinced these fish which jump so are tarpon, as they are just like those described in Dimmock's book of the tarpon; but I did not know they were on this coast.

The dredger *Egerton* was working on the bar, so I went along-side, and the officers gave me a whisky and soda. It's not my habit to drink before sundown, but I wanted it quite badly. The *Egerton* officers had been watching my efforts and were greatly interested, but confirmed the shark question. I went home afterwards, real tired.

Next Sunday there were big long swells coming over the bar, so I dared not risk going out in the dug-out. I therefore went and fished off the beach into the surf with very little hope of getting anything. I got however two good runs and two good fish of a nice size, about twenty pounds each, in the first hour. These fish were of a fine shape, silvery with darker backs, the most noticeable feature being a dull copper colour diffused all over the back of the fish. I wish I had some book which told me what they were.

As things were quite bright I was well on the *qui vive* when I felt my bait picked up, then dropped, then picked up again, and the fish moved off with due deliberation. I let him go for ten or fifteen yards, then struck hard. Nothing occurred, and I waited quite a time for action, then struck again. Things then moved, and my fish went sailing majestically parallel to the coast, about seventy yards out, like a tug, and I was forced to trot along the beach after him. The whole thing was rather ridiculous if there had been an onlooker to see it, but there was only Hassan, and he didn't matter.

Nearly a mile I trotted down the beach, then we returned the same way for some more exercise, until I began to feel a lack of breath; so I stood my ground, only to get a most violent rush which changed the trotting to a fast run. Even then I wasn't holding line. These proceedings went on, I should think, for an hour until I began to see red spots in my eyes. I gave him everything in a desperate effort. I found he was now coming in to me, so I continued until my back nearly broke. On the second breaker we saw a triangular fin and knew our old enemy the shark was around. The next time he surged on the furrow of the wave I realised we had hooked a shark all the time!

I felt a real rage which gave me strength, and I laid into that fish with demoniacal strength until he came in on the last breaker of the surf. What to do with him I didn't know, as I couldn't hold him against the ebb of the surf, and he was done as we saw him roll over several times. The two fishermen with Hassan however followed the wave down, got hold of his tail, and, much to my astonishment, with the incoming surf beached him. I was scared stiff, but they did it off their own bat.

My legs shook so much now it was all over that I hastily sat down whilst my shoulders ached until I could have shouted. The fit passed off, so I went to see my catch. It was a shark all right, quite ten feet long, grey on the back with a white belly. I judged it a sand shark, but what species I don't know. He must have weighed over three hundred pounds and was far and away the biggest fish I had ever caught, bigger in fact than my wildest dreams. My rod had a curve in it like a hoop, but it came right again during the week with a weight tied on it and hung up.

That ended the day for me. The fishermen took the shark off, after getting aid, and, I believe, sold it piecemeal. Anyway, I got my own back on one of the shark family, but I have no great wish to do it all over again, especially as the tackle which I had is not to my mind suitable for the job.

I went out twice more in the dug-out. The first time I lost three of the tarpon with sharks; one brute evidently got the hook into his mouth and steamed out towards the open sea. I luckily had a knife and cut adrift before matters became more serious. I lost over a hundred yards of my twenty-four thread line which makes things too expensive, especially out here, so I am reduced to trade line which is really light cord, but if dressed is not too bad. I cannot get so much on my reel which rather cramps my style.

The second time we started out with a tarpon which changed into a shark. This brute did nothing whatsoever, so we paddled up with great caution. I have ceased to rush things out here. I saw his long grey bulk with the line running to his head, then underneath him, but with no signs of the tarpon. He simply looked at me until my blood ran cold, never moved an eyelid. We got to within fifteen feet of him; that is, he was that much under us, and he was longer than our canoe, which is eighteen feet. I realised with a start what a damned fool I was and how utterly helpless we were, so cut the line in a real good fright. The last I saw of that shark he was in the same position, looking at me with those eyes of his. It was really quite a time before the hair at the back of my neck went down to its normal position.

We went over to the dredger for the needful which they kindly provided free of cost. Feeling better, we went off towards home, and whilst on the way hooked a tarpon. At the final tiring out of this fish there were three attendant sharks, but they just didn't get him, although one had a good try alongside us—so near that I thought he would overturn us.

However, the two men beat the water with their paddles, really in a blue funk, so was I, and Hassan got the tarpon by the gills and heaved him in. One of the sharks followed us in just behind all the way, so my man did not dally that journey.

On landing, I had a good talk to myself about the whole proceedings, and determined that I was every fool under the sun and not to do it again. My nerves wouldn't stand much more of it. I don't mind having two feet on the sand, but that cranky canoe out there was not good enough. For two nights I had the first nightmares of my life as far as I can remember, and shark's eyes formed too large a portion of them for sound sleep.

I took the tarpon to Lagos where it was weighed—eighty pounds. Several fellows came to see it, and one of the doctors told me that the natives catch the same fish at Sierra Leone in nets or hand lines—he had forgotten which. It was not good eating at all, so the boys and their friends polished it off. I am very sorry now I didn't dry the head and keep it for a memento.

That really finished my fishing, which, I think you will admit, was as about as exciting as ever we dreamt about in our wildest dreams. I got on to the mail steamer, went round to Forcados, then up the Niger on a Government mail boat without any untold excitement. I shall be here for a short time and then return to my old station, Ibi.

This letter has gone to a most extraordinary length, but I hope you will be interested. I received your letter on spinning for pike, and it did bring back many memories. I shall be returning on leave in November, so it won't be long now before I am fishing the old places with you and Henry.

With kindest regards to you all,

Yours,

Oliver.

From *The Letters of Two Fishermen*

Baked Carp
with Soft Roe Stuffing

Jane Grigson

There is a world of difference between carp caught from the river and the muted products of a German or Israeli fish farm. For a start they are different varieties, but the freshness of running water with its weeds and tiny forms of floating life are what make the difference. The first carp I ever cooked came from a French river, the Loir. We wrapped it up, with seasoning and butter and a splash of white wine, in a foil parcel, which was laid on a grill over some smouldering charcoal. After 10 minutes we turned the package over to cook the other side. Then we ate it with lemon juice, bread and butter and glasses of white wine. I have persisted with farm carp, but have never found one which came near the perfection of that river fish.

Another way of cooking carp, a recipe for the kitchen, comes from the early nineteenth century:—

For 4–6	6 oz. *175 g*. butter	2 anchovy fillets (or 1
A 2½–3 lb carp	Salt, pepper	generous teaspoon
4 pts water	¼ teaspoon each mace,	anchovy essence)
6 tablespoons vinegar	nutmeg, cloves	1 pint dry white wine
Salt, pepper	Bouquet garni	1 tablespoon flour
	1 onion	Lemon juice

Ask the fishmonger to clean and scale the fish, and also to remove the bitter gall sac at the back of the head. When you get it home, wash it in the water and vinegar very thoroughly.

Choose an ovenproof dish into which the carp will fit closely and snugly. Spread 4 oz of the butter over the base, lay the drained carp on top, and add seasoning, spices, herbs, onion and anchovy. Pour on enough dry white wine barely to cover the fish—you may need less than 1 pt, it depends on the size of the dish. Cover with foil, and put into a fairly hot oven, mark 5–6, 375–400°, until cooked. This will take 30–40 minutes. When the carp is done, put it on to a serving dish and strain the cooking juices into a clean pan. Taste them and correct the seasoning; boil down a little if they seem watery. Mash the remaining butter with the flour, and add it to the barely simmering sauce in little knobs. Keep stirring, and in about 5 minutes the sauce will thicken nicely. Taste and add a little lemon juice to sharpen the flavour. Pour the sauce over the fish and serve.

This method can be applied to any sizeable freshwater fish; or to several small ones—in which case, reduce the cooking time accordingly. The sauce can always be enriched by a spoonful or two of cream, or by a liaison of egg yolk and cream added after the butter-and-flour thickening.

If your carp had a soft roe, use it to make the following stuffing:—

The soft roe, chopped	Heaped tablespoon	1 oz. 25 g. butter
1 oz. 25 g. white breadcrumbs	chopped green herbs	½ teaspoon anchovy essence
Milk	Teaspoonful grated lemon rind	Salt, pepper, lemon juice
1 small onion, chopped		

Put the roe in a basin. Mix the crumbs with just enough milk to turn them into a soft paste. Cook the onion gently in the butter until soft. Mix together all the ingredients, with the seasoning and lemon juice last of all, to taste. Stuff and sew up the fish.

From *English Food*

The Uncatchable Trout

William Faulkner

The narrator in Faulkner's novel The Sound and the Fury
*is a man who committed suicide at Harvard in 1910. The
relevant section of the book is his description of his last day
alive, during which he encounters the boys and the trout.*

Where the shadow of the bridge fell I could see down for a
long way, but not as far as the bottom. When you leave a
leaf in water a long time after awhile the tissue will be gone and
the delicate fibres waving slow as the motion of sleep. They don't
touch one another, no matter how knotted up they once were,
no matter how close they lay once to the bones. And maybe when
He says Rise the eyes will come floating up too, out of the deep
quiet and the sleep, to look on glory. And after a while the flat
irons would come floating up. I hid them under the end of the
bridge and went back and leaned on the rail.

I could not see the bottom, but I could see a long way into the
motion of the water before the eye gave out, and then I saw a
shadow hanging like a fat arrow stemming into the current.
Mayflies skimmed in and out of the shadow of the bridge just above
the surface. *If it could just be a hell beyond that: the clean flame the
two of us more than dead. Then you will have only me then only me then
the two of us amid the pointing and the horror beyond the clean flame.*
The arrow increased without motion, then in a quick swirl the
trout lipped a fly beneath the surface with that sort of gigantic
delicacy of an elephant picking up a peanut. The fading vortex
drifted away down stream and then I saw the arrow again, nose

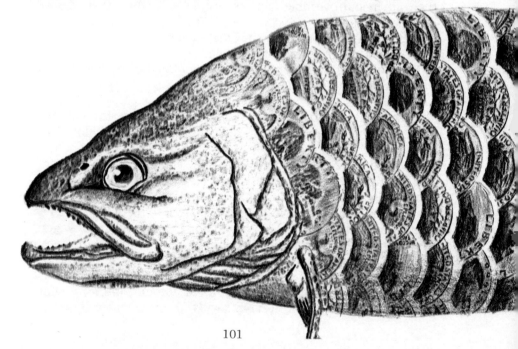

into the current, wavering delicately to the motion of the water above which the Mayflies slanted and poised. *Only you and me then amid the pointing and the horror walled by the clean flame.*

The trout hung, delicate and motionless among the wavering shadows. Three boys with fishing poles came on to the bridge and we leaned on the rail and looked down at the trout. They knew the fish. He was a neighbourhood character.

"They've been trying to catch that trout for twenty-five years. There's a store in Boston offers a twenty-five dollar fishing rod to anybody that can catch him."

"Why don't you all catch him, then? Wouldn't you like to have a twenty-five dollar fishing rod?"

"Yes," they said. They leaned on the rail, looking down at the trout. "I sure would," one said.

"I wouldn't take the rod," the second said. "I'd take the money instead."

"Maybe they wouldn't do that," the first said. "I bet he'd make you take the rod."

"Then I'd sell it."

"You couldn't get twenty-five dollars for it."

"I'd take what I could get then. I can catch just as many fish with this pole as I could with a twenty-five dollar one." Then they talked about what they would do with twenty-five dollars. They all talked at once, their voices insistent and contradictory and impatient, making of unreality a possibility, then a probability, then an incontrovertible fact, as people will when their desires become words.

"I'd buy a horse and wagon," the second said.

"Yes, you would," the others said.

"I would. I know where I can buy one for twenty-five dollars. I know the man."

"Who is it?"

"That's all right who it is. I can buy it for twenty-five dollars."

"Yah," the others said, "He don't know any such thing. He's just talking."

"Do you think so?" the boy said. They continued to jeer at him, but he said nothing more. He leaned on the rail, looking down at the trout which he had already spent, and suddenly the acrimony, the conflict, was gone from their voices, as if to them too it was as though he had captured the fish and bought his horse and wagon, they too partaking of that adult trait of being convinced of any-thing by an assumption of silent superiority. I suppose that people using themselves and each other so much by words, are at least consistent in attributing wisdom to a still tongue, and for a while I could feel the other two seeking swiftly for some means by which to cope with him, to rob him of his horse and wagon.

"You couldn't get twenty-five dollars for that pole," the first said. "I bet anything you couldn't."

"He hasn't caught that trout yet," the third said suddenly, then they both cried:

"Yah, wha'd I tell you? What's the man's name? I dare you to tell. There ain't any such man."

"Ah, shut up," the second said. "Look, Here he comes again." They leaned on the rail, motionless, identical, their poles slanting slenderly in the sunlight, also identical. The trout rose without haste, a shadow in faint wavering increase; again the little vortex faded slowly downstream. "Gee," the first one murmured.

"We don't try to catch him any more," he said. "We just watch Boston folks that come out and try."

"Is he the only fish in this pool?"

"Yes. He ran all the others out. The best place to fish around here is down at the Eddy."

"No it ain't," the second said. "It's better at Bigelow's Mill two to one." Then they argued for a while about which was the best fishing and then left off all of a sudden to watch the trout rise again and the broken swirl of water suck down a little of the sky. I asked how far it was to the nearest town. They told me.

"But the closest car line is that way," the second said, pointing back down the road. "Where are you going?"

"Nowhere. Just walking."

"You from the college?"

"Yes. Are there any factories in that town?"

"Factories?" They looked at me.

"No," the second said. "Not there." They looked at my clothes. "You looking for work?"

"How about Bigelow's Mill?" the third said. "That's a factory."

"Factory my eye. He means a sure enough factory."

"One with a whistle," I said. "I haven't heard any one o'clock whistles yet."

"Oh," the second said. "There's a clock in the Unitarian steeple. You can find out the time from that. Haven't you got a watch on that chain?"

"I broke it this morning." I showed them my watch. They examined it gravely.

"It's still running," the second said. "What does a watch like that cost?"

"It was a present," I said. "My father gave it to me when I graduated from high school."

"Are you a Canadian?" the third said. He had red hair.

"Canadian?"

"He don't talk like them," the second said. "I've heard them talk. He talks like they do in minstrel shows."

"Say," the third said, "Ain't you afraid he'll hit you?"

"Hit me?"

"You said he talks like a coloured man."

"Ah, dry up," the second said. "You can see the steeple when you get over that hill there."

I thanked them. "I hope you have good luck. Only don't catch that old fellow down there. He deserves to be let alone."

"Can't anybody catch that fish," the first said. They leaned on the rail, looking down into the water, the three poles like three slanting threads of yellow fire in the sun.

From *The Sound and the Fury*

Cleopatra's Joke

William Shakespeare

Alexandria.   Cleopatra's palace.
Enter Cleopatra, Charmian, Iras, and Alexas.

Cleo. Give me some music; music, moody food
　Of us that trade in love.

All.　　　　　　　The music, ho!
　　　　　Enter Mardian the Eunuch.

Cleo. Let it alone; let's to billiards: come, Charmian.

Char. My arm is sore: best play with Mardian.

Cleo. As well a woman with an eunuch play'd
　As with a woman. Come, you'll play with me, sir?

Mar. As well as I can, madam.

Cleo. And when good will is show'd, though 'to come to short.
　The actor may plead pardon. I'll none now:
　Give me mine angle; we'll to the river: there,
　My music playing far off, I will betray
　Tawny-finn'd fishes; my bended hook shall pierce
　Their slimy jaws, and as I draw them up,
　I'll think them every one an Antony,
　And say 'Ah, ha! you're caught.'

Char.　　　　　　　　'Twas merry when
　You wager'd on your angling; when your diver
　Did hang a salt-fish on his hook, which he
　With fervency drew up.

Cleo.　　　　　　　　That time—O times!—
　I laugh'd him out of patience, and that night
　I laugh'd him into patience; and next morn,
　Ere the ninth hour, I drunk him to his bed;
　Then put my tires and mantles on him, whilst
　I wore his sword Philippan.

From *Antony and Cleopatra*, Act II, Scene 5

Border Incident

David Pownall

They were both, by nature, competitive men.

Most of the dreariness they were experiencing in retirement was caused by the lack of conflict and struggle. Only in fishing did some of the flavour of life return.

They had never spoken. Facing each other across the River Finn in high or low water, they had remained silent. There was plenty to look at in that stretch of country. They had no need of each other. No need they would admit. The only words were those which were directed at the big brown trout.

This monster specimen's territory was a pool in the River Finn. The rocky bed held many holes and hiding-places. From Castlederg to Ballybofey anglers spoke of this trout and told tales of the day that they had tried to catch it . . . always *nearly* succeeding.

William was tight-lipped about his quest. Always taciturn, his own man, he was partially ashamed of his relentless pursuit of the fish. His enemy on the other side, the long, lugubrious Liam, was less reserved.

He had attempted to talk to William via his address to the great fish.

Forthrightness in his personal relations had never been a strong point of Liam's. His failure to achieve promotion in the hierarchy of the dye works at Strabane was attributable to this factor in his personality. Why William had failed in equal measure in the same test—a lifetime of employment at the smoking, rainbow-encrusted tank-house—was the opposite. He had to face every man and every situation head-on. In this posture he was the victim of frequent collision.

"Will you come to me?" Liam had crooned over the water, past the concentric ripples of the rising big-nosed brownie. For two hours in that long summer twilight he had kept talking, not wanting to stop, having started. The fish ignored him and his old rival did likewise, grey eyes fixed ahead, only moving to follow the trajectory of his fly.

"Well you're an ignorant creature," Liam had murmured after his last long cast. "Which hardly needs saying to a Catholic cold-blooded vertebrate like yourself."

October.

*   *   *

In the last week of the season there were few fishermen left on the Finn as the weather was cold and squally. In that week it was announced that an underground aqueduct would be constructed from the River Finn to a new reservoir near Mourne Beg. The work would start after Christmas and continue for two years, it being a substantial project requiring the mining of a seven-mile tunnel. Some of the fishermen returned and tried again.

The site of the tunnel entrance was to be the pool of the big brown trout.

Rain came, then sleet. High winds streamed over Donegal from the cold Atlantic. The last fishermen packed up and went home with what small catches they had made. The Finn rose; red water came down. Flies became invisible and too light for the plunging current. Letters appeared in the newspapers from all the secretaries of all the angling associations. A public inquiry was called for and the call ignored both in Dublin and Belfast as both authorities were involved in the scheme. Isobars and government conspired.

It was spinning weather.

William was in a fury. He drank more: butted his way into as many arguments with his wife and few friends as he could. And whatever time he chose, with time running out, he would find his enemy on the opposite bank of the doomed pool, rod working, spinner fishing along the dark water. Side by side, the river in between, they combed the coloured flow. William lost his best barspoons. Liam lost his rubber minnow Mep, the only one in the county. Down the swollen river came branches, detritus. When the wind dropped they could hear the boulders rumbling along the river bed. Liam chattered to himself with cold, not even trying to make himself heard.

They caught fish in equal quantities. Half-pounders. Small fry. Even the occasional salmon did not excite them. Both men wanted the big brownie. Through clenched teeth they cursed each other, the weather and the future when their river and their dream would be siphoned away to an underground home.

The final weekend of the season arrived. The big trout remained uncaught.

*   *   *

William and Liam came face to face in Rafferty's Bar, Strabane. This time the Finn was not between them, only bare boards. That morning they had fished through the first three hours of dawn; shifting position, anxious to be as far apart as possible. Both men were tired and wind-reddened and the drink they took worked quickly. They were both in the company of friends and everyone knew of the rivalry between the two old men—so it became the fulcrum of their chat.

It had always been an inarticulate dislike. In fact William and Liam had often been aware of strange urges towards each other which were not clearly aggressive. It was a nervous, insecure, irrational business. That trouble would actually break out into physical reality had always been a fear, but a relished fear. Each fancied his chances.

Now, with drink inside them, they allowed their friends to tempt the old antagonism to the surface. It was done with good humour because the central issue was not a human thing. It was a fish; a catchable, manageable thing which lived and could die without hurtful repercussions.

William and Liam did not look at each other during the fun. Their eyes barely touched before sliding away in long glances to wall decorations or windows. Smiles they managed, and covert squaring of their shoulders inside their jackets. Their friends pursued their joke throughout the lunchtime session until the bet made its inevitable appearance and was clinched with the brightness of eye and loudness of voice which signifies a great life-challenge. The bet mattered. It mattered down to the roots of what the two men had left in this world, down to those deep roots.

"A hundred," William said firmly, his hand palm-down on the table.

"A hundred it is," Liam averred, "and no turning back."

"I will not be turning back."

"Then neither will I."

After a momentary hesitation they shook hands.

As the company spilled out into the street in the late afternoon there were cumulus clouds piling up in the west and the sun was masked.

*   *   *

On that Monday evening, in the quiet hour as the day turned, Liam and William sat opposite each other on the banks of the Finn and watched the water. It was less turbulent now and clearing, but still only good for spinning. They were both hoping for a sign from the fish; some movement in a tranquil sidewater or a leap. Around them the country was mellowing, changing from rich summer greens to more muted colours. Leaves floated over still

surfaces and eddies, sending false messages and alarms. It was a difficult river to read under these conditions.

William struggled with ripple, white water, swirl and the glass of calm runs, trying to interpret the random motions.

What broke that flow? What brought about that turbulence? Kingfisher? Water-rat? Declining dragonfly? Or *him*?

In a long, smooth glide the trout rose with its signal. Waves radiated from the spot in pure geometry and were then bent by the river's flow, sagging, breaking, dispersing. William groaned softly in the back of his throat and cast his lure to the other side of the fading circles, drawing it across.

No check, no stop. The lure flowed through the warped letter O, revolving sadly.

Liam's dry laugh crossed the river.

When William looked up, amazed at his opponent's audacity, he saw Liam standing with his rod at his side. Over his long face was a lop-sided smile.

"Well, you'll need God to guide you if you keep casting like that," he called. "You dropped it in the water with too much of a splash. Now avoid the splash if you can. Any undue disturbance will frighten him out of his normal residence. We don't want him shifting downstream now, do we?"

William gripped his rod and checked the swinging lure with his free hand, letting the treble hooks stick into his palm in his astonished rage.

"Are you talking to me?" he managed to choke. "To me? To me?"

"I am," Liam replied, switching his gaze to a nearby tree and directing his words at that so they, boomeranging, curved round the trunk and approached William from the rear.

"You can shut up then!" William roared.

"Now you're nervous of losing a hundred pounds," chuckled Liam via a flock of starlings and an incipient moon. "Refrain from shouting so close to the water. His honour down there will pick up the vibrations."

William lunged forward, entering the river, his face beetroot-red. As he waded across, staggering over the slippery stones in the bed, Liam retreated and delivered his tormenting comments from further up the bank.

Pausing with the water up to his hips, William realised that he had been deliberately provoked.

Tactics.

As old as the hills.

Turning his back on the chanting Protestant he waded back to his side and resumed fishing.

*   *   *

They forgot food.

They forgot rest.

Salmo trutta fario with his red and silver, blue and brown beauty became the sole object of their desire.

Liam spoke to him through rock and tree-root, sky and earth, light and dark. The Finn became his torrent of words, a home for the great trout.

William faced the ghost he could not see, only sense, and bade him come up fighting.

They entered the last night of the last day of the season, still empty-handed except for fish of no consequence, all of which had been hurled back.

From a deep hole in a tributary stream a mile away the great brownie peered, seeing no light above, only the swarming silk underside of the water which was gently in motion, well protected by a jaw of rocks against the quickening current. The fish had moved there a week ago, tired of the endless assaults on its territory. Its food, the smaller fish, had been caught or scooted away up or downstream to escape the derrick-lines of rods, the constant combing and cunning. In the stony, single-minded nature of the great fish there had appeared a contentment which was akin to peace.

*   *   *

In the last hour before midnight the gale struck the valley of the Finn with a full accompaniment of sound. The low hills deflected little of the roaring sea-wind and the rain hammered down in long columns, nails.

Exhausted, almost sightless, William and Liam clung onto the bank, refusing to leave until the time was up. When they cast it was into darkness and they lost lure after lure, broke line after line.

"Come out and fight you bastard!" William shouted into the face of the storm, there being no other living thing to butt and abuse. "Take that, take that . . ."

His rod cut the turbulent air, swish lost, tip invisible.

"God how you try my patience," Liam wept, his cracking muscles heaving the lure forward again on another blasted parabola. "I'll be the death of you."

On the other side William stiffened, raised his rod, sighed. Cursing he relaxed his reel, thinking he was snagged again.

The rod bent, trembled. What was on the other end was not fixed. It was running, fighting. With a hoarse cry of delight he sank the rod-butt into his abdomen and heaved upwards, overjoyed at the great threshing weight on the other end. He had it! Keeping the tension on the line he advanced into the water, sensing the power of the fish. He prayed that it was not a salmon. It must be the big brown. Immense surges of strength hit the drum of his reel, dragging William further into the river. It was not tiring. Step by step he went in, seeking the flash in the dark storm.

Liam talked and talked to the only thing he could see.

The line flying from his bent rod.

"Will you come to me?" he sang, up to his waist in the water. "I've got you now."

The storm lulled. The clouds parted and an Irish moon poured down its light.

In the middle of the River Finn, lure locked with lure, the old deceivers faced each other, trying to guess which one might find the strength to smile first.

From *The Spectator*

Bear Fishing

John McPhee

John McPhee's river journey through the Alaskan
wilderness took place in 1976.

Fedeler had picked cups of blueberries to mix into our breakfast pancakes. Finishing them, we prepared to go. The sun was coming through. The rain was gone. The morning grew bright and warm. Pourchot and I got into the canoe, which, for all its heavy load, felt light. Twenty minutes downriver, we had to stop for more repairs to the Kleppers, but afterward the patchwork held. With higher banks, longer pools, the river was running deeper. The sun began to blaze.

Rounding bends, we saw sculpins, a pair of great horned owls, mergansers, Taverner's geese. We saw ravens and a gray jay. Coming down a long, deep, green pool, we looked toward the riffle at the lower end and saw an approaching grizzly. He was young, possibly four years old, and not much over four hundred pounds. He crossed the river. He studied the salmon in the riffle. He did not see, hear, or smell us. Our three boats were close together, and down the light current on the flat water we drifted toward the fishing bear.

He picked up a salmon, roughly ten pounds of fish, and, holding it with one paw, he began to whirl it around his head. Apparently, he was not hungry, and this was a form of play. He played sling-the-salmon. With his claws embedded near the tail, he whirled the salmon and then tossed it high, end over end. As it fell, he scooped it up and slung it around his head again, lariat salmon, and again he tossed it into the air. He caught it and heaved it high once more. The fish flopped to the ground. The bear turned away, bored. He began to move upstream by the edge of the river. Behind his big head his hump projected. His brown fur rippled like a field under wind. He kept coming. The breeze was behind him. He had not yet seen us. He was romping along at an easy walk. As he came closer to us, we drifted slowly toward him. The single Klepper, with John Kauffmann in it, moved up against a snagged stick and broke it off. The snap was light, but enough to stop the bear. Instantly, he was motionless and alert, remaining on his four feet and straining his eyes to see. We drifted on toward him. At last, we arrived in his focus. If we were looking at something we had rarely seen before, God help him so was he. If he was a tenth as awed as I was, he could not have moved a muscle, which he did, now, in a hurry that was not pronounced but nonetheless seemed inappropriate to his status in the situation. He crossed low ground and went up a bank toward a copse of willow. He stopped there and faced us again. Then, breaking stems to pieces, he went into the willows.

From Coming into the Country

Fish Soup

Peter Feibleman

The fish soup of the poor people in Sanlúcar is like a light essence of the sea, a kind of seafood consommé, in which the ingredients have been brewed until only shell or bone is left. Little seasoning is used, maybe just a bay leaf and a little salt. The broth is first reduced to a purified liquid about the consistency of expensive scent and about as strong smelling. Sometimes river fish and crabs are cooked in it too, thickening the soup and mingling the elements of ocean and river. The soup can be drunk on even the hottest days, because there is no heaviness in it no matter how much fish it was made with. A bowl of it with half a bottle of cool dry *manzanilla* from one of the Sanlúcar cellars where it is bottled, and you will feel lighter for having eaten. This is perhaps the most important function of the Andalusian kitchen, and the wines of the region have been designed to suit this purpose.

From *The Cooking of Spain & Portugal*

Herring the King

Traditional

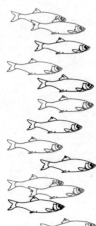

Of all the fish that roam the sea,
The Herring alone our King shall be!
So fill your cups, ye fishers strong,
And drink his health full, deep and long.

Chorus:
Sing hugamar fein an sawra lin,
The storm is o'er, 'tis calm again;
And we have brought the summer in,
In holding chase with Herring our King.

I think with me you'll all agree,
We to our King should thankful be.
He clothes us, feeds us, pays the rent,
And cheers us in the time of Lent.

Oh! who would not a fisher be,
And lead a life so wild and free?
Grim care we leave upon the shore
To wait until our voyage is o'er.

Then once more hearken unto me,
The Herring alone our King shall be!
So fill your cups, ye fishers strong,
And drink his health full, deep and long.

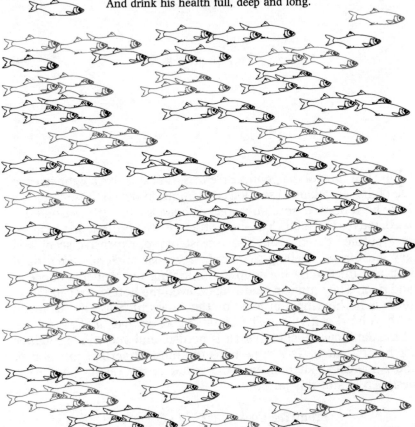

On the Danube

Negley Farson

In 1925, when the Rumanians were shocking the world with their organised murdering of the Russians they were inducing to escape across the Dniester (and then shooting them as they crossed the river to Kichenev) I got into Bessarabia without a permit. I lived with some Russian sturgeon fishermen in the frozen marshes of the Danube delta, sleeping in their clay hut on the top of their clay stove. The Russian peasant is outrageously courageous when it comes to talking; he says everything that is on his mind—if it is a complaint—even though he knows he might get killed for it. And I almost had to shut these people up when they began pouring out what they knew about the Tartar Bunar massacre which had just taken place—Bessarabia was a land of terror in those days.

To get them to the stage of intimacy where they would begin to talk I first had to go out to fish sturgeon with them in their black sailing lodka in the choppy yellow waves of the Black Sea. The days were so cold that I thought my spine would become nothing but a strip of ice. They caught the sturgeon on long lines of bare hooks that lay like a rake before the shallow entrance of this mouth of the Danube. The sturgeon, feeling his way up along the bottom, met these obstructive hooks, gave a flip—and the next instant he was involved in a whirl of hooks—pinioned. With the ice coating the black skiff these three men pulled a sturgeon almost as big as a man into the boat. Then they beat him to death with wooden clubs. Remember, the sturgeon has armour-plated sides and a head hard as a stone, built that way to meet the rocks of the bottom up which he must travel against the swift currents. These hooks, made in Norway, had needle-sharp points. With them flying around my head as the sturgeon flung himself about the skiff, I can truthfully say I have seldom had a more terrifying experience in my life.

Rumanian sentries, with fixed bayonets—also sharp as needle points—challenged us from every bit of solid land in the marsh. But it was so bitterly cold that they did not take their mittens off to examine our papers. A good thing for me—for I had none.

These persecuted fishermen had to "sell" all their sturgeon to the Fish Control—a horrible piece of Government graft—and the big one was duly taken up to the market at Wilkowo; but a smaller one was walking around all that afternoon, cut up in small pieces, in the fishermen's pockets and down inside their boots. That night we made a rich, red soup of him; and we all ate it with the same wooden spoon. It was considered good manners to lick the spoon clean before you passed it on. We drank the last of my vodka, and they suddenly produced some red wine from a blue tea-pot. The hut steamed. The ice boomed and cracked in the moonlit marshes. They sailed me down the Black Sea the next day, where I was arrested at Sulina. But their story had corroborated a story of official terrorism that I had been putting together ever since I left Bucharest. Later, I wired it from Constantinople—with never a hint of these courageous sturgeon fishermen. And it was with a satisfied mind, on my last night with them, that I stretched myself out on their warm stove—to dream of the mighty sturgeon, feeling his way up the Danube, with his cold moonstone eyes.

These stories, my newspaper syndicate discovered, were the things people wanted to read in the United States. They were tired of politicians. So when, in the winter of 1928–29, I asked if I could ride horse-back the next spring over the Caucasus—my editor snapped at the idea. "Tell us how people *live*," he said.

From my newspaper's point of view the series of articles I had been commissioned to write meant stories of the remote, strange tribes which the marches of history had left in nearly every valley in the high Caucasus. For Wicksteed and myself it meant weeks on horseback in the snow-ranged mountains (it turned out that for three of these weeks we never saw a road); it meant living on our own wits and resources almost entirely, sleeping under a tent I had invented, made from a ground sheet and two sleeping bags, cooking our own meals, the subjects of no man's caprice, except our own. "And," I said to old bearded Wicksteed, "it means some of those fine Caucasian snow trout. We should live well, this spring."

Wicksteed was an Englishman who came out to Soviet Russia in 1924 with the Quaker Relief, when there was that hideous famine along the Volga. "Wicker" had seen cannibalism. And what he saw in Russia—the great heart of the Russian people—decided him to make his life there. A good part of this trip I am now describing can be found in Alexander Wicksteed's book, *Life under the Soviets*.

This is a fishing book. I cannot go into the joy of those days in the high Caucasus. One detail makes it particularly interesting, the fact that the tribes were so different, even in some adjacent valleys, that a man from one valley could not be induced to go into the next one. This meant constant changing for us, getting new relays of horses; and while we would wait, sometimes a day or two, until we could get two horses to go on again, I always fished the streams leading down into each valley. They seemed ideal for trout, but for weeks I never could rise one—and the Abbey & Imbrie rod (this trip was the death of it) almost caused me to be pushed over a precipice several times when its stiff, slotted wooden case caught again on some projecting rock as I tried to ride my horse around some narrow ledges.

The hospitality of primitive people is very similar, and nearly

always spontaneous, the world around. When we were in contact
with any tribe they invariably gave us milk, bread and their taste-
less cheese almost as if it were a customary rite; yet, like the African
natives, they disliked eating their sheep or cattle as these animals
were symbols of their owner's wealth, his position in the world.
Primitive people, when you come down to brass tacks, are much
more materialistic and "capitalist" than in the sophisticated
world. And not being on a vegetarian diet Wicksteed and I bought
a sheep every three days, when we could get one. This we grilled
impaled on sticks over our campfires, using the same methods as
the Cossacks and these mountain men had used for centuries; a
chunk of meat, then a chunk of fat, and so on until an entire skewer
was stuffed. They call this "shaslick", when you buy it in London,
although in London they will seldom add the sour cream, which,
smeared on the toasting meat, gives it the most appetising tang.
But fish we did not get for weeks.

The chief reason was that we trekked through heavy rains;
these mountain streams were sluices of greyish water, often carrying good-sized boulders along; and those streams which came
down from the glaciers were almost amalgams of water and rock.
It is doubtful if a trout could have seen a fly.

Then one sunset we came out on a high spur of mountains where
the swift-flowing rivers, the Teberda and the Kuban, meet to
form that eventually long lazy river wandering across the Cossack
steppes. Mt Elbruz, 3,000 feet higher than Mt Blanc, lay behind
us, its cone of straw glowing like a living flamingo in the sunset.
There were one hundred and twenty miles of unbroken snow and
glaciers between its two nipples and Kazbek. And as I sat on my
horse my eyes were still filled with the thunder of the previous
sunset, the thunder of emotions inside me, when I sat in the saddle
and looked along fifty miles of unbroken snows turning all shades
of rose and indigo as night came on.

Below me now lay the junction of these two rivers, the Terek
glacial and grey, the Kuban a vivid bottle-green. Where they met
they ran in two parallel bands of colour until they fused in a rapid-
filled gorge about two miles from where we had come out of the
pine forest. I fished this gorge at sunset that night, getting seven
trout. By an accident, as it was I who put them on the ashes and
embers, using some of our last butter we had bought from a shepherd tribe, they were excellent. I had forgotten them and had let
them get slightly crisp. And that night a Cossack, who informed
me that his official status was Instructor in Communism, ate one
of these, pronounced it marvellous; but said that I was a Capitalist
because I used the fly. The worm, he declared, was the only thing
to be trusted. And he even volunteered to produce an old "charac-

ter" who caught monster-sized fish in these two rivers. He was so much like the local man in either England or the States, always bragging about how *they* caught such whopping big ones, that he could not understand my frequent fits of laughter. Besides, it turned out that he had never seen a fly. Even more, he did not believe I had caught trout on such a thing. His doubts were dispelled only by my showing him my outfit, wherein there was not a hook which did not have these coloured feathers attached. Still he was dubious.

There was a Turco-Tartar village here, named Utsch-Khalan, at which our man with the two horses saw fit to desert us. He and the horses were just not there the next morning. I left it to Wicksteed to go some ten miles up the valley to get us two new ones, I intended to fish. Working upstream I fished all that morning in the most likely places and never rose a fish. I changed flies, I changed tactics, I fished open water in the slow reaches and behind every rock in the swift. I might as well have been casting in a bathtub. I was eating my lunch, sitting on the bank, with a large slab of black bread with another slab of cheese planked on it, and at the same time idly casting a short line into the swift, sun-dappled river flowing past, when I got a rise. It was so unexpected that I dropped my sandwich in the stream and make another cast over the spot without getting up. This cast brought me a beautiful little trout of about a third of a pound. As trout usually take their colouring from the bottom and colour conditions of the stream, this one's back was a vivid apple green and his hundreds of small spots were a bright scarlet. I then discovered that I had nothing to put him in; as if half-suspecting that I would get no fish I had not taken my canvas fish-bag along.

I got thirty-five trout that afternoon—the greatest number in any one day I have ever caught. I do not think I would have caught so many then had it not been for my argument with the Communist the previous night; I wanted to kill him dead with an unanswerable argument. I found out that instead of the wide, open stretches of fairly deep water, all the fish seemed to be lying in the white water, behind every lee of rock or ridge. I would dump those which I had caught out on the bank, wade out into the river and fish every likely rock. I also discovered that they had a passion for a little orange-and-green bodied fly, with an inconspicuous wing—neither teal not grouse nor mallard—that I had always had in my book, but whose name I did not even know, nor could I remember where I had ever come by them. Anyway, I had almost a dozen. And when I found that the trout liked these best I took off the two other flies and fished with these "United Irelands", as

I found out later they were called. It was an unorthodox, bold gesture, but it resulted twice that day in my catching three fish at one time. I had never had more than two on before or since. With three fish I did not know how to land them; which one should I net? My solution, and I am ready to admit that it was possibly not the right one, was to play them as long as I felt safe, then work them towards the shallow lee of a pebbled spit, drag the top fish up on the bank, slip the net under the middle one—and trust that the tail trout was not rubbed off as I pulled the trio ashore. In both cases it worked.

From that day one particular stretch of this swift green river lingers in my memory. It was where a pine had fallen some years back into the stream. Time and the freshet had turned it round and washed it diagonally out into the river. But its roots had held its butt to the bank, thus causing sand and small boulders to deposit behind it, as they do in those jetties that are built to stop shore erosion. This had made a pool about thirty yards long. It was in this long pool that I caught both of these triple-catches. I took eleven of my thirty-five trout out of that pool alone.

While I was fishing I did not notice that two Caucasians had come out of the forest, on their tiny, cat-footed horses, and were watching me. Their sporting instinct had been aroused. They dismounted, like cats themselves, and walked to the river. Then I saw them for the first time and waved them back. That, too, struck them as being peculiar; it had never occured to them before that fish could see them. In fact, I doubt if they had ever held a fish in their hands. Then when I was unhooking a fish, they saw the flies! Now, this *was* magic, according to their way of thinking; they could not believe what I then actually showed them—a trout rising to the fly. They began to laugh like schoolboys. They became so excited that they pressed forward to the river again. I could not speak to them as their dialect was not even Russian at its base. But they then appointed themselves my unofficial gillies, carrying my net—heavy and bulging by now—through the thick underbrush from pool to pool, from rapid to rapid, and up each unfishable racing slant of white water. I pulled one of the feathered hooks against a calloused forefinger of each of them and gave it a tug. They yelled with delight when they saw the tiny hook fixed in them. An eagle seemed to add to their surprise and curiosity as he spread his pinions over our heads and then dropped with a jerk onto a dead branch across the stream.

That night, as I had been unthinkingly fishing upstream all afternoon, without ever thinking of how far away I was getting from the village, I was almost two hours finding my way down the dim trail in the dark. When I got to the board shacks of Utsch-

Khalan I dropped in at the local wine shop and bought two bottles of that purple, heavy Caucasian wine known as Naperiouli. In the shop I found the Instructor in Communism and held up to him the bulging net of fish. I invited him to come to the new schoolhouse, built by the Soviets, and on whose floor I was now sleeping, to share the feast. Wicksteed I found waiting for me, and very hungry. I showed him the trout.

"Good Lord!" said this old hermit philosopher (he was a great Shakespeare and Dante student), "for once I shall have more trout than I can eat. I have always been a poor man, you know. I have *never* had enough trout."

Well, he would tonight, I told him; and I suggested that I was going out to lie in the stream, clinging on to a boulder, to freshen me up. I was dog-tired. Hanging there, like a waving flag, to the tip of a boulder sticking up from the racing river, I regained strength and an appetite that would mean the end of all those thirty-five firm trout that came to my share. I informed Wicker, who really knew nothing whatever about trout, that this catch was a memorable one, that I would probably never again have such a day's luck, and that he must not be misled into thinking I was going to repeat the performance. I could see he was having dreams of trout for dinner every night.

Well, supporting that conceited but likeable Don Cossack in his Communist arguments about fishing had been a pug-nosed young schoolmistress, also a Cossack, whom the Bolshies had sent into these mountains to instruct the Turco-Tartar children, and their parents, in the ideology of the Soviets. She, too, seemed to know the answer to nearly everything. But she didn't know how to cook fish—not trout.

At the first bite the face of Wicksteed contracted as if he had bitten an unripe persimmon. Then he rushed for the door. He tried again, took another nibble, rushed out again. "Perfectly ghastly!" he said.

They were. The Instructress in Communism had cooked them in sunflower-seed oil. Not only that, she had placed the whole thirty-five in *cold* sunflower-seed oil to let them soak! I discovered that when I rushed out into the kitchen.

"*Nu Vot!*" said the Don Cossack comfortably—and he and she ate the whole lot. Poor Wicksteed died later in his one room in a congested Moscow tenement. He never did have all the trout he wanted to eat. Also, and I never knew how it happened, I found the tip of my rod broken in the morning. I think the Instructor in Comminism had been showing some of the Turco-Tartars how to catch fish with a fly.

From *Going Fishing*

The End of Jaws

Peter Benchley

*Probably the most widely-known fishing story this century,
Jaws is set in Amity, a seaside resort on Long Island in
America which is being terrorized by a great white shark.
Quint is a professional fisherman. Brody is the local
police chief.*

When he drove up to the dock, Quint was waiting for him—a
tall, impressive figure whose yellow oilskins shone under
the dark sky. He was sharpening a harpoon dart on a carborun-
dum stone.

"I almost called you," Brody said as he pulled on his slicker.
"What does this weather mean?"

"Nothing," said Quint. "It'll let up after a while. Or even if it
doesn't, it don't matter. He'll be there."

Brody looked up at the scudding clouds. "Gloomy enough."

"Fitting," said Quint, and he hopped aboard the boat.

"Is it just us?"

"Just us. You expecting somebody else?"

"No. But I thought you liked an extra pair of hands."

"You know this fish as well as any man, and more hands won't
make no difference now. Besides, it's nobody else's business."

Brody stepped from the dock on to the transom, and was about
to jump down to the deck when he noticed a canvas tarpaulin
covering something in a corner. "What's that?" he said, pointing.

"Sheep." Quint turned the ignition key. The engine coughed
once, caught, and began to chug evenly.

"What for?" Brody stepped down on to the deck. "You going to
sacrifice it?"

Quint barked a brief, grim laugh. "Might at that," he said. "No, it's bait. Give him a little breakfast before we have at him. Undo my stern line." He walked forward and cast off the bow and spring lines.

As Brody reached for the stern line, he heard a car engine. A pair of headlights sped along the road, and there was a squeal of rubber as the car stopped at the end of the pier. A man jumped out of the car and ran towards the *Orca*. It was Bill Whitman.

"I almost missed you." he said, panting.

"What do you want?" said Brody.

"I want to come along. Or, rather, I've been ordered to come along."

"Tough shit," said Quint. "I don't know who you are, but nobody's coming along. Brody, cast off the stern line."

"Why not?" said Whitman. "I won't get in the way. Maybe I can help. Look, man, this is news. If you're going to catch that fish, I want to be there."

"Fuck yourself," said Quint.

"I'll charter a boat and follow you."

Quint laughed. "Go ahead. See if you can find someone foolish enough to take you out. Then try to find us. It's a big ocean. Throw the line, Brody!"

Brody tossed the stern line on to the dock. Quint pushed the throttle forward, and the boat eased out of the slip. Brody looked back and saw Whitman walking down the pier towards his car.

The water off Montauk was rough, for the wind—from the south-east now—was at odds with the tide. The boat lurched through the waves, its bow pounding down and casting a mantle of spray. The dead sheep bounced in the stern.

When they reached the open sea, heading south and slightly west, their motion was eased. The rain had slackened to a drizzle, and with each moment there were fewer whitecaps tumbling from the top of waves.

They had been around the point only fifteen minutes when Quint pulled back on the throttle and slowed the engine.

Brody looked towards shore. In the growing light he could see the water tower clearly—a black point rising from the grey strip of land. The lighthouse beacon still shone. "We're not out as far as we usually go," he said.

"No."

"We can't be more than a couple of miles offshore."

"Just about."

"So why are you stopping?"

"I got a feeling." Quint pointed to the left, to a cluster of lights farther down the shore. "That's Amity there."

"So?"

"I don't think he'll be so far out today. I think he'll be some-where between here and Amity."

"Why?"

"Like I said, it's a feeling. There's not always a why to these things."

"Two days in a row we found him farther out."

"Or he found us."

"I don't get it, Quint. For a man who says there's no such thing as a smart fish, you're making this one out to be a genius."

"I wouldn't go that far."

Brody bristled at Quint's sly, enigmatic tone. "What kind of game are you playing?"

"No game. If I'm wrong, I'm wrong."

"And we try somewhere else tomorrow." Brody half hoped Quint would be wrong, that there would be a day's reprieve.

"Or later today. But I don't think we'll have to wait that long." Quint cut the engine, went to the stern, and lifted a bucket of chum on to the transom. "Start chummin'," he said, handing Brody the ladle. He uncovered the sheep, tied a rope around its neck, and lay it on the gunwale. He slashed its stomach and flung the animal overboard, letting it drift twenty feet from the boat before securing the rope to an after cleat. Then he went forward, unlashed two barrels, and carried them, and their coils of ropes and harpoon darts, back to the stern. He set the barrels on each side of the tran-som, each next to its own rope, and slipped one dart on to the wooden throwing shaft. "Okay," he said. "Now let's see how long it takes."

The sky had lightened to full, grey daylight, and in ones and twos the lights on the shore flicked off.

The stench of the mess Brody was ladling overboard made his stomach turn, and he wished he had eaten something—anything—before he left home.

Quint sat on the flying bridge, watching the rhythms of the sea.

Brody's butt was sore from sitting on the hard transom, and his arm was growing weary from the dipping and emptying of the ladle. So he stood up, stretched, and facing off the stern, tried a new scooping motion with the ladle.

Suddenly he saw the monstrous head of the fish—not five feet away, so close he could reach over and touch it with the ladle—black eyes staring at him, silver-grey snout pointing at him, gaping jaw grinning at him. "Oh God!" Brody said, wondering in his shock how long the fish had been there before he had stood up and turned around. "There he is!"

Quint was down the ladder and at the stern in an instant. As he jumped on to the transom, the fish's head slipped back into the water and, a second later, slammed into the transom. The jaws closed on the wood, and the head shook violently from side to side. Brody grabbed a cleat and held on, unable to look away from the eyes. The boat shuddered and jerked each time the fish moved its head. Quint slipped and fell to his knees on the transom. The fish let go and dropped beneath the surface, and the boat lay still again.

"He was waiting for us!" yelled Brody.

"I know," said Quint.

"How did he—"

"It don't matter," said Quint. "We've got him now."

"*We've got him?* Did you see what he did to the boat?"

"Give it a mighty good shake, didn't he?"

The rope holding the sheep tightened, shook for a moment, then went slack.

Quint stood and picked up the harpoon. "He's took the sheep. It'll be minutes before he comes back."

"How come he didn't take the sheep first?"

"He got no manners," Quint cackled. "Come on, you motherfucker. Come and get your due."

Brody saw fever in Quint's face—a heat that lit up his dark eyes, an intensity that drew his lips back from his teeth in a crooked smile, an anticipation that strummed the sinews in his neck and whitened his knuckles.

The boat shuddered again, and there was a dull, hollow thump.

Quint leaned over the side and shouted, "Come out from under there, you cocksucker! Where are your guts? You'll not sink me before I get you!"

"What do you mean, sink us?" said Brody. "What's he doing?"

"He's trying to chew a hole in the bottom of the fucking boat, that's what! Look in the bilge. Come out, you Godforsaken sonofabitch!" Quint raised high his harpoon.

Brody knelt and raised the hatch cover over the engine room. He peered into the dark, oily hole. There was water in the bilges, but there always was, and he saw no new hole through which water could pour. "Looks okay to me," he said. "Thank God."

The dorsal fin and tail surfaced ten yards to the right of the stern and began to move again towards the boat. "There you come," said Quint, cooing. "There you come." He stood, legs spread, left hand on his hip, right hand extended to the sky, grasping the harpoon. When the fish was a few feet from the boat and heading straight on, Quint cast his iron.

The harpoon struck the fish in front of the dorsal fin. And then the fish hit the boat, knocking the stern sideways and sending Quint tumbling backward. His head struck the footrest of the fighting chair, and a trickle of blood ran down his neck. He jumped to his feet and cried, "I got you! I got you, you miserable prick!"

The rope attached to the iron dart snaked overboard as the fish sounded, and when it reached the end, the barrel popped off the transom, fell into the water, and vanished.

"He took it down with him!" said Brody.

"Not for long," said Quint. "He'll be back, and we'll throw another into him, and another, and another, until he quits. And then he's ours!" Quint leaned on the transom, watching the water.

Quint's confidence was contagious, and Brody now felt ebullient, gleeful, relieved. It was a kind of freedom, a freedom from the mist of death. He yelled, "Hot shit!" Then he noticed the blood running down Quint's neck, and he said, "Your head's bleeding."

"Get another barrel," said Quint. "Bring it back here. And don't fuck up the coil. I want it to go over smooth as cream."

Brody ran forward, unlashed a barrel, slipped the coiled rope over his arm, and carried the gear to Quint.

"There he comes," said Quint, pointing to the left. The barrel came to the surface and bobbed in the water. Quint pulled the string attached to the wooden shaft and brought it aboard. He fixed the shaft to the new dart and raised the harpoon above his head. "He's coming up!"

The fish broke the water a few yards from the boat. Like a rocket lifting off, snout, jaw, and pectoral fins rose straight from the water. Then the smoke-white belly, pelvic fin, and huge, salami-like claspers.

"I see your cock, you bastard!" cried Quint, and he threw a second iron, leaning his shoulder and back into the throw. The iron hit the fish in the belly, just as the great body began to fall forward. The belly smacked the water with a thunderous boom, sending a blinding fall of spray over the boat. "He's done!" said Quint as the second rope uncoiled and tumbled overboard.

The boat lurched once, and again, and there was the distant sound of crunching.

"Attack me, will you?" said Quint. "You'll take no man with you, uppity fuck!" Quint ran forward and started the engine. He pushed the throttle forward, and the boat moved away from the bobbing barrels.

"Has he done any damage?" said Brody.

"Some. We're riding a little heavy aft. He probably poked a hole in us. It's nothing to worry about. We'll pump her out."

"That's it, then," Brody said happily.

"What's what?"

"The fish is as good as dead."

"Not quite. Look."

Following the boat, keeping pace, were the two red wood barrels.

They did not bob. Dragged by the great force of the fish, each cut through the water, pushing a wave before it and leaving a wake behind.

"He's chasing us?" said Brody.

Quint nodded.

"Why? He can't still think we're food."

"No. He means to make a fight of it."

For the first time, Brody saw a frown of disquiet on Quint's face. It was not fear, nor true alarm, but rather a look of uneasy concern—as if, in a game, the rules had been changed without warning. or the stakes raised. Seeing the change in Quint's mood, Brody was afraid.

"Have you ever had a fish do this before?" he asked.

"Not like this, no. I've had 'em attack the boat, like I told you. But most times, once you get an iron in 'em, they stop fighting you and fight against that thing stickin' in 'em."

Brody looked astern. The boat was moving at moderate speed, turning this way and that in response to Quint's random turning of the wheel. Always the barrels kept up with them.

"Fuck it," said Quint. "If it's a fight he wants, it's a fight he'll get." He throttled down to idling speed, jumped down from the flying bridge and up on to the transom. He picked up the harpoon. Excitement had returned to his face. "Okay, shiteater!" he called. "Come and get it!"

The barrels kept coming, ploughing through the water—thirty yards away, then twenty-five, then twenty. Brody saw the flat plain of grey pass along the starboard side of the boat, six feet beneath the surface. "He's here!" he cried. "Heading forward."

"Shit!" said Quint, cursing his misjudgement of the length of the ropes. He detached the harpoon dart from the shaft, snapped the twine that held the shaft to a cleat, hopped down from the transom, and ran forward. When he reached the bow, he bent down and tied the twine to a forward cleat, unlashed a barrel, and slipped its dart on to the shaft. He stood at the end of the pulpit, harpoon raised.

The fish had already passed out of range. The tail surfaced twenty feet in front of the boat. The two barrels bumped into the stern almost simultaneously. They bounded once, then rolled off the stern, one on each side, and slid down the sides of the boat.

Thirty yards in front of the boat, the fish turned. The head raised out of the water, then dipped back in. The tail, standing like a sail, began to thrash back and forth. "Here he comes!" said Quint.

Brody raced up the ladder to the flying bridge. Just as he got there, he saw Quint draw his right arm back and rise up on tiptoes.

The fish hit the bow head on, with a noise like a muffled explosion. Quint cast his iron. It struck the fish atop the head, over the right eye, and it held fast. The rope fed slowly overboard as the fish backed off.

"Perfect!" said Quint. "Got him in the head that time."

There were three barrels in the water now, and they skated across the surface. Then they disappeared.

"God *damn!*" said Quint. "That's no normal fish that can sound with three irons in him and three barrels to hold him up."

The boat trembled, seeming to rise up, then dropped back. The barrels popped up, two on one side of the boat, one on the other. Then they submerged again. A few seconds later, they reappeared twenty yards from the boat.

"Go below," said Quint, as he readied another harpoon. "See if that prick done us any dirt up forward."

Brody swung down into the cabin. It was dry. He pulled back the threadbare carpet, saw a hatch, and opened it. A river of water was flowing aft beneath the floor of the cabin. We're sinking, he told himself, and the memories of his childhood nightmares leaped into his mind. He went topside and said to Quint, "It doesn't look good. There's a lot of water under the cabin floor."

"I better go take a look. Here." Quint handed Brody the harpoon. "If he comes back while I'm below, stick this in him for good measure." He walked aft and went below.

Brody stood on the pulpit, holding the harpoon, and he looked at the floating barrels. They lay practically still in the water, twitching now and then as the fish moved about below. How do you die? Brody said silently to the fish. He heard an electric motor start.

"No sweat," said Quint, walking forward. He took the harpoon from Brody. "He's banged us up, all right, but the pumps should take care of it. We'll be able to tow him in."

Brody dried his palms on the seat of his pants. "Are you really going to tow him in?"

"I am. When he dies."

"And when will that be?"

"When he's ready."

"And until then?"

"We wait."

Brody looked at his watch. It was eight-thirty.

For three hours they waited, tracking the barrels as they moved, ever more slowly, on a random path across the surface of the sea. At first they would disappear every ten or fifteen minutes, resurfacing a few dozen yards away. Then their submergences grew rarer until by eleven, they had not gone under for nearly an hour. By eleven-thirty, the barrels were wallowing in the water.

The rain had stopped, and the wind had subsided to a comfortable breeze. The sky was an unbroken sheet of grey.

"What do you think?" said Brody. "Is he dead?"

"I doubt it. But he may be close enough to it for us to throw a rope 'round his tail and drag him till he drowns."

Quint took a coil of rope from one of the barrels in the bow. He tied one end to an after cleat. The other end he tied into a noose.

At the foot of the gin pole was an electric winch. Quint switched it on to make sure it was working, then turned it off again. He gunned the engine and moved the boat towards the barrels. He drove slowly, cautiously prepared to veer away if the fish attacked. But the barrels lay still.

Quint idled the engine when he came alongside the barrels. He reached overboard with a gaff, snagged a rope, and pulled a barrel aboard. He tried to untie the rope from the barrel but the knot had been soaked and strained. So he took his knife from the sheath at his belt and cut the rope. He stabbed the knife into the gunwale, freeing his left hand to hold the rope, his right to shove the barrel to the deck.

He climbed on to the gunwale, ran the rope through a pulley at the top of the gin pole and down the pole to the winch. He took a few turns around the winch, then flipped the start switch. As soon as the slack in the rope was taken up the boat heeled hard to starboard, dragged down by the weight of the fish.

"Can that winch handle him?" said Brody.

"Seems to be. It'd never haul him out of the water, but I bet it'll bring him up to us." The winch was turning slowly, humming, taking a full turn every three or four seconds. The rope quivered under the strain, scattering drops of water on Quint's shirt.

Suddenly the rope started coming too fast. It fouled on the winch, coiling in snarls. The boat snapped upright.

"Rope break?" said Brody.

"Shit no!" said Quint, and now Brody saw fear in his face. "The sonofabitch is coming up!" He dashed to the controls and threw the engine into forward. But it was too late.

The fish broke water right beside the boat, with a great rushing whoosh of noise. It rose vertically, and in an instant of horror Brody gasped at the size of the body. Towering overhead, it blocked out the light. The pectoral fins hovered like wings, stiff and straight, and as the fish fell forward, they seemed to be reaching out to Brody.

The fish landed on the stern of the boat with a shattering crash, driving the boat beneath the waves. Water poured in over the transom. In seconds, Quint and Brody were standing in water up to their hips.

The fish lay there, its jaw not three feet from Brody's chest. The body twitched, and in the black eye, as big as a baseball, Brody thought he saw his own image reflected.

"God damn your black soul!" screamed Quint. "You sunk my boat!" A barrel floated into the cockpit, the rope writhing like a gathering of worms. Quint grabbed the harpoon dart at the end of the rope and, with his hand, plunged it into the soft white belly of the fish. Blood poured from the wound and bathed Quint's hands.

The boat was sinking. The stern was completely submerged, and the bow was rising.

The fish rolled off the stern and slid beneath the waves. The rope, attached to the dart Quint had stuck into the fish, followed.

Suddenly, Quint lost his footing and fell backwards into the water. "The knife!" he cried, lifting his left leg above the surface, and Brody saw the rope coiled around Quint's foot.

Brody looked to the starboard gunwale. The knife was there, embedded in the wood. He lunged for it, wrenched it free, and turned back, struggling to run in the deepening water. He could not move fast enough. He watched in helpless terror as Quint, reaching towards him with grasping fingers, eyes wide and pleading, was pulled slowly down into the dark water.

For a moment there was silence, except for the sucking sound of the boat slipping gradually down. The water was up to Brody's shoulders, and he clung desperately to the gin pole. A seat cushion popped to the surface next to him, and Brody grabbed it. ("They'd hold you up all right," Brody remembered Hendricks saying, "if you were an eight-year-old boy.")

Brody saw the tail and dorsal fin break the surface twenty yards away. The tail waved once left, once right, and the dorsal fin moved closer. "Get away, damn you!" Brody yelled.

The fish kept coming, barely moving, closing in. The barrels and skeins of rope trailed behind.

The gin pole went under, and Brody let go of it. He tried to kick over to the bow of the boat, which was almost vertical now. Before he could reach it, the bow raised even higher, then quickly and soundlessly slid beneath the surface.

Brody clutched the cushion, and he found that by holding it in front of him, his forearms across it, and by kicking constantly, he could stay afloat without exhausting himself.

The fish came closer. It was only a few feet away, and Brody could see the conical snout. He screamed, an ejaculation of hopelessness, and closed his eyes, waiting for an agony he could not imagine.

Nothing happened. He opened his eyes. The fish was nearly touching him, only a foot or two away, but it had stopped. And then, as Brody watched, the steel-grey body began to recede downward into the gloom. It seemed to fall away, an apparition evanescing into darkness.

Brody put his face into the water and opened his eyes. Through the stinging saltwater mist he saw the fish sink in a slow and graceful spiral, trailing behind it the body of Quint—arms out to the sides, head thrown back, mouth open in mute protest.

The fish faded from view. But, kept from sinking into the deep by the bobbing barrels, it stopped somewhere beyond the reach of light, and Quint's body hung suspended, a shadow twirling slowly in the twilight.

Brody watched until his lungs ached for air. He raised his head, cleared his eyes, and sighted in the distance the black point of the water tower. Then he began to kick towards shore.

From *Jaws*

The Fish

Rupert Brooke

In a cool curving world he lies
And ripples with dark ecstasies.
The kind luxurious lapse and steal
Shapes all his universe to feel
And know and be; the clinging stream
Closes his memory, glooms his dream,
Who lips the roots o' the shore, and glides
Superb on unreturning tides.
Those silent waters weave for him
A fluctuant mutable world and dim,
Where wavering masses bulge and gape
Mysterious, and shape to shape
Dies momently through whorl and hollow,
And form and line and solid follow
Solid and line and form to dream
Fantastic down the eternal stream;
An obscure world, a shifting world,
Bulbous, or pulled to thin, or curled,
Or serpentine, or driving arrows,
Or serene slidings, or March narrows.
There slipping wave and shore are one,
And weed and mud. No ray of sun,
But glow to glow fades down the deep
(As dream to unknown dream in sleep);
Shaken translucency illumes
The hyaline of drifting glooms;
The strange soft-handed depth subdues
Drowned colour there, but black to hues,
As death living, decomposes—
Red darkness of the heart of roses,
Blue brilliant from dead starless skies,
And gold that lies behind the eyes,
The unknown unnameable sightless white
That is the essential flame of night,
Lustreless purple, hooded green,
The myriad hues that lie between
Darkness and darkness! . . .

                          And all's one
Gentle, embracing, quiet, dun,
The world he rests in, world he knows,
Perpetual curving. Only—grows
An eddy in that ordered falling,
A knowledge from the gloom, a calling
Weed in the wave, gleam in the mud—
The dark fire leaps along his blood;
Dateless and deathless, blind and still,
The intricate impulse works its will;
His woven world drops back; and he,
Sans providence, sans memory,
Unconscious and directly driven,
Fades to some dank sufficient heaven.

O world of lips, O world of laughter,
Where hope is fleet and thought flies after,
Of lights in the clear night, of cries
That drift along the wave and rise
Thin to the glittering stars above,
You know the hands, the eyes of love!

The strife of limbs, the sightless clinging,
The infinite distance, and the singing
Blown by the wind, a flame of sound,
The gleam, the flowers, and vast around
The horizon, and the heights above—
You know the sigh, the song of love!

But there the night is close, and there
Darkness is cold and strange and bare;
And the secret deeps are whisperless;
And rhythm is all deliciousness;
And joy is in the throbbing tide,
Whose intricate fingers beat and glide
In felt bewildering harmonies
Of trembling touch; and music is
The exquisite knocking of the blood.
Space is no more, under the mud;
His bliss is older than the sun.
Silent and straight the waters run.
The lights, the cries, the willows dim,
And the dark tide are one with him.

Munich, March 1911

On Holiness, Foolishness, and the Carp

Herbert Palmer

Herbert Palmer's book of fishing thoughts and reminiscences, The Roving Angler, *was published in 1933.*

Angling, although it is termed "the gentle art", is, I suppose, a sort of relic of primitive hunting. But it is termed "the gentle art", and there is something holy about it. At any rate, there would be something holy if sporting instincts didn't swing uppermost, and the angler felt no joy in a fish's fight for life. That's the real wasp in the font. The fish must struggle, and struggle hard, or there will be little or no fun in catching him. The harder he struggles the better the fishing, and yet the harder he struggles the more certain it is that he objects to being caught. But probably he doesn't feel the hook too painfully. How can he, when he pulls like that! The instinct of a man with a pair of dental forceps jammed in his mouth is to clasp the dentist round the waist, and not push himself furiously backwards in his chair.

But cruelty or no cruelty—and why did God create hunters and sportsmen?—there is something in fishing that is relative to holiness. It makes men good-tempered and quiet-minded. It steadies the nerves and sweetens the understanding. It undermines vulgarity, and prompts simplicity of thought and manners. All this it does in spite of the fact that an unfortunate angler is apt to let forth rushing cascades of bad language. But the total effect of his days by river- or pond-side is to improve both his manners and his language, not to speak of his general disposition and humour. He has had to be by himself and take stock of himself, whether he wanted to or not. A bad man was never a good fisher, and probably never a fisher at all, undesirous even of wetting a line.

The fish, indeed, enters into the ritual of Christianity, for its first prominent symbol was the sign of the fish and not the sign of the Cross. The early Christians scrawled the design of a fish in the catacombs of Rome—a secret sign by which they knew one another. Moreover, in primitive Christian and medieval Christian art the picture of a fish signified Christ. I do not know Greek, but I understand that the origin may be discovered in "the initial letters of the names and titles of Jesus in Greek—Jesus Christ, Son of God, Saviour, which spell together the Greek word for fish". Added to this it must be remembered that some of Christ's early disciples were fishers; Simon Peter, who holds the keys of the gates of heaven, the most important of them.

Another holy fisher was Saint Wilfrid, who was instrumental in converting the heathen inhabitants of Sussex through his knowledge of fishing. When he visited the country the exceedingly ignorant and unskilful people were dying of famine; but St Wilfrid pointed out that there was abundance of food in their waters and showed them how to come by it. "By this benefit the bishop gained the affection of them all, and they began more readily to hope for heavenly blessings, since by his help they had already received those which are temporal."

It is probable that the only sport in which the medieval monks frequently indulged was the sport of fishing. No one, who has not his entire living to make by it, can fish without enjoyment; for fishing, at any rate angling, is like playing tennis with God. Fish was the monks' only permissible flesh food on Fridays and other fast days. At least once a week they had to fish with nets or rod and line. On the Continent, the carp pond was a common feature of the monastery preserves. And, as a relic of all this, Puritan Protestants have generally sat down to fish lunches on Good Fridays.

Fish, too, played an important part in one of the most inexplicable of Christ's miracles—the Feeding of the Five Thousand. And in St Matthew we read that when Christ was asked to pay tribute He told Simon Peter to procure the money in this wise: "Go thou to the sea, and cast an hook, and take up the fish that first cometh up; and when thou hast opened his mouth thou shalt find a piece of money: that take, and give unto them for me and thee." All of which was probably a parable (slightly distorted in its committal to writing), and a way of telling Simon Peter to earn the necessary money by catching fish.

For a long time the fish seems to have figured as a religious symbol. Medieval church pilgrims, called "palmers", who made pilgrimages to the Holy Land, wore the armour of a shell-fish as the symbol of their material aloofness. The cockle-shell or scallop-shell was the insignia of their withdrawal from all riot of worldliness.

But the French, sad to relate, out of their inborn passion for mockery and profanity, have made of the fish a symbol of foolishness and reproach. Medieval French thieves and blackguards, called "coquillards" (a fraternity to which that wild but great poet François Villon belonged), adopted cockle-shells and scallop-shells as symbols of their independence and rascality; while in modern France any kind of finned fish has become the symbol of April Fool's Day, "un poisson d'avril", signifying an April fool. On April the first an unwary person may walk the length of the town with a stale herring dangling down his back, pinned there by the *enfant terrible* when he was unobservantly staring too intently in front of him. Also on that day it is usual to receive a post card with the picture of a fish on it, though most of these post cards are quite inoffensive and just sent "pour rire". Mockery may be mingled with

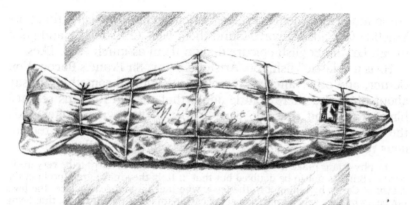

sentimentality—the first of April turned into a sort of St Valentine's Day, and above the symbolical fish a pair of clasped hands, male and female, display themselves. But *la blague* may develop rather too much into *la blague*, and a fish a month old, wrapped up in innumerable pieces of paper with the information that it is valuable and fragile, be carefully delivered by the postman. To be hoaxed in this way or any way is to "swallow the fish".

I remember that many of the chocolate and sugar *poissons moqueurs* which delighted the palates of the French children resembled carp in their shape. So did those designed on the picture post cards—though many of the colours were against nature.

I think that the prominent fish of the Continent (where fresh-water fish are caught with nets for the market) is not the salmon or trout, the cod or the mackerel, but the carp. It is entertaining to pay a visit to a French fish-stall on a town square. You thread your way through eager throngs of buyers and sellers, fierce little fellows in blue blouses, and wizened old white-capped market-women, all jostling and babbling and bawling. Somewhere in the middle stands the fishmonger's stall, the fat brown carp swimming about in a glass case or lying in a moist heap, writhing and palpitating in their hard scale armour—for carp live a long time out of the water. He is a common article of food, probably the commonest of all superior French fish-food, and his sweet, if slightly muddy-flavoured, yellow-brownish-white flesh tastes well enough in water that has been well enriched with red wine. But the Prussians boil him in water that has been enriched with beer or white Rhenish, serve up the whole fish with his armour instead of hacking him into cutlets as do the French, and make of him the finest dish imaginable. Again the Fish becomes something of a sacred symbol, for it is round about Christmas and the New Year that German carp lunches and suppers are so much in evidence. Praises to Heaven for those carp, that holy Yuletide fare, for I always found them very Christmassy and good to eat. Let the English epicure malign them as much as he likes.

He is a "classic" fish, too. Aristotle, Pliny, Sir Francis Bacon, Von Gesner, and other ancient notables have all had something to say about him; and there is little doubt that the old Romans relished him greatly and that the early Christian fish-symbol often took the broad form of a carp. Izaak Walton writes of him with tremendous reverence, and among many strange things tells us:

> The physicians make the galls and stones in the heads of Carps to be very medicinable. But it is not to be doubted but that in Italy they make great profit of the spawn of Carps, by selling it to the Jews, who make it into red caviare; the Jews not being by their law admitted to eat of caviare made of the Sturgeon, that being a fish that wants scales, and (as many appear in Levit. xi) by them reputed to be unclean.

He is an uncanny fish, too. Izaak Walton writes about him, not only with reverence, but also as if he were a little uncanny. And I can also speak from experience, for some remarks I once made about him got me into shocking trouble with an editor—such an absurd storm in a teacup. It is as if he had been bewitched by the medieval monks; for every angler has been strangely frustrated or bewildered by him. That writer of fine angling-essays, Arthur Ransome, tells the following queer anecdote about a big carp:

> On the fourth occasion one of the monsters made a direct run of thirty yards and then broke me, the fine gut cast parting above the float. Then there occurred an incident that illustrates the uncanny nature of these fish. My float, lying out in the middle of the pond, turned and sailed slowly in again to my very feet, towed by the monster who then in some manner freed himself, thus returning me my tackle with a sardonic invitation to try again. No other fish is capable of putting so fine a point on irony.

But I must now confess that I have never caught a carp, though on one or two occasions I have angled for him. Natural indolence and impatience have always conspired to hinder me from probing his depths. One may catch him in the evening, just before and round about sundown, but the best time is the very early morning; and the months should be July, August, and September. I do not like getting up at two, three, and four o'clock, and have generally left such early fishing to my friends.

But though I have never caught carp, I have sometimes watched them. I have seen great quantities of them in a French canal connected with the river Cher; huge fellows up to five pounds in weight, rubbing their sides against the weeds. The French angler armed himself with a strong bamboo pole with a flexible top, a strong gut trace, three or four yards of thin twine (no reel or running-tackle), and a big bottle-cork for a float. I understand that the rush of big carp as soon as he feels the hook is like lightning, so those Frenchmen with their short, primitive lines must have used very strong gut. But an enthusiastic carp-fisher who wished to sophisticate and anglicize his fishing was so impressed by my ten-foot, split-bamboo trout-rod, that he borrowed it for a week to look at, and after procuring some lengths of good bamboo, made such a fine carp-rod of fourteen feet on the same pattern, that he put all other fishing-rods to shame. Nobody could carp at his carp-rod, a marvellous three-jointed feat of hexagonal workmanship, and one which became the admiration of the country-side—a four-guinea rod in these days.

I have spoken of the outside colour of the carp as brown. So he seemed to me, though I think I remember a tinge of green down his sides. But there is more than one kind of carp; and an English friend who lives nearly opposite has just recently told me that he once caught a quantity of big carp which were as "golden as sovereigns", and that they turned the silvery colour of roach after they had been a few hours out of the water.

A peculiar species of carp is the crucian carp, which is allied to the gold-fish, and pictures of him have always made me think of fantastic fishes on Japanese fans. A small, muddy pond on the estate of a Prussian junker where I once spent two strange wild months was full of crucians as well as croaking frogs. The junkers told me that nobody had ever caught one of their crucians with a rod and line, and certainly my own efforts in that direction were quite unsuccessful. But I realize to-day that I fished in the wrong month, that I did not get up at three o'clock on a hot summer's day, and that I did not use the right vegetarian bait—bread-and-honey paste is, I understand, one of the best; for all fish of the carp family (which are more or less vegetarians) bite well at some kind of a paste bait, though the French often used boiled wheat.

The two or three most prominent species of carp have fleshy whiskers similar to the barbel's hanging from their upper jaws. But a species of carp without whiskers, one which everybody is familiar

with, is *Carassius auratus*, the gold-fish of the glass bowl and garden-fountain tank. His real home, I suppose, is China, and so he is the most continental of all carp. But really I ought to say "she", for the gold-fish is the most feminine of all fishes, is the nymph of fishes. But if angles are gold coloured and angels are masculine gender, then the gold-fish is "he" in spite of her nymph qualities. The poet Gray has thought of her in this way, and has written a pretty lyric about her and the tabby cat which tried to catch her and fell into the big bowl and was drowned:

> 'Twas on a lofty vase's side
> Where China's gayest art had dy'd
>   The azure flowers, that blow;
> Demurest of the tabby kind,
> The pensive Selima, reclin'd,
>   Gazed on the lake below.
>
> Her conscious tail her joy declar'd;
> The fair round face, the snowy beard,
>   The velvet of her paws,
> Her coat, that with the tortoise vies,
> Her ears of jet, and emerald eyes,—
>   She saw; and purr'd applause.
>
> Still had she gaze'd; but midst the tide
> Two angel forms were seen to glide,
>   The Genii of the stream. . . .

Ah! I have it. Gold-fishes, which seem to eat nothing at all, are the reincarnations of deceased freshwater fishes which deserve futurity. They are—O my mad brain!—tangible manifestations of fish spirituality, none of which, I presume, include any of those freshwater devils called "pike". But by the Grace of God they do perhaps include those trout which have scorned snags and unfair means in battle and not fled away with the artificial flies of poor anglers. So the gold-fish I last stared at was perhaps the resurrected soul of a certain kicking morsel of trout insanity which one day, long before the War, got into my basket through mistaking my crudest imitation for a suicidal bluebottle. Or it was its glorious, but silly, one-pound grandmother which I slew the day previous with a brandling in the waters of the upper Liffey. How my mind wanders, from gold-fish to trout and bluebottles, from bread-crumbs to brandlings!

From *The Roving Angler*

The Story of the Record Salmon

Saturday, 7 September 1922 started well for Miss Ballantine. In the morning she took three respectable salmon, weighing 17lb., 21lb. and 25lb. At dusk on the same day her father, James Ballantine, who was then fisherman for the Laird of Glendelvine, Sir Alexander Lyle, took her out in the boat for an hour's harling, that curious form of fishing indigenous to the Tay and scarcely practised elsewhere. The boatman, in this case James Ballantine, rows back and forth across the current—the Tay is roughly 60 yards wide—skilfully covering salmon lies that have been known and studied for hundreds of years. Sometimes even three rods are set up to trail fly or lure over the stern.

On this evening there were two rods; a split-cane with a Wilkinson fly, and a great heavy greenheart attached to a now obsolete revolving lure of a mottled brown colour called a "dace". The weather, Miss B. recalls, was quiet and balmy, as fine an autumn evening as one could wish for.

At 6.15 the dace was taken suddenly and violently. The shock nearly pulled the rod from her hands, but she regained control, keeping the line tight and clear of the other rod. Her father held the boat steady; somehow they managed to get the other rod in and clear the scene for action. At that point she knew, "there was something very, very heavy on". The unseen monster led them back and forth across the river in sweeping 50-yard rushes. At one point it slipped behind a rock into a deep lie. Terrified she might lose it, Miss B. kept a tight but delicate control of her line while her father swiftly manoeuvred the boat downstream of the rock to keep the line from rubbing and fraying. Suddenly the fish shot clear, Miss B. kept a tight line and the fish was still hers.

Slowly they were towed down river to a point opposite their cottage. They saw Mrs Ballantine on the river-bank, lantern in hand, peering into what was now a pitch-black night. They shouted to her what was happening and followed the fish hoping for even a glimpse of it. But not once did it surface; there was nothing but the great silent weight and the line slicing through the black water.

A hundred yards below the cottage is Caputh Bridge. The bridge has two pilings, and as the boat hugged the left bank of the river their quarry made a determined rush for the far shore. Inevitably the line would be broken. With waning strength Miss B. applied as great a strain as she dared and slowly the fish turned, slipping between the pilings where James Ballantine, rowing frantically, could just follow. She was ready to drop from exhaustion, but her father refused to touch the rod. This was a challenge only she could answer.

It was nearly two hours since the salmon had been hooked in

the Boat Pool. Now they were half a mile down the stream. Once more, keeping a tight line, Miss B. reeled in, and felt with aching arms that the creature she had not yet seen was almost ready to be taken. It was moving slowly, in short bursts. Gently she urged it closer to the boat until they could see that the line entered the water almost vertically; somewhere, three or four or five feet down was her fish. Certainly it was ready to be gaffed, but gaffing even a normal-sized fish in the dark is not easy. How were they to manage this leviathan?

James inched his way aft, set the gaff against the line and slowly moved it down until he felt the knot of the leader. Had he not made it himself? Did he not know precisely how many blood knots he had made in the expensive silkworm gut? He ran the head of the gaff down into the water, counting each time he felt a tiny protuberance. Three, four, five . . . the fish must be just below. He pushed forward gently, then turned the gaff and drew it up quickly. There was no mistake; with his great strong hands he brought his daughter's catch to the surface and with one big heave, he dragged it over the gunwales.

The fish, even after more than two hours, was by no means exhausted, and leaped and flapped in the bottom of the boat. "Father thought it was going to jump back into the river and threw himself on top of it." Miss B. sipped her tea, her eyes sparkling. "My whole arm felt paralysed, and I was so utterly exhausted I could have lain down beside the fish and slept.

"Well, two men were hailed to carry it slung on a pole to the farm, where it was weighed and witnessed by 16 people." Many times before the morning she woke with nightmares, and found herself clutching the brass railing of her bedstead as she had clung to the rod that afternoon. Her arms remained swollen for two weeks.

Her name was famous when she woke. Papers throughout Britain carried news of her achievement and every detail of the fish. Weight 64lb; length 54in; girth 28½in.

Miss B. said: "Next day, Sunday, the news went round like wildfire and people came from far and near to see the monster. Our laird, Sir Alexander, gifted it to the Perth Royal Infirmary where it went over with both patients and staff. The fun began on Monday when it was taken to Malloch's the tackle shop in Perth. I happened to go round by Scott Street in the afternoon and there was a big crowd around Malloch's window. I thought there had been an accident; instead the fish was displayed in the window with a placard stating its weight and that it had been caught by Miss Ballantine.

"I went round to the back and stood for a moment beside two

old chaps with white side-whiskers. One said to the other 'A woman? Nae woman ever took a fish like that oot of the water, mon, I would need a horse, a block and tackle, tae tak a fish like that oot. A woman—that's a lee anyway.' I had a quiet chuckle up my sleeve and ran to catch the bus."

From *The Field*

On Dry-Cow Fishing
as a Fine Art

Rudyard Kipling

It must be clearly understood that I am not at all proud of this performance. In Florida men sometimes hook and land, on rod and tackle a little finer than a steam-crane and chain, a mackerel-like fish called "tarpon" which sometimes run to 120 pounds. Those men stuff their captures and exhibit them in glass cases and become puffed up. On the Columbia River sturgeon of 150 pounds weight are taken with the line. When the sturgeon is hooked the line is fixed to the nearest pine tree or steamboat wharf, and after some hours or days the sturgeon surrenders himself if the pine or line do not give way. The owner of the line then states on oath that he has caught a sturgeon and he too becomes proud.

These things are mentioned to show how light a creel will fill the ordinary man with vanity. I am not proud. It is nothing to me that I have hooked and played several hundred pounds weight of quarry. All my desire is to place the little affair on record before the mists of memory breed the miasma of exaggeration.

The minnow cost eighteenpence. It was a beautiful quill minnow, and the tackle-maker said that it could be thrown as a fly. He guaranteed further in respect to the triangles—it glittered with triangles—that, if necessary, the minnow would hold a horse. A man who speaks too much truth is just as offensive as a man who speaks too little. None the less, owing to the defective condition of the present law of libel, the tackle-maker's name must be withheld.

The minnow and I and a rod went down to a brook to attend to a small jack who lived between two clumps of flags in the most cramped swim that he could select. As a proof that my intentions were strictly honourable, I may mention that I was using a light split-cane rod—very dangerous if the line runs through weeds, but very satisfactory in clean water, inasmuch as it keeps a steady strain on the fish and prevents him from taking liberties. I had an old score against the jack. He owed me two live-bait already, and I had reason to suspect him of coming up-stream and interfering with a little bleak-pool under a horse-bridge which lay entirely beyond his sphere of legitimate influence. Observe, therefore, that my tackle and my motives pointed clearly to jack, and jack alone; though I knew that there were monstrous big perch in the brook.

The minnow was thrown as a fly several times, and, owing to my peculiar, and hitherto unpublished, methods of fly throwing, nearly six pennyworth of the triangles came off, either in my coat-collar, or my thumb, or the back of my hand. Fly fishing is a very gory amusement.

The jack was not interested in the minnow, but towards twilight a boy opened a gate of the field and let in some twenty or thirty cows and half-a-dozen cart-horses, and they were all very much interested. The horses galloped up and down the field and shook the banks, but the cows walked solidly and breathed heavily, as people breathe who appreciate the Fine Arts.

By this time I had given up all hope of catching my jack fairly, but I wanted the live-bait and bleak-account settled before I went away, even if I tore up the bottom of the brook. Just before I had quite made up my mind to borrow a tin of chloride of lime from the farm-house—another triangle had fixed itself in my fingers—I made a cast which for pure skill, exact judgement of distance, and perfect coincidence of hand and eye and brain, would have taken every prize at a bait-casting tournament. That was the first half of the cast. The second was postponed because the quill minnow would not return to its proper place, which was under the lobe of my left ear. It had done thus before, and I supposed it was in collision with a grass tuft, till I turned round and saw a large red and white bald faced cow trying to rub what would be withers in a horse with her nose. She looked at me reproachfully, and her look said as plainly as words: "The season is too far advanced for gadflies. What is this strange disease?"

I replied, "Madam, I must apologize for an unwarrantable liberty on the part of my minnow, but if you will have the goodness to keep still until I can reel in, we will adjust this little difficulty."

I reeled in very swiftly and cautiously, but she would not wait. She put her tail in the air and ran away. It was a purely involuntary motion on my part: I struck. Other anglers may contradict me, but I firmly believe that if a man had foul-hooked his best friend through the nose, and that friend ran, the man would strike by instinct. I struck, therefore, and the reel began to sing just as merrily as though I had caught my jack. But had it been a jack, the minnow would have come away. I told the tackle-maker this much afterwards, and he laughed and made allusions to the guarantee about holding a horse.

Because it was a fat innocent she-cow that had done me no harm the minnow held—held like an anchor-fluke in coral moorings—and I was forced to dance up and down an interminable field very largely used by cattle. It was like salmon fishing in a nightmare. I took gigantic strides, and every stride found me up to my knees in marsh. But the cow seemed to skate along the squashy green by the brook, to skim over the miry backwaters, and to float like a mist through the patches of rush that squirted black filth over my face. Sometimes we whirled through a mob of her friends—there were no friends to help me—and they looked scandalized; and sometimes a young and frivolous cart-horse would join in the chase for a few miles, and kick solid pieces of mud into my eyes; and through all the mud, the milky smell of kine, the rush and the smother, I was aware of my own voice crying: "Pussy, pussy, pussy! Pretty pussy! Come along then, puss-cat!" You see it is so hard to speak to a cow properly, and she would not listen—no, she would not listen.

Then she stopped, and the moon got up behind the pollards to tell the cows to lie down; but they were all on their feet, and they came trooping to see. And she said, "I haven't had my supper, and I want to go to bed, and please don't worry me." And I said, "The matter has passed beyond any apology. There are three courses open to you, my dear lady. If you'll have the common sense to walk up to my creel I'll get my knife and you shall have all the minnow. Or, again, if you'll let me move across to your near side, instead of keeping me so coldly on your off side, the thing will come away in one tweak. I can't pull it out over your withers. Better still, go to a post and rub it out, dear. It won't hurt much, but if you think I'm going to lose my rod to please you, you are mistaken." And she said, "I don't understand what you are saying. I am very, very unhappy." And I said, "It's all your fault for trying to fish. Do go to the nearest gate-post, you nice fat thing, and rub it out."

For a moment I fancied she was taking my advice. She ran away and I followed. But all the other cows came with us in a bunch, and I thought of Phaeton trying to drive the Chariot of the Sun, and Texan cowboys killed by stampeding cattle, and *"Green Grow the Rushes, O!"* and Solomon and Job, and "'loosing the bands of Orion,'" and hooking Behemoth, and Wordsworth who talks about whirling round with stones and rocks and trees, and "Here we go round the Mulberry Bush," and "Pippin Hill," and "Hey Diddle Diddle," and most especially the top joint of my rod. Again she stopped—but nowhere in the neighborhood of my knife—and her sisters stood moonfaced round her. It seemed that she might, now, run towards me, and I looked for a tree, because cows are very different from salmon, who only jump against the line, and never molest the fisherman. What followed was worse than any direct attack. She began to buck-jump, to stand on her head and her tail alternately, to leap into the sky, all four feet together, and to dance on her hind legs. It was so violent and improper, so desperately unladylike, that I was inclined to blush, as one would blush at the sight of a prominent statesman sliding down a fire escape, or a duchess chasing her cook with a skillet. That flopsome *abandon* might go on all night in the lonely meadow among the mists, and if it went on all night—this was pure inspiration—I might be able to worry through the fishing line with my teeth.

Those who desire an entirely new sensation should chew with

all their teeth, and against time, through a best waterproofed silk line, one end of which belongs to a mad cow dancing fairy rings in the moonlight; at the same time keeping one eye on the cow and the other on the top joint of a split-cane rod. She buck-jumped and I bit on the slack just in front of the reel; and I am in a position to state that that line was cored with steel wire throughout the particular section which I attacked. This has been formally denied by the tackle-maker, who is not to be believed.

The *wheep* of the broken line running through the rings told me that henceforth the cow and I might be strangers. I had already bidden good-bye to some tooth or teeth; but no price is too great for freedom of the soul.

"Madam," I said, "the minnow and twenty feet of very superior line are your alimony without reservation. For the wrong I have unwittingly done to you I express my sincere regret. At the same time, may I hope that Nature, the kindest of nurses, will in due season——"

She or one of her companions must have stepped on her spare end of the line in the dark, for she bellowed wildly and ran away, followed by all the cows. I hoped the minnow was disengaged at last; and before I went away looked at my watch, fearing to find it nearly midnight. My last cast for the jack was made at 6.23 p.m. There lacked still three and a-half minutes of the half-hour; and I would have sworn that the moon was paling before the dawn!

"Simminly someone were chasing they cows down to bottom o' Ten Acre," said the farmer that evening. "'Twasn't you, sir?"

"Now under what earthly circumstances do you suppose I should chase your cows? I wasn't fishing for them, was I?"

Then all the farmer's family gave themselves up to jam-smeared laughter for the rest of the evening, because that was a rare and precious jest, and it was repeated for months, and the fame of it spread from that farm to another, and yet another at least three miles away, and it will be used again for the benefit of visitors when the freshets come down in spring.

But to the greater establishment of my honour and glory I submit in print this bald statement of fact, that I may not, through forgetfulness, be tempted later to tell how I hooked a bull on a Marlow Buzz, how he ran up a tree and took to water, and how I played him along the London-road for thirty miles, and gaffed him at Smithfields. Errors of this kind may creep in with the lapse of years, and it is my ambition ever to be a worthy member of that fraternity who pride themselves on never deviating by one hair's breadth from the absolute and literal truth.

Roach

Jane Grigson

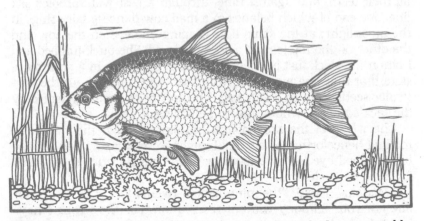

Roach can be a little dull unless they are cooked very quickly after being caught. They are a beautiful fish, with silver to red scales, and reddish eyes and fins. They seem to have caught a sunset light, which goes, unfortunately, when they are scaled.

Here is a simple recipe which makes the most of them. First of all bring 4 oz of butter to the boil in a little pan. Let it bubble for a moment or two then put it aside to cool, while you scale and clean the fish and season it inside. Strain off the transparent butter through a muslin-lined sieve into a frying pan. Now that the butter has been clarified, it will not burn so easily—very important for the slow cooking of fish.

Turn the roach in seasoned flour. Heat up the butter in the pan, and put in the roach. They should cook gently for about 6 minutes a side. If you keep the heat moderate, they will develop a crisp, golden brown skin, and will not be over-cooked. Serve them with quarters of lemon, and brown bread and butter, or boiled new potatoes turned in butter and parsley.

From *English Food*

The Hunchback Trout

Richard Brautigan

*The freewheeling style of Brautigan's book makes the exact
location of this story difficult to calculate. We think he
wanted everywhere to stay a secret.*

The creek was made narrow by little green trees that grew too
close together. The creek was like 12,845 telephone booths in
a row with high Victorian ceilings and all the doors taken off and
all the backs of the booths knocked out.

Sometimes when I went fishing in there, I felt just like a telephone
repairman, even though I did not look like one. I was only a kid
covered with fishing tackle, but in some strange way by going in
there and catching a few trout, I kept the telephones in service.
I was an asset to society.

It was pleasant work, but at times it made me uneasy. It could
grow dark in there instantly when there were some clouds in the
sky and they worked their way on to the sun. Then you almost
needed candles to fish by, and foxfire in your reflexes.

Once I was in there when it started raining. It was dark and
hot and steamy. I was of course on overtime. I had that going in
my favour. I caught seven trout in fifteen minutes.

The trout in those telephone booths were good fellows. There
were a lot of young cutthroat trout six to nine inches long, perfect
pan size for local calls. Sometimes there were a few fellows, eleven
inches or so—for the long distance calls.

I've always liked cutthroat trout. They put up a good fight,
running against the bottom and then broad jumping. Under their
throats they fly the orange banner of Jack the Ripper.

Also in the creek were a few stubborn rainbow trout, seldom
heard from, but there all the same, like certified public accountants.
I'd catch one every once in a while. They were fat and chunky,
almost as wide as they were long. I've heard those trout called
"squire" trout.

It used to take me about an hour to hitchhike to that creek.
There was a river nearby. The river wasn't much. The creek was
where I punched in. Leaving my card above the clock, I'd punch
out again when it was time to go home.

I remember the afternoon I caught the hunchback trout.

A farmer gave me a ride in a truck. He picked me up at a traffic
signal beside a bean field and he never said a word to me.

His stopping and picking me up and driving me down the road
was as automatic a thing to him as closing the barn door, nothing
need be said about it, but still I was in motion travelling thirty-five
miles an hour down the road, watching houses and groves of
trees go by, watching chickens and mailboxes enter and pass
through my vision.

Then I did not see any houses for a while. "This is where I get out," I said.

The farmer nodded his head. The truck stopped.

"Thanks a lot," I said.

The farmer did not ruin his audition for the Metropolitan Opera by making a sound. He just nodded his head again. The truck started up. He was the original silent old farmer.

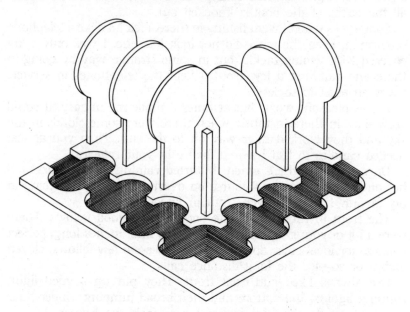

A little while later I was punching in at the creek. I put my card above the clock and went into that long tunnel of telephone booths.

I waded about seventy-three telephone booths in. I caught two trout in a little hole that was like a wagon wheel. It was one of my favourite holes, and always good for a trout or two.

I always like to think of that hole as a kind of pencil sharpener. I put my reflexes in and they came back out with a good point on them. Over a period of a couple of years, I must have caught fifty trout in that hole, though it was only as big as a wagon wheel.

I was fishing with salmon eggs and using a size 14 single egg hook on a pound and a quarter test tippet. The two trout lay in my creel covered entirely by green ferns, ferns made gentle and fragile by the damp walls of telephone booths.

The next good place was forty-five telephone booths in. The place was at the end of a run of gravel, brown and slippery with algae. The run of gravel dropped off and disappeared at a little shelf where there were some white rocks.

One of the rocks was kind of strange. It was a flat white rock.

Off by itself from the other rocks, it reminded me of a white cat I had seen in my childhood.

The cat had fallen or been thrown off a high wooden sidewalk that went along the side of a hill in Tacoma, Washington. The cat was lying in a parking lot below.

The fall had not appreciably helped the thickness of the cat, and then a few people had parked their cars on the cat. Of course, that was a long time ago and the cars looked different from the way they look now.

You hardly see those cars any more. They are the old cars. They have to get off the highway because they can't keep up.

That flat white rock off by itself from the other rocks reminded me of that dead cat come to lie there in the creek, among 12,845 telephone booths.

I threw out a salmon egg and let it drift down over that rock and WHAM! a good hit! and I had the fish on and it ran hard downstream, cutting at an angle and staying deep and really coming on hard, solid and uncompromising, and then the fish jumped and for a second I thought it was a frog. I'd never seen a fish like that before.

God-damn! What the hell!

The fish ran deep again and I could feel its life energy screaming back up the line to my hand. The line felt like sound. It was like an ambulance siren coming straight at me, red light flashing, and then going away again and then taking to the air and becoming an air-raid siren.

The fish jumped a few more times and it still looked like a frog, but it didn't have any legs. Then the fish grew tired and sloppy, and I swung and splashed it up the surface of the creek and into my net.

The fish was a twelve-inch rainbow trout with a huge hump on its back. A hunchback trout. The first I'd ever seen. The hump was probably due to an injury that occurred when the trout was young. Maybe a horse stepped on it or a tree fell over in a storm or its mother spawned where they were building a bridge.

There was a fine thing about that trout. I only wish I could have made a death mask of him. Not of his body though, but of his energy. I don't know if anyone would have understood his body. I put it in my creel.

Later in the afternoon when the telephone booths began to grow dark at the edges, I punched out of the creek and went home. I had that hunchback trout for dinner. Wrapped in cornmeal and fried in butter, its hump tasted sweet as the kisses of Esmeralda.

From *Trout Fishing in America*

The Salmon of Knowledge

Lady Gregory

And then he said farewell to Crimall, and went on to learn poetry from Finegas, a poet that was living at the Boinn, for the poets thought it was always on the brink of water poetry was revealed to them. And he did not give him his own name, but he took the name of Deimne. Seven years, now, Finegas had stopped at the Boinn, watching the salmon, for it was in the prophecy that he would eat the salmon of knowledge that would come there, and that he would have all knowledge after. And when at the last the salmon of knowledge came, he brought it to where Finn was, and bade him to roast it, but he bade him not to eat any of it. And when Finn brought him the salmon after a while he said: "Did you eat any of it at all, boy?" "I did not," said Finn; "but I burned my thumb putting down a blister that rose on the skin, and after that, I put my thumb in my mouth." "What is your name, boy?" said Finegas. "Deimne," said he. "It is not, but it is Finn your name is, and it is to you and not to myself the salmon was given in the prophecy." With that he gave Finn the whole of the salmon, and from that time Finn had the knowledge that came from the nuts of the nine hazels of wisdom that grow beside the wall that is below the sea.

From *Gods and Fighting Men*

In the Andes

Negley Farson

Chile is one of the most sporting countries in the world. The Chileans themselves are quite possibly its finest horsemen; they come as close to being Centaurs as modern man and horse can get—at any rate, when you see them riding either on hacienda or at one of their famous horse shows both man and horse seem made of one piece, with one brain and with one synchronised system of muscles; and an American cavalry team with which I went down to Valparaiso told me after the competition that they had never seen such horsemen in their life. This was from men of the famous U.S.A. cavalry school at Fort Riley, at least one of whom had jumped at Olympia. There is a legend that when the Spaniards first landed on the coast in their conquest of Peru, the Indians (who had never seen a horse) fled in terror because they thought both horse and man were one—were monsters—until one Conquistador was knocked off his horse . . . and the Indians attacked.

But it was an Irishman who introduced fishing to Chile—its magnificent rainbow trout. I saw quite a lot of him in Valparaiso; a big, genial, grey-haired man who had been honorary game warden for the country (self-appointed, I believe), patron of both the horse racing and the famous shows; who, twenty-five years before, had hit on the idea of introducing some rainbow trout into the swift, green, rapid-streaked rivers that flow down from the Southern Andes. The result has been a miracle. These streams are simply crawling with crayfish—and a rainbow likes nothing better; until within even the last few years some of them were never fished; and the rainbow (with that predilection of theirs for travel) have spread all over the country. They might not reach the size of those prodigious rainbow of New Zealand, but if for fitness and fighting quality they may have their equals, I doubt if finer rainbow can be found anywhere else in the world.

The result of this is that in Valparaiso and Santiago you find colonies of Irish, English, Scots, and Americans—men from the old nitrate days or the modern copper mines—who, almost the minute they have met you, take you to their homes and show you their rods and tackle, produce a whisky bottle, and in a few minutes are telling you fish stories that make even you blush to listen.

The funny part of it is, they are true. One Naval Attaché said to me, "When I wrote home and told my friends that the first four rainbows I caught in Chile averaged over 6 lb, they wrote back and called me a liar!" I merely nodded my head—for, only a few days previously at a strange shoot arranged for the Diplomatic Corps on the hitherto preserved lakes supplying the water to Valparaiso, I had seen this same man kill 48 ducks in one morning, shooting through a hole in a blind (which I had in the afternoon) with only a 20-bore shotgun. It was even said that his country had appointed him to Chile in particular simply because its State Department knew his passion and skill with both rod and gun would make him a success with the sporting Chileans.

He was one.

There is a Scot in Valparaiso, the third generation of his family to be born in the country who is reputed to be the best fly-fisherman in Chile. He came into my room in the hospital where I was lying, introduced himself, and said: "When you get out of here I am going to give you some fishing that will take the hair off your head." The Naval Attaché whom I have just mentioned assured me that this was only the bare truth. And the ambassador of my own country (a fanatic fisherman himself) gave me four of the best and biggest Silver Doctors in his book. "You will need plenty of backing on the river where that man is going to take you!" he warned me. When I told him the size of my two reels and the weight of the rod he closed his eyes and said: "Well, then, there's no use going. They'll just run away from you . . . take the lot!"

It didn't sound promising. But I was used to this rod and thought it was better to stick to the devil I knew rather than accept one of the longer and more powerful rods which the Scot tried to lend me. Also, going off with such a reputedly fine fisherman I did not want to take the chance of performing with a rod that might make me look clumsy. So a few nights later he and I, and an English ex-naval officer (who had been in the Secret Service in Chile during the last war), were in a train for southern Chile—for Chillan, the town which was literally wiped off the map by an earthquake a few years later. From Chillan we drove the next day, some forty or fifty miles, I think, to a little village between us and the far, blue, broken silhouette of the Andes. After that there was nothing between us and the mountains but a grim plain of low scrub, roadless and rocky. When the next morning we forced the unfortunate car we had procured through this sea of low undergrowth we passed an occasional horseman who, in this setting, brought back pictures of remote Spain. For he sat his horse with the same idle arrogance; he wore a flat black hat, such as you will see in Andalusia; he was Spanish (with possibly a dash of Indian blood); and about the only essential outward difference was that *this* man held his hat to his head by a strap that was tied to his nose! There is a little black tippet dangling from it that always makes you think these Chilean caballeros' noses must be bleeding. The one or two horsemen we met merely gave us a solemn nod, by way of salute; but an old hag that we came on, a withered old ancient riding sidesaddle, cackled at us when she watched us get out of the car and put our slender rods together by the banks of the racing river. The blue Andes never seemed to have come any nearer; they lay always like a jagged line of broken blue glass along the eastern sky.

What made it even more strange was that the volcano of Chillan, on our left, was erupting every ten minutes. So regularly that you could set your watch by it, it shot a 2,000-foot feather of sulphur yellow into the blue sky every ten minutes. And three times when I had on my first fish I saw that feather shoot up.

This river was the Laja, racing down from the extinct volcano of Antuco in the far Andes. In the long flat sweeps it was a deep bottle-green . . . but swirling. Then it crashed through the rocks it had rounded through the ages, poured white over ledges, and emitted the continuous low roar of broken water. I remembered what the ambassador had told me in Santiago—"plenty of backing on your line"—and my heart sank.

At any rate, I told myself, put on the biggest cast you've got (it was a 2X), soak it well . . . and trust to heaven. It was well I did.

I had picked the side of a broad stretch of white falls where the main river swept past in frothing white sulphur and where there was a lee of green water lying along the main current. I felt that if there were any big trout, waiting for something to come down, this was where they would be. It was easy casting, for there was no high brush behind me, and I kept as long a line as I could in the air, hoping to reach the edge of the white water. I think I must have been even more shocked than the fish when, on my very first cast, just as my fly was sweeping down about opposite me, I got that driving pull of a heavy strike. It was the first cast I made in Chile—and it was the best fish.

Without waiting for any more argument he went straight on down the river, sweeping through the white water, where he seemed to rest, or sulk, for a moment in the green water on the other side. It was lucky for me that he did; practically every foot of my line had been taken out. So there we were. I could not get across to him. Neither could I get him across to me. So I gave him the bend of the rod while I stood there and thought about it.

In these parts of Chile there is a very poor brand of peasant, which exists heaven knows how; they come about as close to living without any visible means of support as you would think man could get. There was the brush-board-and-thatched hovel of one of these ramshackle humans behind me now. Its inhabitants had evidently been watching me for some time. Now, seeing me standing there, apparently doing nothing, a small urchin impelled by curiosity came cautiously up to see what I was doing. We spoke no language in which we could communicate with each other; and when I unhooked my landing-net and snapped it open he almost fainted from fright. But he was a quick-witted little fellow, and, somehow, he comprehended what a net was. I made him take it from me.

So there were two of us standing there now. The fish had remained exactly where he was. I gave him a slow pull. The next instant the fish was going down along his side of the river and the boy and I were stumbling down along the boulders on ours. As I said, these strange, volcanic rocks had been rounded by time, and a more tricky, stumbling, infuriating river journey I have seldom made. For I was deep in the river by now, getting as close to the fish as I could get in order to win back some more line. In this fashion I took several yards back from him. Then I reached a high stretch of bank where the water was too deep, and so came back to land. It was now, I said gloomily to myself, that I would lose this fish. I remembered the big sea trout I had had on for two hours and forty minutes, in the Shetlands. Here was to be another broken heart; for, some fifty yards below me, shone a long sloping shelf of white water in the mid-day sun.

Then the fish took it into his head to command operations. To my confused delight and dismay he came directly at me across the white water, so fast that I could barely strip in the line. I had no chance to reel in. Then he went on up the river, taking the line with him as fast as I could pay it out without fouling it. Then, boring against the line, as if he meant to jump the low falls, he again remained stationary over one spot.

This was exactly what the doctor ordered. I could not have asked him to do anything nicer. Reeling in as swiftly as I could, I worked my way up to him. So there, plus one Chilean boy, we were exactly where we had started over twenty minutes before. I knew it was twenty minutes, because twice during our tussle, I had seen Chillan erupt. That 2,000-foot sulphurous jet!

Now began one of the most beautiful battles I have ever experienced. For I had plenty of line in hand now; when he came past I gave him the bend of the rod for all I thought it could stand—determined he should never cross to the other side of that white water again. And every time I checked him. The green water was so glass-clear that when he swung in the swirls sluicing past me the sun caught and reflected the pinkish stripe along his strong sides. I could watch him fighting the hook. And then he spun in the sun, jumping. He was the very essence of fight. Furious, I think—still not frightened.

There is no doubt that in the ingredients of a fisherman's delight there is nothing comparable to being able to watch a fish fight like this. For I could see him, or his shape, nearly all the time. Chillan erupted once more.

But by now my gallant rainbow was a slow-moving, sullen thing. His tail working heavily, he lay in the green water about twenty yards out from me. And I looked around for the lee of some rocks and slowly worked him in. I had him in a pool. It was almost still water. He was almost resting against the hook. And then, as the bank was high, and I was an idiot, I signalled the little Chilean boy to wade out and slip the net under him. . . .

The boy did. He was an eager boy . . . so eager that he stabbed the net at the fish . . . pushed him with it! Then he tried to scoop him in from the tail. . . . I jumped. As I did, the boy actually got the fish into the net. I seized boy, net, fish, all at the same time, and threw them all up on the bank. There I dived on the fish.

It all goes to prove the hysterical condition into which some fishermen will get themselves. For this rainbow was not much over 6 lb. But he was such a beautiful one! That was the point; that small nose, and those deep shoulders, and those firm fighting flanks. This fish had been living in clean water on crayfish galore. I sat on the bank and looked at him for nearly twenty minutes. I had him.

Then I sighed, got up, and went to fishing again.

I got three more fish that afternoon. The next one was a $5\frac{1}{2}$-pounder. He put up a grand fight. But it was not the same thrill. I felt braver now; I could afford to be more rough with them. I could take time out to watch . . . this great river sweeping down in the sun below me. I noticed that on nearly all the flat rocks were the crushed shells of crayfish. Eaten there by some form of bird, obviously. And then, as I was fishing one point, a flock of reddish duck came round it so swiftly they almost swept into me. The Scot, that beautiful fly-caster (and he certainly was one!) had taken one look at my 6-pounder, and immediately set off down river—determined to catch a bigger one. The English ex-naval officer had also examined it. "Ah," was all he said. Then he went up the river and began fishing furiously below another fall.

Meantime, I caught two more 3-pounders.

I suddenly became aware that I was very fatigued (for I have one leg which is not quite so good as the other), and I hooked the faithful fly into the cork handle of my rod, tipped the little Chilean brat, and worked back to the car. There I found the Scot and the Englishman, who held the bottle out to me. . . .

"Funny, isn't it," smiled the Englishman as I wiped my lips, "how damned *good* it tastes after a day like this! Nothing like the same taste in a city. . . ."

"Ah . . .," I said—and looked eagerly at their catch.

They were all spread out on the grey boulders.We each had four fish. And I had the biggest. "It's been a grand day!" I said comfortably.

From *Going Fishing*

Night Fishing

Hugh Falkus

The man who sets forth with a rod knowing nothing of the environment in which he goes to hunt is only half an angler. He sees without comprehending. The waterside has a language he does not understand. The multitude of stories it offers him he cannot read. He is out of sympathy with his surroundings. In consequence he is, all too often, the man who when darkness falls fears to fish alone.

"Men fear death as children fear to go in the dark." But not only children fear the dark. Many a fisherman has suffered feelings of nameless dread as the dusk closed round him on some lonely river, lake or stretch of coastline. Even on my own water, a friendly little beck, I have known men who would not fish alone at night. "What —go up there alone through those spooky woods? Not me!"

Although few care to admit it, many fishermen do not fancy fishing by themselves after the light has gone, and many a chance of catching sea trout has been missed because some companion failed to arrive on the water at an appointed time. Finding himself alone beside a darkening river, the nervous angler heads for home.

His apprehension is understandable. How different it all seems when daylight disappears—and the darkness becomes full of strange sounds. Things *do* go bump in the night! There are squeaks and grunts and screeches and gurgles and rustles and plops. Stones rattle, shingle slides, bushes move and swish, eyes gleam, ripples spread across the water from unseen swimmers; a fox screams from the fellside; a deer barks; owls hoot from shadowy woods. The creatures of the night are stirring: badger, otter, hedgehog, stoat, weasel, rat, feral mink, nightjar; all of them at some time or another will share the waterside with us. But to the novice who comes unprepared into this elemental and seemingly hostile jungle of the dark, these animals are strangers; the sounds they make he does not understand—and what man does not understand, he fears.

For this reason the owl was long prominent in stories of the supernatural. It is a bird of more than usual interest. For a vertebrate its hunting ability in unique. Probably, no animal has contributed more towards man's feeling of uneasiness at night. Mainly the tawny owl, whose long, wavering call sounds so eerie in the darkness.

Tawny owls are particularly vocal late in the summer when the adults defend their territories against their young. The young owls that fail to establish territories of their own probably die quite soon—of starvation.

Then the barn owl, that glides ghost-like over the water meadows at dusk with its terrifying screech. The sight of a white shape that floated screaming into the night must have started many a ghost story. As Gilbert White noted: "White owls often scream horribly

as they fly along. I have known a whole village up in arms on such an occasion, imagining the churchyard to be full of goblins and spectres."

To our forbears, darkness was a symbol of death. It was natural that the mysterious owls, being pre-eminently creatures of the night, should become associated with death and disaster.

The Romans hated them. As the sight of an eagle before a battle signified victory, so an owl presaged defeat. Ovid called it: "Cowardly owl, an omen dreadful to mortals." To Pliny, it was "The bird of death, and utterly abominable." Virgil's owl ". . . prolonged his mournful and prophetic note", and when Herod Agrippa entered the theatre at Cæsaraea, it was an owl perching on a rope above his head that warned him of his coming end.

Our own literature, too, abounds with references. Chaucer wrote of: "The owl that eke of death the bode bringeth." And Shakespeare: "Out on ye owls, nothing but songs of death." It was his ". . . fatal bellman that gives the stern'st goodnight." And as some anonymous poet observed:

> Thy note that forth so freely rolls,
> With shrill command the house controls.
> And sings a dirge for dying souls.
> Te Whit! Te Whoo!

The belief that owls are birds of ill-omen exists even today. I remember an aged Devonshire angler shaking his head in dismay one sunny afternoon when a barn owl crossed our path as we made our way to the river. "We'll do no good today!" he prophesied. And later, on our way home having caught nothing, the old sage wagged his head knowingly. "It was that bliddy owl, m'dear. I told 'e t'would put a blight on us!" Loving him, I contented myself with thinking of the low water and blinding sunlight (to me, more rational reasons for our failure) and said nothing—not that anything I could have said would have changed his opinion.

Undoubtedly such superstition has its origins in the uncanny ability of some species of owls to hunt not only at night but in utter darkness. The owl has remarkable night vision; but no creature, however good its sight, can *see* in utter darkness.

A recent theory was that an owl's eyes responded to infra-red radiation from its prey. But this has now been disproved. Experiments have shown that in the daytime, on starry nights and in moonlight, owls hunt by sight. But on very dark, cloudy nights they locate and pin-point their prey by *sound*. This is made possible by their noiseless flight and asymmetrical ears—owls being the only vertebrates to have such ears.

Of the ghostly silence of an owl's flight, that fine naturalist and fisherman, St John, observed: "If we take the trouble to examine the manner of feeding and the structure of the commonest birds —which we pass over without observation in consequence of their want of rarity—we see that the Providence that has made them has also adapted each in the most perfect manner for acquiring with facility the food on which it is designed to live. The owl, that preys mostly on the quick-eared mouse, has its wings edged with a kind of downy fringe, which makes its flight silent and inaudible in the still evening air. Were its wings formed of the same kind of plumage as those of most other birds, it is so slow a flier that the mouse, warned by the rustling of its approach, would escape long before it could pounce upon it."

(What St John did not, perhaps, appreciate was that the silence of the owl's wings works two ways: it certainly prevents the mouse from hearing the flight of the owl, but it also enables the owl to hear the rustle of the mouse.)

When we think of their exceptional eyesight and sense of hearing, their soundless flight and eerie, terrifying calls, it is not surprising that owls occupy so large a place in country legend. Nor is it surprising, even in these so-called enlightened days, that for so many people the lonely darkness still holds vague feelings of unease.

But the angler who interests himself in the animals of the waterside and can identify the signs and sounds of his unseen companions, need no longer fear "things that go bump in the night". When he regards the river bank with understanding, it will present a world of fresh interest and fascination, and he will await the coming of dusk with new-found eagerness. Already, he will be a better angler—for he has become a better hunter.

Alone in the summer twilight, with the bats flickering above the tree-tops and a barn owl hunting silently along the hedge, he may remember those evocative lines of Meredith's:

> Lovely are the curves of the White Owl sweeping
> Wavy in the dusk lit by one large star.

And watch his fellow hunter with delight as the owl swoops low over the shadowy fields, with Venus brilliant in the west.

From *Sea Trout Fishing*

Lioness and Fish

John Smith

The lioness prowls through the silent lemon grove
   Savage as history, sinuous as fire;
The lemons open their envious eyes above
   Bitter and acid yellow among their leaves.
Burning with amber flame she stalks that shade
   And melts the black bars with her heat and gold.

   Savage as history, sinuous as fire,
She comes where blank sky fallen from above
   Lies like a vacant blind eye under the leaves:
A fathomless well cold with insidious shade.
   A fever robs that beast of her liquid gold,
Her hot blood drained by that still pool in the grove.

The well below: the lioness above
   Sees in the mirrored pattern of those leaves
A blade as sharp as light cut through that shade:
   Arrogant negative of her positive gold;
God of the well within that fabulous grove
   Hanging like thin smoke under her sullen fire.

   The bright fish cold as steel among the leaves
Waits with unwinking eye deep in that shade;
   His shape of silver wrestles with her red gold.
The lioness roars in the silent lemon grove.
   Majestic fury breaks from her hot as fire,
Fierce as the raging sun that flames above.

The fish within that knife-cold water's shade
  Throbs as his silver fuses with that hot gold,
Then from that fathomless well in the listening grove
  Leaps through the surface down by her radiant fire,
Like a bright lemon dropping from above
  Through the black shining of enamel leaves.

The lioness roars, dripping with molten gold;
But now a chill strikes through the quivering grove,
  A vein of silver eats along her fire
Like the thin sap within those luminous leaves;
  The fierce gold writhes and sears the blank sky above;
Below bright silver flashes in locks of shade.

The fish like crystal dazzles the emerald grove;
  The lioness lifts her head like a golden fire;
Her eyes more bright than lemons yellow above,
  Her glittering teeth sharp as the edge of leaves;
Her bones stronger than silver, cold as shade,
  Her blood like amber flame, her fur white-gold.

Burning the dark with radiant, pure fire,
The lioness prowls through the silent lemon grove.

From *Excursus in Autumn*

Salmon in Danger

Anthony Netboy

T he Atlantic salmon!
The words conjure up visions of a powerful, silvery fish renowned for its vast oceanic migrations and herculean upriver struggles. We see Magdalenian cave men huddling over a blazing fire roasting impaled salmon . . . Neolithic lake dwellers in Scotland and perhaps Switzerland spearing the gamy fish below their pile-built huts . . . and the encamped soldiers of Julius Caesar in Gaul attempting to catch the leaping giants in the rivers. It was the Romans who named the fish "Salmo", the leaper.

"Salmo" was destined to become one of the noblest and most honoured (as well as most harried) of fishes known to man. Born in some humble river, it tarried there from one to four or more years; then, having attained the size of a man's finger, vanished utterly, only to return to this very stream one or more years later as a husky adult. It gave sport fit for kings and its savoury pink flesh was like no other.

Perhaps the cave dwellers (and lake dwellers) already knew some of the secrets of the salmon, its birth and departure from the river and punctilious homecoming. If so, the knowledge died with them because they had no written language. But their delight in and appreciation of this fish is commemorated in the pictures they carved on reindeer bone, smooth as ivory. Such objects have been found in the caves of the Pyrénées region of southern France and in north-western Spain at Altamira, where the river still flows which supplied them with salmon.

The Salmonidae family of fishes to which *Salmo salar* belongs may be traced to a common ancestor in the Pliocene epoch when modern plants and animals developed; the outlines of North America were almost the same as in recent times and in Europe the sea covered small parts of the north-west of the continent and a large area around the present Mediterranean. The Pleistocene (or Great Ice Age) which saw the rise of man is believed to have been specially propitious for the evolution of salmonid species into anadromous fishes—those which spend part of their lives in fresh and part in salt water and breed only in fresh water.

Being cold-water species, the Salmonidae thrived during the Ice Age when an ice cap covered the greater part of the northern hemisphere, blockaded the North American coast as far as Cape Hatteras, blanketed the British Isles, and laid down massive glaciers over Scandinavia and northern Russia, Siberia and Canada. When the glaciers began to retreat and vast quantities of fresh water poured into the northern seas, creating rivers and lakes, the Salmonidae adapted themselves to these new conditions. According to the French ichthyologist Edouard le Danois, "great rivers which opened into the Arctic Ocean flowed freely, at least in summer-time, and there was really little difference in salinity between river and marine waters. So the salmon formed the habit of going from the sea to the rivers to spawn; thereafter to return to the coastal zone to feed."

At this time "the Baltic, the North Sea and the Irish Sea were still immense glacial valleys, while salt waters very diluted with fresh waters from the polar regions even washed the shores of southern Europe." Melting of the glaciers in the Alps, Apennines, Balkan and Atlas mountains lowered the salt content of the surface layers of the Mediterranean. All these changes had an effect on the habits of the salmon (and other anadromous fishes). They left the high latitudes and gradually moved southward, frequenting all the great European rivers, not only those which flowed into the Atlantic Ocean but those like the Ebro, the Rhône and the Po which entered the Mediterranean Sea. In time, however, the glacial waters the salmon had always known departed from parts of Europe in the face of melting snows and encroachment of warm equatorial waters. This happened in the Mediterranean, which ultimately became too warm for the species—none is found there now. Only "unwary fishes which had ventured into this sea at the end of the great glacial period have left some descendants in the lakes of Italy, Albania and even of Algeria", and these are landlocked. Other landlocked varieties of *Salmo salar* are found in various lakes in Russia, Sweden, Norway, and eastern North America.

In North America *Salmo salar* once probably inhabited rivers as far north as the tundra zone.

After thousands of years of adaptation to changing climatic conditions, *Salmo salar* established itself roughly in an area extending from latitudes 41 to 60 degrees north in North America and 40 to about 70 degrees north in Europe, when the landscape assumed modern features, entering rivers which were not too fully icebound and which flowed into, and gave access to, food-rich seas.

Related to the Atlantic salmon are the Pacific salmon (*Oncorhyncus* species), and sea-going steelhead trout (*Salmo gairdneri*) which seems to be biologically a Pacific version of *Salmo salar*.

When man first entered Europe the salmon were plentiful in hundreds of coastal rivers, often wandering far inland for hundreds of miles. They were found in Iceland, Ireland, Scotland, England and Wales, Portugal, Spain, France, the Low Countries, Germany, Switzerland, Denmark, Poland and all the countries bordering the Baltic Sea, Norway as far north as the rivers flowing into the Arctic, and Russia as far east as the Pechora River. They occurred in Greenland and ran up all the suitable waterways on the North American side of the Atlantic from Ungava Bay to the Housatonic which empties into Long Island Sound, and possibly the Hudson. Land-locked salmon swarmed in the streams draining into Lake Ontario and Lake Champlain. They were abundant in nearly every coastal river in Maine as well as in the Connecticut up to its headwaters near the Canadian border. Several hundred rivers in eastern Canada originally harboured regular runs of salmon. Indeed, before the white man came *Salmo salar* was probably as plentiful in eastern North America as Pacific salmon were in the United States and British Columbia.

Salmon is first mentioned in history by Pliny the Elder in his *Historia Naturalis*, written in the first century AD. When the Romans colonized Gaul they found that the inhabitants were avid fish-eating people, and the most esteemed species were salmon in the west and mullet in the Midi. Demand arose for Gaulish fish in the markets of Rome. With the collapse of the Roman Empire this trade vanished.

In the Middle Ages salmon fisheries were highly prized because they were important sources of protein food in areas where meat was scarce and expensive. Moreover, the Church's injunction for-bidding the eating of meat on Fridays and during Lent made it necessary to assure a constant fish supply. In times of local famines, as in parts of France, the abundant salmon and eel and other fresh-water fishes saved the population from starvation.

Magna Carta, the first charter of British freedom, contains a clause stipulating that rivers must be kept unobstructed by agents of the Crown so that migratory fish, including salmon, would have free passage to their spawning grounds. In fact, from earliest times the French, English and Scottish governments took pains to protect their inland fisheries and keep the rivers open. All the early British fishery legislation was concerned with salmon because it was the most valuable and also the largest food fish found in the rivers. Owing to the protection afforded by governments and the solicitude of proprietors, for rivers in western Europe were privately owned, salmon stocks remained at high levels almost everywhere, subject to the normal fluctuations of animal populations, until about the eighteenth century. In some areas there was not only plenty of fish for local use but salmon became an important export commodity.

With the growth of population, spread of agriculture, and espe-cially the coming of the Industrial Revolution, man increasingly tampered with the salmon's habitat, and the leaping fishes could no longer thrive in many of their immemorial haunts. In the later nineteenth and early twentieth centuries we rarely hear of salmon gluts in Europe; instead the fish became increasingly scarce and expensive. They deserted one river after another.

The plight of *Salmo salar* is dramatized by the roll-call of famous rivers it has abandoned. The last naturally produced salmon was caught on the Thames in 1833 and legend says it was sold to the King for a guinea a pound. To mention but a few, salmon no longer come up the Seine or the Moselle; the Rhine (once probably the most productive river in Europe); the Gudenaa, Denmark's largest waterway: the Douro, Portugal's major river and prime salmon stream; the Mino, Lérez, Nalón and Nansa in Spain; the Elbe and Weser in Germany; the Oder in Poland; and the Kemi and Kokemäki in Finland. Some Swedish Baltic rivers once famous for their natural runs have been totally or partly supplanted with artificially-reared fish. The Vistula's runs have dropped precipitously.

The species has utterly vanished from Portugal, Switzerland, Denmark, the Low Countries, and is in danger of extinction in France and Spain.

In North America salmon have deserted such major rivers as the Connecticut, Penobscot, Merrimack and Kennebec, not to mention many streams of less renown in the Maritime Provinces of Canada. No nation, in fact, frittered away its Atlantic salmon wealth more wantonly than the United States.

The River Rhine is a classic example of the ruin of a noble salmon fishery. One branch of the river starts in the Alps of eastern Switzerland, in a bleak mountain of almost 10,000 feet elevation. It flows through wild scenery to join the other branch, gushing out of a glaciated gateway, to form the Alpine Rhine, a substantial river with a rocky and boulder-strewn bed. In Switzerland, amid cerulean skies, the Rhine is a pure Alpine stream, and one may drink from it safely. A few hundred miles downstream it has a different colour and taste, and to drink it unpurified is to court disease and possibly death.

In Germany the river acquires the wastes of hundreds of industrial plants, sewage outflows from towns and villages, and sludge released by the incessant parade of barges. In the Alsace region French potash works pour over 10,000 tons of salts into the Rhine daily. When it crosses the Netherlands the river carries an estimated daily load of 40,000 tons of salts as well as 300 tons of petroleum waste dumped by 8,000 self-propelled freight barges. In some places the bed of the stream is already covered with a thick layer of petroleum sludge that is slowly settling into the ground and may eventually threaten water wells.

As one sails down the Rhine, especially from Mainz to Coblenz, past dreamy medieval villages, Gothic castles standing on islets or perched on beetling cliffs, past steep hillsides covered with vineyards or well-tended green fields, watching the highway on the shore crowded with trucks and motor-cars, while trains shoot past, disappear into tunnels and reappear, it is difficult to believe that salmon once teemed in these busy (and dirty) waters, within the memory of very old men. The huge fish came up from their sojourn in the distant sea, perhaps from as far as Greenland, and ploughed their way across Holland, Germany and France, to spawn in the headwaters above Basle. Many of those that survived the spawning ordeal negotiated the long journey back to sea and eventually, six to eighteen months later, returned to the river.

Up and down the Rhine men had fished for salmon for centuries, and their catches were in such great demand that Rhine salmon was a famous delicacy in Paris and Berlin and other places where gourmets met. At the bend of the river where the cliff stands sheer on which the Lorelei sat and by her beauty and song lured sailors to their destruction, there is a deep pool from which fishermen from St Goar and Goarhausen used to take as many as 6,000 salmon yearly. In the North Sea estuary of the river Dutch set nets and seines made glorious hauls. . . . All that is now but a memory.

Even before the rapid growth of industry along the banks of the Rhine and some of its tributaries had befouled the once crystalline waters, hydro-electric projects made migration of fish to the headwaters in Switzerland quite difficult. By 1930 there was a series of dams on the main stem, 10 to 40 feet high, tapping the flow of the river for the generation of electricity. Several power projects on the upper tributaries further impeded fish migration: Bezner dam (18 feet high), Aarau (20 feet), Olten (27 feet), and Wather (66 feet), all on the Aar River, and Baden dam on the Limmat. As a result of

these barriers built with poor or no fishways, the Upper Rhine
became inaccessible while the polluted Middle and Lower Rhine,
the busiest inland waterway in Europe, could no longer sustain
salmon runs.

In the 1880s the Dutch section of the Rhine alone yielded millions
of pounds of salmon yearly. "The great draft nets at Kralingen dwarf
anything seen in England and Wales", said A. D. Barrington, Chief
Inspector of Salmon Fisheries for England and Wales, in his report
for the year 1886. In 1885 the nets in this area caught 69,500
salmon, averaging 17.1 pounds, for a total of almost 1,200,000
pounds; those at Amerstol took 6,500 and at Gorinchen 6,000 fish,
a grand total of 82,000.

In 1886 a convention was signed by the German Empire, the
Kingdom of the Netherlands and the Swiss Confederation for protection of the salmon and other migratory fishes in the Rhine. It
barred stationary nets that extended over halfway across the
stream at low water, set close seasons in Dutch territory from
August 16 to October 15 and above Dutch territory from August
27 to October 26; and forbade fishing for 24 hours beginning at
6 pm Saturday in the main river and tributaries below Basle.
Further, netting and rod fishing were prohibited in the zones where
the salmon were known to spawn, between the Rheinfall and
Mannheim, from October 15 to December 31. The contracting
parties also promised to make the greatest possible use of fish cul-
ture to augment the salmon stocks. But this convention was of no
avail. Catches held up fairly well through the nineteenth century,
slumped around World War I, and petered out by the 1940s. Thus
died one of the world's greatest salmon rivers.

When I was in France in 1963 I heard some talk of the possibility
of planting salmon ova in "Vibert boxes" on the French side of the
river in Alsace, where promising nursery grounds exist. But it is
difficult to believe that, even if the ova are successfuly incubated,
salmon can ever again thrive in what has been called the longest
and worst sewer in Europe.

There is a little museum on the German side of the river at the
Rheinfall opposite Schaffhausen, much frequented by tourists,
where one may see photographs of salmon fishing in the good old
days. At Stein-am-Rhein, a Renaissance Swiss village preserved in
amber, there are 'Salmon Steubli' with their brass salmon signs
swinging in the doorways, just as they did centuries ago. But not
often is fresh salmon served there nowadays since it has to be im-
ported from Norway or Scotland, or perhaps the Pacific coast of
North America.

From *The Atlantic Salmon*

The Pike

Edmund Blunden

From shadows of rich oaks outpeer
The moss-green bastions of the weir,
Where the quick dipper forages
In elver-peopled crevices,
And a small runlet trickling down the sluice
Gossamer music tires not to unloose.

Else round the broad pool's hush
Nothing stirs,
Unless sometimes a straggling heifer crush
Through the thronged spinney where the pheasant whirs
Or martins in a flash
Come with wild mirth to dip their magical wings,
While in the shallow some doomed bulrush swings
At whose hid root the diver vole's teeth gnash.

And nigh this toppling reed, still as the dead
The great pike lies, the murderous patriarch
Watching the waterpit sheer-shelving dark,
Where through the plash his lithe bright vassals thread.

The rose-finned roach and bluish bream
And staring ruffe steal up the stream
Hard by their glutted tyrant, now
Still as a sunken bough.

He on the sandbank lies,
Sunning himself long hours
With stony gorgon eyes:
Westward the hot sun lowers.

Sudden the gray pike changes, and quivering poises for slaughter;
Intense terror wakens around him, the shoals scud awry,
but there chances
A chub unsuspecting; the prowling fins quicken, in
fury he lances;
And the miller that opens the hatch stands amazed at the whirl
in the water.

About Pike

R. Haig Brown

*Haig-Brown's book is a series of autobiographical stories
based on the life-cycle of a river through a year's seasons.
It was published in 1948.*

To create a legend, time is needed. There must be time for stories
to grow and men's minds to work upon them and build them
larger yet, time for eyes and minds made receptive by tales already
told to collect and magnify new fragments of evidence, time for
partisans of the growing myth to raise about its essential points a
hedge of protecting dogma. So a fish, to make a good subject for a
legend, must belong to one of those species that stay put—migratory
fish, such as salmon, haunting a single locality at most for the brief
span of the season, have little chance to become legendary.

Brown trout are excellent subjects of minor legend. Almost any
village public house in the British Isles has its monstrous, hog-
backed hero who is seen from time to time through the dark depths
of a great pool or under the dim centre arch of the nearest road
bridge. Carp, because they are long-lived and cautious fish, are
favourites of some storytellers. But no fish has inspired such legends
as the pike. He has every necessary quality—size, strength, ferocity,
a cruel cold eye, a wicked head and a love of dark, still waters.

Because, as I have said, it takes time to cultivate good stories, it
is natural that the oldest ones should be the best. In 1497 the
famous Mannheim pike was caught, a neat little fish nineteen feet
long and 267 years old. The age was readily ascertained from a
brass ring in its gills, which was inscribed as follows: "I am the
first fish that was placed in this pond by the hand of Frederick II,
Governor of the World, on the 5th October, 1230." The skeleton
of the fish and the ring were preserved in Mannheim Cathedral for
many years in clearest proof of the tale. True, some busybody
checked the skeleton and found that it had been lengthened by the
addition of a number of vertebrae, but the Mannheim pike has found
its way into more printed records than most fish, and the debunker's
name is quite lost.

Sir John Hawkins slipped a fine pike story into several of his
editions of *The Compleat Angler*. This fish, which weighed 170
pounds, was taken from a pool near Newport that had been drained,
and a contemporary newspaper report has the following note:

> Some time ago the clerk of the parish was trolling in the above pool, when
> his bait was seized by this furious creature, which by a sudden jerk pulled him
> in, and doubtless would have devoured him also, had he not by wonderful
> agility and dexterous swimming escaped the dreadful jaws of this voracious
> animal.

The fishing writers tell that one without a single debunking
note, but it is a long drop down to the next monster—the Kenmure
pike, of seventy-two or sixty-one pounds, depending on who is
telling the tale. From examination of the measurements of the

skull, Tate Regan believes the fish really may have weighed that much.

Irish pike stories are innumerable and for a long while they were regarded with the greatest suspicion by all the authorities. Then the late R. B. Marston, editor of *The Fishing Gazette*, offered a prize of ten pounds for any properly authenticated Irish pike of fifty pounds or over. This was probably the best-spent ten pounds on record and the kindest service ever done for pike fishers throughout the British Isles, because in 1923 John Garvin caught a pike of fifty-two pounds in Lough Conn and received the reward. This gives substance to all the records and reports of Irish thirty- and forty-pounders and makes the ninety-six-pound fish from Killaloe and the sixty-pounder from the Ballina Lakes well worth thinking about.

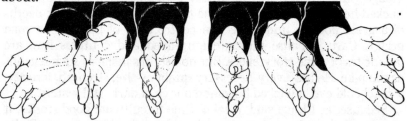

Nearly all these big fish have fine tales built around them; but the fish are unnecessarily big, for a twenty-pounder, under the right circumstances, can do just as well. There is so much about a pike for the imagination to work on—the lean swift body, the love of dark, deep places, the flat head and long jaws filled with sharp teeth, the cold, upward-staring eyes, even the mottled green and olive brown of his sides and back which allow him to melt into invisibility against an underwater background of reeds and rushes. A pike lurks—that is the perfect word—in wait for his prey. When it moves close enough to him, he springs forward or upward upon it. He seizes it crosswise in his huge jaws and sometimes shakes it. When he is ready to do so, he turns it and swallows it. He has a boldness in pursuit that leads him to reach for ducks and grebes on the surface of the water, for a swimming rat and perhaps for other and larger creatures that come within reach. In Svend Fleuron's book about a great pike, his heroine (Grim is her name) graduates into legend through a splendid series of crimes. One unfortunate angler falls from his boat in the excitement of reaching to gaff her and is drowned as she tangles the line about his legs. Another, who unwisely chooses to go swimming when sport is slow, almost loses a leg to the slash of her great teeth. Later she drags down a roe deer fawn that has come to drink at the edge of the lake and after that a swimming dog. She learns to lie in wait at the drinking holes of the cattle and to seize and tear the noses of steers and horses. As her fame spreads through the villages, she becomes a serpent, a dragon, a crocodile. A milkmaid saw her as she shot up out of the deep water and shook herself. The jingling of the scales in her mane was clearly to be heard. Ole, the wheelwright, saw her too. "Such a head! As big as a calf's! And the skin round the corners of its mouth all in great thick folds!"

This is the very stuff of good pike legend: crocodile, serpent, dragon; lurking, lying in wait, dangerous, mysterious; of the swampy marges and the blackest depths; seen only in breathtaking, terrorising glimpses. There must, I think, be American and Canadian pike legends. I have found a trace of one in a book by William Senior, the famous "Red Spinner" of the angling periodicals: "Captain Campbell of the Lake Ontario Beaver Line informs me that he once brought over in a whisky cask the head of a muskinlonge from the St Lawrence that was said to weigh one hundred and forty pounds." There are the bare bones of a fine story, and it would seem that there should be others to be found in lands which have not only the common pike but the pickerel and the muskellunge as well. After all, the muskie commonly attains weights that are the outside limit for ordinary pike. Or perhaps a country that breeds the gator and the catamount, to say nothing of Paul Bunyan and Mike Fink and Daniel Boone and sidehill gougers, need not concern itself with mere fish.

Though I have listened faithfully to all pike stories, I have never yet come close enough to one of these fabled monsters to go out after it myself. I have many times fished waters where every cast gave me a chance of a salmon of forty or fifty pounds, and probably I have never shown a bait to a pike much larger than twenty pounds. But pike fishing has always given me a strange excitement. It is a different excitement, musty as folklore, yet with some of the radiance of mythology, built on curiosity and a sense of vague possibilities rather than on the expectation of a great fish and an uncontrollable fight.

Once I built my own myth. It was only a little myth and all my own, but it was very satisfying and there was room for doubt in the end of it, as there should be in all good myths. It started in a south of England railroad train which stopped, unaccountably, between stations. I saw that my carriage was on a steel bridge over a slow, dark river and stood up to look out of the window. The guard came along as I did so and I asked him, "How long?"

"About ten minutes," he said.

"Can I get out? I'd like to take a look at the river."

He hesitated a moment, then said, "All right. Don't be long. Not more than five minutes."

I climbed out and went to the side of the bridge to look down. The river was big and deep as it passed under the bridge, and I realised that I should not be able to see what I had vaguely hoped to see—a big spring salmon passing upstream. Then the long curve of a backwater caught my eye, and I thought of pike. It was a perfect place, stirring in tiny whirlpools where the easy current swung round against the river's flow, its surface hidden under a raft of little dead sticks and leaves and rushes near the bank. I saw the pike as the guard called me back to the train. A long, still shape, four or five feet down in the water, wide-backed, bronze against the darkness beneath him. I turned away and ran for the train. All the way to London I thought about that pike, and perhaps, as good pike do, he began to grow. Anyhow, I mentally weighed him at twenty-five pounds as I waited for a taxi at Waterloo.

It took me over a year to get back to the backwater under the railroad bridge. The river, as I had known all along, was closely preserved salmon water. But there was an hotel in a nearby town where one could stay and get day tickets on the water to fish for pike and coarse fish of all kinds. A bad case of mumps earned me a February holiday, and I persuaded Mother to spend it with me at this hotel. In the hotel lobby a great pike looked down from a glass case. I began to ask about the fishing. Pike like that were a thing of the past, I was told; the river wasn't what it used to be. I might get something around five or six pounds, but not much more than that.

To reach the main river, we had to cross the millstream at the mill. I stopped to fish through the milltail, and the miller came out to watch me. He was a pale but cheerful man, with flour-whitened clothes and a stoop from lifting heavy sacks. He watched my fishing intently, his head a little on one side as though sizing up what I could do. I asked him about pike, and he gave depressing answers. After a little he said, "There's zalmon up t' river now." His voice was suddenly much softer than it had been.

"I haven't got a salmon ticket," I said. "Only pike."

"If so be 'ee should get one on, 'ee wouldn't think to turn un loose, would 'ee?"

I made another cast. "What else could I do?"

"There's sacks to the mill. There wouldn't be no one the poorer if 'ee was to send t' lady back after one."

I laughed then, because I didn't think I'd hook a salmon. But the miller was too friendly and his conspiracy too flattering for me to turn him down.

"I'll remember that," I said, "if I hook one."

He went back into the mill, and in a little while Mother and I started across the wet meadows towards the main river. I was not in a hurry to try for my big pike, but I began at once to look for the black steel bridge under which he had been lying. We were about half a mile above the railroad, and there were two bridges, one over the millstream, the other over the main river. I realised that I wasn't sure which was the right one. We decided to fish down the main river, then cut back along the railroad to the bridge over the millstream. I told Mother I was sure I could recognise the place as soon as I saw the water.

The big river was a disappointment. Not that it wasn't a fine river—it was broad and strong and deep in wide, flat meadows that climbed almost sharply into low timbered hills a mile or so away on either side. But it was in flood, not in heavy flood, but full to the height of its low banks and soaking back into the meadows so that one could only approach it properly where there was a slight rise in the flat ground. I ploughed in with kneeboots and got wet almost at once. After making a few casts I had to circle back into the meadow to move on; then I could make a few more casts and circle another wet place. So it went, and Mother said, "Why don't you leave it and go back to the millstream? It's just right there."

I thought I knew better. The big river looked like big fish, and in spite of the high water there were beautiful places for pike to lie. I was using a big bait too, something new, the first pike plug I had ever owned. With a one-ounce lead and my silex reel I could get it well across the river and search some of the likely places, but I was not fishing as I had been taught to, moving down only a step or two between casts and working the bait so that it covered the whole river from side to side in slow, careful arcs. The wet places that forced me back from the bank prevented this and made me uneasy and uncomfortable.

When we came to the bridge, I had caught only a single pike, a little fish of about four pounds, which is the same as nothing at all if you are used to such rivers as the Frome and the Dorsetshire Stour, and this was a river at least as famous as either of them. I looked hopefully at the water just above the bridge and tried to see in it the place I had looked down on from the railroad bridge. Mother asked me, "Is this it?"

"No," I said. "I'm sure it isn't. Lord, I hope we find it."

"It must be on the millstream, then," Mother said sensibly. "And that's lucky because you'll be able to get to it without any trouble."

So we crossed to the millstream, and that was it and I could fish it. The wide eddy was under the far bank, almost as I had seen it a year before, with the same scum of little sticks and broken reeds on the surface and the same little whirls where the current turned back. I can never look at such a place in any river without thinking of pike and now I found that my fingers were shaking as I held the plug in my hands and looked carefully at the hooks.

"Do you think he's still there?" Mother said. "I do hope he is."

I nodded. "He's still there—or another one just as big. It's too good a place for them to give a little fish a chance."

I made the first cast carefully and accurately into the upstream tip of the eddy. The plug sidled down into the black water, and I could feel the gentle throb as it worked, suddenly stronger as it came out of the eddy into the current. I fished the eddy for an hour and I don't think I made a bad cast the whole time. I tried every different angle, worked different depths, brought the bait to me at different speeds. I changed the plug to a big rubber wagtail, blue and silver; from that to a brown and gold phantom; from that to a little silver reflex minnow. Nothing touched any of them and at last I had to give up. Mother takes it hard when I don't get what I want. "What a shame!" she said. "He must have moved, or else somebody has caught him."

"Nobody's caught him," I said quickly. That idea hurt. "He's still there. If he wasn't, we'd have caught a little fish like the one we've got. It's too good a place to be empty."

We went back to the mill and ate our lunch of blue vinny cheese with thick, crusty white bread, yellow butter and Dorset beer for a Dorset cheese. The miller came out to us and I offered him the little pike. He accepted it gratefully.

"And 'ee haven't zee'd no zalmon?" He shook his head and clicked his tongue. "Must be that 'ere bait's too durn big for un."

I tried to say again that we were fishing for pike, not salmon. Then he looked at my rod and saw the little silver Devon on it, and his face lighted in a great smile. He winked one eye solemnly as he turned away. "Don't 'ee forget where to come fer t' zack, will 'ee?"

After lunch we went up above the mill and began fishing where the stream split to pass a reedy island. In spite of the miller's confidence in me, I changed the minnow for a wagtail, which has always been my favourite pike bait. The millstream was big, almost as big as the main river itself, but the banks were dry, and I could drop the bait comfortably across it to within six inches of the rushes of the island. To be fishing properly was satisfying in itself, and I was scarcely thinking of fish as I cast across to the mouth of the lesser stream at the lower end of the island. A good fish took the wagtail before it had travelled six feet from the bank. He ran well, and Mother asked, "Is it a salmon?"

"No," I said, "But it's a bigger pike than they said we'd get at the hotel."

"You must get him, my dear. It may be your only chance."

But I didn't feel that when he was on the bank, a fine thick fish of thirteen pounds.

"That's just a beginning for us," I said confidently. "This river grows fish big enough to make a meal of him."

Mother looked at the big, flat head and sharp, backward-pointing teeth as I cut the hooks out. She was used to Frome trout.

"I call him an ugly brute," she said. "I don't think I'd like to see one very much bigger."

For some reason, perhaps because the wagtail was battered and twisted, I changed back to the plug again. For half a dozen casts nothing moved to it; then there was a broad silver flash close behind it under the far bank. I felt nothing and did not strike, but I knew what it was and moved down half a dozen paces before I cast again. I asked Mother if she had seen anything.

"No," she said. "What was it?"

"The miller's salmon," I said. "The bait's too big for him and he only showed at it, but we'll try him again in a minute with something smaller."

"We shouldn't really," Mother said. But it was only a formal protest.

I felt salmon excitement strong in me, and it was hard to keep on and fish out the rest of the pool before going back to him; but I knew he should be rested, and it was easier to keep fishing than to stand quietly on the bank and wait out the time. Then a four-pound chub took the plug at the end of the pool and filled in more time. When he was safely on the bank, I changed to the two-inch silver reflex again, and I was as shaky as I had been when we found the eddy by the bridge. The river was famous for big pike, all right, but it was famous for even bigger salmon.

I had the place exactly marked, but I started a few casts above it and worked down. The minnow was easier and pleasanter to cast than the plug, and it began to spin the moment it hit the water, so that one could work it down deep and slow even under the far bank. The salmon took it there, deep down, with a heavy, solid pull, and started straight out on a run that made the reel talk its loudest.

"I've got him," I said triumphantly.

"Oh, no, my dear," Mother said. "What are we going to do?"

Then the fish broke water, twice and splendidly. He was big and silver and beautiful. Mother started down the river towards the mill.

"We must tell the miller," she said. "We promised him we would."

For another five minutes the fish played me, then I began to feel on top of the fight. Guiltily I looked behind me across the broad meadows. There was a man in the distance coming down towards me. I saw Mother disappear into the mill. The salmon ran again, jumped again, then let me bring him slowly back. The unknown was closer now, and I felt sure he was a keeper or a water bailiff. Mother came out of the mill, and the miller was with her. The salmon was directly below me, lying almost quietly, but not on his side. I knelt on the bank where I could see him very clearly and knew he was nearer thirty pounds than twenty. It might be a chance to tail him; by getting him out that way I should still be free to slip him back if the unknown man upstream of me was too close. I reached down, just touched him and sent him away on another fine run.

He had run against the stream and against heavy pressure and out at the end he rolled over, obviously tiring. He came slowly back, making short downward rushes whenever he felt the surface of the water too close. I looked downstream, then up, and knew that Mother would reach me with the miller and his incriminating sack at almost exactly the same time as the unknown man. The salmon was at my feet again now, really played out, and there seemed only one thing to do. I reached into a pocket for my pliers and knelt down once more. The minnow had been blown up the trace and jammed on the lead, and there was only a single small hook in the side of the salmon's jaw. I gripped it in the pliers, twisted sharply, and he was free. But he lay there quietly under the bank, just moving his great tail. Twice he opened his mouth and forced water out through his gills. Then he began to swim slowly down and away in the dark water. I looked upstream: the unknown man had turned off towards the main river. The miller came up panting, a hundred yards ahead of Mother.

"'E didn't lose un, did 'ee? I came as fast as I could."

"No," I said. "Turned him loose. I had to. That fellow up there," and I pointed to the unknown man out in the middle of the meadow now, "was coming straight down at me. What is he? The keeper?"

The miller snorted in disgust. "Yon's nowt but Jim Ford, going over to look at t' hatches. How big was t' zalmon?"

"Twenty-five pounds," I said. "Perhaps more."

The miller clicked his tongue. "A fi' pun note," he said. "A fi' pun note. That's what 'ee throwed away."

I pointed to the pike on the bank. "How's that one?"

"Yon's big," the miller said, "for what they do be 'ere nowadays. But her beant like the ones they used to catch. And her beant no zalmon neither."

He went sadly back to his mill, and we fished on down. Mother said, "Perhaps it was just as well you let the salmon go. I felt all the time we shouldn't do it, but it was so exciting when he got on I just had to go."

I hooked another small pike of six or seven pounds above the mill, and Mother took the rod and killed him. Below the mill we caught another big chub, and a fair-sized pike came at the bait and missed it. So we came again to the railroad bridge. I stopped to straighten the hooks of the wagtail, and Mother went a little ahead. She said quickly, almost in a whisper, "Look! He's there now."

I looked across and the pike was there, my pike, straight and still as a thick bronze rod, not a foot under the water. He was lying at the lower end of the eddy, nose almost touching the main stream, body slanting in towards the bank. Mother came quietly and slowly back to where I was standing—she knows about fish.

"Do you think you can catch him?"

"Not from this side," I said. "I'll go up on the railway and round. You wait here and tell me what he does."

It must have taken me ten minutes to cross the bridge and get to where I wanted to fish from.

"He hasn't moved at all," Mother said.

I made the first cast right across the stream from well above the eddy, so that the wagtail would swing round to my side opposite the upstream end of the eddy and well away from the waiting pike. I meant to fish right down the length of the eddy step by step that way, so that he would see the bait first at a distance, then gradually closer and closer to him. The second cast swung round. As the line straightened, I let it hang for a minute, then began to reel quite fast. I heard Mother say, "He's gone," and there was a splash and a great swirl in the water twenty or thirty feet below me, directly behind the wagtail. He hadn't touched it, and I let the bait hang there again, then brought it slowly up to me until I was sure he was not following. I lifted it out and felt despair. All too often when a big pike misses the first time, he does not come again. Then Mother said, "He's back in his old place."

"Exactly the same?"

"Exactly the same, except perhaps a little deeper now. I can only just see him."

I supposed I ought to wait and rest him, but I couldn't do it. We had two more days to fish, but he might not be in the mood to take again. I fished on down the eddy, bringing the bait to the edge of it at each cast from clear across the stream. I thought he would come, if he were coming at all, when it swung in three or four feet above him. But he didn't; and he didn't come at the next cast or the next. Mother said, "He doesn't seem to see it even," and I was sure then that we wouldn't get him. I took two steps down and cast again. The bait swung in ten or twelve feet below the eddy, and I began to recover it in quick jerks and stops. He took when it was right opposite him, within two feet of his nose. I don't think I struck. He just ran, pulling the rod down in my hands, tearing at the reel as the salmon had. Fifty or sixty yards down, right under the bridge, he jumped, not like a pike, half out and shaking his head, but like a trout or salmon, clear out so that the drag of the line flopped him over on his side with a splash that echoed splendidly from the bridge girders. There was much more to it than that: at least three good runs, several sulky, head-shaking jumps, a long straining and reaching with the gaff from the high bank above the eddy. But I had him at last and held him up on the hook of the spring balance for Mother to see.

"He's twice as big as the other one," she said. "He must be even bigger than you thought."

But he wasn't; the needle of the spring balance wouldn't quite come down to the eighteen-pound mark. And I still don't know whether he was the same fish I had made into a twenty-five-pounder on Waterloo Station or whether someone had caught that fish and let another take his place. Probably it was the same, though; spring balances are notoriously unfriendly to legends.

The day that all this happened was February 22, 1926. I was eighteen years and one day old at the time and still six or eight months away from American soil, so I probably didn't realise it was Washington's birthday.

From *A River Never Sleeps*

The Culprit

Anton Chekhov

A puny little peasant, exceedingly skinny, wearing patched trousers and a shirt made of ticking, stands before the investigating magistrate. His hairy, pock-marked face, and his eyes scarcely visible under thick, overhanging brows, have an expression of grim sullenness. The mop of tangled hair that has not known the touch of a comb for a long time gives him a spiderish air that makes him look even grimmer. He is barefoot.

"Denis Grigoryev!" the magistrate begins. "Step nearer and answer my questions. On the morning of the seventh of this present month of July, the railway watchman, Ivan Semyonovich Akinfov, making his rounds, found you, near the hundred-and-forty-first milepost, unscrewing the nut of one of the bolts by which the rails are fastened to the sleepers. Here is the nut! . . . With the said nut he detained you. Is this true?"

"Wot?"

"Did all this happen as stated by Akinfov?"

"It did, sure."

"Very well; now, for what purpose were you unscrewing the nut?"

"Wot?"

"Stop saying 'wot' and answer the question: for what purpose were you unscrewing the nut?"

"If I didn't need it, I wouldn't've unscrewed it," croaks Denis, with a sidelong glance at the ceiling.

"What did you want that nut for?"

"The nut? We make sinkers of these nuts."

"Who are 'we'?"

"We, folks. . . . The Klimovo peasants, that is."

"Listen, brother; don't play the fool with me, but talk sense. There's no use lying to me about sinkers."

"I never lied in my life, and here I'm lying . . ." mutters Denis, blinking. "But can you do without a sinker, Your Honor? If you put live bait or worms on a hook, would it go to the bottom without a sinker? . . . So I'm lying," sneers Denis. "What the devil is the good of live bait if it floats on the surface? The perch and the pike and the eel-pout will bite only if your line touches bottom, and if your bait floats on the surface, it's only a bullhead will take it, and that only sometimes, and there ain't no bullhead in our river . . . That fish likes plenty of room."

"What are you telling me about bullhead for?"

"Wot? Why, you asked me yourself! Up our way the gentry catch fish that way, too. Even a little kid wouldn't try to catch fish without a sinker. Of course, somebody with no sense might go fishing without a sinker. No rules for fools."

"So you say you unscrewed this nut to make a sinker of it?"

"What else for? Not to play knucklebones with!"

"But you might have taken a bit of lead or a bullet for a sinker . . . a nail . . ."

"You don't pick up lead on the road, you have to pay for it, and a nail's no good. You can't find nothing better than a nut . . . It's heavy, and it's got a hole."

"He keeps playing the fool! As though he'd been born yesterday or dropped out of the sky! Don't you understand, you blockhead, what this unscrewing leads to? If the watchman hadn't been on the lookout, the train might have been de-railed, people would have been killed—*you* would have killed people."

"God forbid, Your Honor! Kill people? Are we unbaptized, or criminals? Glory be to God, sir, we've lived our lives without dreaming of such a thing, much less killing anybody . . . Save us, Queen of Heaven, have mercy on us! What are you saying, sir?"

"And how do you suppose train wrecks happen? Unscrew two or three nuts, and you have a wreck!"

Denis sneers and screws up his eyes at the magistrate incredulously.

"Well! How many years have all of us here in the village been unscrewing nuts, and the Lord's protected us; and here you talk about wrecks, killing people. If I'd carried off a rail or put a log in the way, then maybe the train might've gone off the track, but . . .ppfff! a nut!"

"But try to get it into your head that the nut holds the rail fast to the sleepers!"

"We understand that . . . We don't unscrew all of 'em . . . We leave some . . . We don't do things without using our heads . . . We understand."

Denis yawns and makes the sign of the cross over his mouth.

"Last year a train was derailed here," says the magistrate. "Now it's plain why!"

"Beg pardon?"

"I say that it's plain why the train was derailed last year . . . Now I understand!"

"That's what you're educated for, our protectors, to understand. The Lord knew to whom to give understanding . . . Here you've figured out how and what, but the watchman, a peasant like us, with no brains at all, he gets you by the collar and pulls you in. You should figure it out first and then pull people in. But it's known, a peasant has the brains of a peasant. . . . Write down, too, Your Honor, that he hit me twice on the jaw, and on the chest, too."

"When your house was searched they found another nut. . . . At what spot did you unscrew that, and when?"

"You mean the nut under the little red chest?"

"I don't know where you kept it, but it was found. When did you unscrew it?"

"I didn't unscrew it; Ignashka, one-eyed Semyon's son, he gave it to me. I mean the one that was under the chest, but the one that was in the sledge in the yard, that one Mitrofan and I unscrewed together."

"Which Mitrofan?"

"Mitrofan Petrov . . . Didn't you hear of him? He makes nets and sells them to the gentry. He needs a lot of those nuts. Reckon a matter of ten for every net."

"Listen. According to Article 1081 of the Penal Code, deliberate damage to a railroad, calculated to jeopardize the trains, provided the perpetrator of the damage knew that it might cause an accident —you understand? Knew! And you couldn't help knowing what this unscrewing might lead to—is punishable by hard labor."

"Of course, you know best . . . We're ignorant folk . . . What do we understand?"

"You understand all about it! You are lying, faking!"

"Why should I lie? Ask in the village if you don't believe me. Only bleak is caught without a sinker. And a gudgeon's no kind of fish, but even gudgeon won't bite without a sinker."

"Tell me about bullhead, now," says the magistrate with a smile.

"There ain't no bullhead in our parts. . . . If we cast our lines without a sinker, with a butterfly for bait, we can maybe catch a chub that way, but even that not often."

"Now, be quiet."

There is silence. Denis shifts from one foot to the other, stares at the table covered with green cloth, and blinks violently as though he were looking not at cloth but at the sun. The magistrate writes rapidly.

"Can I go?" asks Denis, after a silence.

"No. I must put you in custody and send you to prison."

Denis stops blinking and, raising his thick eyebrows, looks inquiringly at the official.

"What do you mean, prison? Your Honor! I haven't the time; I must go to the fair; I must get three rubles from Yegor for lard!"

"Be quiet; don't disturb me."

"Prison . . . If I'd done something, I'd go; but to go just for nothing! What for? I didn't steal anything, so far as I know, I wasn't fighting . . . If there's any question about the arrears, Your Honor, don't believe the elder . . . Ask the permanent member of the Board . . . the elder, he's no Christian."

"Be quiet."

"I'm quiet as it is," mutters Denis; "as for the elder, he's lied about the assessment, I'll take my oath on it . . . We're three brothers: Kuzma Grigoryev, then Yegor Grigoryev, and me, Denis Grigoryev."

"You're disturbing me . . . Hey, Semyon," cries the magistrate, "take him out."

"We're three brothers," mutters Denis, as two husky soldiers seize him and lead him out of the chamber. "A brother don't have to answer for a brother. Kuzma don't pay, so you, Denis, have to answer for it . . . Judges! Our late master the general is dead—the Kingdom of Heaven be his!—or he'd have shown you judges what's for . . . You must have the know-how when you judge, not do it any which way . . . All right, flog a man, but justly, when it's coming to him."

Sea Urchins

Elizabeth David

Sea-urchins were eaten by the Greeks and the Romans, served up, according to Macrobius, with vinegar or hydromel, with the addition of mint or parsley. When Lentulus feasted the priest of Mars, this formed the first dish at supper. Sea-eggs also appeared at the marriage feast of the goddess Hebe.

Sea-urchins (there are several edible varieties) are a menace to bathers on the shores of the Mediterranean, for they cluster by the hundred in shallow waters, hidden in the rocks, and anyone who has ever trodden on a sea-urchin with a bare foot knows how painful and tedious a business it is to remove their sharp little spines from the skin. They are, however, delicious to eat for those who like food redolent of the sea, iodine, and salt. They are served cut in half, and the coral flesh so exposed is scooped out with a piece of bread; they are at their best eaten within sight and sound of the sea, preferably after a long swim, and washed down with plenty of some cold local white wine. Figuier says that they are sometimes also "dressed by boiling, and eaten from the shell like an egg, using long sippets of bread; hence the name of sea-eggs, which they bear in many countries."

Sea-urchins are wrested from their lairs in the rocks with wooden pincers, or can be picked up by hand provided you wear gloves.

From *Italian Food*

The Linn of Logie

Patrick R. Chalmers

*This story was originally published in 1931 and re-printed
in* Great Angling Stories, *an anthology edited by
J. M. Dickie and published in 1941.*

T here was once a young man in a shooting-lodge among the
misty red hills and it was Lammas time. And the rain roared
and hammered on roof and windows and, on such a day as yon,
you would not be driving a grouse were it ever so. And the young
man could not play at bridge for he had not the bridge faculty. But
neither had he a fishing-rod, for he had come to shoot grouse and
not to catch burn trouts. So he stood in the window and listened to
the singing of the showers. And he went to the hall door and opened
it, and the West Wind, sweet with the rain and the smell of the
pinewoods, went by with a shout and bade him follow it. It was then
that his host told that, if a body walked two miles over the hill, that
he would come to the Logie Water wherein were trout for the
catching. The rod to take them on was still the difficulty. But a rod
was borrowed from the bothy. It was a little old two-piece trout-rod
and it was lashed with binding and bound about with twine. But it
was light and whippy and the handicraft of a great maker of old,
and Peter Stuart had had it "in a present" from "her leddyship" at
Druim this long time ago.

But the young man was not concerned for the genesis of the rod
so long as he might get a loan of it. And to this he was kindly welcome.
There was a sufficiency of line on the reel too. And, as it passed the
not too drastic testing of a line, all was well. Peter had some bait-
hooks and a yard or two of gut. The procuring of a "pucklie" worms,
in wet moss and a mustard-tin, would not hinder long. And so the
guest was provided for. And presently he swung a game-bag upon
his back, for creel there was none, and, syne, he was for away. But
not before he had remembered that, in the cap to match with his
Lovat mixture of yesterday's wearing, there were a two or three
trout-flies. So it was that cap that he would put on. And before he
did so he asked about the Logie Water, for he knew it not.

The Logie was, it appeared, a wee stony water on most days and
the trout that lived in it were wee trout. About six to the pound?
They would be just about that, said the angler's host. But they were
plump and golden little trout and dusted on with crimson spots,
and sometimes, maybe, there was a half-pounder to be had. The
Logie ran into the Waupie of course. And the Waupie was a salmon
river? Why, yes, the Waupie was a salmon river, but no salmon
were ever in the Logie because they could not get up the Linn of
Logie. And a very good reason too, thought the angler as he crossed
the hill. And the West Wind was blowing steady and the rain was
going out on it. But the hills were full of the roar of waters where the
burns ran foaming full. And the mist rose out of the glens and the

corries and shifted, like grey smoke, and through it the hills, what a man might see of them, were very dark and blue. And when the angler got to the Logie Water he thought that it was a real bonny little river.

Like all the hill waters the Logie rose like a rocket. But she cleared soon and then she ran in good and swirling ply for a whole fishing day before she fell in and went trickling among the humpbacked stones that huddled in the course of her like a herd of sheep that lie in a park. But there were none of these river-sheep to show to-day. A sleek back here and a sleek back there perhaps, a swirl, a curl, a brown eddy to mark, you'd say, a likely cast, a likely resting place for a running fish. That is, did salmon run the Logie. But no salmon ever ran the Logie because none, as we know, may mount the Linn of Logie. Which was a sad pity, said the angler, for it is a pretty little river, this Logie, and if he, the angler, were Lord Pittenweem, his host's landlord, he'd have the Linn, and the rocks that made it roar, dynamited out of that and a passage made for my lord the salmon.

"This is no worm water, anyhow," thought the fisherman. And he sat down and considered the flies that he wore in his bonnet. There, tied on gut, were a male March brown, a red palmer, two teals-and-red, and a couple more that he could put no name to. "They'll serve," said he, "and if I fish them single they'll see me through the day."

So our angler took the worms out of the mustard-tin and howked a hole and buried them, moss and all; for he was a young man solicitous of all living things. He mounted the March brown, the March brown that kills well everywhere and, in spite of its specialist title, all the year round.

As he makes his first cast, a slant of sun kisses the water simultaneously with his March brown, and an ouzel speeds upstream and under the angler's very line. The angler notes the pucker where the March brown alights on the Logie Water, and almost before that miniature ring has disappeared there is a flash of gold at the fly. The angler twitches the rod-top, but the trout has missed the March brown. To the repeated cast the fingerling responds with a dash and, hooking himself, tears, for all that he weighs scarce the poor quarter of a pound, a goodly yard of line off a stiffish reel. He is beached (for the angler has never a net) where the Logie, fringed with a lace of foam, sweeps round a tiny curve of sand and small gravel.

The report on the trouts of the Logie has been a true report. This is a remarkable pretty trout, fat and well-liking, high in the shoulder, deep in the golden flank and dotted upon, as it was said that he would be, in crimson dots. So, with a quick tap on his head, the *coup de grâce* that every takeable trout should get ere he be basketed, the game-bag receives him to lie upon two handfuls of hill grass and heather. He is not long alone there for, to the next cast, there is a glancing rise and a trout that might be the twin of the first is making "her leddyship's" little rod bend and curtsey as he leaps and leaps again. A game and a gallant little fighter he is, but in a minute or so he also is drawn up on to the little circle of sand and his troubles, if ever he had any until now, are over.

The sun is hot by this time and the wet heather is steaming in the kindliness of light and day. The angler can hear the pop of guns somewhere over the march. The tenant of Waupie Lodge has evidently gone to the hill for an after-luncheon hour or two. But our friend is very well content to be where he is. The little Logie trout are worth a lot of grouse and, moreover, none so little as all that are some of them. For on the edge of a smooth *break*, a streaming swirl that marks the sunken boulder, Troll-tossed a million years ago from a mountain top to lie for all time in Logie as the shelter of great trout, the March brown is taken with a devil of a tug. And almost before the angler can raise the point of "her Leddyship," for, as such, he has come to know lovingly the little engine at his command, a great trout, every ounce of three-quarters of a pound, fat as butter, golden as guineas, leaps with a shattering leap and, falling with a splash, has gone and the March brown with him.

Well now, that's a pity and all, but there are over two dozen trout in the game-bag and an uncommon pretty creel they are and uncommon well, no doubt, they will taste, split and fried and eaten with cold fresh butter and a sprig of parsley. And talking of eating it is now three-thirty and the angler has not yet eaten the egg sandwiches that Maggie came running after him with as he went out. He will eat them now therefore. And that done, shall it be the Palmer as a second horse, or one of the anonymous insects—or a teal-and-red?

A teal-and-red it is, and now the angler will catch another five trouts to make the three dozen and then be facing the lodge-ward two miles up along the march burn, over the rigging, down hill again, and so home. This pool is a real picture of a pool and it is a thousand sorrows that salmon cannot loup the Linn of Logie, for, if they could, you'd say, in this water, that it is here you'd get into a fish. The river shoots and tumbles in peacock tails of amber, over an upheaval of granite it goes, with a flounce of foam, and so, into a deep, fast, porter-coloured pool—a pool that thins out on to a wide shallow of gravel that, in turn, contracts into the rough-and-tumble neck of another important-looking piece of water.

Very quickly the angler catches a further three of the game little trout to whom he has grown accustomed. And the teal-and-red now explores the glassy honey-coloured glide, the fan of clearing water, and it all happens in a second of time, there is a welt of sudden silver that shoots athwart just where the teal-and-red—ah, no salmon can loup—but "her Leddyship's" slight nose is pulled, for all that, most savagely a-down and the line goes off the stiff reel with a shriek.

Twenty yards out and the hooked fish, finding the shallow, throws himself sideways out of the water, clean and beautiful and swift, the salmon who has louped the Linn—the sea-silver salmon who has established a precedent! And back he comes into the dark water with a dash that takes him upstream, up till almost he'd leave the pool at the top of it. Indeed, for a moment he hangs in the very tumult of the entry, then as the angler comes opposite to him, he goes down, down under the boughs of the birks on the far bank and the line buzzing like bees.

Splash, he is on the shallow once more. He jolts and he lunges, and then "her Leddyship" is pulled almost straight as the rough water at the neck of the next pool takes charge of the fish. Headlong down he goes and headlong the angler follows after him—fifty dividing yards after him, fifty of the sixty yards of line that the reel runs to. The next pool is a bonny pool too—bonny from an artistic point of view anyhow—but rock-staked and swirling, a bad place to beat a fish in. And beaten he must be, for at the tail of this pool boils the Linn itself and plunges over and down in spouts and waterfalls. However, there is seventy yards of water to go or ever the fish may make the fall, and half-way thereto is a bit of shelving gravel and backwater which the angler notes well. The fish, six pounds is he, eight perhaps, has had a rattling and if he can be brought to the gravel the rod shall do yet. And so "her Leddyship" bends and condescends with all her slim might.

And gradually the fish comes to her, heavily now and sometimes with the wedge of his steel-grey tail cutting the surface. The angler holds him as tightly as he dares, gives him such of the butt as he presumes. And the gods are on his side, for, rolling this way and that way, the fish comes to hand. And the angler, with a last guiding pressure, lays him, head and shoulders, on the beach, and dropping "her Leddyship," he tails the only salmon that ever louped Logie's Linn.

From *Where the Spring Salmon Run*

How the Whale got his Throat

Rudyard Kipling

In the sea, once upon a time, O my Best Beloved, there was a Whale, and he ate fishes. He ate the starfish and the garfish, and the crab and the dab, and the plaice and the dace, and the skate and his mate, and the mackereel and the pickereel, and the really truly twirly-whirly eel. All the fishes he could find in all the sea he ate with his mouth—so! Till at last there was only one small fish left in all the sea, and he was a small 'Stute Fish, and he swam a little behind the Whale's right ear, so as to be out of harm's way. Then the Whale stood up on his tail and said, "I'm hungry." And the small 'Stute Fish said in a small 'stute voice, "Noble and generous Cetacean, have you ever tasted Man?"

"No," said the Whale. "What is it like?"

"Nice," said the small 'Stute Fish. "Nice but nubbly."

"Then fetch me some," said the Whale, and he made the sea froth up with his tail.

"One at a time is enough," said the 'Stute Fish.

"If you swim to latitude Fifty North, longitude Forty West (that is Magic), you will find, sitting *on* a raft, *in* the middle of the sea, with nothing on but a pair of blue canvas breeches, a pair of suspenders (you must *not* forget the suspenders, Best Beloved), and a jack-knife, one shipwrecked Mariner, who, it is only fair to tell you, is a man of infinite-resource-and-sagacity."

So the Whale swam and swam to latitude Fifty North, longitude Forty West, as fast as he could swim, and *on* a raft, *in* the middle of the sea, *with* nothing to wear except a pair of blue canvas breeches, a pair of suspenders (you must particularly remember the suspenders, Best Beloved), *and* a jack-knife, he found one single, solitary shipwrecked Mariner, trailing his toes in the water. (He had his Mummy's leave to paddle, or else he would never have done it, because he was a man of infinite-resource-and-sagacity.)

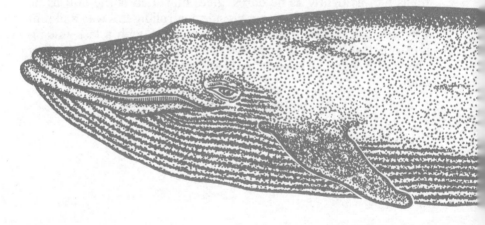

Then the Whale opened his mouth back and back and back till it nearly touched his tail, and he swallowed the shipwrecked Mariner, and the raft he was sitting on, and his blue canvas breeches, and the suspenders (which you *must* not forget), *and* the jack-knife. He swallowed them all down into his warm, dark, inside cupboards, and then he smacked his lips—so, and turned round three times on his tail.

But as soon as the Mariner, who was a man of infinite-resource-and-sagacity, found himself truly inside the Whale's warm, dark, inside cupboards, he stumped and he jumped and he thumped and he bumped, and he pranced and he danced, and he banged and he clanged, and he hit and he bit, and he leaped and he creeped, and he prowled and he howled, and he hopped and he dropped, and he cried and he sighed, and he crawled and he bawled, and he stepped and he lepped, and he danced hornpipes where he shouldn't, and the Whale felt most unhappy indeed. (*Have* you forgotten the suspenders?)

So he said to the 'Stute Fish, "This man is very nubbly, and besides he is making me hiccough. What shall I do?"

"Tell him to come out," said the 'Stute Fish.

So the Whale called down his own throat to the shipwrecked Mariner, "Come out and behave yourself I've got the hiccoughs."

"Nay, nay!" said the Mariner "Not so, but far otherwise. Take me to my natal-shore and the white-cliffs-of-Albion, and I'll think about it." And he began to dance more than ever.

"You had better take him home," said the 'Stute Fish to the Whale. "I ought to have warned you that he is a man of infinite-resource-and-sagacity."

So the Whale swam and swam and swam, with both flippers and his tail, as hard as he could for the hiccoughs; and at last he

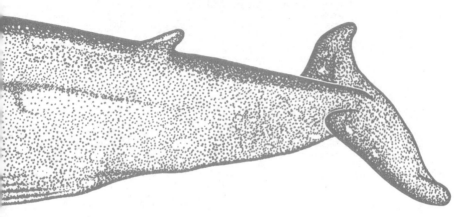

saw the Mariner's natal-shore and the white-cliffs-of-Albion, and he rushed half-way up the beach, and opened his mouth wide and wide and wide, and said, "Change here for Winchester, Ashuelot, Nashua, Keene, and stations on the *Fitch*burg Road"; and just as he said "Fitch" the Mariner walked out of his mouth. But while the Whale had been swimming, the Mariner, who was indeed a person of infinite-resource-and-sagacity, had taken his jack-knife and cut up the raft into a little square grating all running criss-cross, and he had tied it firm with his suspenders (*now* you know why you were not to forget the suspenders!), and he dragged that grating good and tight into the Whale's throat, and there it stuck! Then he recited the following *Sloka*, which, as you have not heard it, I will now proceed to relate:

> By means of a grating
> I have stopped your ating.

For the Mariner he was also an Hi-ber-ni-an. And he stepped out on the shingle, and went home to his Mother, who had given him leave to trail his toes in the water; and he married and lived happily ever afterward. So did the Whale. But from that day on, the grating in his throat, which he could neither cough up nor swallow down, prevented him eating anything except very, very small fish; and that is the reason why whales nowadays never eat men or boys or little girls.

The small 'Stute Fish went and hid himself in the mud under the Door-sills of the Equator. He was afraid that the Whale might be angry with him.

The Sailor took the jack-knife home. He was wearing the blue canvas breeches when he walked out on the shingle. The suspenders were left behind, you see, to tie the grating with; and that is the end of *that* tale.

From *Just So Stories*

Fisherman's War

Maurice Wiggin

The tempo of invasion preparations quickened: there was no time for fishing. But before we drove the lorry aboard an LCT, on Gosport Hards, perch had been snatched from a pool near Maidstone and from another near Ashford, and there had been one wonderful benign evening on a brook in Hampshire, when I caught trout. I imagine that no man of the millions encamped in Hampshire during those unforgettable days of May 1944 will ever forget the feeling that was in the very air, a champagne feeling, or the kindness of the villagers whose lives we so thoroughly upset. We made ourselves free of almost every road and meadow, and the people made us free of their homes. It may not have been the dizzy send-off Kitchener's army got, but it was even better: we had a month or so during which the irritations and frustrations of Service life were somehow forgotten, when for the first time we really felt that we were on the brink of doing what we had joined up to do, and that it was marvellously worth while. And the people of Hampshire, whom we elbowed almost out of house and home, showed us a quiet confidence and friendship which was as touching and invigorating as anything that happened (to me, at any rate) in the whole war.

I cannot name the gentleman, but I thank him now. I was walking past his lawn one evening, and in the manner of people then, he bade me Good Evening, and invited me to step in and take a cup of tea. He was a retired professional man. In a few minutes we were talking about trout.

So it came to pass that I cast a dry fly on Hampshire water, a very few days before all last and lingering contacts with the life of peaceful England were to be broken. Very discreetly, on my next free evening, I left his back door, happily carrying a little

brook rod, and furnished with a precious cast and flies. He led me
to the brook, and like the good soul he is, he left me to it.

It was a tiny stream, in all conscience; but it was a distant relative to a famous river, it was Hampshire trout water gliding through
hallowed land. As I put up the minute sedge, I trembled with eagerness. Frankly, the incongruity of the situation was lost on me: I
only realised later—a few days later, when we were rolling gently
in Cowes Roads—how ironical it was that I should achieve the
ambition of a lifetime, at such a point in a lifetime, one which might
well have been the last of a lifetime.

The brook was difficult, as good brooks are. It was overhung in
a perfectly terrifying manner, and of course I was sadly out of
practice. But I made a vastly lucky start, which encouraged as
much as it thrilled me. I spotted a rise close to the bank at the first
bend, where the water ran deeper, and the first, tentative, far-from-
confident switch cast covered it. To my incredulous delight the
fly cocked and floated down superbly, without drag, within six
inches of the ring. A small snout poked up, a voice within me
screamed "Wait for it!"—and I felt the line tighten as the trout
bored down. I hauled him brutally downstream and soon had him
on the grass—a fine deep little golden fish, all of half a pound. The
thrill of having a real Hampshire trout lying in the hollow of my
hand, his delicate colours gleaming in the light that came shafting
through the leaves, remained with me for many a long and dusty
day, and ridiculous though it undoubtedly sounds, that pretty
trout did his bit to "boost the morale" of His Majesty's Forces.
Reluctantly, and gently, I slipped him back into the water, and he
wiggled madly away, into the deep water beneath his small,
overhanging fortress-bank.

Nothing now had power to break the spell, nor diminish the
exultant joy, of the airman who went creeping and crawling up
the brook, mostly on his knees, ruining a pair of battledress trousers
and collecting numberless scratches and insect bites and stings.
I made many sad mistakes, and spent ages (it seemed) in recovering
that precious cast and fly from the surrounding jungle. (Tackle
was nigh impossible to come by, in 1944.) I caught one more
trout, about six ounces, in a weedy glide where he was feeding
steadily on flies very different from the one I had up. I guess the
sheer brazen novelty of it attracted him. He nearly got away,
being lightly hooked and fond of the weed bed. But I don't believe
in giving a hooked fish time to plan a disengaging campaign. I
missed several more fish.

The sun was down when I crept in through the back gate and
returned the rod and tackle. We drank a cup of tea and ate a sandwich together, talking of the rough Teme, and the southern water

meadows; of the perverse attractions of live-baiting and the dubious character of an Alexandra; "of gut, and gimp, and cunning casts, and reels, and agate rings." At least, my host talked, in the sense that he conversed rationally. I'm afraid I was slightly incoherent: "a babbled o' green fields." We walked to his gate together and stood for a moment. The hamlet was lightless and silent, and all around us, bearing the bloom of night, the immemorial English fields. Faint night sounds pricked the silence: a dog in the hamlet barked, one answered. A nightjar called, and from the village a mile away came crumping up the unmistakable heavy sound of a tank.

We shook hands. I said, "Goodnight, and thank you for the fishing." "Goodbye," he said. "Good luck." Everyone in my tent was asleep when I slipped in, except Johnny. He murmured cynically, "Drunk again," and turned over to sleep. Well he wasn't far wrong. I dreamed I was fishing with my host, and caught a two-pound trout from the deep hole in the brook.

Next day we were confined to camp, for Operation Overlord.

From *The Passionate Angler*

Estuary Night

Henry Williamson

An hour before midnight, in bright moonlight, a dozen crews of four men each, silently in rubber thighboots, went down to their salmon boats moored on the sandbank at the edge of the deep water of the fairway. "Let'n come," said one, truculently, with a glance up the estuary. All the fishermen felt an angry but subdued sense of injustice against water-bailiffs employed by the Board of Conservators. They believed that the laws were imposed only for the benefit of rich sportsmen; while they themselves were poor men with families to feed and clothe from what they got by fishing. The Board, they said, stops us fishing before the big fall run of fish, declaring they must run through to spawn; but the rod-and-line men aren't stopped for six weeks after the nets be off. Yet when the spring run begins, they stop us fishin' for to stock the rivers for the rich gentry's pleasure. So most of the fishermen ignored the limits of the season for net-fishing, and fished for salmon all the year through when the weather was favourable. During the close season they fished only at night, beginning two hours before low ebb, and continuing until the returning flow made the drag on the nets too heavy. The tide ebbed brightly; the water looked white, the shapes of boats going down were indiscernible. There was no wind. The night was in the moon's unreal power. Curlew and other wading birds were crying on sandbank and gravel ridge. In each boat two men pulled at the sweeps, a youth sat in the bows, the owner sat in the stern, where the net was piled.

An old man in the stern of one boat sat upright as light flicked on the starboard bow and was scattered in a loud splash. The oarsmen, dipping enough to keep way on the boat, looked over their left shoulders. Salar had leapt near the Pool buoy, at the tail of The String, where the ebbing waters of the Two Rivers met and bickered.

Salar has gone up with the estuary tide in daylight as far as Sunken Tree bend, where the salt water pressing against river water was so cold that he and the grilse had dropped back with the tide, avoiding fresh water and the plates of ice riding down with the river. The salmon's excitement arising from crammed power was chilled by the sleet water. Now in the Pool, below The String, with its irregular line of froth, many salmon were hovering head to stream, avoiding sometimes playfully the currents of cold water by rising or swimming sideways or drifting backwards before them, always nosing into the water-flow.

The Sharshook Ridge, a gravel bank bound with mussels, grew longer and higher as the tide ebbed at five knots. The Pool buoy rolled with the weight of assaulting water, leaning ocean-wards on its iron chain which the salt never ceased to gnaw in darkness, sunlight, and the moon's opalescent glimmer. Ocean's blind

purpose is to make all things sea; it understands nothing of the
Spirit that moves in air and water.

On the shillets of the lower ridge known among fishermen as
the Fat and the Lean, the keel-shoe of the salmon boat grated,
the man in the bows sprang out and held the gunwale. The boat
swung round to the shore, noisy with the water streaming against
its length. When the other three men had clambered out, he short-
ened the anchor rope in the ring and carried the anchor a little
way up the slope of the ridge, putting it down carefully lest the
clank of metal be heard over the water. The tide was too strong for
shooting a draught, and they waited there quietly, talking in low
voices and sometimes standing silent to listen for sound of the
water-bailiff's motor boat.

Soon the boat was heeling over, and they shoved it down into
the lapsing water. Splash! My Gor, that was a master fish, thirty
pound by the noise of'n. Shall us shoot, feyther? Bide a bit, 'tes
rinning too strong yet.

They waited. The youth struck a match to light a cigarette.
Put 'n out, I tell 'ee! Aw, I ban't afraid of no bliddy bailies. Nor be us,
but us wants fish to-night, don't us? 'Tes no sense hadvertisin' us
be yurr, be ut? Okay. American films were shown nightly in the
converted shed called The Gaiety Theatre. The youth wished he
had a machine-gun in the bows of the boat for the water-bailiffs.

Other boats were going down, gliding fast on the ebb and in
silence but for the occasional squeak of sweeps in thole pins. A
flight of shelduck went by overhead, wind sibilating in a wing where
a quill had dropped. Far away down the estuary the piping and
trilling of birds running and feeding by the wavelap line was changing to cries of alarm as the first boats reached their stances on
shore and sandbank. Two sets of flashes beyond the hollow roar of
the bar came from lighthouses north and south of the Island twenty
miles away. There was no horizon to the earth, no shape or form

to its objects, the moon's light was dead light.

Fish were dropping back with the tide, new schools were coming in over the bar, on whose pitted and shifting sandbanks the lines of waves plunged and broke with a roar, filling the shimmering hollow midnight.

In lessening tide the boat put out, leaving one man on the ridge. He took a turn of the rope round back and shoulder, trod a firm stand, and gripped the rope in his hands, watching the boat drifting down and across and shedding net from stern as it glided into luminous obscurity. It was a flake of darkest shadow in the moon-dazzle on the water, and then was lost to sight. He braced himself and affirmed his footholds, to take the weight of water on rope and net which hung aslant in the tide between head-rope buoyed with corks and heel-rope weighted with lead. The boat turned into the tide, and he leaned against the curved drag of the net with its two-inch mesh stipulated by Conservancy by-law for the escape of smolts.

He heard the noise of the boat touching uptide, the others clambering out, the clank of anchor, and one of his mates hastening to help him. Together they took strain on the rope and waited for their mates, who were trudging down to meet them with the other rope. The arc cast by the two hundred yards of net was now an elongated and narrowing bulge, which must be drawn in as quickly as possible before any fish enclosed by the netting walls found a way out by the space between ropes and the ends of the net.

They hauled slowly, steadily, hand under hand, leaning back against the scarcely yielding ropes, pulling against an area of water restrained by eight hundred thousand meshes. The two coconut fibre ropes came in four yards a minute. Each rope ended at a wooden stretcher, to which were tied the head-rope and the heel-rope. At every concerted tug on these less water was restrained, and the net came in not so dead. Now the skipper became more anxious, and ordered two of the crew to haul at the heel-rope to foreshorten the net under any fish which might be dashing about the enclosed water. The men at the heel-rope hauled rapidly, bending down, their hands near the gravel to keep the bottom of the net as low as possible. The seine, or purse net, came in swiftly, seeming to hiss in the water. There was nothing in the net.

The fishermen showed no disappointment. They had been wet in sea-labour since boyhood. The youth fetched the boat and they shook small crabs and seaweed from the net and repiled it in the stern of the boat. After a few minutes' rest they shot another draught, and hauled in again, bending low as before when the seine came fast and easy near the top of the water, which was asplash and glinting: they lifted the seine and ran back a few paces, while the youth dropped on hands and knees, and gripping a fish by the wrist, his thumb by the tail-fin, lugged it out and struck vigorously the base of its head with a wooden thole pin. It ceased to slap the gravel, and lay still. He killed four other fish, three of them being grilse. A good draught! One twenty-pounder, another fifteen, and the others between five and six pound apiece.

The fish were flung in the well of the boat, and covered with sacks.

Two more draughts were shot, taking three more fish, one of them a lean brown kelt with fungus growing on tail-fin and jaw. They knocked the kelt on the head, and threw it into the water. The kelt had entered fresh water as a clean-run fish weighing eighteen pounds a year previously; it languished in the lower pools of the river all spring and summer, and travelled at the fall to the spawning redds under the moor. During the twelve months it had lived on its stored power; when taken in the net it weighed under ten pounds. A few of the older fishermen killed kelts because it was a Conservancy law that kelts or unclean fish, must be returned to the sea. One or two very old fishermen remained in the village who refused to believe that a kelt could mend itself in salt water, and return again the following season as a clean fish. They said it was another lie of the Board to take away the living of poor men. The hard times in which these old fellows had been schooled were passed away, but their effect would remain throughout the rest of their lives.

After a pause of slackwater, the tide began to flow, and with the flow came Salar and the school of grilse led by Gralaks, forerunners of larger schools to arrive from the feeding banks in later spring.

Salar and the eight grilse swam a little ahead of the flow, to breathe and control the current. Suddenly alarmed by a fearful apparition, Salar shot up and across, breaking the water with a bulging splash and a glittering ream or travelling wavelet. Gralaks also leapt, and the watchers saw the arrowy glints of their reaming. They saw too a broader, slower flash, and thought this to be the roll of an immense fish. The boat was already afloat, the rowers waiting at the sweeps, the fourth man holding the post-staff. Immediately the boat put out, the rowers bending the sweeps with full strength across the tide, then with it, and back across: they shipped sweeps and ran ashore: the skipper threw out the anchor and hastened to help the fourth man. They heard and saw splashing, and imagined a great haul, bigger than the record of seventeen fish a few years before. As they hauled he exhorted the heel-rope men in a voice hoarsely earnest to pull faster, and together. Although only half the net was in, they could feel the jags on the walls as fish struck them trying to escape.

Then a shout from the direction of the Pool told them of danger: the water-bailiffs had landed on the ridge. The fishermen did not fear being fined if caught and convicted: they dreaded confiscation and destruction of their net, and their licence for the season, soon to open, not being renewed.

Glancing over his left shoulder, the skipper saw several moving spots of light from electric torches, and realized the bailies were there in force. He knew they could not search without a warrant, and he could plead he was rough-fish-catching; but if the bailies arrived while they were giving salmon a dapp on the head, they would have all the proof, needed. Gladly he heard the sound of raised voices upalong, and hoarsely exhorted the others to get the seine in, and away. He began to speak rapidly to himself, wife and children needing food and covering, one law for the rich another for the poor, but if they bailies comed near they'd find what they wasn't looking for. An extraordinary plunging and beating of the water inside the distorted horseshoe of corks made him pause in his mental tirade, and haul the stronger on his rope. He realized something other than fish was in the seine; the tugging plunges against the net made him anxious lest it be broken.

The shouts from the upper end of the ridge had ceased; the water-bailiffs, having come upon a boat with net piled for a draught, were moving down, hoping to find one in the act of taking salmon.

'Errin' 'ogs, cried the skipper, with a roar of disgust. Fetch the boat, he ordered his son. Seven porpoises were clashing and threshing about in the seine. Gralaks was there, too, her side and shoulders scored criss-cross where she had driven against the net and broken her scales. Quick, into the boat, cried the skipper, shouting as a spot of approaching light wavered and dazzled his eyes an instant. Holding the head-rope, he shoved off and scrambled aboard. Pull like something, he cried, taking a turn with the head-rope round a thwart, and hauling over the stern. The skipper did not swear— he was Chapel through and through, as he occasionally informed those who did. Several torchlights were flashing as the water-bailiffs hastened over the gravel bank, wary of falling into pits left by the barges digging gravel. Make'n spark, cried the skipper, and the rowers grunted with their efforts. Then, seeing that the net was safe, the skipper bellowed indignantly, Why don't you chaps stop they witherin' 'errin' 'ogs, can you answer me that, tho'?

The youth wanted to leave the net trailing in the water, to taunt the bailies into giving chase, and then clog the screw of their motor-boat with the mesh. Tidden no sense, grunted his father, who was in shape not dissimilar from the shape of a herring hog. Besides, the tide be flowin', if 'twere ebbin', might be some use, 'twould serve the bailies right to be drov' out to sea and wrecked.

The net was taken aboard, with one small porpoise, which was soon battered to death, and the boat made for the sandbank below the sea-wall of the village.

There they were met by the skipper's wife, who whispered in a voice deep and hoarse that two bailies with a policeman were waiting by the slip, up which they must walk to get home. They witherin' bailies, they deserve to get their boat rammed and zunk below 'em, declared the skipper in great disgust.

The salmon were taken from under the sack. While the two hands and the youth lit cigarettes at a discreet distance, the skipper's wife removed a wide black skirt much speckled with dried fish-scales. Rapidly the skipper threaded a stout cord through gill and mouth of each salmon. The cord was then tied round the wife's waist, after which the skirt, by a feat of balancing made more difficult on the wet and infirm sand, was put on and fastened. Having anchor'd the boat, and carrying the oars, the crew went slowly towards the slip leading to the quay.

"What have you got in that bag?" one of the waiting water-bailiffs demanded, pointing to the bulging sack on the skipper's shoulder.

"My own property," replied the skipper.

"Of what nature?"

" 'Og."

"I don't want no sauce," threatened the bailiff. "I have a constable here. What's in that sack?"

" 'Og, I tell 'ee."

"Turn it out."

"You can't make me. Where's your search warrant?"

"I know what you've got. You're caught this time. Do you want me to go to a magistrate and get a warrant, when you'll lose your renewal of licence. I'll ask you once more, what have you got in that sack?"

" 'Og, I tells 'ee. For a bailie's breakfast, if you likes."

"Turn it out."

"If you promise to fry it for to-morrow's breakfast."

"I promise nothing."

"Why don't you try and search me?" screeched the old woman, amidst laughter.

"For the last time I ask you, will you turn out that bag?" shouted the water-bailiff. "Or shall I give you in charge?"

"Aw, don't 'ee vex yourself so," said the skipper, in a gentle voice. "Here's an Easter egg for 'ee," and he dropped the heavy weight, and tugged the sack from the blubbery mass.

"It's yours, Nosey Parker," yelled the fishwife, as she staggered away, holding the arm of her husband and laughing stridently.

The curlews made their spring-trilling cries over the water flowing fast up the estuary. Soon the birds would be flying to the high moor for nesting.

Salar swam up with the tide, alone. Within and around and making the muscle-cluster of his body were fats and albuminous matter sufficient for five hundred and seventy ascents of the river, without restoration by feeding, from its mouth in the sea to its source on the moor. The moon declined to the west, and the estuary was silent.

From *Salar the Salmon*

Quenelles de Brochet

Rosemary Hume and Muriel Downes

6 oz. pike, free from skin and bone (whiting, hake, or codling can be used); salt; pepper; grated nutmeg; 1 oz. butter; $\frac{1}{2}$ oz. flour; $\frac{1}{2}$ gill milk; $2\frac{1}{2}$ oz. butter; 1 egg white; 2 egg yolks; 2–3 tablespoons thick cream.

Cut the fish into cubes and pound with the seasonings in the pestle and mortar until smooth. Prepare a panada with the 1 oz. butter, flour, and milk, and allow to get quite cold. Work the cold panada into the fish, then add the creamed butter, the unbroken egg white, and the egg yolks. Pass through a fine sieve or work in the blender, then add the cream very slowly, beating well between each addition. Keep the mixture in a cool place for 1 hour then shape and poach for 10 minutes (see below). Serve in a cream or velouté sauce.

Shaping:
1. The mixture can be placed in small quenelle moulds, which may be bought.

2. Shape with two dessertspoons in the same way as meringues, cleaning the spoons in a small bowl of hot water after making each quenelle.

3. Use a piping-bag fitted with an éclair pipe and cut away the mixture cleanly with a knife when the desired size and length is obtained.

4. Most simply of all the mixture can be rolled and shaped by hand on a lightly floured board.

Poaching: Have ready a sauté pan or frying-pan full of boiling, salted water. Slide in only just enough quenelles to cover the bottom of the pan as they rise during cooking. Draw the pan to the side of the stove, cover, and allow barely to simmer for 10 minutes. Lift carefully and drain on a cloth before serving in a sauce.

From *Penguin Cordon Bleu Cookery*

Fish are such Liars!

Roland Pertwee

There had been a fuss in the pool beneath the alders, and the small rainbow trout, with a skitter of his tail, flashed upstream, a hurt and angry fish. For three consecutive mornings he had taken the rise in that pool, and it injured his pride to be jostled from his drift just when the Mayfly was coming up in numbers. If his opponent had been a half-pounder like himself, he would have stayed and fought, but when an old hen fish weighing fully three pounds, with a mouth like a rat hole and a carnivorous, cannibalistic eye rises from the reed beds and occupies the place, flight is the only effective argument.

But Rainbow was very much provoked. He had chosen his place with care. Now the Mayfly was up, the little French chalk stream was full of rising fish, and he knew by experience that strangers are unpopular in that season. To do one's self justice during a hatch, one must find a place where the fly drifts nicely overhead with the run of the stream, and natural drifts are scarce even in a chalk stream. He was not content to leap at the fly like a hysterial youngster who measured his weight in ounces and his wits in milligrams. He had reached that time of life which demanded that he should feed off the surface by suction rather than exertion. No living thing is more particular about his table manners than a trout, and Rainbow was no exception.

"It's a sickening thing," he said to himself, "and a hard shame." He added: "Get out of my way," to a couple of fat young chub with negroid mouths who were bubbling the surface in the silly, senseless fashion of their kind.

"Chub indeed!"

But even the chub had a home and he had none—and the life of a homeless river dweller is precarious.

"I will not and shall not be forced back to midstream," he said.

For, save at eventide or in very special circumstances, trout of personality do not frequent open water where they must compete for every insect with the wind, the lightning-swift sweep of swallows and martins, and even the laborious pursuit of predatory dragon-flies with their bronze wings and bodies like rods of coloured glass. Even as he spoke he saw a three-ouncer leap at a dapping Mayfly which was scooped out of his jaws by a passing swallow. Rainbow heard the tiny click of the Mayfly's body cracked against the bird's beak. A single wing of yellowy gossamer floated downward and settled upon the water. Under the shelving banks to right and left, where the fly, discarding its nymph and still too damp for its virgin flight, drifted downstream, a dozen heavy trout were feeding thoughtfully and selectively.

"If only some angler would catch one of them, I might slip in and occupy the place before it gets known there's a vacancy."

But this uncharitable hope was not fulfilled, and with another whisk of his tail he propelled himself into the unknown waters upstream. A couple of strands of rusty barbed wire, relic of the war, spanned the shallows from bank to bank. Passing beneath them he came to a narrow reach shaded by willows, to the first of which was nailed a board bearing the words Pêche Réservée. He had passed out of the communal into private water—water running languidly over manes of emerald weed between clumps of alder, willow herb, tall crimson sorrel and masses of yellow iris. Ahead, like an apple-green rampart, rose the wooded heights of a forest; on either side were flat meadows of yellowing hay. Overhead, the vast expanse of blue June sky was tufted with rambling clouds. "My scales!" said Rainbow. "Here's water!"

But it was vain to expect any of the best places in such a reach would be vacant, and to avoid a recurrence of his unhappy enencounter earlier in the morning, Rainbow continued his journey until he came to a spot where the river took one of those unaccountable right-angle bends which result in a pool, shallow on the one side, but slanting into deeps on the other. Above it was a water break, a swirl, smoothing, as it reached the pool, into a sleek, swift run, with an eddy which bore all the lighter floating things of the river over the calm surface of the little backwater, sheltered from above by a high shelving bank and a tangle of bramble and herb. Here in this backwater the twig, the broken reed, the leaf, the cork, the fly floated in suspended activity for a few instants until drawn back by invisible magnetism to the main current.

Rainbow paused in admiration. At the tail of the pool two sound fish were rising with regularity, but in the backwater beyond the eddy the surface was still and unbroken. Watching open-eyed, Rainbow saw not one but a dozen Mayflies, fat, juicy and damp from the nymph, drift in, pause, and carried away untouched. It was beyond the bounds of possibility that such a place could be vacant, but there was the evidence of his eyes to prove it; and nothing if not a trier, Rainbow darted across the stream and parked himself six inches below the water to await events.

It so happened that at the time of his arrival the hatch of fly was temporarily suspended, which gave Rainbow leisure to make a survey of his new abode. Beyond the eddy was a submerged snag—the branch of an apple-tree borne there by heavy rains, water-logged, anchored, and intricate—an excellent place to break an angler's line. The river bank on his right was riddled under water with old rat holes, than which there is no better sanctuary. Below him and to the left was a dense bed of weeds brushed flat by the flow of the stream.

"If it comes to the worst," said Rainbow, "a smart fish could do a get-away here with very little ingenuity, even from a canni-balistic old hen like—hullo!"

The exclamation was excited by the apparition of a gauzy shadow on the water, which is what a Mayfly seen from below looks like. Resisting a vulgar inclination to leap at it with the vio-lence of a youngster, Rainbow backed into the correct position which would allow the stream to present the morsel, so to speak, upon a tray. Which it did—and scarcely a dimple on the surface to tell what had happened.

"Very nicely taken, if you will accept the praise of a complete stranger," said a low, soft voice, one inch behind his line of sight.

Without turning to see by whom he had been addressed, Rain-bow flicked a yard upstream and came back with the current four feet away. In the spot he had occupied an instant before lay a great old trout of the most benign aspect, who could not have weighed less than four pounds.

"I beg your pardon," said Rainbow, "but I had no idea that any one—that is, I just dropped in *en passant*, and finding an empty house, I made so bold . . ."

"There is no occasion to apologise," said Old Trout seductively.

"I did not come up from the bottom as early to-day as is my usual habit at this season. Yesterday's hatch was singularly bountiful and it is possible I did myself too liberally."

"Yes, but a gentleman of your weight and seniority can hardly fail to be offended at finding . . ."

"Not at all," Old Trout broke in. "I perceive you are a well-conducted fish who does not advertise his appetite in a loud and splashing fashion."

Overcome by the charm of Old Trout's manner and address, Rainbow reduced the distance separating them to a matter of inches.

"Then you do not want me to go?" he asked.

"On the contrary, dear young sir, stay by all means and take the rise. You are, I perceive, of the rainbow or, as they say here in France, of the Arc-en-ciel family. As a youngster I had the impression that I should turn out a rainbow, but events proved it was no more than the bloom, the natural sheen of youth."

"To speak the truth, sir," said Rainbow, "unless you had told me to the contrary, I would surely have thought you one of us."

Old Trout shook his tail. "You are wrong," he said. "I am from Dulverton, an English trout farm on the Exe, of which you will have heard. You are doubtless surprised to find an English fish in French waters."

"I am indeed," Rainbow replied, sucking in a passing Mayfly with such excellent good manners that it was hard to believe he was feeding. "Then you, sir," he added, "must know all about the habits of men."

"I may justly admit that I do," Old Trout agreed. "Apart from being hand-reared, I have in my twelve years of life studied the species in moods of activity, passivity, duplicity and violence."

Rainbow remarked that such must doubtless have proved of invaluable service. It did not, however, explain the mystery of his presence on a French river.

"For, sir," he added, "Dulverton, as once I heard when enjoying 'A Chat about Rivers' delivered by a much-travelled sea trout, is situated in the west of England, and without crossing the Channel I am unable to explain how you arrived here. Had you belonged to the salmon family, with which, sir, it is evident you have no connection, the explanation would be simple, but in the circumstances it baffles my understanding."

Old Trout waved one of his fins airily. "Yet cross the Channel I certainly did," said he, "and at a period in history which I venture to state will not readily be forgotten. It was during the war, my dear young friend, and I was brought in a can, in company with a hundred yearlings, to this river, or rather the upper reaches of this river, by a young officer who wished to further an entente between English and French fish even as the war was doing with the mankind of these two nations."

Old Trout sighed a couple of bubbles and arched his body this way and that.

"There was a gentleman and sportsman," he said. "A man who was acquainted with our people as I dare to say very few are acquainted. Had it ever been my lot to fall victim to a lover of the rod, I could have done so without regret to his. If you will take a look at my tail, you will observe that the letter W is perforated on the upper side. He presented me with this distinguishing mark before committing me, with his blessing, to the water."

"I have seldom seen a tail more becomingly decorated," said Rainbow. "But what happened to your benefactor?"

Old Trout's expression became infinitely sad. "If I could answer that, " said he, "I were indeed a happy trout. For many weeks after he put me into the river I used to watch him in what little spare time he was able to obtain, casting a dry fly with the most exquisite precision and likeness to nature in all the likely pools and runs and eddies near his battery position. Oh, minnows! It was a pleasure to watch that man, even as it was his pleasure to watch us. His bravery too! I call to mind a dozen times when he fished unmoved and unstartled while bullets from machine-guns were pecking at the water like herons and thudding into the mud banks upon which he stood."

"An angler!" remarked Rainbow. "It would be no lie to say I like him the less on that account."

Old Trout became unexpectedly stern.

"Why so?" he retorted severely. "Have I not said he was also a gentleman and a sportsman? My officer was neither a pot-hunter nor a beast of prey. He was a purist—a man who took delight in pitting his knowledge of nature against the subtlest and most suspicious intellectual forces of the wild. Are you so young as not yet to have learned the exquisite enjoyment of escaping disaster and avoiding error by the exercise of personal ingenuity? Pray, do not reply, for I would hate to think so hard a thing of any trout. We as a race exist by virtue of our brilliant intellectuality and hyper-sensitive selectivity. In waters where there are no pike and only an occasional otter, but for the machinations of men, where should we turn to school our wits? Danger is our mainstay, for I tell you, Rainbow, that trout are composed of two senses—appetite, which makes of us fools, and suspicion, which teaches us to be wise."

Greatly chastened not alone by what Old Trout had said but by the forensic quality of his speech, Rainbow rose short and put a promising Mayfly on the wing.

"I am glad to observe," said Old Trout, "that you are not without conscience."

"To tell the truth, sir," Rainbow replied apologetically, "my nerve this morning has been rudely shaken, but for which I should not have shown such want of good sportsmanship."

And with becoming brevity he told the tale of his eviction from the pool downstream. Old Trout listened gravely, only once moving, and that to absorb a small blue dun, an insect which he keenly relished.

"A regrettable affair," he admitted, "but as I have often observed, women, who are the gentlest creatures under water in adversity, are a thought lacking in moderation in times of abundance. They are apt to snatch."

"But for a turn of speed she would certainly have snatched me," said Rainbow.

"Very shocking," said Old Trout. "Cannibals are disgusting. They destroy the social amenities of the river. We fish have but little family life and should therefore aim to cultivate a freemasonry of good-fellowship among ourselves. For my part, I am happy to line up with other well-conducted trout and content myself with what happens along my own particular drift. Pardon me!" he added, breasting Rainbow to one side. "I invited you to take the rise of Mayfly, but I must ask you to leave the duns alone." Then, fearing this remark might be construed to reflect adversely upon his hospitality, he proceeded: "I have a reason which I will explain later. For the moment we are discussing the circumstances that led to my presence in this river."

"To be sure—your officer. He never succeeded in deluding you with his skill?"

"That would have been impossible," said Old Trout, "for I had taken up a position under the far bank where he could only have reached me with a fly by wading in a part of the river which was in view of a German sniper."

"Wily!" Rainbow chuckled. "Cunning work, sir."

"Perhaps," Old Trout admitted, "although I have since reproached myself with cowardice. However, I was at the time a very small fish and a certain amount of nervousness is forgivable in the young."

At this gracious acknowledgement the rose-coloured hue in Rainbow's rainbow increased noticeably—in short, he blushed.

"From where I lay," Old Trout went on, "I was able to observe the manoeuvres of my officer and greatly profit thereby."

"But excuse me, sir," said Rainbow, "I have heard it said that an angler of the first class is invisible from the river."

"He is invisible to the fish he is trying to catch," Old Trout admitted, "but it must be obvious that he is not invisible to the fish who lie beside or below him. I would also remind you that during the war every tree, every scrap of vegetation, and every vestige of natural cover had been torn up, trampled down, razed. The river banks were as smooth as the top of your head. Even the buttercup, that very humorous flower that tangles up the back cast of so many industrious anglers, was absent. Those who fished on the Western Front had little help from nature."

Young Rainbow sighed, for, only a few days before, his tongue had been badly scratched by an artificial alder which had every appearance of reality.

"It would seem," he said, "that this war had its merits."

"My young friend," said Old Trout, "you never made a greater mistake. A desire on the part of our soldiery to vary a monotonous diet of bully beef and biscuit often drove them to resort to villainous methods of assault against our kind."

"Nets?" gasped Rainbow in horror.

"Worse than nets—bombs," Old Trout replied. "A small oval black thing called a Mills bomb, which the shameless fellows flung into deep pools."

"But surely the chances of being hit by such a . . ."

"You reveal a pathetic ignorance," said Old Trout. "There is no question of being hit. The wretched machine exploded under water and burst our people's insides or stunned us so that we floated dead to the surface. I well remember my officer coming upon such a group of marauders one evening—yes, and laying about him with his fists in defiance of King's Regulations and the Manual of Military Law. Two of them he seized by the collar and the pants and flung into the river. Spinning minnows, that was a sight worth seeing! 'You low swine,' I heard him say; 'you trash, you muck! Isn't there enough carnage without this sort of thing?' Afterward he sat on the bank with the two dripping men and talked to them for their souls' sake.

" 'Look ahead, boys. Ask yourselves what are we fighting for? Decent homes to live in at peace with one another, fields to till and forests and rivers to give us a day's sport and fun. It's our rotten job to massacre each other, but, by gosh, don't let's massacre the harmless rest of nature as well. At least, let's give 'em a running chance. Boys, in the years ahead, when all the mess is cleared up, I look forward to coming back to this old spot, when there is alder growing by the banks, and willow herb and tall reeds and the drone of insects instead of the rumble of those guns. I don't want to come back to a dead river that I helped to kill, but to a river ringed with rising fish—some of whom were old comrades of the war.' He went on to tell of us hundred Dulverton trout that he had marked with the letter *W*. 'Give 'em their chance,' he said, 'and in the years to come those beggars will reward us a hundred times over. They'll give us a finer thrill and put up a cleaner fight than old Jerry ever contrived.' Those were emotional times, and though you may be reluctant to believe me, one of those two very wet men dripped water from his eyes as well as his clothing.

"'Many's the 'appy afternoon I've 'ad with a roach pole on Brentford Canal,' he sniffed, 'though I've never yet tried m' hand against a trout.' 'You shall do it now,' said my officer, and during the half-hour that was left of daylight that dripping soldier had his first lesson in the most delicate art in the world. I can see them now—clumsy, wet fellow and my officer timing him, timing him—'one and two, and one and two, and . . .' The action of my officer's wrist with its persuasive flick was the prettiest thing I have ever seen."

"Did he carry out his intention and come back after the war?" Rainbow asked.

"I shall never know," Old Trout replied. "I do not even know if he survived it. There was a great battle—a German drive. For hours they shelled the river front, and many falling short exploded in our midst with terrible results. My own bank was torn to shreds and our people suffered. How they suffered! About noon the infantry came over—hordes in field grey. There were pontoons, rope bridges, and hand-to-hand fights on both banks and even in the stream itself."

"And your officer?"

"I saw him once, before the water was stamped dense into liquid mud and dyed by the blood of men. He was in the thick of it, unarmed, and a German officer called on him to surrender. For answer he struck him in the face with a light cane. Ah, that wrist action! Then a shell burst, smothering the water with clods of fallen earth and other things."

"Then you never knew?"

"I never knew, although that night I searched among the dead. Next day I went downstream, for the water in that place was polluted with death. The bottom of the pool in which I had my place was choked with strange and mangled tenants that were not good to look upon. We trout are a clean people that will not readily abide in dirty houses. I am a Dulverton trout, where the water is filtered by the hills and runs cool over stones."

"And you have stayed here ever since?"

Old Trout shrugged a fin. "I have moved with the times. Choosing a place according to the needs of my weight."

"And you have never been caught, sir, by any other angler?"

"Am I not here?" Old Trout answered with dignity.

"Oh, quite, sir. I had only thought, perhaps, as a younger fish enthusiasm might have resulted to your disadvantage, but that, nevertheless, you had been returned."

"Returned! Returned!" echoed Old Trout. "Returned to the frying-pan! Where on earth did you pick up that expression? We are in France, my young friend; we are not on the Test, the Itchen, or the Kennet. In this country it is not the practice of anglers to return anything, however miserable in size."

"But nowadays," Rainbow protested, "there are Englishmen and Americans on the river who show us more consideration."

"They may show you consideration," said Old Trout, "but I am of an importance that neither asks for nor expects it. Oblige me by being a little more discreet with your plurals. In the impossible event of my being deceived and caught, I should be introduced to a glass case with an appropriate background of rocks and weeds."

"But, sir, with respect, how can you be so confident of your unassailability?" Rainbow demanded, edging into position to accept an attractive Mayfly with yellow wings that was drifting downstream toward him.

"How?" Old Trout responded. "Because . . ." Then suddenly: "Leave it, you fool!"

Rainbow had just broken the surface when the warning came. The yellow-winged Mayfly was wrenched off the water with a wet squeak. A tangle of limp cast lapped itself round the upper branches of a willow far upstream and a raw voice exclaimed something venomous in French. By common consent the two fish went down.

"Well, really," expostulated Old Trout, "I hoped you were above that kind of thing! Nearly to fall victim to a downstream angler. It's a little too much! And think of the effect it will have on my prestige. Why, that incompetent fool will go about boasting that he rose me. Me!"

For some minutes Rainbow was too crestfallen even to apologise. At last:

"I am afraid," he said, "I was paying more heed to what you were saying than to my own conduct. I never expected to be fished from above. The fly was an uncommonly good imitation and it is a rare thing for a Frenchman to use Four-X gut."

"Rubbish," said Old Trout testily. "These are mere half-pound arguments. Four-X gut, when associated with a fourteen-stone shadow, should deceive nothing over two ounces. I saved your life, but it is all very provoking. If that is a sample of your general demeanour, it is improbable that you will ever reach a pound."

"At this season we are apt to be careless," Rainbow wailed. "And nowadays it is so hard, sir, to distinguish the artificial fly from the real."

"No one expects you to do so," was the answer, "but common prudence demands that you should pay some attention to the manner in which it is presented. A Mayfly does not hit the water with a splash, neither is it able to sustain itself in midstream against the current. Have you ever seen a natural insect leave a broadening wake of cutwater behind its tail? Never mind the fly, my dear boy, but watch the manner of its presentation. Failure to do that has cost many of our people their lives."

"You speak, sir," said Rainbow, a shade sulkily, "as though it were a disgrace for a trout ever to suffer defeat at the hands of an angler."

"Which indeed it is, save in exceptional circumstances," Old Trout answered. "I do not say that a perfect upstream cast from a well-concealed angler, when the fly alights dry and cocked and dances at even speed with the current, may not deceive us to our fall. And I would be the last to say that a grasshopper skilfully dapped on the surface through the branches of an overhanging tree will not inevitably bring about our destruction. But I do most emphatically say that in such a spot as this, where the slightest defect in presentation is multiplied a hundredfold by the varying water speeds, a careless rise is unpardonable. There is only one spot—and that a matter of twelve yards downstream—from which a fly can be drifted over me with any semblance to nature. Even so, there is not one angler in a thousand who can make that cast with success, by reason of a willow which cramps the back cast and the manner in which these alders on our left sprawl across the pool."

Rainbow did not turn about to verify these statements because it is bad form for a trout to face downstream. He contented himself by replying, with a touch of acerbity:

"I should have thought, sir, with the feelings you expressed regarding sportsmanship, you would have found such a sanctuary too dull for your entertainment."

"Every remark you make serves to aggravate the impression of your ignorance," Old Trout replied. "Would you expect a trout of my intelligence to put myself in some place where I am exposed to the vulgar assaults of every amateur upon the bank? Of the green boy who lashes the water into foam, of the purblind peasant who slings his fly at me with a clod of earth or a tail of weed attached to the hook? In this place I invite attention from none but the best people—the expert, the purist."

"I understood you to say that there were none such in these parts," grumbled Rainbow.

"There are none who have succeeded in deceiving me," was the answer. "As a fact, for the last few days I have been vastly entranced by an angler who, by any standard, is deserving of praise. His presentation is flawless and the only fault I can detect in him is a tendency to overlook piscine psychology. He will be with us in a few minutes, since he knows it is my habit to lunch at noon."

"Pardon the interruption," said Rainbow, "but there is a gallant hatch of fly going down. I can hear your two neighbours at the tail of the pool rising steadily."

Old Trout assumed an indulgent air. "We will go up if you wish," said he, "but you will be well advised to observe my counsel before taking the rise, because if my angler keeps his appointment you will most assuredly be *meunièred* before nightfall."

At this unpleasant prophecy Rainbow shivered. "Let us keep to weed," he suggested.

But Old Trout only laughed, so that bubbles from the river bed rose and burst upon the surface.

"Courage," said he; "it will be an opportunity for you to learn the finer points of the game. If you are nervous, lie nearer to the bank. The natural fly does not drift there so abundantly, but you will be secure from the artificial. Presently I will treat you to an exhibition of playing with death you will not fail to appreciate."

He broke off and pointed with his eyes. "Over you and to the left."

Rainbow made a neat double rise and drifted back into line. "Very mellow," he said—"very mellow and choice. Never tasted better. May I ask, sir, what you meant by piscine psychology?"

"I imply that my angler does not appreciate the subtle possibilities of our intellect. Now, my officer concerned himself as vitally with what we were thinking as with what we were feeding upon. This fellow, secure in the knowledge that his presentation is well-nigh perfect, is content to offer me the same variety of flies day after day, irrespective of the fact that I have learned them all by heart. I have, however, adopted the practice of rising every now and then to encourage him."

"Rising? At an artificial fly? I never heard such temerity in all my life," gasped Rainbow.

Old Trout moved his body luxuriously. "I should have said, appearing to rise," he amended. "You may have noticed that I have exhibited a predilection for small duns in preference to the larger *Ephemeridae*. My procedure is as follows: I wait until a natural dun and his artificial Mayfly are drifting downstream with the smallest possible distance separating them. Then I rise and take the dun. Assuming I have risen to him, he strikes, misses, and is at once greatly flattered and greatly provoked. By this device I sometimes occupy his attention for over an hour and thus render a substantial service to others of my kind who would certainly have fallen victim to his skill."

"The river is greatly in your debt, sir," said Young Rainbow, with deliberate satire.

He knew by experience that fish as well as anglers are notorious liars, but the exploit his host recounted was a trifle too strong. Taking a sidelong glance, he was surprised to see that Old Trout did not appear to have appreciated the subtle ridicule of his remark. The long, lithe body had become almost rigid and the great round eyes were focused upon the surface with an expression of fixed concentration.

Looking up Rainbow saw a small white-winged Mayfly with red legs and a body the colour of straw swing out from the main stream and describe a slow circle over the calm surface above Old Trout's head. Scarcely an inch away a tiny blue dun, its wings folded as closely as the pages of a book, floated attendant. An upward rush, a sucking kerr-rop, and when the broken water had calmed, the dun had disappeared and the Mayfly was dancing away downstream.

"Well," said Old Trout, "how's that, my youthful sceptic? Pretty work, eh?"

"I saw nothing in it," was the impertinent reply. "There is not a trout on the river who could not have done likewise."

"Even when one of those two flies was artificial?" Old Trout queried tolerantly.

"But neither of them was artificial," Rainbow retorted. "Had it been so the angler would have struck. They always do."

"Of course he struck," Old Trout replied.

"But he didn't," Rainbow protested. "I saw the Mayfly go down with the current."

"My poor fish!" Old Trout replied. "Do you presume to suggest that I am unable to distinguish an artificial from a natural fly? Are you so blind that you failed to see the prismatic colours in the water from the paraffin in which the fly had been dipped? Here you are! Here it is again!"

Once more the white-winged insect drifted across the backwater, but this time there was no attendant dun.

"If that's a fake I'll eat my tail," said Rainbow.

"If you question my judgment," Old Trout answered, "you are at liberty to rise. I dare say, in spite of a shortage of brain, that you would eat comparatively well."

But Rainbow, in common with his kind, was not disposed to take chances.

"We may expect two or three more casts from this fly and then he will change it for a bigger. It is the same programme every day without variation. How differently my officer would have acted. By now he would have discovered my little joke and turned the tables against me. Aye me, but some men will never learn! Your mental outfit, dear Rainbow, is singularly like a man's," he added. "It lacks elasticity."

Rainbow made no retort and was glad of his forbearance, for every word Old Trout had spoken was borne out by subsequent events. Four times the white-winged Mayfly described an arc over the backwater, but in the absence of duns Old Trout did not rise again. Then came a pause, during which, through a lull in the hatch, even the natural insect was absent from the river.

"He is changing his fly," said Old Trout, "but he will not float it until the hatch starts again. He is casting beautifully this morning and I hope circumstances will permit me to give him another rise."

"But suppose," said Rainbow breathlessly, "you played this game once too often and were foul hooked as a result?"

Old Trout expanded his gills broadly. "Why, then," he replied, "I should break him. Once round a limb of that submerged apple bough and the thing would be done. I should never allow myself to be caught and no angler could gather up the slack and haul me into midstream in time to prevent me reaching the bough. Stand by."

The shadow of a large, dark Mayfly floated cockily over the backwater and had almost returned to the main stream when a small iron-blue dun settled like a puff of thistledown in its wake.

The two insects were a foot nearer the fast water than the spot where Old Trout was accustomed to take the rise. But for the presence of a spectator, it is doubtful whether he would have done so, but Young Rainbow's want of appreciation had excited his vanity, and with a rolling swoop he swallowed the dun and bore it downward.

And then an amazing thing happened. Instead of drifting back to his place as was expected, Old Trout's head was jerked sideways by an invisible force. A thin translucent thread upcut the water's surface and tightened irresistibly. A second later Old Trout was fighting, fighting, fighting to reach the submerged apple bough with the full weight of the running water and the full strength of the finest Japanese gut strained against him.

Watching, wide-eyed and aghast, from one of the underwater rat holes into which he had hastily withdrawn, Rainbow saw the figure of a man rise out of a bed of irises downstream and scramble upon the bank. In his right hand, with the wrist well back, he held a light split-cane rod whose upper joint was curved to a half-circle. The man's left hand was detaching a collapsible landing net from the ring of his belt. Every attitude and movement was expressive of perfectly organised activity. His mouth was shut as tightly as a steel trap, but a light of happy excitement danced in his eyes.

"No, you don't, my fellar," Rainbow heard him say. "No, you don't. I knew all about that apple bough before ever I put a fly over your pool. And the weed bed on the right," he added, as Old Trout made a sudden swerve half down and half across stream.

Tucking the net under his arm the man whipped up the slack with a lightning-like action. The manoeuvre cost Old Trout dear, for when, despairing of reaching the weed and burrowing into it, he tried to regain his old position, he found himself six feet farther away from the apple bough than when the battle began.

Instinctively Old Trout knew it was useless to dash downstream, for a man who could take up slack with the speed his adversary had shown would profit by the expedient to come more quickly to terms with him. Besides, lower down there was broken water to knock the breath out of his lungs. Even where he lay straining and slugging this way and that, the water was pouring so fast into his open mouth as nearly to drown him. His only chance of effecting a smash was by a series of jumps, followed by quick dives. Once before, although he had not confessed it to Rainbow, Old Trout had saved his life by resorting to this expedient. It takes the strain off the line and returns it so quickly that even the finest gut is apt to sunder.

Meanwhile the man was slowly approaching, winding up as he came. Old Trout, boring in the depths, could hear the click of the check reel with increasing distinctness. Looking up, he saw that the cast was almost vertical above his head, which meant that the moment to make the attempt was at hand. The tension was appalling, for ever since the fight began his adversary had given him the butt unremittingly. Aware of his own weight and power, Old Trout was amazed that any tackle could stand the strain.

"Now's my time," he thought, and jumped.

It was no ordinary jump, but an aërial rush three feet out of the water, with a twist at its apex and a cutting lash of the tail designed to break the cast. But his adversary was no ordinary angler, and at the first hint of what was happening he dropped the point of the rod flush with the surface.

Once and once more Old Trout flung himself into the air, but after each attempt he found himself with diminishing strength and with less line to play with.

"It looks to me," said Rainbow mournfully, "as if my unhappy host will lose this battle and finish up in that glass case to which he was referring a few minutes ago." And greatly affected, he burrowed his nose in the mud and wondered, in the event of this dismal prophecy coming true, whether he would be able to take possession of the pool without molestation.

In consequence of these reflections he failed to witness the last phase of the battle, when, as will sometimes happen with big fish, all the fight went out of Old Trout, and rolling wearily over and over, he abandoned himself to the clinging embraces of the net. He never saw the big man proudly carry Old Trout back into the hayfield, where, before proceeding to remove the fly, he sat down beside a shallow dyke and lit a cigarette and smiled largely. Then, with an affectionate and professional touch, he picked up Old Trout by the back of the neck, his forefinger and thumb sunk firmly in the gills.

"You're a fine fellar," he said, extracting the fly; "a good sportsman and a funny fish. You fooled me properly for three days, but I think you'll own I outwitted you in the end."

Rummaging in his creel for a small rod of hard wood that he carried for the purpose of administering the quietus, he became aware of something that arrested the action. Leaning forward, he stared with open eyes at a tiny W perforated in the upper part of Old Trout's tail.

"Shades of the war! Dulverton!" he exclaimed. Then with a sudden warmth: "Old chap, old chap, is it really you? This is red-letter stuff. If you're not too far gone to take another lease of life, have it with me."

And with the tenderness of a woman, he slipped Old Trout into the dyke and in a tremble of excitement hurried off to the *auberge* where the fishermen lodged, to tell a tale no one even pretended to believe.

For the best part of an hour Old Trout lay in the shallow waters of the dyke before slowly cruising back to his own place beneath the overhanging bank. The alarming experience through which he had passed had made him a shade forgetful, and he was not prepared for the sight of Young Rainbow rising steadily at the hatch of fly.

"Pardon me, but a little more to your right," he said, with heavy courtesy.

"Diving otters!" cried Young Rainbow, leaping a foot clear of the water. "You, sir! You!"

"And why not?" Old Trout replied. "Your memory must be short if you have already forgotten that this is my place."

"Yes, but . . ." Rainbow began and stopped.

"You are referring to that little circus of a few minutes ago," said Old Trout. "Is it possible you failed to appreciate the significance of the affair? I knew at once it was my dear officer when he dropped the artificial dun behind the natural Mayfly. In the circumstances I could hardly do less than accept his invitation. Nothing is more delightful than a re-union of comrades of the war." He paused and added: "We had a charming talk, he and I, and I do not know which of us was the more affected. It is a tragedy that such friendship and such intellect as we share cannot exist in a common element."

And so great was his emotion that Old Trout dived and buried his head in the weeds. Whereby Rainbow did uncommonly well during the midday hatch.

From *Fish are such Liars! and Other Stories*

My Moby-Dick

William Humphreys

*The home of the great trout which Humphreys pursued
with such obsessive care was in a pool on a tributary
of the Housatonic river near Stockbridge, Massachusetts.*

The Boston symphony orchestra was in its summer home and
the concert season on up at Tanglewood, drawing music-
lovers from all over the northeast. On Sundays a steady stream of
cars passed over the bridge in Interlaken—over me—on their
way there, then when the concert ended, came down in a stampede.
On one rather sombre Sunday, when the people of the settlement
were all shut indoors and when the low cover of clouds put a lid
on things and sounds carried far and wide, down from above
came the distant thunder of Beethoven's "Ode to Joy." The music
seemed to be coming from light-years off, and so vast was the
number of voices in the choir that had been assembled, it sounded
like the hosts of heaven: ethereal harmony, music of the spheres.

Conscious that my time was short, I applied myself closely,
and under the fish's strict tutelage I was becoming a better fisherman. He demanded nothing less than perfection. A careless cast,
that missed its aim by an inch or that landed with the least disturbance, and he was gone. Such ineptness seemed not so much
to frighten as to affront him. He then retired beneath the bridge
as though to allow me to beat an unwatched retreat. How fatuous
of me it seemed then ever to have thought I was going to catch that
wonder of the world. In this feeling I was unfailingly seconded by
my companion, the towheaded frecklefaced little boy on the bank.

Until, that is, he gave me up as a hopeless case, lost interest, and
no longer appeared at the pool. The appeal of fishing as a spectator
sport is limited at best; with never a nibble, I provided no excitement whatever, only the laughable spectacle of a wrong-headed
and stubborn fool, deaf not just to local wisdom but to plain common sense. I was relieved to be rid of him.

I was improving steadily, and all the same I remained as far short
as ever of the mastery, the magic, needed to entice this phenomenon
of a fish into taking my fly. The longer I fished for him and the better
I got at it, the more elusive he seemed to grow, as though he were
leading me—as he alone among trout could do—into the most
rarefied realms of trout fishing. I got good enough, or so I felt, to
be justified in wondering whether there was a man alive who could
catch this fish.

Steadily forcing me to yield to him in the battle of the lengthening
leader, he now had me down to one eighteen feet long, spidery thin.
With that I could see I was beginning to interest him. So big was
he that even at my distance from him I could detect that rippling
of his spots which denoted that he was tensing, readying himself

to pounce upon his approaching prey. He looked then like a jet plane, throbbing as its engines are revved up for the take-off. I too throbbed with tension at those times. He would raise himself, wait, watch. Then at the last moment he always had second thoughts, sank back and let my fly drift past. I had said it to myself before, I now became convinced that this fish had attained his extraordinary size, his uncommon age, thanks to some faculty that made him unique among his kind, perhaps in the history of his kind. I alternated between cursing him for his invulnerability and feeling that I had been uniquely privileged to have made the acquaintance of so remarkable, so rare a creature.

I grew increasingly conscious of my debt to him, yet I remained ungrateful. He was giving me incomparable training in how to catch trout—lesser trout than himself, that is, and that included them all. He was testing me against the highest possible standards. Few fishermen had ever had such coaching as his of me. I should have been content with that. I was not. He himself was the fish I wanted to catch, I hardly cared whether I ever caught another, and, forgetting now that I owed my betterment all to him, in my increasing pride and vainglory I grew more and more confident that I could, that I would. Right up to the season's closing day I continued to believe that.

"Closing day," my small companion met me with at poolside.

"Has come. Aye, Caesar. But not gone," I rejoined.

"Huh?" My talking in riddles was all that was needed to convince him that I was hopelessly addled.

"Still using them artificial flies, I see."

"Mmh."

"Ever get him to bite one of them yet?"

"Can't say I have."

"Then what makes you think he's going to now at the last minute?"

"Don't think he's going to—just hoping he might. You never know when your luck will change."

But the truth was, the boy had dashed my hopes. Closing day it was, and that alone would be the thing to make this one different from all the other days I had sunk in this folly of mine. At midnight tonight the Fish and Game Commission of the Commonwealth of Massachusetts would extend legal protection over its most venerable trout, and he would live out his pensionage in this little pool. It was only out of a sense of obligation and to round out the fitness of things that I waded into the water. A sense that, having challenged the fish, I owed him his total triumph over me. It was I who had made today's appointment with him, and there he was.

As often happens, now that I had lost confidence, and, with it, the compulsion to perform, I excelled myself in my casting that day. Four times running I placed my fly—a No. 12 Black Gnat it was, to match the ones that were biting me—over the fish without rousing his suspicions, putting him off his feed and sending him to sulk beneath the bridge. Those repeatedly ignored casts made my young companion smirk; I, though rather ruefully, admired my unproductive accomplishment.

My fifth cast would have alighted in the same spot, some four feet in front of the fish, as the others had. However, it never did. Exploding from the water, the fish took it on the wing, a foot above the surface. Why that cast and none of the countless others, nobody will ever know. Instantly he felt the barb. Not fright, but fight, was what it brought out in him.

Out of the water he rose again like a rocket—out and out, and still there was more to him, no end to him. More bird than fish he seemed as he hovered above the water, his spots and spangles patterned like plumage. I half expected to see his sides unfold and spread in flight, as though, like the insects he fed upon, he had undergone metamorphosis and hatched. His gleaming wetness gave an iridescent glaze to him, and as he rose into the sunshine his multitudinous markings sparkled as though he were studded with jewels. At once weighty and weightless, he rose to twice his own length. Then, giving himself a flip like a pole-vaulter's, down he dove, parting the water with a wallop that rocked the pool to its edges.

The next moment I was facing in another direction, turned by the tug of my rod, which I was surprised to find in my hand. Nothing remotely resembling his speed and power had I ever experienced in my fishing. Nothing I might have done could have contained him. It was only the confines of the pool that turned him.

Straight up from the water he rose again. Higher than before he rose. It was not desperation that drove him. There was exuberance in his leap, joy of battle, complete self-confidence, glory in his own singularity. Polished silver encrusted with jewels of all colours he was, and of a size not to be believed even by one who had studied him for weeks. I believed now that he had taken my fly for the fun of it. I was quite ready to credit that superfish with knowing this was the last day of the season, even with knowing it was his last season, and of wanting to show the world what, despite age and impairment, he was capable of. Reaching the peak of his leap, he gave a thrash, scattering spray around him. In the sunshine the drops sparkled like his own spots. It was as though a rocket had burst, showering its scintillations upon the air.

Another unrestrainable run, then again he leaped, and for this

one the former two had been only warm-ups. Surely he must have a drop of salmon in his blood! Up and up he went until he had risen into the bright sunshine, and there, in defiance of gravity, in suspension of time, he hung. He shook himself down his entire length. The spray that scattered from him caught the light and became a perfect rainbow in miniature. Set in that aureole of his own colours that streamed in bands from him, he gave a final toss of his head, breaking my leader with insolent ease, did a flip, dove and re-entered the water with a splash that sent waves washing long afterward against my trembling and strengthless legs.

"Dummy!" cried the boy on the bank. "You had him and you let him get away!"

From *My Moby-Dick*

The Royal Fisherman

Traditional

As I walked out one May morning,
　　When May was all in bloom,
O there I spied a bold fisherman,
　　Come fishing all alone.

I said to this bold fisherman,
　　How come you fishing here?
I'm fishing for your own sweet sake
　　All down the river clear.

He drove his boat towards the side,
　　Which was his full intent,
Then he laid hold of her lily-white hand
　　And down the stream they went.

Then he pulled off his morning gown
　　And threw it over the sea,
And there she spied three robes of gold
　　All hanging down his knee.

Then on her bended knees she fell:
　　Pray, sir, pardon me
For calling you a fisherman
　　And a rover down the sea.

Rise up, rise up, my pretty fair maid,
　　Don't mention that to me,
For not one word that you have spoke
　　Has the least offended me.

Then we'll go to my father's hall,
　　And married we shall be,
And you shall have your fisherman
　　To row you on the sea.

Then they went to his father's house,
　　And married now they be;
And now she's got her fisherman
　　To row her down the sea.

The Weir at Galway

C. Conor O'Malley

The weir at Galway City is in the heart of Ireland West. This is where the waters of Carra Mask and Corrib flow down to the sea. The stretch of Corrib River from the weir gates above to the salmon weir bridge below, approximately 200 yards, is possibly one of the best known 200 yards of salmon water in the world. Hitherto, before deepening, it was less than a quarter of a mile from the sea. Now, with each full tide, it is estuarine all the way to the weir falls. For this reason the Galway weir salmon is really never far from the sea, and so he is in prime condition on the hook or on the hotel menu.

Probably the ancestors of our salmon passed up and down through Galway when it was only *Baile na Shruthan*—"The Village of the Streams"—a little fishing village long, long ago, where St Nicholas's medieval church now stands. In the Middle Ages salmon in Galway were associated with the Fathers of St Francis. The Fathers no doubt had their methods, like the monks of Cong, who made that clever fish trap, to be seen there today, where each salmon as he entered rang a bell to say "Here I am." One of the seven markets of old Galway dealt entirely with fresh-water fish. Professor M. Donovan O'Sullivan in her learned book, *Old Galway*, quotes this city law for fishermen in the Town of Galway: "In 1585 it was enacted:

> that no fysherman should take in hande the ploughe or spade that would bar them from fyshing both to serve themselves and the common wealthe with fyshe in consideration whereof that the said fysshers with their wyffs and familie be served before others with all necessaries sustenunce and food of provition as cometh to the market whereby they mought be better hable to earne their said livings and have better hope."

There is a record in the city archives that stonemasons repairing holes in the city walls, (no doubt to keep out the native "O's and the Macs") went on strike against having to eat salmon on too many days a week. A recent tale of tourist Galway is that in a certain hostelry in Galway where salmon was on the menu too frequently, a tourist guest, when asked, "What would you like to do today, sir?" replied, "I think I'll go down to the river to spawn."

We suggest that the salmon should be a symbol of Galway City, after the manner of Boston and its sacred codfish. In the First National Bank there hangs a great carved pinewood codfish, symbol of old Boston:

> "The towne of the bean and the cod,
> Where the Lowells speak only to Cabots
> And the Cabots speak only to God."

In this 200-yards stretch of weir river the salmon lie in hundreds, almost immobile as in a painting, with their heads pointing to Loch Corrib, where they are going; their tails pointed to the great ocean, whence they have come. Come and look at this river in summer, when all 14 gates of the dam are closed and the waters of Corrib, Mask and Carra are held up in a reservoir. Sometimes only a trickle of water comes through, scarcely enough to keep the salmon decently covered with breathing space. The medial swiftly flowing channel is about 18 feet wide and 2 to 3 feet deep. This is where all the salmon lie. The bottom is rocks, shingle, uneven bedrock projections that break the current into eddies—lies beloved by salmon. They lie in groups sheltering behind any barrier in the swift current. In this crystal clear water, against a background of white rockbottom and polished shingle, one sees the details of each fish as clearly as if he were on the slab of a fishmonger's shop. This has been an aquarium where Eddie Lydon looked at salmon for a seven-hour day, a six-day week, from February to September for 59 years. He had an opportunity given to few, to study salmon in all shapes and sizes. He has been in touch with them in the trickling crystal clear waters of summer and the muddy peaty spates of spring, when the river may be a roaring torrent 40 yards wide and 13 feet deep.

When the salmon arrive in the river home from his high living in the ocean, he is full of life and silver sparkle, light colour on the back, bright silver on the sides and snow-white under the belly. The longer he is in fresh water, the more he loses this sparkle and silver sheen. His appearance changes to resemble a somewhat debunked brown trout, with red fins and a "stale" look.

These thousands of handsome fish lying in crystal clear summer water is a wondrous sight for hundreds of people leaning on the parapet of the weir bridge. This sight is a "must" for tourists who visit Galway each summer in ever-increasing numbers. The salmon pose there beneath the bridge, as if by arrangement with *An Bord Failte*. They lie practically immobile, just maintaining station against the stream, seemingly in suspended animation, heedless of gesticulating mankind on the parapet above, and the roar of traffic over the bridge. This strange contempt for all life in the air above them is a never-failing source of wonder to the onlookers; almost always someone is asking, "Are those fish alive?"

Personally, I have always been trying to find the answer to the question, "How far away in terms of human vision and hearing can a salmon see and hear?" Doubtless all objects as far away as the parapet of the bridge, whether moving or not, are far beyond the range of vision of the salmon in the river beneath. From my observation of hundreds of salmon in the low summer water on the weir, I conclude their vision in terms of human vision is very limited. They do not appear to see the angler moving on the bank ten feet away and one can approach to within four or five feet without scaring them, provided one is slow and deliberate. The angler's shadow at rest on the water or moving very slowly does not seem to scare the salmon, but his shadow moving smartly across them on the water always does scare them, temporarily, from their lies in the stream. Rapid jerky movements within the fish's range of vision frighten him, as the sudden upturned face and gun of a fowler scares a bird approaching him in the air. To our sorrow, we have seen how the salmon makes the last successful effort to break away when he sees the landing net suddenly thrust at him by unskilled hands. It is said that salmon in the alevin stage freeze into immobility in their redds when the shadow of a predator bird overhead falls on them. Does this explain the adult salmon's fear of a moving shadow on the water?

I think the salmon must be almost altogether unaware or un-afraid of sounds. Eddie says that during the five years, 1955–59, the weir river was deepened by blasting four feet deep of hard granite off the river bed. In the midst of all the noise and turmoil the salmon came in there as usual. A coffer dam 200-yards long ran from the weir above to the bridge below, dividing the river into two parallel parts. Each part was alternately dried up for blasting, which went on most of the day for years. While blasts were exploding on one side the salmon came up the other side and rested there as usual or passed up into the lake. They behaved as if the blasting, which went on only a few yards away, did not worry them at all. They took, or ignored, flies and baits as usual. Again, quite recently, in the August low water, the eel weir was being renewed and heavy hammering went on each day, yet I observed salmon a few yards away upstream in no way disturbed.

Sometimes the watchers on the parapet of the weir bridge are rewarded by seeing an angler on the catwalk tense with bent rod "stuck in a fish." This is excitement even for those who never saw an angler in action. At the sight of a great leaping salmon making powerful rushes to get away, all leaners on the parapet become fishermen. Many rejoice and give the angler an ovation when the fish is landed. Some, no doubt, are sorry if the fish gets away. Some, possibly, are not. This whole scene is one that is full of beauty ever new—one of the highlights of Galway. The weir dam above with fourteen great steel gates holding back the water of Loch Corrib; the handsome six-arch weir bridge of cut limestone; gaily coloured crowds of tourists leaning on the parapet of the bridge; and in recent years a magnificent new Romanesque cathedral replacing the old jail wall. The salmon steps is a feature of the weir that always catches the passing eye. This laneway of foaming water forever falling down from the Corrib River above to the weir river fourteen feet below mystifies the leaners on the parapet. When told that this is the salmon steps, they say, "Why don't we see them going up the steps with great leaps as salmon do?"

The explanation is this: the steps constitute a ramp with a gradient of one-in-two, through which a constant depth of water flows from the upper to the lower river. In the sides and bottom of the ramp there are baffle plates set in sites slanted against the current, breaking it into foaming eddies and backwaters that cut down its force. Unseen beneath the foam, the salmon "walk" up this "escalator" with comparative ease through the baffled water. Dan Madden, keeper of the gates, tells me that the salmon pass up mainly at dusk and dawn. At the top they swim into the Corrib River. Each fish as it passes breaks an electronic current and so is counted, but two fish passing simultaneously register as only one. Fish less than 2 pounds weight do not break the circuit, and so do not register. Salmon while still in the Corrib River above are the property of the Fishery; but with the owner's consent, the salmon fishing there is free to all State salmon licence holders.

There are other interesting inhabitants of the weir river. In June, with the grilse or small summer salmon, there come the lampreys, those strange nightmare sort of parasitic half-"fish," half-worm, which they say Henry I of England ate too much of. Those stone-suckers come in numbers into the river and with frenzied energy, twisting and writhing their suckers, attach to stones great and small, which they drag downstream to make a rampart across the strong current, under which they spawn and some, perhaps, make off to sea again; more die in the river. Spectators on the bridge who see these eel-like animals furiously in action think they are engaged in civil war, destroying one another. The opposite is the truth; these primitive "fish," jawless vertebrates, are intensely active spawning, preparing to raise a new generation of their kind.

Incidentally, Eddie never saw a lamprey attached to a salmon in the river sucking its blood as they do to fish in the sea where they fatten on living blood. He never heard of this occurrence from any of his people and, taking all of them, they must have observed myriads of salmon closely for nearly a century and a half. Such an unpleasant sight would surely be remembered.

The lamprey, in fact, like the salmon, goes on hunger strike in fresh water when spawning. I have seen dead and dying lampreys in the river after spawning, but have not seen babies of the lamprey family: they are, no doubt, deep under the gravel of the parados formed by the parent lampreys. The parents, having spawned approximately 250,000 eggs each, almost all disappear overnight from the spawning redds, and almost all die, they say. Lampreys are not seen again in the river until the coming of the summer salmon in June.

I have watched a spawning lamprey quiver like a bowstring. I do not know at what state the little ones leave the river, nor where they go. One only presumes they go to sea and grow up. Do they return to spawn in the spot where they were born? The parados of stones and gravel made by the lampreys in June may be utilised by the salmon as spawning beds in December, and as lies to break the current when resting en route to spawn—accidental co-existence, chance good-neighbour relations.

Then there are the eels inhabiting the fissures in the bedrock of the river. They lie there, invisible, but alert, for if you dangle a shrimp close to their hiding holes and let it rest only for a moment, they dart out and seize it. Their sense of smell, or smell and sight, seems to be very keen. We see the little elvers, young eels, coming in from the Sargasso Sea in limitless myriads in April. They climb up via the hay-ropes over the steps arranged for them into the Corrib River, en route for the rivers and streams of Corrib, Mask and Carra. Unlike salmon, eels go up and come down through the Mark-Corrib underground channels.

A number of sea trout come into the river in August and September. Some of them ascend the salmon steps into the Corrib River above, but they do not go into the lake. Some of them spawn in the lower reaches of Corrib River. It is said that sea trout do not feel at home in limestone or medium chalk waters like Corrib. They seem to be happy only in low pH, granite acid, boggy water, where there is no lime. Salmon, on the other hand, seem to make their spawning ground in either type of water. No one has come up with a complete answer as to why sea trout spawn in alkaline Corrib River, but avoid Corrib Lake. Piggins suggests they spawn in the acid patches of river adjacent to boggy terrain.

I am an admirer of the great black-backed gull which in low water keeps watch over the foaming salmon steps with the keen eye of a water bailiff. Now and again he is rewarded when a foolish fish jumps out of the foam on to the dry apron of the weir. Eddie has seen this gull drag a small salmon out of the shallow water up on to the stones, pick out his eyes and wait till he is dead, and then proceed to eat him, starting at the head region.

Even when this gull, called in Irish *Wheelawn*, flies downriver and is absent for a time, the smaller gulls on the apron do not dare to touch this half-eaten salmon. Several times I have seen him nail a river eel, dragging it from its hiding hole in the bottom. With powerful chops of his beak, he breaks the eel's spine and so stops its writhing. Then *Wheelawn* throws back his head like a sword swallower, and in a jiffy the eel is inside. After this treat he drinks quantities of water like any compleat angler who "wets his fish" as we all do—but not with water!

When shoals of sea-trout are climbing the steps of the weir in July, August and September Eddie has seen *Wheelawn* do big business. He catches his fish and retires to a quiet corner to eat. Observing this, Dan, the keeper of the gates, comes on the scene, scares the bird away and adds the seatrout to his own menu. Eddie never mentioned that he had seen naughty *Wheelawn* grab his fish and fly away when he sees Dan in the offing. *Wheelawn* has learnt the hard way.

In 1971, during an unprecedented spell of low water on the weir river, there was no fishing for *Wheelawn* at the weir falls, so I saw him move his fishing grounds down nearer the sea, to the Claddagh Bridge. There one could see him sweeping round and round on great wings, his head turning rhythmically from left to right, scanning the river bottom for eels that are quite invisible to the human eye against the dark green slime of the bottom. Suddenly the gull dives to the bottom and comes up with a juicy twisting eel. I have never seen him miss.

I think that like the peregrine falcon, the great black-backed gull eats only his own kill. I never saw him dine on sewage like lesser gulls.

The otter has a bad name with anglers since the time of Izaak Walton. Although there are two otter dens in the weir banks Eddie never saw them prey on the salmon, but they do love eels and can be observed walking on the bottom scratching eels out of their hiding holes in the fissures of the rocks. They can shoot through the water with the speed of a salmon. One day one of Eddie's clients was playing a fish in medium deep water when an otter shot by. The salmon leaped clean out of the water and there was quite a commotion among all the neighbouring fish. Sometimes a fish is seen with a bite taken out of it, probably a victim of an otter, and not a seal as some say, since a seal would scarcely be content with one bite. The perch and pike trappers of the Inland Fisheries Trust sometimes find otters drowned in their traps, where the traps are completely submerged. The otters are lured to their death to eat the pike and perch trapped inside. If, however, there is even a little air space at the top of the trap, the otter eats his way through the strong wire netting and escapes.

Perch enter these wire traps spontaneously at spawning time. Who can tell why, since there is no bait to lure them in? The Inland Fisheries Trust trappers think pike go in to eat the perch, and the otter goes in to eat both. Eels do not seem to enter the traps; they do, however, eat pike trapped in gill nets, but trappers say they do not eat perch so trapped.

The otter is called a "water dog" by country people, who do not like him. In smaller streams where salmon spawn they are easy prey to the "water dog" who takes only one bite and leaves the rest of the fish on the bank. This is like the wanton fox, that kills all the hen roost and eats only one hen. Country folk always use the sinister definite article "the" when telling of the villainy of "the" fox, "the" otter, "the" grey crow, "the" hawk.

Some years ago seals probably took a big toll of salmon in the Bay. Inishlee, the "grey island" near Barna, was a seal breeding ground. It does not seem to be so any longer. The great seal colony at Tawin, where one could count 100 seals forty years ago, now seems extinct also. One rarely sees a seal now off shore. They were once an attraction off Salthill Prom, but now a seal is a rare sight there. Inspector Varley of the Galway Fishery Conservators tells me he pays a seal hunter for ten seals shot each year in the Bay to protect the salmon.

"In general it is true to say that coarse fish (pike, bream, rudd, roach and tench) enter these traps simply because they are there with the mouth opening towards them; probably curiosity plays a large part in the whole procedure. Perch enter the traps only around spawning time (April–May) and presumably they fancy the traps as an ideal location to spawn on because at spawning time you get the traps covered in spawn, both inside and outside. Trout do not enter traps in any of our lakes, except in Lake Inchiquin, Co. Clare, and why they should be so inclined there, I am afraid I cannot offer any explanation. Also we find that if one or two fish enter the trap, it is very likely that more will follow. The traps are usually set at the margins of lakes (except for perch at spawning time) among or near weeds; the fish do not seem to treat the traps with any kind of suspicion." (Fitzmaurice.)

In committing suicide unwittingly they resemble the lemmings of Norway.

From *With a Fishing Rod in Ireland*

Cannibal Trout
David Pownall

As a predator you always seem
oddly guiltless in your stream,
casting quiet to hook your lip,
waiting for my float to dip,
strikes me as a quasi-crime—
you have killed from time to time.

When I reel in all my cast,
You, the cannibal, come last,
Stuffed with brothers, sisters, sons,
Fighting as the nylon runs:
I offer death on decent terms
And feel far friendlier to worms.

The Fisherman

Martin Armstrong

The road, diving downwards off the bridge, slid away to the left; but tucked into a low recess on the right, so that it looked down upon the river and up at the high, foreshortened mass of the bridge, the George Inn opened its comfortable, L-shaped front, thick with climbing greenery. Behind it a flourishing kitchen-garden stood embanked above the river to which steps descended under a canopy of ancient elm-trees.

Michael Dunne, having finished his breakfast, appeared in the doorway and stood looking up at the sky. Then he lowered his eyes to the scene before him and slowly drew in his breath. It was delicious to be in the country again. The trees, loaded mound upon mound with fresh young green; the pervading hush of the river; the soft clean air tinged with the smell of wet earth and standing water breathed up from the river edge, thrilled him with indescribable delight. He glanced again at the sky. It was bright, too bright, at present, but there were light clouds in the blue and a gentle breeze: there would certainly be intervals of dullness. Not, on the whole, a bad day for fishing. He had made up two fishing-casts overnight, seated in the bow-window of the sitting-room with half a dozen trout-flies hanging from his mouth. When the gut was sufficiently soaked, he drew out the flies one by one and carefully knotted them on the cast. He had decided to use nothing but March Browns, and old Wales, the landlord, had entirely agreed when Dunne had mentioned it to him.

He was ready to start now at any moment, and he stood there in the doorway with his hands in his breeches-pockets, impatiently waiting for the sun to stop shining. From time to time in the inn behind him footsteps tapped along the stone-floored passage and died away. But at last he was roused by some that came closer and closer still and finally stopped just behind his back. He swung round. Somebody was waiting to be allowed to pass: a young woman. With a quick apology Dunne moved out of her way and she came out, thanking him with a smile as she passed him, and moved away along the front of the inn, a slim figure in a brown coat and skirt. A white-handled umbrella hung from her left arm: her right hand carried a camp-stool and a satchel.

Dunne stood watching her. It was as if in its flying course an invisible flame had swept over him, for the brief glimpse of her face had thrilled him suddenly and profoundly. Only two or three times before had that curious experience befallen him, for he was not easily attracted by women. He stood now, immovable, gazing after her with flushed face, till she vanished round the corner of the house: then he turned back into the inn, his senses resounding with the impression of her. In a few minutes, he reappeared, pre-ceded by the slim point of his rod. He had put on his waders and an old cap stuck with one or two gaudy salmon-flies; a creel hung at his left side. His emotion at the sight of the beautiful girl had died down; he was calm again, and now he began to make his way down the little garden path under the elm-trees, carefully pointing the wavering tip of the rod into the spaces between the thick hanging foliage. At the river's edge he paused to survey again the grey and golden bridge whose four stone arches towered above him a stone's throw away to his right. Under the two nearest, at this time of the year, there was nothing but dry gravel, thickly overgrown near the bank with a jungle of wild rhubarb. Under the third, the water, brown and clear as ale, babbled shallow over the pebbles. It was only under the fourth, where it washed the farther bank, that the water was deep.

Dunne clambered down, holding his rod carefully in front of him, and began to push through the great funnel-shaped rhubarb leaves. Then, crunching across the gravel-bed, he waded through the shallows to a little island within a short cast of a round pool, the very place for a trout. He had watched them rising there on the previous evening as he stood, an hour after his arrival, leaning idly over the parapet of the bridge. It was a deep, round pool, slowly stirred by a circular eddy which swung the streaks of floating spume into narrowing whorls, so that it looked, from above, like a huge polished ammonite. He had decided to fish upstream from that point.

It was years, four years at least, since he had last had a day's fishing, but as he began casting up to the head of the pool, he recovered at once that delicious mood peculiar to the fisherman—mood composed of conscious craft, expectation, and at the same time a quiet passivity laying the mind open to streams of thoughts and ideas which flow through the brain easily as the flowing of the river, washing it clean of complexities.

The breeze had almost died down. Not a fish was stirring. And, moving slowly upstream, he worked leisurely on for half an hour without getting a single bite. But just as he reached the lower end of another promising pool—a gently swirling pool fed by a narrow and copious flow—the breeze freshened again and the day clouded over. It was ideal now—grey, and with just the right purl on the water.

The fish were beginning to feed. A small one rose in the pool a few yards from where he stood; then, just under the bank, another, a larger one. The sudden musical splash sounded clear and sharp above the monotonous babbling of the water. Then, as though his line were a nerve identifying the finger that held it with every movement of the floating fly, he felt three electric tugs. The end of his rod curved into a hoop, and he began to play the trout.

It was only, he knew at once, a small one—something over a quarter of a pound perhaps; and, though it fought gamely, as a trout always does, Dunne landed it at once. It lay for a moment motionless on the pebbles with helpless, gaping mouth: but as he stooped to take hold of it, suddenly it began to twist and wriggle, tense as a steel spring. Dunne caught it, grasping the firm, wincing body in his left hand while with his right he began to work the hook free of its mouth, twisting and wrenching the pale, talc-like flesh. Then, stooping again, he struck its head against a stone. It lay motionless in his palm now, a limp, exquisite shape of silver, gold, and brown. The delicate cucumber scent of it rose to his nostrils. Between a quarter and half a pound he thought, and dropped it into his creel.

A few minutes later, soon after he had begun to cast again, Dunne experienced a curious repetition of the physical sensation of striking the soft, unresisting creature against the stone. A little shudder ran through his vitals. Curious! Could it have been something disagreeable in the sound of it, or in the sense of the too hard striking the too soft? He shuddered again, but less perceptibly, and then the ceaseless tinkle of the water smoothed the faint scar from his mind. Peaceably, incoherently his thoughts swirled with the swirling clusters of bubbles.

But soon he was thinking coherently again. What was it that happened when he struck the trout's head against the stone and all its exquisite mechanism stopped for ever? Was it nothing more than that he broke the delicate motor housed in the little box in the skull? No more than the smashing of a watch? Years ago, old Mr Worston, the peppery old gentleman who always gave him a sovereign when he went back to school after the summer holidays, smashed his watch against the wall in Hexham station because it was slow and had made him miss the express. Smash! Swinging it the full length of the heavy gold chain. A pulp of little gold wheels and broken glass. Delightful thought! It had delighted him as a boy and it delighted him still. But a watch is hard. To smash something hard . . . a bottle or an egg against a wall . . . how satisfying! But to hit a fish . . . a limp, soft fish . . . and alive! Another faint shudder. All the leaves on the river bank hissed and rustled suddenly: hurrying grey spearheads shot along the surface of the stream. The wind was freshening.

A twitch. A palpitating tug. He had hooked another; and a few minutes after that there was another, and then another—a much larger one. Such a game one it was that Dunne thought for a moment that it must be a salmon-trout. When he landed it, the hook was fixed in the extreme tip of the lower jaw: it was a wonder it had held. A fine fish, fully a pound, the tarnished silver sides spotted with rose. Dunne gazed at it fascinated, curiously inspecting the staring, expressionless eyes, set like the work of a master jeweller in the subtly moulded bronze of the head. The slippery body thrilled and stiffened spasmodically in his clenched fingers. Its slipperiness was beginning already to grow viscous against his palm. The foolish mouth gaped patiently, sufferingly, and Dunne suddenly recalled the blanched, tight-lipped mouth of a dying man whom, years ago, he had visited in hospital. He felt his heart contract under his ribs. Then, throwing off his morbid fancies, he stooped down and struck the trout's head against a stone, as he had struck the other. The body stiffened: the tail curved up tensely like a spring. He struck it again and then loosened his grip. The second blow had done it: the body was limp and flaccid now: the life was gone.

Gone where? Could the life be something distinct from the body actuated . . . could it fly out and escape from the killed fish? A shadow . . . a little puff of cigarette-smoke, detaching itself from the fish's mouth . . . floating away? Life must be the same as what some people call the soul. . . . The immortality of the soul. . . . A fish's soul. . . . Jesu, lover of my soul. A flood of the emotion which that hymn always produced in him as a boy. Ancient memories . . . sentimental . . . absurd!

A touch on his face, soft, fluttering. Here he was, standing up to his thighs in water, fishing. A gust of wind was furrowing the water and blowing his line along in a great bow. He reeled in a few yards of it. The breeze stiffened: all his fisherman's skill was needed now, and for the next few minutes his attention was concentrated on throwing a clean line in defiance of the breeze. But it had only been a momentary flurry: soon it had swept on downstream and with the return of calm Dunne dropped back into his former line of thought. . . .

Fishes are cold-blooded creatures without feeling. A comforting idea, but false—mere metaphor and simile drawn from human experience. We know nothing outside our own narrow circle of experience, can never escape into the universal where everything is true and equal. A simple thing to beat the life out of a trout; and yet, when we have done it, what have we done? A mystery. A tremendous act of whose consequences we know nothing. Who can tell? perhaps the death of a fish changes irrevocably the whole hidden scheme of things. And yet, wherever there is life, there must be death. All life devours life, even the sheep and cows that munch grass. Life feeding on life. Life destroying life that it may live. An endless process . . . process . . progress . . . progression . . . the scheme of things . . . stream of things. . . .

The stream had caught his mind again, caressing it, floating it safely away from all those jarring, sharp-edged thoughts. But now the fish had stopped taking and during the next hour Dunne caught nothing. Yet he fished on, soothed by the peacefully sliding river, his mind sliding with the water over rough and smooth, deep and shallow. Then, discovering that he was hungry, he looked at his watch and began to wade towards the bank.

There he sat down and took out his flask and sandwiches. But before beginning to eat he opened his creel, tumbled out the contents, and arranged them in a row on the grass. They were a nice lot—seven fish ranging from a quarter to half a pound and, at the end, the noble one-pounder. They were dull and gummy now; their clean slipperiness was gone, their iridescence faded. Dunne gazed at them until his mind slipped out of the grooves of habit and again he was gazing at fish for the first time in his life. Strange, unbelievable creatures; mysterious slips of life, swift and spear-like, marvellously designed and coloured. He stared at their eyes; for a man, baffled by man or beast, always stares at the eye, that smouldering window of the spirit, and there finds some partial answer to his question. But these quaint metallic disks, stark as the painted eyes of a mask, told him nothing except that their secret was undiscoverable or that there was nothing to discover. They did not even rebuke him, like the eye of a dead bird or animal, for snatching them from their secret world and slaughtering them. Dunne sighed and next moment shrugged his shoulders. After all, such questions as he was asking have no answer. Neither philosophy nor religion casts any light on them. To what category, then, can they belong? To poetry, perhaps: and Dunne, being no poet, but a solicitor and a fisherman, threw the trout back one by one into the creel and began to eat his sandwiches.

The sun came out. He looked anxiously at the sky: this would play the devil with his afternoon. But meanwhile it was delicious to feel its warmth on his back, stealing through coat and shirt. He finished his last sandwich, lit a cigarette, and leaned back full length on the grass. Although the sun was still shining, clouds covered more than half the sky: there was certainly some hope, now, for the afternoon. A luxurious drowsiness overcame him: he closed his eyes for a moment, then opened them again. Then he closed them again, and this time they remained closed. The cigarette fell from his fingers and lay twining a blue spiral among the tall green glass-blades. . . .

He was still fishing. The little brass rings on his rod had sprouted into green leaf-buds. He was fishing in a stream of liquid gold, the Gulf Stream. All at once he noticed that his line was running out noiselessly . . . longer . . . longer . . . longer. He clasped it to the butt of the rod, gripped it with all his strength. When he had almost

given up hope, he succeeded at last in holding it. Then slowly he
began to reel in, and as he did so the reel tinkled a little tune like a
musical-box. It was a heavy fish—a pound at least. He reeled away
strenuously until he had reeled the cast right out of the water.

A beautiful wooden fish, streaked with scarlet and blue, hung
from the end of it. A Chinese fish. Each eye was a gold disk with a
daisy in the centre of it. He began to sway the rod so that the fish
swung to and fro. When it was at the top of its swing he suddenly
dipped the rod and the fish dropped on the bank. But the moment
it touched earth it began to cry—a horrible human cry. "No! No!"
it cried. "No! No! No!" He stood staring at it, appalled, not daring
to touch it. Then, bracing himself, he suddenly put his foot on it
and immediately swooped upon it to remove the hook. The fish did
not move, but its mouth opened and shut spasmodically like an
automatic toy and, to his horror, it began to cry again. But soon
its voice flagged, died away, fainter . . . fainter. . . . It had become
almost inaudible when suddenly, as if summoning its last strength,
it shouted aloud a single sharp "Ah!"

Dunne awoke. A shaggy dog stood looking at him, wagging
its tail. He held out his hand to it and sat up, but the dog flounced
away and trotted off along the bank with its tail down. Dunne
looked about him. The sun had gone in: conditions were perfect
once again. He felt refreshed and clear-headed after his sleep and,
scrambling to his feet, he pocketed his flask, took up his rod and
creel, and began to work slowly downstream.

During the afternoon he added eight good fish to his catch, and
by five o'clock he had got back to the point from which he had
started. He reeled in and, securing his cast, waded to the bank.
He was looking forward to showing the fish to old Wales. Mrs
Wales would fry the best of them for dinner: she knew how to fry
trout perfectly, rolling them first in oatmeal and serving them
with melted butter. He climbed up the bank to the little path and,
with his rod pointed in front of him, began to make his way
cautiously under the elm-trees. In the creel behind him a trout
not yet dead kept up a dry, persistent rustling.

As he came out in front of the inn he became aware of something
unusual. A little group of people was moving towards the door.
They were stooping as if carrying something. A few yards from
the bridge an empty motor stood at the roadside.

When Dunne came up with the moving group they had reached
the inn door. They were carrying something laid on a large sack,
as on a stretcher, and with a sudden constriction of the heart he
caught sight, between two of the bearers, of an end of brown skirt
hanging over the edge of the sack. Hardly knowing what he did,
he propped his rod against the house-wall and, turning his back on

the door, walked away towards the standing car. His instinct had been to escape from something unbearable. Then, pausing dazed where the road dipped from the bridge, he saw lying at the roadside between him and the car a white-handled umbrella. He stooped and gently picked it up and began to carry it to the inn. He felt vaguely that he had found something that he could do for her.

The bearers had vanished indoors. Dunne entered the stone-flagged hall with its pleasant, humble smell of beer and sawdust. A group of women—Mrs Wales and the three servants—stood with their backs to him at an open door, their heads craning into a great bare room. It was a room unused except in summer-time when large parties came to the inn for lunch or tea. Several people were inside. A table was being moved. Dunne, still holding her umbrella, paused beside the women.

"What happened?" he whispered.

One of the maids turned a white face to him. "The car knocked her down," she replied. "It must have come on her when she was crossing the road."

Another turned. "They come so unexpected over that bridge," she said.

Old Mrs Wales was leaning against the door-post with her apron to her eyes. Dunne touched her arm. "Is she . . . is she much hurt?" he asked.

The old woman raised her bleared face from the apron and stared at him vacantly. Then her chin began to tremble. "Hurt? She's dead, poor thing!" she whispered.

Twenty-five years later Dunne himself died. He was a bachelor, and his things went to his nephews. They had spent several days in his house, going through cupboards and drawers. Last of all they looked into the attic. It was half dark, but one of them rummaging among old hat-boxes and portmanteaux, pulled out a creel and a fishing-rod in a canvas case. Both the creel and the case were cloaked with the grey wool of cobwebs.

"I say, look at this!" the young man called to his brother. "I never knew the Uncle was a fisherman."

From *Sir Pompey and Madame Juno*

Bleak

Izaak Walton

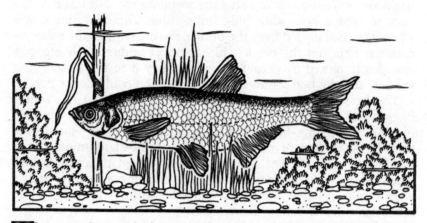

There is also a Bleak, or fresh-water sprat, a fish that is ever in motion, and therefore called by some the river-swallow; for just as you shall observe the swallow to be most evenings in summer ever in motion, making short and quick turns when he flies to catch flies in the air, by which he lives, so does the bleak at the top of the water. Ausonius would have him called bleak from his whitish colour: his back is of a pleasant sad or sea-water green, his belly white and shining as the mountain snow; and doubtless, though he have the fortune, which virtue has in poor people, to be neglected, yet the bleak ought to be much valued, though we want Allamot salt, and the skill that the Italians have to turn them into anchovies. This fish may be caught with a Paternoster line; that is, six or eight very small hooks tied along the line, one half a foot above the other: I have seen five caught thus at one time, and the bait has been gentles, than which none is better.

Or this fish may be caught with a fine small artificial fly, which is to be of a very sad brown colour, and very small, and the hook answerable. There is not better sport than whipping for bleaks in a boat, or on a bank, in the swift water, in a summer's evening, with a hazel top about five or six foot long, and a line twice the length of the rod. I have heard Sir Henry Wotton say, that there be many that in Italy will catch swallows so, or especially martins; this bird-angler standing on the top of a steeple to do it, and with a line twice as long as I have spoken of. And let me tell you, scholar, that both martins and bleaks be most excellent meat.

From *The Complete Angler*

An Early Spring Day with "Bob"

William Nelson

After passing through the village of whitewashed houses we turned down to the river through the farmyard, and into the wood, under whose big trees I used to see old Dick so mysteriously disappear on June nights just as dusk was setting in.

Before reaching our fly water we had a good long mile to walk, but I knew "Bob" would be talking all the way and noticing everything. The opening days of spring set the blood of this middle-aged man a-tingling very much in the same way that it affected all the wild things in wood and water.

I shall never forget that glorious morning—*the* red letter day in a long fishing life. The spring sun was shining through the leafless elms and chestnuts, and striking the clean, scaly, russet trunks of the great Scotch firs. Well Bank Wood was alive with the excited, mating twitter of small birds, and the thrushes were singing in the tree tops. Otherwise all was still, and we might well have thought that we were miles away from a busy working world. We met no one, and most likely would not do so until we got back to the village at night.

This was my first real outing with "Bob," and the outcome of the promise that when the rudiments of casting had been mastered he would take me to fresh water. The winter evening apprentice was now on the way to actual practice and felt serenely happy. I remember trying to keep step with him, so imbued was I with the idea of living up to the great honour he was doing me. The consciousness of a certain timing of the master's stride was present, and I noticed how his right foot always seemed to drop into its proper resting-place, as we crossed the rough ditches, without any interruption to the rhythm of his pace.

Shortly we emerged from the old wood into a large, open, rough pasture, where the peewits flew around us, and the curlews rose with swift flight and plaintive cry from the marshy places.

Wild Boar Fell at the southern end of the valley came into view, and "Bob" remarked that, as the night mist was rising to its top, we should have a fine day. "If ivver yer to be a fisherman worth yer saut ye'll hev to ken summat aboot t' weather." It is of no use trying to give expression to "Bob" apart from the dialect. He is only to be realised in his own words, and what is known in the north country as the lilt of them.

He said in regard to early spring fishing that the weather did not matter so much then as later on. "Ah've often hed a real good day when t' sleet and snow was blawen i' mi faice, and mi fingers were so cauld ah could hardly tee on a fresh flee." He talked about the quietness and often of the absence of visible rise of the fish at this time of the year, and before they had got their full strength. "Sometimes ye'll not see a fish risen all t' day through, but ye may be

sure they'll be feeden efter t' sun's up at tail et streams and in t'
flats. In wild stormy weather t' flees ther feeden on often come doon
to them from t' rough streams hauf drooned and under t' watter.
It's nea use fishen in t' strang watter at this time o' year."

He spoke about a strong rise of flies, like Duns or March Browns,
sometimes occurring during the afternoon in April, and the trout
feeding on them voraciously. "If it's March Broons ah put on a
Partridge and Orange, and if it's Duns ah put on a Blue Hawk."

"If ye finnd trout are not feedin' et top, which is likely eneugh at
this time o' t' year, let yer flees sink and keep a sharp watch on t'
line. It'll straighten befoor ye feel owt, but ye mun allus strike
quietly doon t' stream baith et seet and touch."

We were almost at our starting point, and stepping over a wide
field runner when we saw a dead heron lying in the rushes. "Bob"
remarked in passing, "Nivver on any account stoop down to pick
up a langneck that isn't dead. They strike straight at yer eyes, and
are good shots."

By this time we had arrived at the first of "Bob's" favourite
reaches, a long, quiet, gently flowing, flat shallow at our side,
and deepening towards the far, high wooded bank to four or five
feet of water. He decided that we should both put on a light Snipe
at the tail of the cast, a Blue Hawk on the middle dropper, a Partridge
and Orange on the top dropper, and that he would start in where
we were and fish to the top of Black Scar Dub, and that I could get
in at the first flat above him.

"Ye mun use a short line, fish up and across towards t' far bank,
and mind ye keep raisen t' point o' yer rod efter t' flees are on t'
watter, but doan't click back as ther fawen. Ye'll freeten t' fish if
they see a row o' flies trailen ower their heeds. Yer cast mun come
doon wi t' watter, and when it's gitten a yard or twea below ya and
beginnin' to trail throw again."

Have you ever seen a novice standing at the side of the tee to watch a great golfer drive off? Well, it was in like manner that I watched "Bob" wade carefully in, and make a few preliminary casts over the water above him. This was carrying out to the letter what he had often told his apprentices. "Nivver alloo yersels, lads, to splash into t' middle et stream reet off. Ye'll often finnd t' trout feeden et edge just where it's shallow and varra tempten to waide. Ye'll be tekken for a toonsman if ye dea that. Them chaps is nivver content without they're up to t' top of ther waiders."

He flicked out several sharp dexterous casts up by the low, near bushes, gradually, at the same time slightly, lengthening his line, and just when he seemed to have satisfied himself on this point, and without, to me, any apparent strike, a trout was drawn quietly into his net. There was next to no sign of disturbance in the water, and very little movement of the body and arms. With a short step upwards and outwards the rhythmic movement of the forearm went on again; so quietly that, if you had not known he was there, he might easily have been mistaken in his faded suit, and at short distance, for a bleached old tree-stump.

Turning away to my own job it struck me forcibly how much more there was in fishing than the mere casting of a straight line.

On the reach allotted me I managed to get hold of an odd trout or two here and there on the Snipe, and a few annoying smelts on the gay Partridge and Orange. Natural excitement, and too heavy striking, undoubtedly accounted for the loss of several fish, but I was having my first good time and could have stayed where I was all day.

Shortly "Bob" was passing behind me, well back on the bank, and on the way to his next reach, when he shouted, "It's time ye gave them a rist theer noo. Come oot and strike in abune me." The lesson he wanted to teach me was that too continuous flogging of a small stretch of water does not pay. The trout get alarmed, and particularly is this so in the comparatively small upper waters of the Eden when a novice is at work. Since that time, in the larger, lower Eden, I have often spent a whole day in one big stream without unduly alarming the fish.

When I came out, and was following him, a trifle too near his shallow side perhaps, he was at it again. "Keep weel back, it's raither glishy and they'll aither see ye or yer shadow on t' bank." I have often wished since that day that some of the fishermen one meets on the river nowadays could have had a few early lessons of the kind from "Bob."

Making, therefore, a wide detour, I crossed at the stream below the Scar, and waded in as soon as I could above the deep pool. I know now how unselfish "Bob" was not to go straight to that particularly fine stretch himself. In the days that were to come it was destined to be one of my choicest reaches.

The take had considerably improved as the early spring day reached its warmest hours, and I did much better here than in the flat below where I wanted to stay. But there was a sharpish wind blowing in my face from this side, and probably partly owing to excitement I was putting too much brute force into the casting, the tail fly in consequence was every now and then, curling back towards me.

In passing me again "Bob" stopped for a moment, noticed this, and said, "Yer forcen yer rod ower much, be a bit quieter in yer throwin' and keep yer elbow in." With that he went his way again, and after a short interval I followed to watch him fish a length of water rather too deep to wade from our side.

It was a gently flowing, dark piece, with gaps between the alder bushes along the stretch of its bank. "Bob" approached these gaps very quietly, with a few quick curls of his line behind his head, as if trying to dry it, and then, stepping lightly forward, he dropped his flies on the water above him, at an angle of not more than thirty degrees to the bank, that they might come down well under it. Each cast either hooked a trout or was quickly repeated from gap to gap.

He fished the length without much waste of time, and at the end remarked, "Ye should nivver pass such spots at this time o' t' year if yer fishen up. They doan't tak much time and often carry good fish."

We had now reached the bend of the river opposite the old barn-like church of the neighbouring village, and sat down together to eat our sandwiches. From this corner we could see both up and down the river. "Bob's" big wooden pannier was half full of nice trout, and I proudly opened mine to show him that I had not altogether failed. He picked out two or three of the smallest and explained in his quiet humorous way that they were "raither smaw" and would have been better left in t' watter to grow a bit. "Ah's nut finden any faut wi' ye noo, but some day ye'll come to leuk on t' as murder to tak t' babbys oot o' t' watter in t' spring. If ye tak t' smaw uns at any time thers not much eatin' on them. But ah's pleased to see yev takken nea smelts. Live and let live's a good motto, and wi' mun remember t' salmon fishers."

At our feet was a gently flowing pool fed by a strong rough stream from above. This stream was skirted on our side by a high grassy bank, between which, and the strong middle stream, ran a quiet dark flat for a length of about eighty yards. On the opposite bank, in the inner bend of the river, was a long gravel bed, skirting both the pool below and the stream above.

As we sat eating our lunch we noticed odd trout just pricking the surface of this stream-flat. In a few minutes a big rise of March Browns came on below the bank sheltering the flat, and it was soon alive with rising trout. I wanted at once to be up and at them, but "Bob's" reply was that there was too much of a rise there for fish to see any odd fly we could drop amongst them. He said, however, that it would be well for him to cross and try them, but that, first of all, he would substitute a Partridge and Orange for his Light Snipe tail fly.

On taking off the Snipe he put it carefully back in his book, re-marking that he did not believe in the lazy fashion of sticking odd flies in his hat. "It's a way o' spoilen good gut." He then waded over to the other side, at a place where it would have been too deep for me, and began to fish the flat where the big rise was then taking place. Watching him I was surprised to notice that he only got a couple of trout.

Then, leaving the rough stream, he made his way across the inner angle of the bend to the bottom of the pool below. Keeping well back on the bank I followed down to a place opposite his new start, and expressed surprise at the failure above. "Oh! ye'll get used to that soort a thing in time. Ah think they'll dea summat here wher t' flees are comen doon under t' watter hauf drooned." There was not a ripple to be seen on this lower pool, but the steady quiet flow of deepish water, with a few little ships of white froth on it, showing a quiet pace in the middle, and a slightly more urgent movement towards the outer, deep bend.

"Bob's" intuition, or experience, or whatever one may like to call it, was not at fault. Wading in no more than knee-deep, and fishing almost directly across water, from the bottom to the top of the pool, he caught fish after fish. When he found they were doing so well he called. "Come and tak my plaice and ah'll watch ye." I felt, however, that there was some mystery I could not fathom attached to his method, and that it would be wise to remain a looker-on and await explanations.

When he at last came out, and I questioned him, he replied, "They were takken t' flee under t' top o' t' watter. Ah hed to let me cast sink a bit. Ah know this plaice of old. It isn't first time ahve come across what heppened just noo. Thers lots o' sek like plaices on t' beck, and ye'll mebbe remimber, fra what yev seen, that there are lots o' feeden fish below strang streams at this time o' year that ye can't see brek t' top o' t' watter."

In the meantime I had changed my own tail fly, and we moved farther up, where "Bob" sat down and lit his pipe and watched me get a few more trout behind the island; remarking at the finish that I ought to be quieter in netting my fish. "Doan't show t' net

ower much. Stand quietly and hod it riddy for them under t' watter
as ye draw them in. Ye should allus dip yer net heed oot o' seet.
The hooks are nobbut smaw things and it's better not to scare yer
trout wi' t' net. In t' flat spring watter they see ye mair than in t'
streams later on, and they'll generally come alang quietly eneugh
if yer nut waiving things aboot."

These and many other dictums were of the kind "Bob" employed in the course of his teaching. They were always practical
and to the point, and bit so deep, at that time, into an uncrowded
memory that recalling them requires no conscious effort.

We were both nature lovers, and the joy of the river itself was
but a practical part of our pleasure—even as the chasing on the
links of a little white ball. It gave us an object which led us through
sun-warmed fields and dark woods, and on to pleasant headlands,
where we could rest and look around at the glorious country we
called "home."

On the particular day of which I speak, and as we trudged back,
the rooks were gathering together in great flocks on the hilly fields.
Some fields were black with them, and they appeared to me like a
great army standing at attention for the command of its general.
We stood watching them for a minute or two, admiring the glossy
black of their feathers, and then, the signal being given, perhaps
by some old centenarian rook, they all rose together, breaking
with loud cawing the curious waiting silence of the moment before,
and making straight for their ancient home in the great Ash Trees
of the Castle Park.

From *Fishing in Eden*

Action Begins

Michael Mason

The sun blazed down from a sky of scorching molten blue and shone up from the deep blue water. The shore was a line of living green, from the tall coconut-palms. Boobies, frigate-birds and occasional pelicans were in the air, and now and then our bait-lines started to shake and we reeled in bonito or other fish suitable for marlin-bait. Bonito are the best, for their flesh is hard and firm. Most of them run from 3 lbs. to 6 lbs.—and they are the same tunny-fish as in the Mediterranean and the Bay of Biscay. They sometimes run to 18 lbs. but are not to be confused with the giant bluefin, yellowfin and bigeye tuna found in the same waters.

These were cleverly sewn up by Oliver, with a large hook inside them, and streamed from the outriggers. I will describe the method in detail later. We sometimes went to one reef or both, and always came back with some catch of good fish. But more and more we were fishing for the blue marlin in the blue water and catching only bonito and other bait-fish. We never saw a marlin. And the days slid by.

At last, Doctor Baillie suggested that I should go up much further, to the S.W. point of the island; that he, Oliver and I should sleep in the boat and Jim should remain ashore. We did this, taking a basket of provisions and enough petrol; but the first day we caught nothing special.

We anchored off a Negro village, and the people came out to us in an amazing flotilla of small boats—some of them well made dug-outs and some just bits of wood pinned together somehow. They paddled these, rowed them and sometimes sailed with a crude sort of lug-lateen rig; and these men were very skilful boatmen.

A pleasant, simple, friendly people. Not very pretty to look at but childlike and likeable, though I found it hard to understand their talk. Doctor Baillie altered his speech to suit them, and so did Oliver to a lesser degree. It was English but much altered. Oliver asked if they had seen any 'piper', which was their local name for a blue marlin. They hadn't for quite some days, but they thought there might be one or two round Booby Island. These poorly equipped people, who lived partly from the sea and partly from their primitive farming enterprises, had not the lines or the boats to enable them to fight a 'piper'. They simply cut the line and their loss.

They were mostly very poor, and neither had nor ever thought of having more equipment than was sufficient to keep themselves and their dependants alive. They had a perfect climate, so they worked as little as possible, enjoyed the sea breezes and the rustle of the palm-leaves, ate enough, and never bothered about cudgelling their limited intellects more than absolutely necessary. The factory clock-puncher can well envy them. They just sat in the sun and smiled. Who dares to say they were unwise?

The Doctor seemed to know them all and asked the Head man of the village on board with three or four others. They were very agreeable and well-behaved, and the Head man seemed an intelligent and responsible person. Baillie gave them glasses and handed them the whisky to pass round and help themselves. They did so, happily but moderately. We spent the night "sleeping rough" but comfortable on floorboards and wooden bunks. No night is really uncomfortable if you are not cold, or shackled in chains, or in pain or fever, or under sentence of death, or worrying about someone else.

Next day, it poured with a real tropic rainstorm. We dried ourselves and our clothes by peeling everything off and hanging it up when the sun came out again. We came to Booby Island—which was just another little bit of land sticking out of the sea, covered with waving feathery palm trees. Frigate-birds soared majestically over our heads and boobies flew up and down among a few terns and gulls.

Suddenly, a remarkably violent snatch on one of the baitrods. Oliver instantly said, "Get into the chair. It's a dolphin." I took the rod and fixed the butt in the socket. There was no need for the harness belt, for the rod and line were very light and a dolphin is not very big. This one weighed under 20 lbs. But, by gum, he did fight!

Much has been written about the beauty of the dolphin, but no poet that ever was foaled could do justice to the glorious colours of this extraordinary fish. While he is fighting he fights like hell, and as he is a surface fish he often breaks water and sometimes jumps well clear—always fighting with tremendous power, considering his weight. Every jump he makes, and all his continual contacts with the surface as he fights, are decorated by wonderful flashes of blazing golden yellow, brilliant electric iridescent green, and strong streaks and patches of vivid blue. Not only is the fish all these colours at once, but the water he moves through as he fights assumes something of these colours too. There is no room for wonder that the hard-cased old shellbacks of the sailing era, and even the mutton-headed Captains and officers, blind as beetles to the wonders they so often beheld, were so impressed by the dolphin that they sometimes did try to express the impact his beauty had made upon them. Clumsily, one may be sure, but with a genuine, earnest conviction which somehow connected and impressed people who had never seen the fish. So it became a common heraldic emblem among people and institutions concerned with the sea.

The Spaniards call it *dorado* (golden) because that furiously shining gold is perhaps the strongest colour of the three. They made more of it than the English sailors because Spaniards have more natural poetry than Englishmen. They get it from their Moorish-Arab blood in greater part and from their Latin blood in a smaller degree. We Englishmen have little poetry in our make-up but admire it in others (even if it is damnably inferior), but we have a natural feeling of compassion towards the animals, birds and even fishes which we always take for granted were given to us by God to prey upon and exploit. Such a beautiful thing as a dolphin makes an impression, first by its beauty and later by its pathos, upon the hardest heart and dullest intellect.

The fish came in, still fighting gamely and with amazing strength —but he came in. Oliver snatched him out with the small gaff and he lay gasping and flapping on the floorboards of the cockpit. An Irishman, Oliver naturally has a 'priest' of heavy blackthorn for killing big fish. One blow of this and that beautiful dolphin—shining like a straight flush of humming-birds in three wonderful colours— died. And the colours died with him. One minute he was alive, blazing with colour—three minutes later he was dead. Just a dead fish, and rather an ugly one at that. It was as if a lovely light had gone out. I was looking down upon a fine big fish, true—but a dull, mud-coloured thing.

The dolphin is what the pundits call "laterally compressed". That sounds an unkind thing to happen to a fish, but it really means he is narrow sideways and tall up and down. Almost a flat-fish turned edgeways again. His face is very ugly. He has a cruel, pre-datory mouth with small but very effective teeth, no chin, but an immense, high forehead in the bull-fish and a more sloping one in the female. The forehead is most impressive. It makes one think of Charles Darwin and Sir Oliver Lodge. A great rising dome, cram-med with tremendous thoughts. But laterally compressed. Still, this narrowness of habit probably helps the dolphin in going through the water, for he is entirely fish-eating and his tail is a rather mingy little affair with small narrow flukes. He lives on flying-fish and others of similar size or smaller. His mouth is not very big. But he is swift enough to catch anything he fancies. The smaller ones hunt in big shoals.

Well, to catch a dolphin is quite something. I have caught many since then, on light lines. They are the most beautiful fish in the sea, though never very big or at all shapely. But they fight like mad— and, watching them die, I have felt rather like King Henry VIII seeing Sir Andrew Barton's severed head and wishing so brave an enemy might come to life again.

> "Fight on, my men," said Sir Andrew Barton,
> "I am hurt, but I am not slain.
> I'll lay me down, bleed awhile,
> And then I'll rise and fight again."

King Hal had many failings, but lack of courage was not among them. He could appreciate sheer guts, even in a Scottish pirate.

Fishermen seeking for dolphins often visit any floating object, such as a wooden beam or box, especially if there is weed attached to it. It is thought that the little fish that surround these objects attract the dolphin; but the dolphin has a natural manner of curiosity which is often his undoing. When hooked, he often leaps to show you what you've got on the line and then makes a run of fantastic speed. You would think a 10 lbs. dolphin was four times that weight by the power and energy of his rush. But if one considers the shape of this fish compared to that of a tuna one will see that the latter, with his thick strong body, has little flexibility to give him driving force other than his very powerful tail on its very slim peduncle. The thin-bodied dolphin can wriggle his whole body and combine strength of tail with the swimming action of a ling or a conger eel.

Dolphins are common in the warmer oceans of the world and the smaller ones run in schools of hundreds. The biggest of them are not known to weigh much more than 70 lbs. There are many millions of dolphins in the sea, with no immediate danger of any sudden shortage of supply. Like a swordfish, any dolphin you catch is something tremendously worth catching. Though he is not big— and quite apart from the sheer glamour of this beautiful creature —it would not be unreasonable to claim the dolphin as one of the finest game fish for his weight in the oceans of the world. A dolphin over 20 lbs. is reckoned a big one. But size is not everything.

Some confusion is naturally caused in people's minds by the word 'dolphin', for not only is it applied to the true fish just described but also to several species of smaller whales (*delphinidae*, in the bastard Latin of scientists), ranging from the familiar little porpoise, the blackfish or pilot whale, up to twenty-eight feet in length, and even including the terrible killer whale (*orca gladiator*), which exceeds thirty feet, and the narwhal with his long ivory spear. This doesn't help to make things easier, but most people are sensible enough to call everything they see jumping 'porpoises'. Most of the species of dolphins running in great schools and jumping freely have shorter or longer beaks, rather flattened. All are true whales (*cetacea*), breathing through the tops of their heads.

The fish-dolphin, or *dorado*, is also named *coryphaena*. A good name for a call-girl—but I prefer 'dorado' for the fish, and will use it from now on.

It was just south of Booby Island where the marlin rose and struck, all in an instant. I did not see it, but Oliver suddenly shouted and galvanised me into action, though I was still only half-aware of what I had to do and what was involved in doing it.

The bonito bait, streaming about thirty yards from the starboard quarter, was gone with the big fish; the piece of stopping-cotton had parted from the outrigger tip and the twenty-four-thread line was reeling freely off the rod in the nearby socket, offering no resistance to the fish. This rod was quickly moved into position on the fighting chair, which I got into and snapped the belt round my back and on to the reel while Doctor Baillie, Oliver and Clifford madly wound in all other lines—clearing the deck for action.

The line went spinning wildly from the reel for what seemed like minutes but was really only seconds. From three to four hundred yards of it must have gone when Oliver said, "Clamp on the brake. Strike!" I clamped it on and struck—once, twice, and again.

Afar off, nearly a quarter of a mile away, a great, blue, shining fish leaped from the water—his own ten feet of length above the surface—and leaped again and again: beautiful, swift and incredibly strong. Never an enemy: but an antagonist, and a worthy one—like a good man in a twenty-four-foot square ring.

We settled down to fight. From the moment I clamped down the brake on the reel, according to IGFA rules, nobody was allowed to touch me or the rod or line until the wire cast, or leader, came up to the tip of the rod. The only help I was allowed was having my chair turned on its pintle to face the direction of the line. Clifford stood behind me and did this. Oliver stood alert and in command, muttering and swearing and keeping control. Eric, the coxswain, kept the boat in the best position—which was mostly at speed 'stop', for the fish was fighting astern. Doctor Baillie—wise man—stood watching and never said a word.

The first thing I realised was that I had to use not brute strength but patience and judgment. The belt round my back was snapped to the reel. The reel was strongly clamped to the rod. The rod,

one hoped, was clamped to the fish by a line with a breaking-strain
—new and wet—of 75 lbs. With my back against the pull on the
rod and my feet against a wooden rest that turned with the chair,
I realised that with my strength I could fight such a fish all day.
But I had to reckon with the strength of line, and with the star-
shaped wheel on the reel Oliver had adjusted to stand the pull
without parting but to put quite a strain on the fish.

That fish fought like blue murder. I counted eight jumps in
about as many seconds. He ran off with more line, but every time
the pressure slackened a bit and the line stopped whining and
spinning away I was able to 'pump' a bit back again—lifting the
rod tip to get the line in and then reeling in swiftly as I bent it forward
again.

He was still a long way out, fighting like fury, when the line
parted. I had him hooked for eight minutes. When the slack line
came back, we saw it had been cut clean a long way from the fish.
Oliver thought it was probably a companion marlin, swimming
frenziedly about, that cut the line. These things happen. The best
attitude to take is to recognise that nothing can be lost if you have
never owned it. I certainly never owned that fish; I was only trying
to own it. But I had seen quite a bit of life in those eight minutes,
and we went home to England with a fixed determination to come
out again and catch a marlin and get him right into the boat. One
each, at least.

From *In Pursuit of Big Fish*

On Pike

Francis Francis

One of the great fishing authorities of the Victorian era
Francis Francis wrote several books including The Art of
Angling *(1867), and* Sporting Sketches *from which*
this extract is taken.

Dear J.,—*I've got a day on Lord Thompson's water for self and friend.*
I meant to go the first open day in February, so rig out some big
live snaps and watch the weather. I'll take the lunch, and I will leave the
drinks and baits to you.

Thine Piscatorially . . .

Thus I wrote, some years ago, to my friend J., a slayer of mighty pike, indeed, his friends call him "Jack-the-Giant killer". Now, I am not going to tell you where Lord Thompson's water is—old pike fishers keep these things to themselves; and you need not look for Lord Thompson's name in the peerage, and so on to his country seat, because it isn't in it, and I shan't give what old Nicholas used to call "my sportive readers" a chance to mob Lord T. with letters for asking permission. The cheek and perseverance of the London pike fisher in pursuit of permissions for his recreation is unbounded; and the ingenious multiplicity of pleas which he will put in to a perfect stranger, of whom he knows nothing save that he has some pike fishing, is wonderful.

Old D., the well-known cricketer, was a desperate hand at ferreting out permissions; but he got a rebuff once, which made him look all round the compass, and wonder whether he was D. or someone else who had been "stumped" for a "duck's egg". There was a grand match on at Lord's, and old Squire L. of L. always attended all the matches at Lord's. D. happened to hear that he had about the best pike fishing in the Kingdom, but was rather "sticky" in giving orders; but thinking that when he got him well on in a chat over his favourite pastime he might slip in a request for a day, he laid his plans accordingly. The stumps were set; the match about to begin; old D. on the look out. When he saw the Squire drive up four-in-hand and enter the ground, D. carefully meandered round till he came upon him.

"Ah, D.! What sort of a match shall we have today?" and the conversation began; and D., who as a rule was a most disputatious cantankerous man, was highly deferential. The Squire was jolly chatty, and D. saw that day's fishing coming nearer and nearer. At length he made a dash for it.

"I hear, Squire, that you have some good pike fishing at L. I should like to try my luck there very much if you would allow me."

I have said the squire was "sticky" in giving permission, but "sticky" is not the word. He never gave permission at all save under very unusual circumstances. He hated to give leave; he didn't fish himself, but he couldn't abide to see any one else fishing. His countenance changed, and the *suaviter in modo* gave place to the *fortiter in re*, or perhaps *in modo* too, would be more correct.

"I keep my fishing for my friends, Mr D.," said the squire, frigidly, and with emphasis on the "friends" and the "mister"—"and you're not one of them—good morning," and off went the squire to back old D.'s tip, while D. said something naughty under his breath, and wished he had the squire before the wicket and without pads on.

Time went over; February set in mild but not too warm and sunny. The day was fixed; the morning came. An early repast of sausages, ham, toast, coffee, eggs, and marmalade, put me in fettle; a large luncheon basket, duly stuffed with varieties, another basket with sundries, a large double hand rush basket and a pair of rods made my outfit when I met J. at the Knockemdown station on the Pick-me-up-in-pieces line. J. was tremendously picturesque, and what with kettles, &c., &c., we looked like Robinson Crusoe and his man Friday in pursuit of the savages. J. was a prodigious smoker, and he had a bowsprit in the shape of a Regalia Elephanta about a foot or so long.

"*Standard*! *Telegraph*!" "Here, boy, give us both," and in five minutes J. was deep in the markets, and I was in the telegrams, as we sped on to our destination. At Bunkemout junction we found a trap waiting. A drive of three miles brought us to the keeper's cottage, a paradise of woodbine, china, roses, &c., in the summer, and pretty enough even now. Alfred was waiting for us, and getting the cans and baskets led the way down through a sunken lane with high sandy banks, across a field to a line of pollards, and there we were. It was a lovely backwater with a stage of bucks in the middle of it, and looked, as J. said, "doosedly like pike". There were holes and long eddies and shallows, with rushes and reeds here and there, and a proper complement of stubs and piles, of course put there on purpose to lose fish.

"Well, Alfred, got any fish for us today?"

"There be plenty there if you can catch 'em, sir. There's one as I do wish you may; he's the biggest I've sin here this many a day; he've yeat a hull brood o' ducks wi' the down for stuffin', drat 'im."

"What'll he weigh, Alfred?"

"He'll goo ower thirty pound, sir. He mostly lies in that long deep eddy by the pollards, just above the bucks, which is the wust thing in the way as can be; but there's plenty good ones aside he; we allus has 'em in here when there's a flood, and the big flood last month have stocked us finely. I think we'll put all the things we don't want to use under the wall by the bucks yanner," and he did so.

"I shall spin this lower reach below the bucks down, I think, J., unless you prefer to."

"No, I'll put on a live snap, and try the pool above the bucks," said J., and the rods being soon together, the tackle fixed, and the baits on, I turned down stream and began.

It was rather more streamy below the bucks, and that was why I chose spinning. I had, too, a recollection of a good fish I had lost formerly near a willow stump half way down, and good fish have a knack of always occupying a good lair. I had a Chapman spinner —one of Woods' pattern. It saves a lot of trouble—preserves the bait, and always spins fairly—and, as your tail triangle flies loose, it does not miss many fish. I now generally carry three or four of different sizes to suit the baits and the fish, and in five minutes thirty yards of line were flying across the water.

I don't mean to brag, but I learnt of the best master on the Thames, have practised a great deal, and think I do it pretty well. Across the stream with a slight splash, just to attract the fish's notice, and the bait comes spinning and whirling round in a seductive curve, as if it were going round a ball room in the Walpurgis Waltz. Once more the line is gathered in; a slight heave and a swing, and away flies the bait again, and along it comes like a streak of silver. The third time, as I was watching it, I saw a slight ridge in the water, and the bait seemed to disappear. There was a check, followed by "sshuck" from me, and I let him have it smartly. "Whizz!" and out went a dozen yards of line. One doesn't part with much, as a rule, to a pike; but this fellow, being in a stream, was a lively chap, and made a strong fight of it before I could get him near Alfred's landing net; but at length he got near enough, the net slipped under him, and out he came, a handsome six-pound fish, like a green tiger, and kicking like old Joe.

"Hi, hi, hi!" from J. broke in here.

"Run to Mr J. with the net; he's in a tidy fish by the bend of his rod," and Alfred sped away, while I straightened the dace on my Chapman, it being little damaged.

There seemed to be a little more difficulty with J.'s fish than mine, which was accounted for when Alfred came back with the intelligence that J. had broken his ice with a good ten-pounder.

Away flew my bait again clean across the water, dropping with a light splash just clear of the opposite bushes. Half a dozen casts, and I saw a bulge in the water of a good fish following, but he shied off and didn't take. Another cast, but he didn't take, so I left him.

"That's a tidy fish there, sir. I see him t'other day just under that bush. He'll go a dozen pounds when you get him out." But as he didn't take I marked him down, and went on a few yards lower

down, where I turned over a fair fish, but he was away directly.
I cast again instantly to the spot without a second's delay, and he
came like a lion at it, and I had him, but only for a moment or two,
for once more he got off, and this time he had had enough of me.
He seemed to be a nice fish of 7 lb, or thereabouts. My bait being
rather done up now, I put on a new one, and while I was doing so,
"Hi, hi, hi!" came down the bank, and away went Alfred to assist
J. in landing a five-pounder, while I spun on for twenty or thirty
yards without a touch.

Alfred had returned, and was relating to me the incidents of the
last course, when in mid-stream I got a heavy pull, and, giving
the fish a severe "rugg", I was soon at the old game again. Up
stream he went, and then up again, and then, like a salmon, he
made two leaps into the air, falling back with a bang, and showing
inches which seemed about the counterpart of the last fish, and
brought my heart into my mouth.

Fortunately, the hooks held, and after ten or twelve minutes'
tender handling, for, having just lost a good one twice, he rather
alarmed me into the prevalent notion that he was lightly hooked
in consequence of his jumping; but it was not so, he was well
hooked, only the flying tail hooks had caught him outside near
the eye, poor beast! After ten or twelve minutes, I repeat, Alfred
managed to spoon him out, and, having earned it, I lighted a weed,
and thought the day was hopeful. After this I got a nice little fish
of 4 lb, which was the lowest size allowed, but, resolved to do the
liberal thing, I turned him in again, as I did a three-pounder just
after. Then there was another "Hi, hi, hi!" from J., and once more
Alfred made tracks, and assisted in the landing of an eight-pounder.

I still worked on down towards the willow tree I mentioned.
The stump projected out over the water, and there was a deep
hole and eddy under it, any fisherman would spot it for a good
fish; halfway across the stream the hole shallowed up to about
three or four feet deep. "Now, carefully, carefully," and seeing
that my bait spun well, and that all was clear, I sent it careering
across the shallow and brought it whirling round the hole, "heave
and pull, heave and pull." It works into a straight line just below
the stump, and comes darting past the stump. "Now or never."

"Confound the fish, he's either not at home or not hungry."

"I see him feeding on the shaller and makin' the baits fly, rarely,"
said Alfred, "and I judge he's a 17 lb or 18 lb fish; I've seed him
many times."

Round came the bait again, but no result followed.

"Not today, Alfred," I said, as I turned round to get below the
tree.

At that moment there was a loud splash—a deuce of a tug at

my rod point, and as the rod was firmly over my shoulder, he got it pretty hot; nevertheless, to make sure I gave him another rugg. The bait was just hanging on the water, turning lazily round on the surface, as the stream caught the fans, and the temptation was too much for him, so he rose like a salmon at a fly, and took it, and I held him. Down he dashed to the very end of the hole, then out of it, on to the shallow, where he made fine play among the small fry, then back and into the hole again.

"He'll be making for his holt presently, sir," said Alfred, "can't you lean down and pass the rod under the tree to me, so as to get below it, and keep him away. If he works up and bolts in under your feet you can't help it; and what old roots and snags there is there Lord only knows."

At the risk of a ducking, and hanging on to the tree by one arm and my eyelids, I passed the rod under, so that Alfred got hold of it by the middle joint. The reel went two feet under water when I let go; but Alfred soon got a tight line on the fish again, which was grubbing along under the bank, and having recovered the rod I hurried down below, and putting a good strain on, brought him away from danger down stream again; and after a little more than a quarter of an hour's tussle, I worked him in on the shallow below where Alfred stood knee deep with the net, and in another minute we had him out, a fine male fish of 16½ lb. We regarded him with satisfaction, and drank his health, and so forth.

While we had been busy with him, sundry "hi, hi, hi's" came down the bank, but, as they could not be attended to, J. was left to his own devices, as he had a pocket gaff. Alfred now went to him. He had hooked a good fish of a dozen pounds or so, played him home, and scratched him severely with the gaff, without hooking him, so the fish got off. Just as Alfred came up he hooked and landed a five-pounder, which he returned, and then another, which was equally lucky.

I went on, and spun the rest of the water down to the bottom for a good hundred yards, but only got hold of one or two small fish. I then went up and tried the fish I had marked down. He came and pulled at me, but very cautiously, so I missed him. As we had breakfasted early, it was pretty well luncheon time, so I shouldered my rod and walked up the bucks, where Alfred was engaged in lighting a fire. My sundry basket produced a fire pot, kettle, saucepan, &c. The luncheon basket, turned out a big basin full of jelly, which being turned into the saucepan soon resolved itself into about three pints of fine mock-turtle soup. A shout brought J. upon the scene, who flavoured the soup with a bottle of old East India sherry, and a bottle of very choice Irroy. How we did enjoy that soup. The day was not by any means warm, and we sat in a triangle round the fire, and swallowed a couple of platefuls each. A cold duck was then reduced to bones, and then, in fear the sherry and fizz should not mix properly, I produced a bottle labelled "cognac" and "1834", and the kettle being now in full sing, we had just one glass of steaming hot grog.

"What's that you say? It was a shame to mix it"—well, perhaps —but after all *que voulez vous?* The best brandy makes the best grog, and if any one manes to deny that proposhition let him just put the print of his big ugly fut on the tail of me coat; whooroo! A comforting pipe, and then we fell to it again.

I won't describe the capture of each fish *seriatim*. I got four more, 6 lb, 7 lb, 10 lb, and 11 lb. J. got two of 8 lb and 9 lb, and lost the sockdolager, and we threw in some seven or eight small ones. About one hundred yards above the bucks the cut narrowed and grew deep—twenty yards above was an old pile or two, part of some broken down framework. J. was about to pitch his bait out into the middle of this cut, which he had not yet fished, when Alfred brought him in the landing net a small Jack about ten or eleven inches long which he had just spooned out of a ditch close by.

"Put him on, sir, put him on," said Alfred. "If there's ever a whopper handy he's bound to fetch him."

"But he's too large for my hooks, Alfred. What shall I do?"

"Never mind, sir. If a fish takes it give him plenty o'time and let him gorge. I'll forgive ye if ye kills a little 'un; but ye wun't."

Thus assured, J. put the fish on somehow, and, pitching it out with a tremendous splash into the very middle of the cut, waited the event. Of course the float went down at once.

"Ain't the bait strong? That's 'ow I likes to see 'em; and don't he keep the float down? Just tighten the line or he'll be getting foul o' weeds." J. did so, and there was a fierce jag at the rod point.

"Why, that ain't the bait; something's took the bait already," said J., quite excited, as the line began to cut the water slowly, the fish moving up towards a big bank of weeds and rushes about twenty yards above.

"That's the big 'un, for a million. I see him lay there at the tail o' them weeds once or twice last week; he must 'a took it as soon as ever it fell in the water. Give him plenty o' time sir, plenty. Don't worry him whatever you doo's. Let 'n get the 'ooks well in his gullet. Eat my ducks will 'e, ye ould varmint? Jest you swaller that nice little great-great-grandson o' yourn, that's all"; and the fish evidently meant to, for he laid up at the tail of the weeds quietly pouching for nearly a quarter of an hour, while J. stood watching, all of a twitter.

Presently the fish showed an inclination to move, and as he was coming out from his lair into the cut J. let him have it. The

stroke was a shrewd one and hurt, for the pike made one dart clean
through the reed and rush bed, mowing them down as if with a
scythe. Fortunately, J.'s line was stout and new, and the tackle
stood it. When he came out into the stream, he made tracks rather,
and took out forty or fifty yards of line at a dash; but the stream
was pretty clear, the tackle sound, and the hold certain—at least,
as Alfred said, "he'll turn hisself inside out afore he gets rid of them
hooks." Then he began dropping down the cut with a short dash
and a heavy drag, every now and then towards the bucks, which
were seventy or eighty yards below.

"Drat 'im; take care ye doesn't lev'n get near the bucks, or
he'll break ye on them piles as sure as fate, for they're full o' rusty
old nails."

J. did his best, and fought a good fight, but five and thirty pounds
is five and thirty pounds, and you can't do as you like with it. The
fish was obstinate, and meant going for the bucks; and, in spite of
every dodge—in spite of dashing, splashing, stoning to frighten him
up again—he merely sheered over to the other side and kept on.

J.'s eyes were half out of his head with indignation at the pike's
base behaviour. He'd "pay him; hang him!"

"Yes, I'm afraid you will; and you won't get through after all.
I never saw such a dour headed beast; he's as obstinate as a mule.
But he's an awful big 'un," I said, as J. laid the rod well on, and
actually checked the fish for a moment, till the big brute fairly
lashed the water into foam as he tumbled and walloped on the
surface. The next moment, however, he was away again forty
miles an hour down to the bucks.

"I'll pay him. D—n his picture," said J., panting after. "By Gad!
he'll beat me after all; he's got into the stream that sets for these
piles, and I can no more stop him than fly. I'll smash the rod. I'll—"

But the next minute the line grated across the outer pile. There
was a plunge and a dash; the rod straightened; the line floated like
a pennant in the wind; and J. collapsed.

"Never mind, old man. Take a drop of '34, and never say die.
You fought him splendidly, and had the water been clear you must
have killed him."

"Forty pound if he was an ounce," said J. in a hoarse whisper,
as he accepted the flask.

"Getting that way, at any rate, though hardly in the fours."

Still J. lamented and wouldn't be comforted. "*If* he'd only killed
that fish."

"What odds will you lay, old man, you haven't killed him?"

"Bet you a new hat."

"Done with you. You'll have that fish within a week. Remember
there's a float to him with a double hitch, and unless he can jam

that very hard somewhere he can't break it, but it will hang up every where and wring his soul out. You'll have him in less than a week." And so he had, for three days after a parcel about four or five feet long, done up in straw, reached the office directed to him, and when he opened it it was the pike, with his own gimp and float, and about four or five yards of line hanging from his mouth. Alfred found the float in the water near the bucks; he got hold of it, and found the fish utterly done, and with little trouble got him ashore, rather wasted, poor beast! He was hooked in the gullet; and even then he weighed $35\frac{1}{2}$ lb. Our great taxidermist Cooper set him up gorgeously, and he is the pride of J.'s ancestral halls.

This fight about finished the day. It was then about half-past four, and we didn't care to fish after. So we collected the spoil, we re-kindled the fire, and sat round it for half an hour or so and punished the '34, till the fly was due.

The fish made a brave show. There was exactly a dozen of them: a 5, two 6's, two 7's, two 8's, one 9, two 10's, one 11, and my $16\frac{1}{2}$, or over 100 lb weight. Besides this we threw back over a dozen more of three or four pounders; and that shan't be a bad day.

From *Sporting Sketches*

Fish

D. H. Lawrence

Fish, oh Fish,
So little matters!

Whether the waters rise and cover the earth
Or whether the waters wilt in the hollow places,
All one to you.

Aqueous, subaqueous,
Submerged
And wave-thrilled.

As the waters roll
Roll you.
The waters wash,
You wash in oneness
And never emerge.

Never know,
Never grasp.

Your life a sluice of sensation along your sides,
A flush at the flails of your fins, down the whorl of your
    tail,
And water wetly on fire in the grates of your gills;
Fixed water-eyes.
Even snakes lie together.

But oh, fish, that rock in water,
You lie only with the waters;
One touch.

No fingers, no hands and feet, no lips;
No tender muzzles,
No wistful bellies,
No loins of desire,
None.

You and the naked element,
Sway-wave.
Curvetting bits of tin in the evening light.

Who is it ejects his sperm to the naked flood?
In the wave-mother?
Who swims enwombed?
Who lies with the waters of his silent passion, womb-
    element?
—Fish in the waters under the earth.

What price *his* bread upon the waters?

Himself all silvery himself
In the element,
No more.

Nothing more.

Himself,
And the element.
Food, of course!
Water-eager eyes,
Mouth-gate open
And strong spine urging, driving;
And desirous belly gulping.

Fear also!
He knows fear!
Water-eyes craning,
A rush that almost screams,

Almost fish voice
As the pike comes . . .
Then gay fear, that turns the tail sprightly, from a
        shadow.

Food, and fear, and joie de vivre,
Without love.

The other way about:
Joie de vivre, and fear, and food,
All without love.

Quelle joie de vivre
Dans l'eau!
Slowly to gape through the waters,
Alone with the element;
To sink, and rise, and go to sleep with the waters;
To speak endless inaudible wavelets into the wave;
To breathe from the flood at the gills,
Fish-blood slowly running next to the flood, extracting
        fish-fire;
To have the element under one, like a lover;
And to spring away with a curvetting click in the air,
Provocative.
Dropping back with a slap on the face of the flood.
And merging oneself!

To be a fish!

So utterly without misgiving
To be a fish
In the waters.

Loveless, and so lively!
Born before God was love,
Or life knew loving.
Beautifully beforehand with it all.

Admitted, they swarm in companies,
Fishes.
They drive in shoals.
But soundless, and out of contact.
They exchange no word, no spasm, not even anger.
Not one touch.
Many suspended together, forever apart,
Each one alone with the waters, upon one wave with
        the rest.

A magnetism in the water between them only.

I saw a water-serpent swim across the Anapo,
And I said to my heart, *look, look at him!*
With his head up, steering like a bird!
He's a rare one, but he belongs . . .

But sitting in a boat on the Zeller lake
And watching the fishes in the breathing waters
Lift and swim and go their way—

I said to my heart, *who are these?*
And my heart couldn't own them . . .

A slim young pike, with smart fins
And grey-striped suit, a young cub of a pike
Slouching along away below, half out of sight,
Like a lout on an obscure pavement . . .

Aha, there's somebody in the know!

But watching closer
That motionless deadly motion,
That unnatural barrel body, that long ghoul nose, . . .
I left off hailing him.

I had made a mistake, I didn't know him,
This grey, monotonous soul in the water,
This intense individual in shadow,
Fish-alive.

I didn't know his God.
I didn't know his God.

Which is perhaps the last admission that life has to
        wring out of us.

I saw, dimly,
Once a big pike rush,
And small fish fly like splinters.
And I said to my heart, *there are limits*
To you, my heart;
And to the one God.
Fish are beyond me.

Other Gods
Beyond my range . . . gods beyond my God . . .

They are beyond me, are fishes.
I stand at the pale of my being
And look beyond, and see
Fish, in the outerwards,
As one stands on a bank and looks in.

I have waited with a long rod
And suddenly pulled a gold-and-greenish, lucent fish
        from below,
And had him fly like a halo round my head,
Lunging in the air on the line.

261

Unhooked his gorping, water-horny mouth,
And seen his horror-tilted eye,
His red-gold, water-precious, mirror-flat bright eye;
And felt him beat in my hand, with his mucous, leaping
      life-throb.

And my heart accused itself
Thinking: *I am not the measure of creation.*
This is beyond me, this fish.
His God stands outside my God.

And the gold-and-green pure lacquer-mucus comes off
      in my hand,
And the red-gold mirror-eye stares and dies,
And the water-sauve contour dims.

But not before I have had to know
He was born in front of my sunrise,
Before my day.

He outstarts me.
And I, a many-fingered horror of daylight to him,
Have made him die.

Fishes
With their gold, red eyes, and green-pure gleam, and
      under-gold,
And their pre-world loneliness,
And more-than-lovelessness,
And white meat;
They move in other circles.

Outsiders.
Water-wayfarers.
Things of one element.
Aqueous,
Each by itself.

Cats, and the Neapolitans,
Sulphur sun-beasts,
Thirst for fish as for more-than-water;
Water-alive
To quench their over-sulphureous lusts.

But I, I only wonder
And don't know.
I don't know fishes.

In the beginning
Jesus was called The Fish . . .
And in the end.

Crocker's Hole

R. D. Blackmore

T he Culm, which rises in Somersetshire, and hastening into a
fairer land (as the border waters wisely do) falls into the Exe
near Killerton, formerly was a lovely trout stream, such as perverts
the Devonshire angler from due respect toward Father Thames
and the other canals round London. In the Devonshire valleys it
is sweet to see how soon a spring becomes a rill, and a rill runs on
into a rivulet, and a rivulet swells into a brook; and before one has
time to say, "What are you at?"—before the first tree it ever spoke
to is a dummy, or the first hill it ever ran down has turned blue,
here we have all the airs and graces, demands and assertions of a
full-grown river.

But what is the test of a river? Who shall say? "The power to
drown a man," replies the river darkly. But rudeness is not argument. Rather shall we say that the power to work a good undershot
wheel, without being dammed up all night in a pond, and leaving
a tidy backstream to spare at the bottom of the orchard, is a fair
certificate of riverhood. If so, many Devonshire streams attain that
rank within five miles of their spring; aye, and rapidly add to it.
At every turn they gather aid, from ash-clad dingle and aldered
meadow, mossy rock and ferny wall, hedge-trough roofed with
bramble netting, where the baby water lurks, and lanes that
coming down to ford bring suicidal tribute. Arrogant, all-engrossing
river, now it has claimed a great valley of its own; and whatever
falls within the hill scoop, sooner or later belongs to itself. Even
the crystal "shutt" that crosses the farmyard by the wood-rick,
and glides down an aqueduct of last year's bark for Mary to fill
the kettle from; and even the tricklets that have no organs for
telling or knowing their business, but only get into unwary oozings
in and among the water-grass, and there make moss and forget
themselves among it—one and all, they come to the same thing
at last, and that is the river.

The Culm used to be a good river at Culmstock, tormented
already by a factory, but not strangled as yet by a railroad. How it
is now the present writer does not know, and is afraid to ask, having
heard of a vile "Culm Valley Line." But Culmstock bridge was a
very pretty place to stand and contemplate the ways of trout;
which is easier work than to catch them. When I was just big
enough to peep above the rim, or to lie upon it with one leg inside
for fear of tumbling over, what a mighty river it used to seem, for
it takes a treat there and spreads itself. Above the bridge the factory
stream falls in again, having done its business, and washing its
hands in the innocent half that has strayed down the meadows.
Then under the arches they both rejoice and come to a slide of
about two feet, and make a short, wide pool below, and indulge
themselves in perhaps two islands, through which a little river

always magnifies itself, and maintains a mysterious middle. But after that, all of it used to come together, and make off in one body for the meadows, intent upon nurturing trout with rapid stickles, and buttercuppy corners where fat flies may tumble in. And here you may find in the very first meadow, or at any rate you might have found, forty years ago, the celebrated "Crocker's Hole."

The story of Crocker is unknown to me, and interesting as it doubtless was, I do not deal with him, but with his Hole. Tradition said that he was a baker's boy who, during his basket-rounds, fell in love with a maiden who received the cottage-loaf, or perhaps good "Households," for her master's use. No doubt she was charming as a girl should be, but whether she encouraged the youthful baker and then betrayed him with false *rôle*, or whether she "consisted" throughout—as our cousins across the water express it— is known to their *manes* only. Enough that she would not have the floury lad; and that he, after giving in his books and money, sought an untimely grave among the trout. And this was the first pool below the bread-walk deep enough to drown a five-foot baker boy. Sad it was; but such things must be, and bread must still be delivered daily.

A truce to such reflections—as our foremost writers always say, when they do not see how to go on with them—but it is a serious thing to know what Crocker's Hole was like; because at a time when (if he had only persevered, and married the maid, and succeeded to the oven, and reared a large family of short-weight bakers) he might have been leaning on his crutch beside the pool, and teaching his grandson to swim by percept (that beautiful proxy for practice)—at such a time, I say, there lived a remarkably fine trout in that hole. Anglers are notoriously truthful, especially as to what they catch, or even more frequently have not caught. Though I may have written fiction, among many other sins—as a nice old lady told me once—now I have to deal with facts; and foul scorn would I count it ever to make believe that I caught that fish. My length at that time was not more than the butt of a four-jointed rod, and all I could catch was a minnow with a pin, which our cook Lydia would not cook, but used to say, 'Oh, what a shame, Master Richard; they would have been trout in the summer, please God! if you would only a' let 'em grow on.' She is living now, and will bear me out in this.

But upon every great occasion there arises a great man; or to put it more accurately, in the present instance, a mighty and distinguished boy. My father, being the parson of the parish, and getting, need it be said, small pay, took sundry pupils, very pleasant fellows, about to adorn the universities. Among them was the original "Bude Light," as he was satirically called at Cambridge, for he came from Bude, and there was no light in him. Among them also was John Pike, a born Zebedee, if ever there was one.

John Pike was a thick-set younker, with a large and bushy head, keen blue eyes that could see through water, and the proper slouch of shoulder into which great anglers ripen; but greater still are born with it; and of these was Master John. It mattered little what the weather was, and scarcely more as to the time of year, John Pike must have his fishing every day, and on Sundays he read about it, and made flies. All the rest of the time he was thinking about it.

My father was coaching him in the fourth book of the *AEneid* and all those wonderful speeches of Dido, where passion disdains construction; but the only line Pike cared for was of horsehair. "I fear, Mr Pike, that you are not giving me your entire attention," my father used to say in his mild dry way; and once when Pike was more than usually abroad, his tutor begged to share his meditations. "Well, sir," said Pike, who was very truthful, "I can see a green drake by the strawberry tree, the first of the season, and your derivation of 'barbarous' put me in mind of my barberry dye." In those days it was a very nice point to get the right tint for the mallard's feather.

No sooner was lesson done than Pike, whose rod was ready upon the lawn, dashed away always for the river, rushing head-long down the hill, and away to the left through a private yard, where "no thoroughfare" was put up, and a big dog stationed to enforce it. But Cerberus himself could not have stopped John Pike; his conscience backed him up in trespass the most sinful when his heart was inditing of a trout upon the rise.

All this, however, is preliminary, as the boy said when he put his father's coat upon his grandfather's tenterhooks, with felonious intent upon his grandmother's apples; the main point to be understood is this, that nothing—neither brazen tower, hundred-eyed Argus, nor Cretan Minotaur—could stop John Pike from getting at a good stickle. But, even as the world knows nothing of its greatest men, its greatest men know nothing of the world beneath their very nose, till fortune sneezes dexter. For two years John Pike must have been whipping the water as hard as Xerxes, without having ever once dreamed of the glorious trout that lived in Crocker's Hole. But why, when he ought to have been at least on bowing terms with every fish as long as his middle finger, why had he failed to know this champion? The answer is simple—because of his short cuts. Flying as he did like an arrow from a bow, Pike used to hit his beloved river at an elbow, some furlong below Crocker's Hole, where a sweet little stickle sailed away downstream, whereas for the length of a meadow upward the water lay smooth, clear, and shallow; therefore the youth, with so little time to spare, rushed into the downward joy.

And here it may be noted that the leading maxim of the present period, that man can discharge his duty only by going counter to the stream, was scarcely mooted in those days. My grandfather (who was a wonderful man, if he was accustomed to fill a cart in two days of fly-fishing on the Barle) regularly fished downstream; and what more than a cartload need anyone put into his basket?

And surely it is more genial and pleasant to behold our friend the river growing and thriving as we go on, strengthening its voice and enlargening its bosom, and sparkling through each successive meadow with richer plenitude of silver, than to trace it against its own grain and good-will toward weakness, and littleness, and immature conceptions.

However, you will say that if John Pike had fished up stream, he would have found this trout much sooner. And that is true; but still, as it was, the trout had more time to grow into such a prize. And the way in which John found him out was this. For some days he had been tormented with a very painful tooth, which even poisoned all the joys of fishing. Therefore he resolved to have it out, and sturdily entered the shop of John Sweetland, the village blacksmith, and there paid his sixpence. Sweetland extracted the teeth of the village, whenever they required it, in the simplest and most effectual way. A piece of fine wire was fastened round the tooth, and the other end round the anvil's nose, then the sturdy blacksmith shut the lower half of his shop door, which was about breast-high, with the patient outside and the anvil within; a strong push of the foot upset the anvil, and the tooth flew out like a well-thrown fly.

When John Pike had suffered this very bravely, "Ah, Master Pike," said the blacksmith, with a grin, "I reckon you won't pull out thic there big vish"—the smithy commanded a view of the river—"clever as you be, quite so peart as thiccy."

"What big fish?" asked the boy, with deepest interest, though his mouth was bleeding fearfully.

"Why that girt mortial of a vish as hath his hover in Crocker's Hole. Zum on 'em saith as a' must be a zammon."

Off went Pike with his handkerchief to his mouth, and after him ran Alec Bolt, one of his fellow-pupils, who had come to the shop to enjoy the extraction.

"Oh, my!" was all that Pike could utter, when by craftily posting himself he had obtained a good view of this grand fish.

"I'll lay you a crown you don't catch him!" cried Bolt, an impatient youth, who scorned angling.

"How long will you give me?" asked the wary Pike, who never

made rash wagers.

"Oh! till the holidays if you like; or, if that won't do, till Michaelmas."

Now the midsummer holidays were six weeks off—boys used not to talk of "vacations" then, still less of "recesses."

"I think I'll bet you," said Pike, in his slow way, bending forward carefully, with his keen eyes on this monster; "but it would not be fair to take till Michaelmas. I'll bet you a crown that I catch him before the holidays—at least, unless some other fellow does."

The day of that most momentous interview must have been the 14th of May. Of the year I will not be so sure; for children take more note of days than of years, for which the latter have their full revenge thereafter. It must have been the 14th, because the morrow was our holiday, given upon the 15th of May, in honour of a birthday.

Now, John Pike was beyond his years wary as well as enterprising, calm as well as ardent, quite as rich in patience as in promptitude and vigour. But Alec Bolt was a headlong youth, volatile, hot, and hasty, fit only to fish the Maëlstrom, or a torrent of new lava. And the moment he had laid that wager he expected his crown piece; though time, as the lawyers phrase it, was "expressly of the essence of the contract." And now he demanded that Pike should spend the holiday in trying to catch that trout.

"I shall not go near him," that lad replied, "until I have got a new collar." No piece of personal adornment was it, without which he would not act, but rather that which now is called the fly-cast, or the gut-cast, or the trace, or what it may be. "And another thing," continued Pike; "the bet is off if you go near him, either now or at any other time, without asking my leave first, and then only going as I tell you."

"What do I want with the great slimy beggar?" the arrogant Bolt made answer. "A good rat is worth fifty of him. No fear of my going near him, Pike. You shan't get out of it that way."

Pike showed his remarkable qualities that day by fishing exactly as he would have fished without having heard of the great Crockerite. He was up and away upon the mill-stream before breakfast; and the forenoon he devoted to his favourite course—first down the Craddock stream, a very pretty confluent of the Culm, and from its junction, down the pleasant hams, where the river winds toward Uffculme. It was my privilege to accompany this hero, as his humble Sancho; while Bolt and the faster race went up the river ratting. We were back in time to have Pike's trout (which ranged between two ounces and one-half pound) fried for the early dinner; and here it may be lawful to remark that the trout of the Culm are of the very purest excellence, by reason of the flinty bottom, at any rate in these the upper regions. For the valley is the western outlet of the Blackdown range, with the Beacon hill upon the north, and Hackpen long ridge to the south; and beyond that again the Whetstone hill, upon whose western end dark portholes scarped with white grit mark the pits. But flint is the staple of the broad Culm Valley, under good, well-pastured loam; and here are chalcedonies and agate stones.

At dinner everybody had a brace of trout—large for the larger folk, little for the little ones, with coughing and some patting on the back for bones. What of equal purport could the fierce rathunter show? Pike explained many points in the history of each fish, seeming to know them none the worse, and love them all the better, for being fried. We banqueted, neither a whit did soul get stinted of banquet impartial. Then the wielder of the magic rod very modestly sought leave of absence at the tea time.

"Fishing again, Mr Pike, I suppose," my father answered pleasantly; "I used to be fond of it at your age; but never so entirely wrapped up in it as you are."

"No, sir; I am not going fishing again. I want to walk to Wellington, to get some things at Cherry's."

"Books, Mr Pike? Ah! I am very glad of that. But I fear it can only be fly-books."

"I want a little Horace for eighteen-pence—the Cambridge one just published, to carry in my pocket—and a new hank of gut."

"Which of the two is more important? Put that into Latin, and answer it."

"Utrum pluris facio? Flaccum flocci. Viscera magni." With this vast effort Pike turned as red as any trout spot.

"After that who could refuse you?" said my father. "You always tell the truth, my boy, in Latin or in English."

Although it was a long walk, some fourteen miles to Wellington and back, I got permission to go with Pike; and as we crossed the bridge and saw the tree that overhung Crocker's Hole, I begged him to show me that mighty fish.

"Not a bit of it," he replied. "It would bring the blackguards. If the blackguards once find him out, it is all over with him."

"The blackguards are all in factory now, and I am sure they cannot see us from the windows. They won't be out till five o'clock."

With the true liberality of young England, which abides even now as large and glorious as ever, we always called the free and enlightened operatives of the period by the courteous name above set down, and it must be acknowledged that some of them deserved it, although perhaps they poached with less of science than their sons. But the cowardly murder of fish by liming the water was already prevalent.

Yielding to my request and perhaps his own desire—manfully kept in check that morning—Pike very carefully approached that pool, commanding me to sit down while he reconnoitred from the meadow upon the right bank of the stream. And the place which had so sadly quenched the fire of the poor baker's love filled my childish heart with dread and deep wonder at the cruelty of women. But as for John Pike, all he thought of was the fish and the best way to get at him.

Very likely that hole is "holed out" now, as the Yankees well express it, or at any rate changed out of knowledge. Even in my time a very flood entirely altered its character; but to the eager eye of Pike it seemed pretty much as follows, and possibly it may have come to such a form again.

The river, after passing through a hurdle fence at the head of the meadow, takes a little turn or two of bright and shallow indifference, then gathers itself into a good strong slide, as if going down a slope instead of steps. The right bank is high and beetles over with yellow loam and grassy fringe; but the other side is of flinty shingle, low and bare and washed by floods. At the end of this rapid, the stream turns sharply under an ancient alder tree into a large, deep, calm repose, cool, unruffled, and sheltered from the sun by branch and leaf—and that is the hole of poor Crocker.

At the head of the pool (where the hasty current rushes in so eagerly, with noisy excitement and much ado) the quieter waters from below, having rested and enlarged themselves, come lapping up round either curve, with some recollection of their past career, the hoary experience of foam. And sidling towards the new arrival of the impulsive column, where they meet it, things go on, which no man can describe without his mouth being full of water. A "V" is formed, a fancy letter V, beyond any designer's tracery, and even beyond his imagination, a perpetually fluctuating limpid wedge, perpetually crenelled and rippled into by little ups and downs that try to make an impress, but can only glide away upon either side or sink in dimples under it. And here a grey bough of the ancient alder stretches across, like a thirsty giant's arm, and makes it a very ticklish place to throw a fly. Yet this was the very spot our John Pike must put his fly into, or lose his crown.

Because the great tenant of Crocker's Hole, who allowed no other fish to wag a fin there, and from strict monopoly had grown so fat, kept his victualling yard—if so low an expression can be used concerning him—within about a square yard of this spot. He had a sweet hover, both for rest and recreation, under the bank, in a placid antre, where the water made no noise, but tickled his belly in digestive ease. The loftier the character is of any being, the slower and more dignified his movements are. No true psychologist could have believed—as Sweetland the blacksmith did, and Mr Pook the tinman—that this trout could ever be the embodiment of Crocker. For this was the last trout in the universal world to drown himself for love; if truly any trout has done so.

"You may come now, and try to look along my back," John Pike, with a reverential whisper, said to me. "Now don't be in a hurry, young stupid; kneel down. He is not to be disturbed at his dinner, mind. You keep behind me, and look along my back; I never clapped eyes on such a whopper."

I had to kneel down in a tender reminiscence of pasture land, and gaze carefully; and not having eyes like those of our Zebedee (who offered his spine for a camera, as he crawled on all fours in front of me), it took me a long time to descry an object most distinct to all who have that special gift of piercing with their eyes the water. See what is said upon this subject in that delicious book, *The Game-keeper at Home*.

"You are no better than a muff," said Pike, and it was not in my power to deny it.

"If the sun would only leave off," I said. But the sun, who was having a very pleasant play with the sparkle of the water and the twinkle of the leaves, had no inclination to leave off yet, but kept the rippling crystal in a dance of flashing facets, and the quivering verdure in a steady flush of gold.

But suddenly, a May-fly, a luscious grey-drake, richer and more delicate than canvas-back or woodcock, with a dart and a leap and a merry zigzag, began to enjoy a little game above the stream. Rising and falling like a gnat; thrilling her gauzy wings, and arching her elegant pellucid frame, every now and then she almost dipped her three long tapering whisks into the dimples of the water.

"He sees her! He'll have her as sure as a gun!" cried Pike, with a gulp, as if he himself were "rising." "Now, can you see him, stupid?"

"Crikey, crokums!" I exclaimed, with classic elegance; "I have seen that long thing for five minutes; but I took it for a tree."

"You little"—animal quite early in the alphabet—"now don't you stir a peg, or I'll dig my elbow into you."

The great trout was stationary almost as a stone, in the middle of the "V" above described. He was gently fanning with his large clear fins, but holding his own against the current mainly by the wagging of his broad-fluked tail. As soon as my slow eyes had once defined him, he grew upon them mightily, moulding himself in the matrix of the water, as a thing put into jelly does. And I doubt whether even John Pike saw him more accurately than I did. His size was such, or seemed to be such, that I fear to say a word about it; not because language does not contain the word, but from dread of exaggeration. But his shape and colour may be reasonably told without wounding the feeling of an age whose incredulity springs from self-knowledge.

His head was truly small, his shoulders vast; the spring of his back was like a rainbow when the sun is southing; the generous sweep of his deep elastic belly, nobly pulped out with rich nurture, showed what the power of his brain must be, and seemed to undulate, time for time, with the vibrant vigilance of his large wise eyes. His latter end was consistent also. An elegant taper run of counter, coming almost to a cylinder, as a mackerel does, boldly developed with a hugeous spread to a glorious amplitude of swallow-tail. His colour was all that can well be desired, but ill-described by any poor word-palette. Enough that he seemed to tone away from olive and umber, with carmine stars, to glowing gold and soft pure silver, mantled with a subtle flush of rose and fawn and opal.

Swoop came a swallow, as we gazed, and was gone with a flick, having missed the May-fly. But the wind of his passage, or the skir of wing, struck the merry dancer down, so that he fluttered for one instant on the wave, and that instant was enough. Swift as the swallow, and more true of aim, the great trout made one dart, and a sound, deeper than a tinkle, but as silvery as a bell, rang the poor ephemerid's knell. The rapid water scarcely showed a break; but a bubble sailed down the pool, and the dark hollow echoed with the music of a rise.

"He knows how to take a fly," said Pike; "he has had too many to be tricked with mine. Have him I must; but how ever shall I do it?"

All the way to Wellington he uttered not a word, but shambled along with a mind full of care. When I ventured to look up now and then, to surmise what was going on beneath his hat, deeply set eyes and a wrinkled forehead, relieved at long intervals by a solid shake, proved that there are meditations deeper than those of philosopher or statesman.

Surely no trout could have been misled by the artificial May-fly of that time, unless he were either a very young fish, quite new to entomology, or else one afflicted with a combination of myopy and bulimy. Even now there is room for plenty of improvement in our counterfeit presentment; but in those days the body was made with yellow mohair, ribbed with red silk and gold twist, and as thick as a fertile bumble-bee. John Pike perceived that to offer such a thing to Crocker's trout would probably consign him— even if his great stamina should overget the horror—to an uneatable death, through just and natural indignation. On the other hand, while the May-fly lasted, a trout so cultured, so highly refined, so full of light and sweetness, would never demean himself to low bait, or any coarse son of a maggot.

Meanwhile Alec Bolt allowed poor Pike no peaceful thought, no calm absorption of high mind into the world of flies, no placid period of cobbler's wax, floss-silk, turned hackles, and dubbing. For in making of flies John Pike had his special moments of inspiration, times of clearer insight into the everlasting verities, times of brighter conception and more subtle execution, tails of more elastic grace and heads of a neater and nattier expression. As a poet labours at one immortal line, compressing worlds of wisdom into the music of ten syllables, so toiled the patient Pike about the fabric of a fly comprising all the excellence that ever sprang from maggot. Yet Bolt rejoiced to jerk his elbow at the moment of sublimest art. And a swarm of flies was blighted thus.

Peaceful, therefore, and long-suffering, and full of resignation as he was, John Pike came slowly to the sad perception that arts avail not without arms. The elbow, so often jerked, at last took a voluntary jerk from the shoulder, and Alec Bolt lay prostrate, with his right eye full of cobbler's wax. This put a desirable check upon his energies for a week or more, and by that time Pike had flown his fly.

When the honeymoon of spring and summer (which they are now too fashionable to celebrate in this country), the hey-day of the whole year marked by the budding of the wild rose, the start of the wheatear from its sheath, the feathering of the lesser plantain, and flowering of the meadow-sweet, and, foremost for the angler's joy, the caracole of May-flies—when these things are to be seen and felt (which has not happened at all this year), then rivers should be mild and bright, skies blue and white with fleecy cloud, the west wind blowing softly, and the trout in charming appetite.

On such a day came Pike to the bank of Culm, with a loudly beating heart. A fly there is, not ignominious, or of cowdab origin, neither gross and heavy-bodied, from cradlehood of slimy stones, not yet of menacing aspect and suggesting deeds of poison, but elegant, bland, and of sunny nature, and obviously good to eat. Him or her—why quest we which?—the shepherd of the dale, contemptuous of gender, except in his own species, has called, and as long as they two co-exist will call, the "Yellow-Sally." A fly that does not waste the day in giddy dances and the fervid waltz, but undergoes family incidents with decorum and discretion. He or she, as the case may be—for the natural history of the river bank is a book to come hereafter, and of fifty men who make flies not one knows the name of the fly he is making—in the early morning of June, or else in the second quarter of the afternoon, this Yellow Sally fares abroad, with a nice well-ordered flutter.

Despairing of the May-fly, as it still may be despaired of, Pike came down to the river with his masterpiece of portraiture. The artificial Yellow Sally is generally always—as they say in Cheshire —a mile or more too yellow. On the other hand, the "Yellow Dun" conveys no idea of any Sally. But Pike had made a very decent Sally, not perfect (for he was young as well as wise), but far above any counterfeit to be had in fishing-tackle shops. How he made it, he told nobody. But if he lives now, as I hope he does, any of my readers may ask him through the G.P.O., and hope to get an answer.

It fluttered beautifully on the breeze, and in such living form, that a brother or sister Sally came up to see it, and went away sadder and wiser. Then Pike said: "Get away, you young wretch," to your humble servant who tells this tale; yet being better than his words, allowed that pious follower to lie down upon his digestive organs and with deep attention watch. There must have been great things to see, but to see them so was difficult. And if I huddle up what happened, excitement also shares the blame.

Pike had fashioned well the time and manner of this overture. He knew that the giant Crockerite was satiate now with May-flies, or began to find their flavour failing, as happens to us with asparagus, marrow-fat peas, or strawberries, when we have had a month of them. And he thought that the first Yellow Sally of the season, inferior though it were, might have the special charm of novelty. With the skill of a Zulu, he stole up through the branches over the lower pool till he came to a spot where a yard-wide opening gave just space for spring of rod. Then he saw his desirable friend at dinner, wagging his tail, as a hungry gentleman dining with the Lord Mayor agitates his coat. With one dexterous whirl, untaught by any of the many books upon the subject, John Pike laid his Yellow Sally (for he cast with one fly only) as lightly as gossamer upon the rapid, about a yard in front of the big trout's head. A moment's pause, and then, too quick for words, was the thing that happened.

A heavy plunge was followed by a fearful rush. Forgetful of current the river was ridged, as if with a plough driven under it; the strong line, though given out as fast as might be, twanged like a harp-string as it cut the wave, and then Pike stood up, like a ship dismasted, with the butt of his rod snapped below the ferrule. He had one of those foolish things, just invented, a hollow butt of hickory; and the finial ring of his spare top looked out, to ask what had happened to the rest of it. "Bad luck!" cried the fisherman; "but never mind, I shall have him next time, to a certainty."

When this great issue came to be considered, the cause of it was sadly obvious. The fish, being hooked, had made off with the rush of a shark for the bottom of the pool. A thicket of saplings below the alder tree had stopped the judicious hooker from all possibility of following; and when he strove to turn him by elastic pliance, his rod broke at the breach of pliability. "I have learned a sad lesson," said John Pike, looking sadly.

How many fellows would have given up this matter, and glorified themselves for having hooked so grand a fish, while explaining that they must have caught him, if they could have done it! But Pike only told me not to say a word about it, and began to make ready for another tug of war. He made himself a splice-rod, short and handy, of well-seasoned ash, with a stout top of bamboo, tapered so discreetly, and so balanced in its spring, that verily it formed an arc, with any pressure on it, as perfect as a leafy poplar in a stormy summer. "Now break it if you can," he said, "by any amount of rushes; I'll hook you by your jacket collar; you cut away now, and I'll land you."

This was highly skilful, and he did it many times; and whenever I was landed well, I got a lollypop, so that I was careful not to break his tackle. Moreover he made him a landing net, with a kidney-bean stick, a ring of wire, and his own best nightcap of strong cotton net. Then he got the farmer's leave, and lopped obnoxious bushes; and now the chiefest question was: what bait, and when to offer it? In spite of his sad rebuff, the spirit of John Pike had been equable. The genuine angling mind is steadfast, large, and self-supported, and to the vapid, ignominious chaff, tossed by swine upon the idle wind, it pays as much heed as a big trout does to a dance of midges. People put their fingers to their noses and said: "Master Pike, have you caught him yet?" and Pike only answered: "Wait a bit." If ever this fortitude and perseverance is to be re-covered as the English Brand (the one thing that has made us what we are, and may yet redeem us from niddering shame), a degenerate age should encourage the habit of fishing and never despairing. And the brightest sign yet for our future is the increasing demand for hooks and gut.

Pike fished in a manlier age, when nobody would dream of cowering from a savage because he was clever at skulking; and when, if a big fish broke the rod, a stronger rod was made for him, according to the usage of Great Britain. And though the young angler had been defeated, he did not sit down and have a good cry over it.

About the second week in June, when the May-fly had danced its day, and died—for the season was an early one—and Crocker's trout had recovered from the wound to his feelings and philan-thropy, there came a night of gentle rain, of pleasant tinkling upon window ledges, and a soothing patter among young leaves, and the Culm was yellow in the morning. "I mean to do it this after-noon," Pike whispered to me, as he came back panting. "When the water clears there will be a splendid time."

The lover of the rose knows well a gay voluptuous beetle, whose pleasure is to lie embedded in a fount of beauty. Deep among the incurving petals of the blushing fragrance, he loses himself in his joys sometimes, till a breezy waft reveals him. And when the sun-light breaks upon his luscious dissipation, few would have the heart to oust him, such a gem from such a setting. All his back is emerald sparkles; all his front red Indian gold, and here and there he grows white spots to save the eye from aching. Pike put his finger in and fetched him out, and offered him a little change of joys, by putting a Limerick hook through his thorax, and bringing it out between his elytra. *Cetonia aurata* liked it not, but pawed the air very naturally, and fluttered with his wings attractively.

"I meant to have tried with a fern-web," said the angler; "until I saw one of these beggars this morning. If he works like that upon the water, he will do. It was hopeless to try artificials again. What a lovely colour the water is! Only three days now to the holidays. I have run it very close. You be ready, younker."

With these words he stepped upon a branch of the alder, for the tone of the water allowed approach, being soft and sublustrous, without any mud. Also Master Pike's own tone was such as becomes the fisherman, calm, deliberate, free from nerve, but full of eye and muscle. He stepped upon the alder bough to get as near as might be to the fish, for he could not cast this beetle like a fly; it must be dropped gently and allowed to play. "You may come and look," he said to me; "when the water is so, they have no eyes in their tails."

The rose-beetle trod upon the water prettily, under a lively vibration, and he looked quite as happy, and considerably more active, than when he had been cradled in the anthers of the rose. To the eye of a fish he was a strong individual, fighting courageously with the current, but sure to be beaten through lack of fins; and mercy suggested, as well as appetitite, that the proper solution was to gulp him.

"Hooked him in the gullet. He can't get off!" cried John Pike, labouring to keep his nerves under; "every inch of tackle is as strong as a bell-pull. Now, if I don't land him, I will never fish again!"

Providence, which had constructed Pike, foremost of all things, for lofty angling—disdainful of worm and even minnow—Providence, I say, at this adjuration, pronounced that Pike must catch that trout. Not many anglers are heaven-born; and for one to drop off the hook halfway through his teens would be infinitely worse than to slay the champion trout. Pike felt the force of this, and rushing through the rushes, shouted: "I am sure to have him, Dick! Be ready with my nightcap."

Rod in a bow, like a springle-riser; line on the hum, like the string of Paganini; winch on the gallop, like a harpoon wheel, Pike, the head-centre of everything, dashing through thick and thin, and once taken overhead—for he jumped into the hole, when he must have lost him else, but the fish too impetuously towed him out, and made off in passion for another pool, when, if he had only retired to his hover, the angler might have shared the baker's fate—all these things (I tell you, for they all come up again, as if the day were yesterday) so scared me of my never very steadfast wits, that I could only holloa! But one thing I did, I kept the nightcap ready.

"He is pretty nearly spent, I do believe," said Pike; and his voice was like balm of Gilead, as we came to Farmer Anning's meadow, a quarter of a mile below Crocker's Hole. "Take it coolly, my dear boy, and we shall be safe to have him."

Never have I felt, through forty years, such tremendous responsibility. I had not the faintest notion how to use a landing net; but a mighty general directed me. "Don't let him see it; don't let him see it! Don't clap it over him; go under him, you stupid! If he makes another rush, he will get off, after all. Bring it up his tail. Well done! You have him!"

The mighty trout lay in the nightcap of Pike, which was half a fathom long, with a tassel at the end, for his mother had made it in the winter evenings. "Come and hold the rod, if you can't lift him," my master shouted, and so I did. Then, with both arms straining, and his mouth wide open, John Pike made a mighty sweep, and we both fell upon the grass and rolled, with the giant of the deep flapping heavily between us, and no power left to us, except to cry, "Hurrah!"

From *Tales from the Tellinghouse*

Fish Recipes

Henri de Toulouse-Lautrec and Maurice Joyant

Perch with Anchovies *Perches aux Anchois*

Put the well-cleaned perch into a saucepan, bathing in equal parts of bouillon and some good dry white wine. Add a laurel leaf, two cloves, a clove of garlic, leek, parsley, sliced carrots, celery, fennel, thyme. Cook gently. Drain the fish and keep them hot.

Put the bouillon from the cooking through a sieve; work some butter in a saucepan with a little flour; let it brown lightly, moisten with the stock, and stir until your sauce is well *bound* and cooked.

Away from the fire, add anchovy butter—the weight of an egg—pour this sauce over the perch, encircle the dish with slices of bread fried in butter.

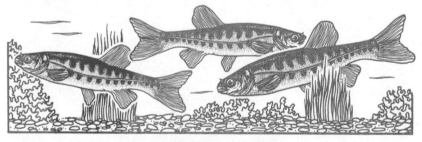

Fried Minnows *Vairons Frits*

Catch some minnows with bottles when they come out of a pure water stream or a fast-flowing river; press the bellies between the thumb and index finger, and empty them through the anus in one operation.

Wash them and dry them in a napkin.

Soak them in milk, roll them in flour and throw them into a fry of boiling oil.

Salt; pepper with white pepper or paprika, or red cayenne pepper; bless them with the juice of a lemon.

Lay the minnows on a dish wreathed with garden cress and serve very hot.

Man Fishing

John McPhee

*John McPhee's river journey through the Alaskan
wilderness took place in 1976.*

In the night, the air and river balanced out, and both were forty-six at seven in the morning. Walking in the water promised to be cold, and, given the depth of the river at the riffles, that was apparently what we were going to do. We took a long time packing, as anyone would who apparently had twenty per cent more cargo than there was capacity in the boats. Duffel was all over the gravel bar. I had brought my gear in a Duluth sack—a frameless canvas pack in every way outsized. It had a tumpline and shoulder straps, all leather, and, stuffed to the bulge point, it suggested Santa Claus on his way south. My boat for the day was one of the single kayaks. I spread out the gear on the gravel beside it, turned the empty Duluth sack inside out and rolled and trussed it so that it was about the size of a two-pound loaf of bread. This went into the bow of the kayak. I poked it up there with a stick. Anyone with a five-foot arm could easily pack a Klepper. The openings in the rib frames were less than the breadth of two spread hands. Stowing gear fore and aft was like stuffing a couple of penholders, but an amazing amount went in. All excess was taken by the canoe, and it was piled high—our aluminium mule. I tied the caribou antler across the stern deck of the kayak, and we moved out into the river. The current was going about four miles an hour, but we travelled a great deal more slowly than that, because we walked almost as far as we floated. If we had a foot of water, we felt luxuriously cushioned. Often enough, we had an inch or two. Pool to riffle, pool to riffle, we rode a little and then got out and walked, painters in our hands. The boats beside us were like hounds on leashes, which now and then stopped and had to be dragged. Getting into a kayak just once is awkward enough, let alone dozens of times a day. You put your hands behind you on the coaming, then lower yourself into place, all in the same act removing your legs from the river and shaking off water. Hession, at the start, showed me how to do this, and then he sat down lightly in his own kayak and floated away. I flopped backward into mine and nearly rolled it over; but the day would hold, if nothing else, practice in getting in and out of a kayak. When the boats scraped bottom at the tops of riffles, we got up, sought the channel of maximum depth, moved the boats through, and then got back into them where the water was fast and deepening in the lower parts of the rips. The problem of getting in was therefore complicated by generally doing so in the middle of rapids. In the first such situation, I lost all coördination, lurched backward onto the boat, nearly sat in the river, and snapped a toe, ripping the ligaments off the second joint. By noon, however,

I was more or less competent, and further damage seemed unlikely.

I was not disappointed that the Salmon was low. In a lifetime of descending rivers, this was the clearest and the wildest river. Walking it in places made it come slow, and that was a dividend in itself. A glance at the gravel bars, ledges, and cut banks told where the river at times would be—high, tumbling, full of silt, and washing down. I would prefer to walk in water so clear it seemed to be polished rather than to ride like a rocket down a stream in flood. For all of that, another two inches would have helped the day.

The water was cold by anyone's standards, for had it been much colder it would not have been water. Pourchot and Hession were wearing sneakers, and I did not envy them. Fedeler and Newman wore hip boots. Kauffmann and I had wet-suit boots—foam-rubber socks, more or less, that keep wet feet completely warm. The water that is arrested in the foam takes on the temperature of blood. I had on thick wool socks as well, and my feet were never cold. The sun was circling a cloudless sky, and needles of light came flashing off the river. The air went into the seventies. We walked along in T-shirts—feet warm, legs cool in soaking trousers, shoulders hot in the Arctic sun.

A couple of tributaries came into the river, the first from the east, the second from the west, and they deepened the pools and improved the rips. Somewhere up the easterly stream, said Pourchot, nineteen placer gold claims had been filed in 1968. The claims had not been kept up with yearly "assessment work," however. No mining had begun, and now would not begin as long as the claims were in national-interest land. This was not important gold country. Perhaps the most unusual event in the experience of the forest Eskimos was the arrival in 1898 of more than a thousand prospectors who had heard glistering rumors about the Kobuk valley. They looked around, did not find much, and lasted, for the most part, a single winter. About ten years later, gold of modest but sufficient assay was discovered on a creek near Kiana. Claims there were worked by placer mining—sluicing gravels, flushing out the gold. Where gold is mined in Alaska now, bulldozers, for the most part, move the gravels. The clear water that comes in from the upstream side goes on its way—brown and turbid—with a heavy load of fresh debris. Early in Fedeler's time with the Habitat Section of the Alaska Department of Fish and Game, he was shifted from pipeline surveillance to gold-mining surveillance —going from one site to another to check effluent standards in placer operations. He might better have waltzed with grizzlies than approach some of the miners, who told him to pack up his permit applications and get the hell off their claims. So what if some fish got a gutful of silt? Fedeler was only a few short years from his

family's farm in Iowa, his master's thesis on the life cycle of pheasants, but he was quickly learning the folkways of Alaska. "Get out!" the miners suggested. "We've always done things when we want to, where we want to, how we want to, and that is what we're going to do now."

The forest around us, to the extent that it could be called forest, consisted of bands of spruce and cottonwood. Occasionally, it made sallies up the hillsides onto protected slopes or into dry ravines, but mainly it pointed north like an arrow, and gradually it widened as we moved downstream. Close to the river edge, much of the way, were clumps of willow and alder, backed by the taller trees, which in turn had bands of alder backing them, before the woods gave way altogether to open, rising ground—to the lichens, the sedges, and mosses of the high tundra. The leaves of alder, chewed to break out the sap, relieve itching when rubbed on mosquito bites. The forest Eskimos make red dyes from alder bark—American green alder, the only species that grows so far north. Willow, as a genus, is hardier. The Sitka spruce is the state tree, in recognition of its commercial distinction, for Sitka spruce is the most negotiable thing that grows from roots in Alaska. It grows only in the south, however, and while the Sitka spruce goes off to the sawmill, the willow vegetates the state. There are only a hundred and thirty-three species of trees and shrubs in all Alaska, and thirty-three of those are willows. Before the importation of nylon, fishnets were made from willow—from long pliant strips of the bark, braided with the split roots of spruce. Rope, dog collars, and hunters' bows were made from willow and snares for small game and birds. Willow still goes into snowshoe frames, and fish traps, and wicker baskets. Young leaves, buds, and shoots of willow are edible and nourishing. The inner bark, chewed like cane, is full of sugar. Willow sap, scraped together with a knife, is sweet and delicious. At least twelve kinds of willow were growing along the Salmon—among them little-tree willow, halberd willow, netleaf, skeleton-leaf, and diamond-leaf willow, Arctic willow, barren-ground willow, Alaska bog willow. Oranges are easier to tell apart. We called all willows willows. The wood was agreeable in fires, and became almost as hot as the coals of alder.

On a broad acreage of gravel, we stopped now for lunch, and built a fire of willow and alder. The sun was hot to the point of headache, but there was a factor of chill in the day. Gradually the kayaks were acquiring water, dripping from us as we got out and in. One's buttocks, after several hours in cold kayak bilge, began to feel like defrosting meat. However warm one's head and shoulders might have been, a shiver went into the bones. The fire was piled high with wood that had bleached on the gravel in the sun, and a light breeze tilted the flame. Standing in the downwind heat was like standing in the Grand Canyon on a summer day. In a few minutes, our clothes had dried.

Three more tributaries came into the river, and its navigable stretches lengthened through the afternoon. Still, though, we did a lot of walking. Mergansers—a mother and six—fled ahead of us, running on the water like loons. Now and again, big ledges of bedrock jutted into and under the river, damming water, framing pools. Below one ledge, where water ran white from a pool, we stopped to fish. Stell Newman caught an Arctic char. Bob Fedeler caught another. They were imposing specimens, bigger than the

Salmon's salmon. They were spotted orange and broad-flanked, with lobster-claw jaws. Sea-run Arctic char. They could be described as enormous brook trout, for the brook trout is in fact a char. They had crimson fins with white edges and crimson borders on their bellies. Their name may be Gaelic, wherein "blood" is *"cear."* The Alaska record length for an Arctic char is thirty-six inches, and ours were somewhat under that. I tossed a small Mepps lure across the stream, size zero, and bringing it back felt a big one hit. The strike was too strong for a grayling—more power, less commotion. I had, now, about ten pounds of fish on a six-pound line. So I followed the fish around, walking upstream and down, into and out of the river. I had been walking the kayak all day long, and this experience was not much different. After fifteen minutes or so, the fish tired, and came thrashing from the water. I took out my tape and laid it on him, from the hooking jaw to the tip of the tail. Thirty-one and a half inches. Orange speckles, crimson glow, this resplendent creature was by a long measure the largest fish I had ever caught in freshwater. In its belly would fit ten of the kind that I ordinarily keep and eat. For dinner tonight we would have grilled Arctic char, but enough had been caught already by the others. So, with one hand under the pelvic fins and the other near the jaw, I bent toward the river and held the fish underwater until it had its equipoise. It rested there on my hands for a time, and stayed even when I lowered them away. Then, like naval ordnance, it shot across the stream. The best and worst part of catching that fish was deciding to let it go.

From *Coming into the Country*

The Fisherman

W. B. Yeats

Although I can see him still,
The freckled man who goes
To a grey place on a hill
In grey Connemara clothes
At dawn to cast his flies,
It's long since I began
To call up to the eyes
This wise and simple man.
All day I'd looked in the face
What I had hoped 'twould be
To write for my own race
And the reality;
The living men that I hate,
The dead man that I loved,
The craven man in his seat,
The insolent unreproved,
And no knave brought to book
Who has won a drunken cheer,
The witty man and his joke
Aimed at the commonest ear,
The clever man who cries
The catch-cries of the clown,
The beating down of the wise
And great Art beaten down.

Maybe a twelvemonth since
Suddenly I began,
In scorn of this audience,
Imagining a man,
And his sun-freckled face,
And grey Connemara cloth,
Climbing up to a place
Where stone is dark under froth,
And the down-turn of his wrist
When the flies drop in the stream;
A man who does not exist,
A man who is but a dream;
And cried, "Before I am old
I shall have written him one
Poem maybe as cold
And passionate as the dawn."

Two Friends

Guy de Maupassant

Paris was blockaded, starving, in the throes of death. The sparrows were becoming scarce on the rooftops and the sewers' population low: people ate whatever they could find.

On a bright morning in January, Mr Morissot, a watchmaker by trade and stay-at-home on occasion, was walking along the boulevard, sad, hungry, with his hands in the pockets of his uniform trousers, when he came face to face with a fellow tradesman whom he recognised as a friend. It was Mr Sauvage, a riverside acquaintance.

Every Sunday, before the war, Morissot would leave at daybreak with a fishing rod in one hand and a tin box on his back. He would take the train to Colombes and walk from there to the Isle of Marante, the place of his dreams, where he would immediately start fishing and carry on until dark.

Every Sunday he would meet there a dumpy little man, Mr Sauvage, who kept a haberdasher's shop in the Rue Notre-Dame-de Lorette, a jovial fellow and, like himself, passionately fond of fishing. They would often spend half a day side by side, fishing rod in hand, feet dangling, and had grown to be friends.

Some days they wouldn't say a word. Sometimes they chatted; but they understood each other without speaking, sharing similar tastes and identical feelings.

On spring mornings at about ten o'clock, when the young sun brought to the surface of the river that thin mist which flows with the current, and poured the pleasant warmth of the new season down the backs of the two keen fishermen, Morissot would sometimes say, "How delightful!", and Mr Sauvage would answer, "There's nothing like it!", and that was enough: they understood and respected each other.

On autumn evenings, when the setting sun turned the sky blood-red, throwing scarlet reflections on to the water, setting the horizon ablaze, enveloping the two friends in a fiery glow and pouring gold on the already rust-coloured trees, Mr Sauvage would look at Morissot and say with a smile, "What a grand sight!". "It beats the boulevard, doesn't it?", Morissot would answer, filled with wonder, without taking his eyes off his float.

As soon as they had recognised each other they shook hands warmly, greatly excited at meeting under such different circumstances. "What terrible events!", sighed Mr Sauvage. "And what weather!", groaned Morissot sadly. "This is the first nice day we have had this year."

The sky was indeed clear and blue.

They started walking side by side, dreamy and sad. Morissot went on, "Do you remember our fishing expeditions? How nice they were!"

"Shall we ever go again?", asked Mr Sauvage.

They went into a little café, had a glass of absinthe and then resumed their walk.

Morissot suddenly stopped. "What about another drink?" Mr Sauvage agreed and they went into another café.

When they came out again they felt quite dizzy, light-headed, as one does after drinking alcohol on an empty stomach. It was a mild day. A soft breeze caressed their faces.

The balmy air made the drinks go to Mr Sauvage's head. He stopped and said, "Suppose we go?"

"Where?"

"Fishing."

"Fishing! Where?"

"To our island, of course. The French soldiers are stationed near Colombes. I know Colonel Dumoulin; they'll let us through."

Morissot quivered with anticipation. "All right; count me in." And they parted to fetch their fishing tackle.

An hour later they were walking side by side along the main road. They soon reached the villa the Colonel occupied. He smiled at their request and agreed to satisfy their whim. Off they set again with a pass.

They soon crossed the outposts, walked through a deserted Colombes and found themselves at the edge of the small vineyards which slope down to the Seine. It was about eleven o'clock.

Opposite, the village of Argenteuil looked dead. The heights of Orgemont and Sannois dominated the whole area. The vast plain, with its bare cherry trees and grey expanse of ground, stretching as far as Nanterre, was quite empty.

"The Prussians are up there!", Mr Sauvage whispered, pointing to the top. Fear paralysed the two friends as they surveyed the deserted area.

"The Prussians!" They had never seen any, but they had been conscious of their presence around Paris for months, destroying, pillaging, massacring, starving France, invisible and all-powerful. This added a kind of superstitious terror to the heat they felt towards this unknown and victorious people.

"What if we meet any?", stammered Morissot.

"We'll offer them some fish!", Mr Sauvage answered, his Parisian banter coming to the surface in spite of everything.

But they were reluctant to venture into the countryside; the silence frightened them.

Mr Sauvage finally made up his mind: "Come on, let's go. But carefully!", and they made their way down into a vineyard, bent double, crawling, taking cover behind every bush, looking and listening tensely.

An exposed strip of land had to be crossed to get to the river. They started to run; as soon as they reached the bank they sank into the dry reeds.

Morissot put his ear to the ground to listen for footsteps. He heard nothing; they were alone, quite alone.

Reassured, they started to fish.

Opposite, the deserted Isle of Marante prevented them from being seen from the other bank. The little restaurant was shut up, it looked as if it had been abandoned years ago.

Mr Sauvage caught the first fish, Morissot the second, and every minute up came their lines with a little silvery fish wriggling on the ends of them—they were miraculously lucky.

Gently they slipped the fish into a fine-mesh keep-net which lay in the water at their feet. They were filled with delight, the delight which one feels on taking up a pleasant pastime again after having been deprived of it for a long time.

The kindly sun poured its warmth between their shoulders. They were no longer listening for anything, nor thinking of anything. The rest of the world was forgotten; they were fishing.

But suddenly they heard a muffled sound which seemed to come from underground, making the earth shake. The cannon had started booming again.

Morrisot looked round and over the bank to the left he could see in the distance the tall outline of Mont Valerien bearing a white plume on its brow, a mist of powder which it had just spat out.

Then, straight away, another jet of smoke came from the top of the fortress, and a few moments later another explosion.

Others followed, and every minute the mountain exhaled its ominous breath and blew forth its milky vapour, which rose slowly against the peaceful sky, forming a cloud above it.

"Here they go again," said Mr Sauvage, shrugging his shoulders.

Mr Morissot was a peace-loving man and as he watched the feather on his float dip twice in succession, anger suddenly seized him at the thought of these madmen who were fighting there.

"They must be daft to kill each other like that." he grumbled.

"Worse than animals." continued Mr Sauvage.

And Morissot, who had just caught a bleak, declared, "And to think that it will always be like that as long as there are governments."

Mr Sauvage cut in, "The Republicans wouldn't have declared war . . ."

Morissot interrupted him: "With a king you have war outside, with a republic inside."

And quietly they started to discuss great political problems with the sound reasoning of simple, peaceable men, both agreeing on one point—there was no freedom to be had. And Mont Valerien went on booming ceaselessly, demolishing French houses with its cannonballs. crushing lives, putting an end to many a dream, to many expected joys and hoped for happiness, bringing suffering to the hearts of women, girls, and mothers far away in other countries, suffering which would never end.

"That's life!" declared Mr Sauvage.

"You mean death!" said Morissot, laughing.

Suddenly they started—someone was walking behind them. They turned and saw four men standing right behind them, four tall, bearded men dressed like servants in livery with flat caps on their heads, and pointing rifles right at them.

They both dropped their fishing rods which floated away down the river.

In a few seconds they were caught, bound, dragged off and thrown into a boat which the soldiers then rowed across to the island.

Behind the house which the two friends had thought to be deserted, they saw a score of Prussian soldiers.

A kind of hairy giant who was sitting astride a chair smoking a big porcelain pipe, asked them in excellent French, "Well, gentlemen, how was the fishing?"

Just then a soldier deposited at the officer's feet the net full of fish which he had taken care to bring along.

The Prussian smiled. "Ah! I see it was going rather well, but that's not the point. Listen to me and don't panic."

"As far as I am concerned, you are two spies sent to watch me. I have captured you and will shoot you. You were pretending to fish as a cover to your real purpose. You fell into my hands; bad luck—war is war. But as you came past the outposts, you must have had the password to get through. Give it to me and you can go free."

The two friends stood side by side, pale and shaking, and remained silent. The officer went on: "No one will ever know, you will go back home quietly and the secret will disappear with you. If you refuse that means immediate death. The choice is yours."

They remained motionless and silent.

Keeping calm, the Prussian went on, pointing to the river. "Think, in five minutes' time you will be at the bottom of that river. In five minutes' time! You both have families, don't you?"

Mont Valerien was still booming.

The two fishermen remained standing in silence. The German gave orders in his own tongue. Then he moved his chair away from the prisoners and twelve men positioned themselves twenty paces away, rifles at the ready.

"I give you one minute, not a second more."

Suddenly he got up, came towards the Frenchmen, grabbed Morissot's arm and taking him aside, whispered: "Quick—the password. Your friend will not know, it will look as if I relented."

Morissot did not answer.

The Prussian then took Mr Sauvage aside and asked him the same question. Mr Sauvage did not answer.

Once again they stood side by side.

The officer gave orders. The soldiers raised their guns.

At that moment Morissot happened to catch sight of the net full of fish left lying on the grass a few feet away.

A ray of sunshine made the still wriggling fish glisten and he suddenly felt weak. In spite of his efforts, tears welled in his eyes.

"Farewell, Mr Sauvage", he faltered.

"Farewell, Mr Morissot", answered Mr Sauvage.

They shook hands, trembling uncontrollably from head to foot.

"Fire!" shouted the officer.

The twelve shots sounded as one.

Mr Sauvage fell straight on his face. Mr Morissot, who was taller, swayed, pivoted and fell sideways across his friend's body, face up, with blood welling up from the hole in his chest.

The German gave further orders. His men scattered then came back with ropes and stones which they tied to the feet of the two corpses, then they carried them to the river bank.

Mont Valerien continued to rumble, topped now by a mountain of smoke.

Four soldiers took hold of Morissot and Mr Sauvage by their arms and legs, swung them back then threw them as far as they could. The bodies curved in the air, hit the water feet first and sank rapidly, dragged down by the stones.

A splash, a few ripples and the water resumed its former calm as tiny waves reached the banks.

Calm and collected, the officer murmured: "The fish will get even now."

Then he walked back to the house.

Suddenly he saw in the grass the net full of fish. He picked it up, examined it, smiled and shouted: "Wilhelm!"

A soldier in a white apron came running. The Prussian, throwing him the two friends' fish, ordered: "Fry me these little things right away while they are still alive. They will be delicious."

Then he went back to smoking his pipe.

Mackerel Recipes

Mackerel with Mustard Hollandaise

8 mackerel fillets (skin left on)	2 tablespoons oil
2 tablespoons lemon juice	1 teaspoon minced garlic
2 tablespoons melted butter	6 tomatoes, skins removed

Rinse mackerel in cold water. Drain on absorbent paper. Place in greased heatproof baking dish. Combine lemon juice and butter and pour over fish. Cover with waxed paper and tuck in around the edges. Bake in hot oven (400°F) 20 minutes. Heat oil in skillet. Add garlic and cook slowly 1 minute. Slice tomatoes $\frac{1}{2}$ inch thick and add to garlic and oil. Cook briskly 2 minutes. Arrange on bottom of hot serving platter. Place mackerel on tomatoes and top with Mustard Hollandaise Sauce. Yield: 8 portions.

Mackerel in Red Wine

6 fillets mackerel	$\frac{3}{4}$ cup red wine	4 tablespoons light
1 cup sliced mushrooms	$\frac{3}{4}$ cup stock	cream
2 tablespoons butter, melted	2 tablespoons chopped fresh dill	2 tablespoons grated cheese
3 tablespoons Sherry	1 teaspoon minced garlic	2 tablespoons shredded blanched almonds
1 teaspoon salt		2 tablespoons butter
$\frac{1}{8}$ teaspoon pepper	2 tablespoons minced onion	
3 tablespoons flour		

Arrange fillets in greased heatproof dish. Combine mushrooms and melted butter and simmer 3 minutes. Add Sherry, salt and pepper and simmer 2 minutes. Remove from heat. Stir in flour and gradually add red wine and stock. Cook over low heat, stirring constantly, until mixture comes to a boil. Add dill, garlic, onion and cream. Pour over mackerel. Sprinkle with cheese and almonds and dot with butter. Bake in moderate oven (350°F) 25 to 30 minutes. Yield: 6 portions.

From *The American Cookbook*

Heaven

Rupert Brooke

Fish (fly-replete, in depth of June,
Dawdling away their wat'ry noon)
Ponder deep wisdom, dark or clear,
Each secret fishy hope or fear.
Fish say, they have their Stream and Pond;
But is there anything Beyond?
This life cannot be All, they swear,
For how unpleasant, if it were!
One may not doubt that, somehow, Good
Shall come of Water and of Mud;
And, sure, the reverent eye must see
A Purpose in Liquidity.
We darkly know, by Faith we cry,
The future is not Wholly Dry.
Mud unto mud!—Death eddies near—
Not here the appointed End, not here!
But somewhere, beyond Space and Time,
Is wetter water, slimier slime!
And there (they trust) there swimmeth One
Who swam ere rivers were begun,
Immense, of fishy form and mind,
Squamous, omnipotent, and kind;
And under that Almighty Fin,
The littlest fish may enter in.
Oh! never fly conceals a hook,
Fish say, in the Eternal Brook,
But more than mundane weeds are there,
And mud, celestially fair;
Fat caterpillars drift around,
And Paradisal grubs are found;
Unfading moths, immortal flies,
And the worm that never dies.
And in that Heaven of all their wish,
There shall be no more land, say fish.

The Death of Far

H. E. Towner Coston

Far was bred on the same trout-farm as Ika (see p. 30).
Towner Coston's book tells the very different
life-stories of the two fish.

By the time Far was six years old, he had paid three visits to the spawning grounds, and left a fine breed in his wake. He was no longer the beautiful fish of his youth but still a coveted trophy of every fisherman who visited the Silver River and who heard of his wiles. By now he had reached the unusual weight of over five pounds and more than one man enjoyed the thrill of seeing his huge form lurking in the darkness of the deep pools.

Far had still fewer things to fear now. Even Esox the Killer found him too large to trouble. But if his enemies were fewer, his troubles were scarcely less. Far's huge bulk needed a lot of fuel to keep it growing, or at least in condition, and he had now to concentrate more than ever on the larger foods of which small fish and crayfish formed a large proportion. He still liked an occasional nymph and fly, but they were insufficient for his needs and so it was that he was seldom seen to be rising.

Even in this state, Far could not resist the mayflies when they came. Then he would drift nearer the surface and thrill the fishermen by his cataclysmic rises or deceive them as he quietly sucked in the spinners at evening. During the day, he seldom rose except perhaps once, quite casually. Apart from the mayfly, his only weaknesses were for the large sedges and an occasional moth; these were mostly taken in the dark.

Far had tried many different holts in the river by this time, and was free to choose a summer home where he cared; there were none large enough to say him nay. Ash Tree Bend had exerted its spell; the twenty feet of water at the bend offered a really fine home for one so large, and following the year of its discovery he returned there every time after spawning.

His tastes had coarsened with age. Should salmon parr or even parr of his own breed come within the precincts of his domain, he made little or no to-do about capturing them for food. But they seldom did, and he was frequently forced to desert his hole and make foraging expeditions to keep going. No longer was he a welcome inhabitant, but came to be regarded in the light of a probable pest. Poor Far—yet he had had a fine lease of life, longer than many. A longer life in the river would only render him a poor thing, gaunt and ugly, a misery to himself and a nuisance and a menace to everything else. Silver River could supply the needs of good fish but not the needs of monsters; Far had outgrown the river.

One who had leased a rod on that stretch of the Silver River that year was not only a famous surgeon but had in the past been a famous cricketer as well. With the hard training demanded by his exacting profession, his hands—and beautiful hands they were—had become closely coordinated with his brain, but entirely dissociated from false nerves, acquiring a touch as delicate as it was positive. The Surgeon was also one to whom were credited many important researches, proving that he was a man of observant eye and constructive thought. To him the river was a relaxation. Although he caught few fish, those fish were fine ones, and although his rod work was not as beautiful as many other fishermen's to watch, it was sufficiently effective to enable him to place a fly just wheresoever he wished.

The story of Far fascinated him, and in his usual unhurried way he settled down to puzzle the thing out. Whenever the beat which included Ash Tree Bend was his, he spent longer watching for signs of Far than he did in fishing for smaller and less important fish. This was something after his own heart. On these days he would arrive early and stay late.

One evening, as he was sitting on a fishing seat resting in the dusk, he saw a mole struggling in the water. This attracted his attention and he watched it as it struggled blindly to reach the bank again, all the while being drawn along by the current. How it got there he was puzzled to say, nevertheless there it was. Just then the mole reached the swirl above the ash tree, there was a surge, a huge snout was thrust out of the water, and the mole disappeared. The Surgeon was astonished. Here at least was a possible clue, or cue. He had been told that Far was wanted out of the river, by fair means if possible.

He assumed that it had been Far who had taken the mole and not a pike; in this he was correct. This immediately suggested a large fuzzy sort of fly, to be employed at dusk, and possibly a hair mouse which he had used when fishing for black bass in North America.

But the experiment failed when he tried it on his next visit, for Far had not found the mole very much to his liking.

Next, as the season progressed, the Surgeon discovered that the time when Far rose most freely was at the merging of dusk and moonrise; this was the result of several weeks of observation. But when there are fixed dates for certain beats it is difficult to arrange things accordingly.

Then came a still calm evening, when the darkness swept over the land, and the silence was broken only by the chatter of the nightjar, and an occasional silvery splash of a late rising trout. On the fishing seat opposite the Ash the Surgeon sat and smoked in infinite peace. He waited.

Presently a huge silver-winged death's head moth flitted by, soon to be followed by another. Then came the slithering splash of a water vole as it sought its evening meal. Other moths and sedges flitted round, settling on his face and neck. The mosquitoes and gnats, finding a focal point, assembled to the attack. Still the figure smoked and waited, unmoved and yet conscious that the moment for which he had waited so long was near.

A silver rim pushed itself above the encircling hills, and shadows came out to dance as the night world awoke. And then Far made a splashing rise at an unfortunate moth which hovered round the overhanging sedge mat.

The figure stirred, picked up his rod, but still waited.

Again Far rose, this time at something the Surgeon could not see. Far rose again, and again, and at last the fisherman got to his feet.

There was no sign of urgency in his movements, nor was there any hesitation. He crept forward to the bank fringe, then drawing his line off his reel began to work it out, but as yet he made no attempt to cast. The gut which tipped the tapered line was tested and heavier than usual, and the fly which it carried was a No. 12 Silver Sedge; not a large fly for such a purpose, but his use of it was the result of observation and a well thought-out plan.

Far rose again.

The tempo of the weaving rod quickened. As the line snaked out, the left hand delicately fed it until but a coil or so was left. The cast was made, and as the fly sped forward the loose coil was allowed to shoot, gaining greater distance and enabling the line to fall in little zigzags which would have to be taken up before a warning drag could occur. The fly fell right in the outer ripple of the rise-rings and danced attractively.

Far, now really hungry, and knowing that darkness always brought safety, rose unhesitatingly at the fly and sucked it in, turning down as he did so.

Not a quiver came from the Surgeon. He knew that this was the supreme moment; and now his magnificent nerve control stood him in good stead. He allowed Far to get well down with the fly, risking the fact that the steel might reveal the deception. Then, with a well-controlled strike, the hook was driven home!

As the rod arched, the kneeling figure came to life. Without a moment's hesitation the slack was taken up and the line tautened positively from reel to fish. This was no small fellow to be played by hand, but a man-sized fish to whom no advantage could be conceded.

The pull of less than one pound against Far's huge bulk was not particularly noticeable, and Far, though annoyed, was slow in realising that at last he was well and truly hooked. For a time he swam stolidly around endeavouring, without wasting too much energy, to rid himself of the encumbrance. Then he came to the surface in a vicious swirl.

Instantly he recognised that a strange presence was there, and long acquaintance with such beings had taught him that they were dangerous. Simultaneously he connected the tugging at his mouth with the figure on the bank. Then he went mad.

Back he plunged to the bottom, seeking to find a weed bank sufficiently thick to place between himself and the line.

There was none.

He swept to the surface, making a flashing half-roll, then flung himself into the air, so that the water danced about him in the moonlight. Now he disdained all thought of cover, fought clean and hard.

Downstream he rushed, tearing line off the reel. The reel screamed to a thrilling crescendo; the sound died only to sing out in a different key as the man frantically reeled in loose line when Far suddenly changed direction.

Upstream and down. In the air and down in the depths. Ever on the move, following desperately the long runs, reeling in against the charges, wrists aching as the strain of the ever bowed rod told both on fish and man. It was a terrific fight and a worthy one.

Five minutes—ten minutes—fifteen and the ash-tree was but a dark shadow in the distance. But now the rushes were shorter, more sullen, and without their former dash. Far was tiring, but not beaten.

Now the other took the battle to Far. This was going to be no waiting game. The Surgeon realised that if he was to get the maximum out of this, it was to be fight and fight all the way, and chance whether the hook broke or pulled from its hold or not. It must be give and take.

Not for a moment did the tension relax. On the contrary the pressure on the line increased and varied until Far felt himself being inexorably drawn to that shadowy figure.

But it was not all over. For a moment Far rested and allowed himself to be drawn in without protest. Then, gathering together his failing energies, he made one last effort and set the reel screaming yet again. But the tackle somehow held, and at last, struggling feebly but with his belly gleaming whitely in the pale light of the moon, Far was drawn in to the bank, quietly netted and lifted from the water.

Then the Surgeon relaxed, but he paid his homage to the magnificent specimen he had captured. Indeed, it was as well that Far had finished his days in this manner, for he would have been black-listed in time and considered fair game by any method. His end was noble as befitted such a fish. Instead of passing into oblivion, he was set up and carefully preserved in order that other men might pay their homage, and his fame last for ever.

Salute! O mighty one!

From *The Swift Trout*

The Fish of the Côte Niçoise

Tobias Smollet

Nice is not without variety of fish; though they are not counted so good in their kinds as those of the ocean. Soals, and flat-fish in general, are scarce. Here are some mullets, both grey and red. We sometimes see the dory, which is called *Saint-Pierre*; with rock-fish, bonita, and mackerel. The gurnard appears pretty often; and there is plenty of a kind of large whiting, which eats pretty well, but has not the delicacy of that which is caught on our coast. One of the best fish of this country is called *Le Loup*, about two or three pounds in weight; white, firm, and well-flavoured. Another, no-way inferior to it, is the *Moustel*, about the same size; of a dark-grey in colour, and short blunt snout; growing thinner and flatter from the shoulders downwards, so as to resemble an eel at the tail. This cannot be the *mustela* of the antients, which is supposed to be the sea lamprey. Here too are found the *vyvre*, or, as we call it, weaver; remarkable for its long, sharp spines, so dangerous to the fingers of the fisherman. We have abundance of the *sœpia*, or cuttle-fish, of which the people in this country make a delicate ragoût; as also of the *polype de mer*, which is an ugly animal, with long feelers, like tails, which they often wind about the legs of the fishermen. They are stewed with onions, and eat something like cow-heel. The market sometimes affords the *écrevisse de mer*, which is a lobster without claws, of a sweetish taste; and there are a few rock oysters, very small and very rank. Sometimes the fishermen find under water, pieces of a very hard cement, like plaister of Paris, which contain a kind of muscle, called *la datte*, from its resemblance to a date. These petrifications are commonly of a triangular form, and may weigh about twelve or fifteen pounds each; and one of them may contain a dozen of these muscles, which have nothing extraordinary in the taste or flavour, though extremely curious, as found alive and juicy in the heart of a rock, almost as hard as marble, without any visible communication with the air or water. I take it for granted, however, that the inclosing cement is porous, and admits the finer parts of the surrounding fluid. In order to reach the muscles, this cement must be broke with large hammers, and it may be truly said, the kernal is not worth the trouble of cracking the shell. Among the fish of this country there is a very ugly animal of the eel species, which might pass for a serpent; it is of a dusky, black colour, marked with spots of yellow, about eighteen inches, or two feet long. The Italians call it *murena*; but whether it is the fish which had the same name among the antient Romans, I cannot pretend to determine. The antient murena was counted a great delicacy, and was kept in ponds for extraordinary occasions. Julius Caesar borrowed six thousand for one entertainment; but I imagined this was the river lamprey. The murena of this country is in no esteem, and only eaten by the poor people. Craw-fish and trout are rarely found in the rivers among the mountains. The sword fish is much esteemed in Nice, and called *l'empereur*, about six or seven feet long; but I have never seen it. They are very scarce; and when taken, are generally concealed, because the head belongs to the commandant, who has likewise the privilege of buying the best fish at a very low price. For which reason, the choice pieces are concealed by the fishermen, and sent privately to Piedmont or Genoa. But, the chief fisheries on this coast are of the sardines, anchovies, and tunny. These are taken in small quantities all the year; but spring and summer is the season when they mostly abound. In June and July a fleet of about fifty fishing-boats puts to sea every evening about eight o'clock, and catches anchovies in immense quantities. One small boat sometimes takes in one night twenty-five rup, amounting to six hundred weight; but it must be observed, that the pound here, as in other parts of Italy, consists but of twelve ounces. Anchovies, besides their making a considerable article in the commerce of Nice, are a great resource in all families. The noblesse and burgeois sup on sallad and anchovies, which are eaten on all their meagre days. The fishermen and mariners all along this coast have scarce any other food but dry bread, with a few pickled anchovies; and when the fish is eaten, they rub their crusts with the brine. Nothing can be more delicious than fresh anchovies fried in oil; I prefer them to the smelts of the Thames. I need not mention that the sardines and anchovies are caught in nets; salted, barrelled and exported into all the different kingdoms and states of Europe. The sardines, however, are largest and fittest in the month of September. A company of adventurers have farmed the tunny-fishery of the king, for six years; a monopoly, for which they pay about three thousand pounds sterling. They are at a very considerable expense for nets, boats, and attendance. Their nets are disposed in a very curious manner across the small bay of St Hospice, in this neighbourhood, where the fish chiefly resort. They are never removed, except in the winter, and when they want repair; but there are avenues for the fish to enter, and pass, from one inclosure to another. There is a man in a boat, who constantly keeps watch. When he perceives they are fairly entered, he has a method of shutting all the passes, and confining the fish to one apartment of the net, which is lifted up into the boat until the prisoners are taken and secured. The tunny-fish generally runs from fifty to one hundred weight; but some of them are much larger. They are immediately gutted, boiled, and cut in slices. The guts and head afford oil; the slices are partly dried, to be eaten occasionally with oil and vinegar, or barrelled up in oil, to be exported. It is counted a delicacy in Italy and Piedmont, and tastes not unlike sturgeon. The famous pickle of the antients, called *garum*, was made of the gills and blood of the tunny or thynnus. There is a much more considerable fishery of it in Sardinia, where it is said to employ four hundred persons; but this belongs to the duc de St Pierre. In the neighbourhood of Villa Franca, there are people always employed in fishing for coral and sponge, which grow adhering to the rocks under water. Their methods do not savour much of ingenuity. For the coral, they lower down a swab, composed of what is called spunyarn on board our ships of war, hanging in distinct threads, and sunk by means of a great weight, which, striking against the coral in its descent, disengages it from the rocks; and some of the pieces being intangled among the threads of the swab, are brought up with it above water. The sponge is got by means of a cross-stick, fitted with hooks, which being lowered down, fastens upon it, and tears it from the rocks. In some parts of the Adriatic and Archipelago, these substances are gathered by divers, who can remain five minutes below water. But I will not detain you one minute longer; though I must observe, that there is plenty of fine samphire growing along all these rocks, neglected and unknown.

From *Travels through France and Italy*

Rod and Line

Arthur Ransome

Arthur Ransome (1884–1967), the author of Swallows
and Amazons, *was for many years on the staff of the*
Manchester Guardian, *to which he contributed a long
series of regular articles on fishing. These were eventually
published in a collection called* Rod and Line, *from
which the following four pieces are taken.*

SEEING OR BELIEVING?

This year, the Lune seems likely to miss the crowning glory of its
autumn colouring. The sharp night frosts have already brought
many of the leaves from the trees before they have wholly lost the
green of summer and before they have caught the golds and reds
and oranges with which, as a rule, they flare up before being
quenched for the winter. To-day the water was low and so clear
that it was possible in all but the fastest streams to watch the leaves
rolling along the bottom, or drifting in mid-water. To these conditions I owe an experience that I am not likely to repeat. On account
of the low bright water I was spinning with the lightest possible
tackle, what is known as a 2x line and a very light 8-foot 6-inch
trout rod. My minnow was not heavily weighted, and I could
watch it the whole time it was spinning and, almost always, help
it to dodge the leaves.

Below the foot bridge is a rocky gorge with several deep holes
and strong current. Below these again is a true pool, with a narrow,
fastish entrance, a steady slightly curling stream down the middle
which affects all the water except a strip of slack at either side.
From the rocks at the neck, I thought I saw something move among
the stones on the bottom near the middle of the pool. I threw my
minnow into the slack water on the far side, spun it into the edge
of the stream and then let it swing, spinning slowly, over the place
where I thought I had seen a fish. As it came towards my side of
the pool a big fish rose from under it and swung with it, a foot below
it, but did not take. With that a miracle seemed to have been worked
upon the pool. The passage of the minnow at that place seemed in
some way to have excited more fish than the one that followed it.
Two others appeared as if from nowhere and, I think, a fourth.
One after another they did a corkscrew curl deep in the pool. Head
up-stream and tail down, they twirled over sideways. They moved
continually in a space of not more than a few yards. I put the minnow
over them again and it was as if they had been dancing a slow
quadrille and the music had suddenly quickened. The minnow
came into the still water and I brought it up fast and threw it out
again, putting the rod well out to keep the minnow hanging as

long as possible over this ballroom of blue and green crystal. There was a frenzy under water, great shapes moving round, getting out of each other's way, but still not taking. The river watcher told me in the evening that he had seen a similar mad dance when fishing with a prawn in a clear deep pool at his feet. The swirl of a moving fish broke the surface. For a moment I could not see fish or minnow and in that moment I saw my line describe a half-circle outwards at the point where it entered the water. I lifted the little rod. For a few seconds I felt a steady strain. Then the reel buzzed like a wasp in a spider's web and I was scrambling over the rocks, making the best going I could in waders and brogues, to get below my fish. When I had got below him he was away on the other side of the pool. I could see him and he seemed a very little one. For one moment I thought he was a sea-trout foul-hooked, so much less did he seem than the partners of the strange dance I had observed. He came up and broke water, as if to restore my respect for him. He was a good salmon, not a big one, but well over ten pounds. He went fast up the middle of the stream. I thanked him for that, but too soon. Down he came again and as he passed through some bright smooth water I thought I saw another fish with him. But he gave me no time to make sure, coming down on the far side of one of those long sharp edged rocks that rise from the bed of the river. That had to be stopped and for a moment it seemed too late to stop it. Giving him very little strain, just keeping taut and no more so as not to help him to cut the line, I got above him, cleared the line and getting below him again tricked him into moving and with a side strain got his head athwart the stream. He was already near the tail of the pool. Obviously he would have to go down to the pool below. I struggled down ahead of him just in time to save the line as he slipped through the rapids into a deep narrow pool like those immediately below the bridge. I could not hold him here either and we shot another cataract together. Again I had had an impression that he was not alone. Now, in a piece of glass clear water I could see that he was not. With him was a much larger salmon. My salmon got his nose down against a rock, and while he was trying to free himself there and I was trying to get him moving, this other larger salmon stood by. My salmon found the side strain too much for him and slipped down a few yards. The other salmon came with him. Then occurred the incident on account of which I am writing this paper. My salmon was holding his own against the current, low in the water. The other salmon was circling round the line (I describe what I thought I saw at the time) and, after doing this several times, suddenly let himself be swept broadside on against the cast immediately above my salmon's head. My distance from the two fish would be about five yards. I felt suddenly a new weight on my rod and could see the cast strained round the larger salmon at a point some foot and a half above the minnow which I could see equally plainly hanging at my salmon's mouth. The whole incident lasted only a moment. Both fish swept down. The big fish rolled off my line and the story ended with my salmon letting me gaff him and lift him out. But though he was a nice fish, weighing close on fifteen pounds when he was weighed later in the day, my interest was already not in him but in his big companion. Did the big fish consciously try, in that most practical manner, to help his fellow to escape. Did I have the extraordinary good fortune to witness that? Or did he, out of curiosity alone, follow him down two pools and, while looking at him suddenly feel the touch of the line and so be moved to that sudden gesture that looked exactly as if he had, on purpose, flung the whole weight of himself against the line? Was it seeing or believing? At the time, as I sat sweating on the bank beside my salmon, I had no doubts at all. It was only afterwards that I began to look for other explanation than purpose in the fish. I realize now that if my best friend had told me that tale I should have looked him very squarely in the eyes. Dozens of times, of course, fishermen have seen their fish accompanied almost to landing net or gaff. But I know of no other instance of anything that could seem, as this most certainly did seem, to be an attempt at rescue. And I am sure that I may fish for the rest of my life in water as low and clear as was the Lune to-day without seeing anything like this again.

FISH AND THE ECLIPSE

Fish, during the eclipse, were rather disappointing. Their reactions to it were entirely negative, and as, both before and after the eclipse, their positive activity was not great, such difference in behaviour as was caused in them by the eclipse was less noticeable than it might have been. During previous eclipses it had been observed that cattle stopped feeding and that birds, mistaking the approaching shadow for evening, flew to their roosting places. Hens are said to be much worried by such phenomena. I had a sort of hope that fish would show their feelings in some remarkable way, and, in spite of previous testimony on the behaviour of animals of other kinds, had somehow allowed the optimism that is as important to the fisherman as his line to persuade me that the trout would show their interest by coming to the top of the water. I had thought that the Astronomers-Royal of the Fish would be about in prominent places, and that I might catch one and put him in a glass case with a diagram of the obscured sun. I could find no mention of the effect of the eclipse on fish, but if cattle stopped feeding that would not necessarily mean that fish would do the same, and if birds flew to their roosting places that would seem to mean that they thought night was upon them, and, if fish should reason in the same way, there might at 6.24 in the morning of June 29 (1927) be a very satisfactory Evening Rise.

In any case, it was my business to go and see, so I broke all rules by being on the water of the tarn at 5.30 in the morning, thinking that, as there is to be no other such eclipse for some seventy years, I was not likely to break the rules in this way again, and could almost count on being forgiven for a first offence. In the valley I had left great quantities of human beings who were being affected by the eclipse in different ways. Between Settle and this place, at that early hour, I had heard mouth organs, accordions, and at least one brass band. I had seen men walking up the hills as fast as if they wished to escape the shadow. I had seen other men practising for looking at the sun by looking through smoked glass at the young woman who accompanied them. I had, however, seen that a great many people were making use of the eclipse for their own livelihood. They were trying to entice motor-cars into fields for their own profit. They were, at this unusual time, doing a roaring trade in lemonade and petrol. The eclipse was giving them an improved chance of making a living, and they were grabbing at that chance with both hands. The fish, I thought, would probably do the same. But, just then, I saw a ginger cat going home in the dawn and remembered that, whereas the human being had foreknowledge of the coming shadow, the cat had none, or it would have lurked out in the fields to spring in the shadow of the moon on a startled rabbit. The trout would be like the cat, not like human beings, in that the darkness and the shadow would come up upon them unawares.

A flock of geese moved protesting from the tarn as I arrived. It was, of course, quite light. There was hardly a breath of wind. Here and there were quiet rings on the water. There were big clouds over the Yorkshire hills, but among them open spaces dazzling with the glow of the rising sun. I put up my rod with the sort of cast that I should put up for an evening rise and, with an occasional pull at the oars to help, drifted down the tarn, wetting my flies as I drifted and wondering what it was the fish were taking, seemingly close under but not on the surface of the water. (I found out, after I had packed up to go away, that they were taking swimming nymphs.) It was very cold, and I landed and looked for a meadow pipit's nest and walked to keep warm. At 5.40 I saw a good splashing rise and a fish come half out of the water. The sun showed through the clouds like a brass saucer out of which some mad hatter had taken a bite. A wind came up. I pulled into the middle of the tarn. Fish were still feeding, and I caught a small one under half a pound who went back, not to be deprived of the experience that was coming, but, though coming so soon, was so little foreshadowed. The light was waning, but not much more noticeably than it often does under a thunder-cloud. The geese, up on the hillside, moved off rapidly. Three human beings showed on the skyline far above me. The sheep stopped feeding and moved restlessly about in little groups. Fish still rose. Then the speed of events seemed to quicken. Everything went suddenly dark. The noise of the curlews, peewits, and small upland birds stopped. There was absolute silence, and it was as if a roof had suddenly been put over the tarn. I had a glimpse of the shrouded sun, but no attention for it, casting carefully in places where a few moments before the fish had been rising, and watching and listening for the movement of a fish. The tarn was dead. I saw no rise and heard no rise. It was exactly like fishing a pool in a river over which a fisherman has inadvertently moved his own shadow. That, I think, is what the eclipse seemed to the trout. It was the sudden passing of a tremendous shadow, the shadow not of a cloud but of a solid body, and they reacted to it exactly as they would to the shadow of a rod or a fisherman, and buried themselves in the weeds or the deepest water.

The shadow passed and the tarn was again in daylight, but it was twenty minutes later that I saw the first fish rise. I drifted down on him, and, getting my flies over him just where he had risen beside a weed bed, had him in the boat a minute or two later, a small fish just over the limit. He was presently followed by a smaller one just under the limit, who went back. After that, the morning of the eclipse was an ordinary fishing morning and one of the worst. I could not rise many fish and I could catch none. One hooked himself in the tail and escaped by taking out thirty yards of line and bolting into a reed bed. Another, hooked on the dropper, caught the tail fly in the weeds and so freed himself. I was very sleepy and was startled by the only good fish I met, who went off with half a cast and two of my best flies, tied specially for the eclipse. These things, unsatisfactory in themselves, were, however, enough to prove that trout, feeding normally before the eclipse, stopped feeding altogether at the passage of the moon's shadow, ceased to feed for about as long as when put down by the shadow of a careless fisherman, and, plucking up heart with the second dawn that day, resumed their feeding. All of which was precisely what might have been expected.

ON WATCHING FISHERMEN

If I am walking with a man and we pass an urchin fishing with a bent pin in a ditch and my companion is unwilling to linger, I suspect that he is a poor specimen of a human being and I am certain that he is no fisherman. In any case, I should not be keen to go for a walk with him again. I should feel for him the same resentment that I felt for the liner in the Bay of Biscay that carried me all too fast past the tunny-fisher with his huge fishing rods hinged to the foot of his mast while, looking back through glasses, I hoped and hoped, till the tunny-fisher was a blob on the horizon, that I should see that seventy-foot rod flutter and spring under the tugs of a gigantic fish. Out of many years of travel, the moments that need least remembering, because their detail is still as bright and clear as when it was first burnt into my mind, are the moments spent in watching fishermen. I think of the Arab with his long bamboo whom I watched till dusk catching mullet (I think) in the harbour of Alexandria; of the workmen in Petrograd, sitting on the stern-post of a barge in the Neva, fishing for perch while the revolution was noisily proceeding in the town; of waking at night during a long journey with post-horses and seeing the yellow flashing of the torches carried by the fish-spearers in the river; of the eel-fisher in a Riga canal who held me for an hour when I should have been hurrying back to my little ship with the stores for which I had come ashore; of the rows of long rods dangled perpendicularly downwards from the embankments of the Seine; of the sheepskin-coated, felt-booted crowd fishing through the ice under the Kremlin walls; and of that spectacle that welcomes the returning traveller, that row of men in oilskins who seem to fish in all weathers from the piers of Dover habour.

I am never likely to do any netting, but I cannot see a net being drawn without waiting to see what is in it. How much more difficult do I find it to move on when I have come across a fisherman using rod and line. Another man's float will satisfy me for hours. Most interesting of all is it to watch the fly-fisher. It is interesting and, I fancy, unnecessarily humbling. Watching an angler is like reading the biography of a man whose life in some way closely resembles our own. We do not often assume equality with him. It is very seldom that we watch a fisherman who seems to cast as badly as we know we sometimes cast ourselves. Nearly always the watched fisherman seems to cast with enviable skill. That is because only the trout is as conscious as the actual fisherman of the bungled cast and the splash of the line in the water. The observer on the bridge sees the general movement, not the detail. He sees the line lift, fly back and, coming forward, unroll itself with easy precision. The thing seems a miracle and yet, in nine cases out of ten, observer and fisherman could change places without affecting the impression made. Criticism is usually not of the casting but of the fisherman's use of his obvious, astonishing skill. The observer, looking at the river, knows just where, if he were fishing it, he would wish the fly to alight. The fisherman omits to send it into just that place. I remember watching one of the most skilful casters and worst fishermen I have ever seen. His action was beautiful,

effortless, rhythmic with never a jerk, never a tussle with one of those jack-in-the-box hawthorn bushes that were not there when we looked round, but bob up out of the earth just in time to catch our fly. But cast after cast dropped his fly perfectly on precisely those spots where, unless by the accident of travel, no trout would ever be. This fisherman chose the places where the trout lay, not to fish over but to stand in. I have never seen a more delicate or a more unprofitable performance. And then I remember watching another man who, though his casting was not pretty to watch, always managed to get his share of fish. Again and again he would pick up a trout from a place I should certainly have passed over, though, after he had taken a trout from it, it was easy to see just why it was a proper station for a feeding fish. Both these men were worth watching. There was something to learn from them. But, if they had been simply down-stream raking with wet flies, I should have watched them just the same. There is no need for any sordid utilitarian excuse for doing what we should do whether we hoped to profit by it or not. Fishing of any kind is to the fisherman one of the vividest forms of life and other fishermen watch him and live vicariously in so doing, much as we intensify our consciousness of existence by going to the play. We share his excitement and, so primitive are we in this matter that we are apt, at the great moments (when he has a good fish on) to shout advice from the gallery. It is only the man who is himself highly developed as a fisherman who can refrain at such moments from seeking to thrust himself from among the audience upon the stage itself.

Fishermen are those who get most out of watching other people fish. But they are not the only folk who watch them. Nearly everybody does. Everybody, I should say, except those who have been thoroughly disheartened by life. Even old ladies who do not know salmon from cod except when boiled, cannot tear themselves away from the bridge. The sight of a man running towards a railway station makes people stop and wonder if he will catch his train. But this interest is mild and colourless compared to that with which on seeing an angler they will neglect all duties to watch if he will catch a fish. The train is hidden by nothing more mysterious than the bricks and mortar of the railway station. Also the catching of a train is something calculable. Even the biggest trains do not elude us, if we take our seats in time. Not so with the fish. He is in another element and the fisherman, plain to view, is fishing as it were into the fourth dimension, into the unknown. This, perhaps, explains his universal interest for other men. He shares the wondering interest (veiled sometimes in a joke), with which men stare after philosophers. The philosopher is sometimes unrecognized, because he does not wear a Druidic robe or carry a fishing rod to show that he is seeking to cozen something out of the unknown. The fisherman cannot disguise himself and everyone who sees what he is about must stop, if only for a moment, to see what he gets out of it, or if, as so often happens, he does not get anything at all.

I hope I shall remember all these reasons for forgiveness, the next time that, after I have laboriously crawled within casting distance of the big trout under the bridge, a group of spectators appear on the parapet and, pointing out with parasols both fisherman and quarry, send the one to shelter and the other to seek some other fish to stalk.

A KETTLE OF FISH

"A rare kettle of fish I have discovered at last," said Squire Western. "Who the devil would be plagued with a daughter?" There, already, a kettle of fish has its modern significance. But at that time real kettles of fish were still being boiled on the banks of the Tweed. That remarkable footman, John Macdonald, who introduced the umbrella into England, saw Sterne die, travelled widely, enjoyed "the keen searching air" which he found at St. Helena but preferred the view from the Castle of Stirling to any out of Scotland, describes very well the real kettle of fish that were known in the eighteenth century. "The noblemen and gentlemen that have estates by the Tweed side, in the summer and harvest give what they call a kettle of fish. The entertainment is conducted in the following manner. They all have marquees for the purpose, which they pitch near the banks of the river. Orders are given for a large dinner, and plenty of wine and punch. The fishermen take the salmons out of the water and that moment cut them in pieces, throw them into boiling water, and when done, serve them up on table. This treat is called a 'krab of fish.' There is always music to play after dinner. Some of the company walk along the banks of the Tweed; others play at cards; and the younger part of the ladies and gentlemen dance country dances on the grass. They conclude with tea and syllabubs; and then go home." Even the Oxford

English Dictionary, though it notes both meanings of the phrase, does not explain how the name of this simple pastoral entertainment came to be applied to such troubles as those of Squire Western over his refractory daughter. Nowadays, "pretty," "nice" and "fine" kettles of fish are common enough in the affairs of men, but are no longer boiled to the accompaniment of music and dancing, wine, punch and syllabubs on the grassy banks of Tweed. The nearest thing to a kettle of fish that is known to-day is the admirable *ukhá* or fish soup boiled at the riverside by Russian fishermen. But that is made with the kind of fish that is scorned by the cooks of Scotland and England.

There are fashions in fish. It is possible in angling literature to watch, for example, the decline and fall of the pike from the eminence he once enjoyed. He was once for the angler "my joy of all the scaly shoal" and when cooked "too good" for any but those who fished for him "or very honest men." With the pike the other coarse fish have lost their kitchen reputations. Yet once upon a time a pike would be the chief dish at a banquet and many another fish now seldom cooked was valued as highly as trout or salmon. At the Assizes in Derby in 1613, the bill of fare included "15 several sorts of fowl, among others young swans, knots, herns, bitterns, etc., three venison pasties appointed for every meal, 13 several sorts of sea-fish, 14 several sorts of freshwater fish, each appointed to be ordered a different way . . ." Eleven of these several sorts must have been fish without adipose fins. In the seventeenth century the lack of an adipose fin in no way barred a fish from honour at the table. Fish ponds were still being stocked, not for angling alone but for food, with the same fish that fed the monks on Fridays and in Lent. In 1674 Sir John Reresby stored two fish ponds at Thryburgh near Rotherham with tench and carp. Fifty years later Defoe observed a regular trade between the Fen country and London "for carrying fish alive by land carriage." "This they do by carrying great buts fill'd with water in waggons, as the carriers draw other goods: the buts have a little square flap, instead of a bung, about ten, twelve, or fourteen inches square, which, being open'd, gives air to the fish, and every night, when they come to the inn, they draw off the water, and let more and sweet water run into them again. In these carriages they chiefly carry tench and pike, perch and eels, but especially tench and pike, of which here are some of the largest in England."

Seventy years later, coarse fish were honoured still. Mrs Elizabeth Raffald, who flourished towards the end of the century, was housekeeper to the Lady Elizabeth Warburton and subsequently kept a cook-shop in Manchester, crowned her life by the writing of a book called, *The Experienced English Housekeeper*, "for the use and

ease of Ladies, Housekeepers, Cooks, etc., Written purely from
Practice." My copy of the great work, with as frontispiece a portrait
of the author in a mob-cap, her eyes sparkling with demure pride
in her profession, was printed by G. Bancks in Manchester, in 1798
(the same year as the *Lyrical Ballads*). Mrs Raffald (like Wordsworth) had none of the modern contempt for coarse fish. She puts
trout and perch together, with just a hint of a superior respect for
perch. She describes a stew of carp and tench as "a top-dish for a
grand entertainment."

With the development of our sea fisheries, of our means of transport and of the laziness of cooks, fresh-water-fish other than trout
and salmon fell out of favour. They are still prized abroad. In the
markets of Russia may be seen huge tubs full of big perch and
pike and other fish. The marketing housewife chooses her fish alive
and so is assured of its freshness. Barges half full of water like vast
floating bait-cans lie long the quays of the Neva and the fishermen
use a long handled net to dip out their fish for their customers.
Over vast areas of Russia the "game" fish are unknown and the
"coarse" fish still enjoy the reputation which they had in eighteenth-
century England. A cookery book in my possession, used by an
officer's mess on the Russian front during the war, gives 23 ways
of cooking pike, 8 ways of cooking carp and 12 ways of cooking
tench. It offers 9 recipes for eels, 11 for bream, 8 for perch, 6 for trout
and 7 for salmon. The pike-perch (*Lucioperca*), an excellent sporting
fish, which has, I think, been introduced into England, is honoured
by the description of 24 methods of cooking him. These recipes
do not include a number of different rissoles, vinaigrettes and mayon-
naises of pike, tench, carp, and perch and special fish dishes for Lent.
Nor do they include the fish soups, of which some well-thumbed
pages give a score, to be made from carp, eel, tench, pike, perch,
ruffe and burbot, besides sturgeon and other specially Russian fish.
"For the best soup," authority tells us, "there must be a pound of
fish for each plateful of soup. For ordinary soup half that quantity
suffices."

In Russia to this day a kettle of fish (*ukhá*) is often the most important part of a banquet. Curiously enough the two fish chiefly
prized for this purpose are two which are not often eaten in England,
the ruffe and the burbot. *Ukhá* for a banquet is made by putting
ruffes or perch (preferably ruffes) in a vessel of cold water and then
thoroughly boiling it. Into this boiling stock are thrown choice
bits of burbot and other fish. The liver of the burbot is particularly
prized and there is a tradition that the poor burbot should be beaten
before cooking, so that his liver may be enlarged, a practice ana-
logous to that cruel whipping to death of sucking pigs which Lamb
described as refining the violet. The whole brew is sometimes

enlivened by the addition of wine. But the *ukhá* which corresponds most nearly to the Tweedside kettles of fish is made by parties of fishermen at the waterside. This *ukhá* is made from whatever fish are caught. Towards evening the camp fire is made on the bank and in a warm luminous hollow in the river mist the fishermen sit and burn their throats with fresh-made soup. If only one could be as sure of catching fish in England, who would carry sandwiches? Beside the fish nothing is needed but salt, pepper and an onion. A bait-can makes an admirable kettle.

Fishing Records

*Selected from the complete list of the U.S. National Fresh
Water Fishing Hall of Fame to January 1980. Records
for the British Isles, marked *, are included for some
species for comparison, and are taken from the lists ratified
by the British Record Fish Committee of the National
Anglers' Council, and the Irish Specimen Fish Committee.*

Arapaima or **Pirarucu** *Arapaima gigas*	161lb 73.030kg	Stu Apte	Rupununi River, Guyana, 1973
Barbel *Barbus barbus*	13lb 12oz 6.237kg	J. Day	Royalty Fishery, Christchurch, Dorset, U.K., 1962
Bass, Landlocked Striped *Morone saxatilis*	59lb 12oz 27.102kg	Frank W. Smith	Colorado River, Arizona, U.S.A., 1977
Bleak *Alburnus alburnus*	3oz 15dr 0.111kg	D. Pollard	Staythorpe pond, Nr. Neward, Nottinghamshire, U.K., 1971
Bowfin or **Dogfish** *Amia calva*	19lb 12oz 8.958kg	M. R. Webster	Lake Marion, S. Carolina, U.S.A., 1972
Bream, Bronze *Abramis brama*	13lb 8oz 6.123kg	A. R. Heslop	Private water, Staffordshire, U.K., 1977
Burbot, Ling or **Cusk** *Lota lota*	15lb 8oz 7.031kg	Irvin E. Glanville	Garrison Dam Terrace, Riverdale, N. Dakota, U.S.A., 1979
Carp *Cyprinus carpio*	55lb 5oz 25.089kg	Frank J. Ledwein	Clearwater Lake, Minnesota, U.S.A., 1952
	*44lb 19.957kg	Richard Walker	Redmire Pool, Hereford and Worcester, U.K., 1952
Carp, Crucian *Cavassius cavassius*	5lb 10oz 8dr 2.565kg	G. Halls	Near King's Lynn, Norfolk, U.K., 1976
Catfish, Blue *Ictalurus furcatus*	97lb 43.988kg	Edward B. Elliott	Missouri River, S. Dakota, U.S.A., 1959
Catfish, Channel *Ictalurus punctatus*	58lb 26.308kg	W. B. Whaley	Sautee-Cooper Reservoir, S. Carolina, U.S.A., 1964
Catfish, European *Silurus glanis*	43lb 8oz 19.731kg	R. J. Bray	Wilstone Reservoir, Hertfordshire, U.K., 1977
Catfish, Flathead *Pylodictis olivaris*	79lb 8oz 36.061kg	Glenn T. Simpson	White River, Indiana, U.S.A., 1968
Char, Arctic *Salvelinus alpinus*	29lb 11oz 13.466kg	Jeanne Branson	Arctic River, North West Territory, Canada, 1968
Chub *Leuciscus cephalus*	7lb 6oz 3.345kg	W. L. Warren	River Avon, Hampshire, U.K., 1957
Dace *Leuciscus leuciscus*	1lb 4oz 4dr 0.574kg	J. L. Gasson	Little Ouse, Thetford, Norfolk, U.K., 1960
Eel *Anguilla anguilla*	11lb 2oz 5.046kg	S. Terry	Kingfisher Lake, Ringwood, Hampshire, U.K., 1978
Gar, Alligator *Lepisosteus spatula*	279lb 126.552kg	Bill Valverde	Rio Grande, Texas, U.S.A., 1951
Gar, Shortnose *Lepisosteus platostomus*	3lb 5oz 4dr 1.509kg	J. Pawlowski	Lake Francis Case, S. Dakota, U.S.A., 1977

Grayling, Arctic *Thymallus arcticus*	5lb 15oz 2.693kg	Jeanne Branson	Katseyedie River, North West Territory, Canada, 1967
Grayling, European *Thymallus thymallus*	2lb 6oz 1.077kg	Simon R. Smith	River Dee, Clwyd, U.K., 1978
Gudgeon *Gobio gobio*	4oz 4dr 0.120kg	M. J. Bowen	Fish pond, Ebbw Vale, Gwent, U.K., 1977
Gwyniad or **Whitefish** *Coregonus lavaretus*	1lb 4oz 4dr 0.567kg	J. R. Williams	Llyn Tegid, Gwynedd, U.K., 1965
Herring, River, or Skipjack *Alosa chrysochloris*	3lb 6oz 1.566kg	Mac Roy Gasque	Watt's Bar Lake, Kingston, Tennessee, U.S.A., 1979
Miller's Thumb or **Bullhead** *Cottus gobio*	10dr 0.018kg	Edward Harrison	Leeds & Liverpool Canal, U.K., 1978
Minnow *Phoxinus phoxinus*	9dr 0.016kg	R. Guy	River Rother, Midhurst, Sussex, U.K., 1978
Muskellunge *Esox masquinongy*	69lb 15oz 31.723kg	Arthur Lawton	St Lawrence River, New York, U.S.A., 1957
Nile Perch *Lates niloticus*	62lb 28.208kg	Denton Hill	Lake Turkana, Nairobi, Kenya, 1970
Orfe, Golden *Leuciscus idus*	4lb 3oz 1.899kg	B. T. Mills	River Test, Hampshire, U.K., 1976
Perch *Perca fluviatilis*	5lb 8oz 2.494kg	S. Drum	Lough Erne, Eire, 1946
Perch, White *Morone americana*	4lb 12oz 2.155kg	Mrs Earl Small	Messalonskee Lake, Maine, U.S.A., 1949
Perch, Yellow *Perca flavenscens*	4lb 3oz 8dr 1.914kg	Dr C. C. Abbot	Bordentown, New Jersey, U.S.A., 1865
Pickerel, Chain *Esox niger*	9lb 6oz 4.252kg	Baxley McQuaig Jr	Homerville, Georgia, U.S.A., 1961
Pike, Amur *Esox reicherti*	28lb 12.705kg	M. J. Chulyak	Glendale Lake, Pennsylvania, U.S.A., 1976
Pike, Northern *Esox lucius*	46lb 2oz 20.922kg *42lb 19.050kg	Peter Dubuc M. Watkins	Sacandaga Reservoir, New York, U.S.A., 1940 River Barrow, Eire, 1964
Roach *Rutilus rutilus*	4lb 1oz 1.842kg	R. G. Jones	Gravel pits, Colwich, Nottinghamshire, U.K., 1975
Rudd *Scardinius erythrophthalmus*	4lb 8oz 2.041kg	Rev. E. Alston	Mere, near Thetford, Norfolk, U.K., 1933
Ruffe *Gymnocephalus cernua*	5oz 0.141kg	P. Barrowcliffe	River Bure, Norfolk, U.K., 1977
Salmon, Atlantic *Salmo salar*	79lb 2oz 35.891kg *64lb 29.029kg	Henrik Henriksen Miss G. W. Ballantyne	Tana River, Norway, 1928 River Tay, Tayside, U.K., 1922
Salmon, Chinook *Oncorhynchus tshawytscha*	92lb 41.731kg	Heinz Wichman	Skeena River, British Columbia, Canada, 1959
Shad *Alosa sapidissima*	9lb 2oz 4.139kg	Edward P. Nelson	Engfield, Connecticut, U.S.A., 1973

Sturgeon, Lake *Acipenser fulvescens*	76lb 8oz *34.670kg*	Joseph Lavota	Lake Superior, Wisconsin, U.S.A., 1977
Sturgeon, White *Acipenser* *transmontanus*	407lb *184.575kg*	Raymond Pihenger	Sacramento River, Colusa, California, U.S.A., 1979
Tench *Tinca tinca*	10lb 1oz 2dr *4.567kg*	L. W. Brown	Brick pit, Peterborough, U.K., 1975
Trout, Brown *Salmo trutta*	33lb 10oz *15.250kg*	Robert L. Bringhurst	Flaming Gorge Reservoir, Dutch John, Utah, U.S.A., 1977
	*26lb 2oz *12.359kg*	William Meares	Lough Ennell, Eire, 1894
Trout, Rainbow *Salmo gairdneri*	26lb 2oz *12.359kg*	Del Cantry	Flaming Gorge Reservoir, Dutch John, Utah, U.S.A., 1979
	*19lb 8oz *8.344kg*	A. Pearson	Avington Trout Fisheries, Itchen Abbas, Hampshire, U.K., 1977
Zander or Perch Pike *Stizostedion lucioperca*	17lb 4oz *7.824kg*	D. Litton	Great Ouse Relief Channel, Norfolk, U.K., 1977

Sources
and Acknowledgements

"Seven Marlin Swordfish in One Day" by Zane Grey: from *Tales of Fishes*

"Pike" by Ted Hughes: reprinted by permission of Faber and Faber Ltd from *Lupercal* (1972)

"It Came as a Big Surprise" by Byron Rogers: from *The Sunday Telegraph Magazine*

"Caviare" by Helen and George Papashvily: from Foods of the World/*Russian Cooking* by H. & G. Papashvily and the editors of Time-Life Books, © Time Inc.

"The Mahseer" by Jocelyn Lane: reprinted by permission of the author from *Fly Fisherman's Pie* (1954)

"The Mighty Mahseer": reprinted by permission from *The Abu Catalogue 1979*

"Trout with Shrimp" by Robert Carrier: from *Cooking for You* (Hamlyn, 1973)

"The Inmates' Fishing Trip" by Ken Kessey: from *One Flew Over the Cuckoo's Nest* (Methuen 1963)

"Piping in the Salmon" by J. F. Todhunter: reprinted by permission of the author

"Fish and the Shadow" by Ezra Pound: reprinted by permission of Faber and Faber Ltd from *Collected Shorter Poems* (1928)

"Big Two-Hearted River" by Ernest Hemingway: reprinted by permission of the Executors of the Ernest Hemingway Estate from *The First Forty-Nine Stories* (Jonathan Cape, 1944)

"Ancient Anglers" by Charles Chenevix Trench: reprinted by permission of Granada Publishing Ltd from *A History of Angling*

"The Bishop Browne Story" by Derek Barker: from *The Fisherman's Bedside Book* by BB (Eyre and Spottiswoode, 1946)

"Baked Carp with Soft Roe Stuffing" and "Roach" by Jane Grigson: reprinted by permission of Macmillan, London and Basingstoke, from *English Food* (1974)

"The Uncatchable Trout" by William Faulkner: from *The Sound and the Fury* (Chatto and Windus, 1954)

"Border Incident" by David Pownall: reprinted by permission of the author from *The Spectator*

"Bear Fishing" and "Man Fishing" by John McPhee: from *Coming into the Country* (Hamish Hamilton, 1977)

"Fish Soup" by Peter Feibleman: from Foods of the World/*The Cooking of Spain and Portugal* by Peter S. Feibleman and the Editors of Time-Life Books, © 1969 Time Inc.

"On the Danube" and "In the Andes" by Negley Farson: reprinted from *Going Fishing* (1942)

"The End of Jaws" by Peter Benchley: reprinted from *Jaws* (André Deutsch, 1974)

"The Story of the Record Salmon": from *The Field*

"On Dry-Cow Fishing as a Fine Art" by Rudyard Kipling: reprinted by permission of The National Trust and Macmillan (London) Ltd

"The Hunchback Trout" by Richard Brautigan: from *Trout Fishing in America* (Jonathan Cape, 1970)

"Salmon in Danger" by Anthony Netboy: reprinted from *The Atlantic Salmon* (André Deutsch, 1979)

"The Pike" by Edmund Blunden: reprinted by permission of Duckworth & Co. Ltd

"About Pike" by Roderick Haig-Brown: from *A River Never Sleeps* (1948)

"Sea Urchins" by Elizabeth David: reprinted by permission of Macdonald Publishers and Penguin Books from *Italian Food*

"How the Whale Got His Throat" by Rudyard Kipling: reprinted by permission of The National Trust and Macmillan (London) Ltd from *Just So Stories*

"Fisherman's War" by Maurice Wiggin: reprinted by permission of the author from *The Passionate Angler* (1951)

"Estuary Night" by Henry Williamson: reprinted by permission of Faber and Faber Ltd from *Salar the Salmon* (1972)

"Quenelles de Brochet" by Rosemary Hume and Muriel Downes: from *Cordon Bleu Cookery* (Penguin Books, 1963)

"Fish are such Liars!" by Roland Pertwee: reprinted by permission of the author's estate

"My Moby-Dick" by William Humphrey: from *My Moby-Dick* (Chatto and Windus, 1978)

"The Weir at Galway" by C. Conor O'Malley: from *With a Fishing Rod in Ireland* (Vantage Press, 1975)